BENCHMARK SERIES

Microsoft® Word

2016
Desktop Publishing

Roggenkamp • Rutkosky • Arford

PARADIGM
EDUCATION SOLUTIONS

St. Paul

Senior Vice President	Linda Hein
Editor in Chief	Christine Hurney
Managing Editor	Cheryl Drivdahl
Assistant Developmental Editor	Katie Werdick
Testers and Instructional Support Writers	Janet Blum, Fanshawe College; Traci J. H. Post; Brienna McWade
Director of Production	Timothy W. Larson
Production Editor	Jen Weaverling
Cover and Text Designer	Valerie King
Senior Design and Production Specialist	Jack Ross
Copy Editor	Communicáto, Ltd.
Proofreader	Shannon Kottke
Indexer	Terry Casey
Vice President Information Technology	Chuck Bratton
Digital Projects Manager	Tom Modl
Vice President Sales and Marketing	Scott Burns
Director of Marketing	Lara Weber McLellan

Trademarks: Microsoft is a trademark or registered trademark of Microsoft Corporation in the United States and/or other countries. Some of the product names and company names included in this book have been used for identification purposes only and may be trademarks or registered trade names of their respective manufacturers and sellers. The authors, editors, and publisher disclaim any affiliation, association, or connection with, or sponsorship or endorsement by, such owners.

We have made every effort to trace the ownership of all copyrighted material and to secure permission from copyright holders. In the event of any question arising as to the use of any material, we will be pleased to make the necessary corrections in future printings.

Cover Photo Credits: © Photomall/Dreamstime.com; page 4 (left): © Yulia Nikulyasha Nikitna/Shutterstock.com; (right) © Hector Sanchez/Shutterstock.com.

Paradigm Publishing is independent from Microsoft Corporation, and not affiliated with Microsoft in any manner. While this publication may be used in assisting individuals to prepare for a Microsoft Office Specialist certification exam, Microsoft, its designated program administrator, and Paradigm Publishing do not warrant that use of this publication will ensure passing a Microsoft Office Specialist certification exam.

ISBN 978-0-76387-425-4 (print)
ISBN 978-0-76387-426-1 (digital)

© 2018 by Paradigm Publishing, Inc.
875 Montreal Way
St. Paul, MN 55102
Email: educate@emcp.com
Website: ParadigmEducation.com

Printed in the United States of America

25 24 23 22 21 20 19 18 17 16   1 2 3 4 5 6 7 8 9 10

Brief Contents

Contents

Contents

Benchmark Series: Microsoft® Word 2016: Desktop Publishing, by Audrey Roggenkamp, Ian Rutkosky, and Joanne Arford, focuses on advanced Word 2016 features with an emphasis on desktop publishing concepts and terminology. Microsoft Word 2016 allows users to create professional-looking documents with attractive graphics, text effects, and eye-catching design elements. Publishing from the desktop computer greatly reduces production costs, combines the tasks of page design and layout, offers immediate results, and allows control of production from start to finish.

Well-designed textbook pedagogy is important, but students learn technology skills through practice and problem solving. Technology provides opportunities for interactive learning as well as excellent ways to quickly and accurately assess student performance. To this end, this textbook is supported with SNAP 2016, Paradigm's web-based training and assessment learning management system. Details about SNAP as well as additional student courseware and instructor resources can be found on page xvi and xvii.

Textbook and Chapter Features

Microsoft® Word 2016: Desktop Publishing is designed for students who are proficient in word processing but have little to no design experience. This textbook assumes that students are using Microsoft Word 2016 in a computer lab or home-study setting.

Course Outcomes

Students who successfully complete a course based on this textbook will be able to do the following:

- Use and apply the design concepts of focus, balance, proportion, contrast, directional flow, consistency, and color
- Evaluate documents for the use of basic design concepts
- Use desktop publishing features of Microsoft Word 2016 to integrate basic layout and design concepts in order to enhance the readability of multiple-page, portrait, or landscape documents such as letterheads, postcards, business cards, certificates, flyers, brochures, announcements, and newsletters
- Produce and enhance business and personal documents with variable page layouts using standardized type and graphic design techniques while incorporating updated Word 2016 features such as watermarks, cover pages, page borders, themes, style sets, shapes, WordArt, SmartArt, quick parts, picture tools, table tools, and Microsoft Office templates

What's New in This Edition

Users familiar with *Microsoft® Word 2013: Desktop Publishing* and other previous editions of this textbook will notice the following enhancements to the textbook and software:

- All Word skills have been updated to correspond with Word 2016, including all features, steps, and screen captures.
- All chapter assessments have been moved to the student ebook, where students can also access the Study Tools, Concepts Checks, and Recheck quizzes.
- The book now contains two units, with four chapters in each unit and an additional performance assessment for each unit.
- Unit 1 focuses on desktop publishing concepts and eases students into creating personal and business documents.
- Unit 2 moves on to more complex documents such as flyers, newsletters, brochures, and other specialty promotional documents.
- Links within the student ebook show how student files should look throughout a project and upon completion of the project.
- Tutorials from Paradigm Education's *Benchmark Series: Microsoft® Word 2016* provide interactive, guided review of skills necessary to complete chapter work.

Instructional Design

Most of the key desktop publishing concepts addressed in this textbook are presented in Chapter 1. Subsequent chapters reinforce the concepts through instruction and projects in which students create commercial-quality documents. Projects are designed to help students not only build proficiency in the desktop publishing features of Word 2016 but also develop critical-thinking, decision-making, and creativity skills. Many assessments reinforce collaborative learning as students work in teams to plan, design, and evaluate business and personal documents for publication. Case studies, found in the *Workbook*, incorporate a scenario framework in which basic information for a task is supplied as it might be presented in a real-life situation.

Students who wish to build a portfolio of documents for course requirements or job applications should take special note of the assessments identified with a portfolio icon in the *Workbook*. The final portfolio can be printed and bound in hard-copy format, or the documents can be saved in PDF format, organized as a portfolio, and then viewed electronically.

Numerous images combined with clearly written instruction offer a highly effective visual learning experience. Screen captures of the entire Word screen highlight ribbon elements and other tools and help students connect concepts with clicks. As students follow the step-by-step projects, they can confirm they are performing the correct actions by comparing their screens with the screen captures displayed and the Check Your Work files in the student ebook. Key steps are labeled on the screen captures to make following the project directions as easy as possible. In addition, images of the completed documents are displayed in the textbook or directly accessed via the student ebook so students can check their work. Sample model answers also are provided for workbook assessments and end-of-unit performance assessments.

Textbook Elements

The textbook contains two units with a total of eight chapters. Each chapter contains the following elements:

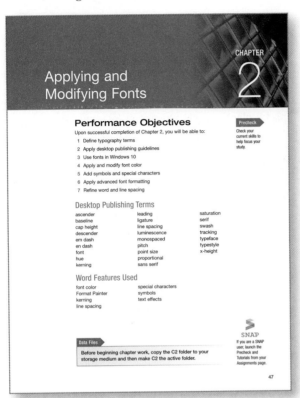

Chapter Openers present an overview of the skills taught.

Precheck quizzes allow students to check their current skills before starting chapter work. Precheck quizzes are accessed in SNAP and also through links in the student ebook.

Performance Objectives outline learning goals for the chapter.

Desktop Publishing Terms and **Word Features Lists** lists prepare students for the chapter work.

Data Files instructions remind students to copy the appropriate chapter data folder from a link in the ebook and make the folder active. Data files are accessed through links in the student ebook.

SNAP instructions remind students with SNAP access to launch the Precheck quiz and tutorials from their SNAP Assignments page.

Multipart Projects provide a framework for instruction and practice on software feature. A project overview identifies tasks to accomplish and key features to use in completing the work.

Preview Finished Project PDFs show how the file will look after students complete the project.

DTP Pointers reinforce key ideas.

Tutorials provide interactive, guided training and measured practice of basic skills.

Word 2016 Button Images help students navigate the application's interface.

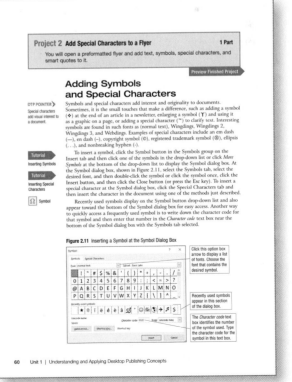

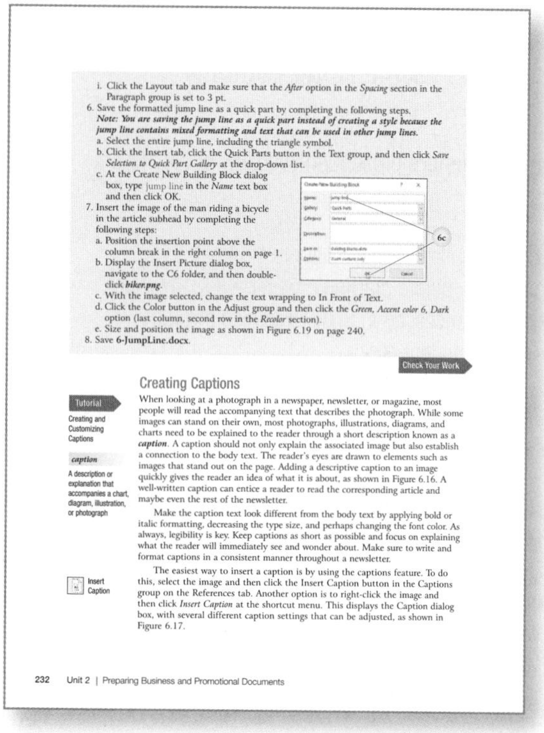

i. Click the Layout tab and make sure that the *After* option in the *Spacing* section in the Paragraph group is set to 3 pt.

6. Save the formatted jump line as a quick part by completing the following steps.
Note: You are saving the jump line as a quick part instead of creating a style because the jump line contains mixed formatting and text that can be used in other jump lines.
   a. Select the entire jump line, including the triangle symbol.
   b. Click the Insert tab, click the Quick Parts button in the Text group, and then click *Save Selection to Quick Part Gallery* at the drop-down list.
   c. At the Create New Building Block dialog box, type jump line in the *Name* text box and then click OK.
7. Insert the image of the man riding a bicycle in the article subhead by completing the following steps:
   a. Position the insertion point above the column break in the right column on page 1.
   b. Display the Insert Picture dialog box, navigate to the C6 folder, and then double-click ***biker.png***.
   c. With the image selected, change the text wrapping to In Front of Text.
   d. Click the Color button in the Adjust group and then click the *Green, Accent color 6, Dark* option (last column, second row in the *Recolor* section).
   e. Size and position the image as shown in Figure 6.19 on page 240.
8. Save **6-JumpLine.docx**.

Check Your Work

Creating Captions

Tutorial

Creating and Customizing Captions

caption

A description or explanation that accompanies a chart, diagram, illustration, or photograph

When looking at a photograph in a newspaper, newsletter, or magazine, most people will read the accompanying text that describes the photograph. While some images can stand on their own, most photographs, illustrations, diagrams, and charts need to be explained to the reader through a short description known as a ***caption***. A caption should not only explain the associated image but also establish a connection to the body text. The reader's eyes are drawn to elements such as images that stand out on the page. Adding a descriptive caption to an image quickly gives the reader an idea of what it is about, as shown in Figure 6.16. A well-written caption can entice a reader to read the corresponding article and maybe even the rest of the newsletter.

Make the caption text look different from the body text by applying bold or italic formatting, decreasing the type size, and perhaps changing the font color. As always, legibility is key. Keep captions as short as possible and focus on explaining what the reader will immediately see and wonder about. Make sure to write and format captions in a consistent manner throughout a newsletter.

Insert Caption

The easiest way to insert a caption is by using the captions feature. To do this, select the image and then click the Insert Caption button in the Captions group on the References tab. Another option is to right-click the image and then click *Insert Caption* at the shortcut menu. This displays the Caption dialog box, with several different caption settings that can be adjusted, as shown in Figure 6.17.

232 Unit 2 | Preparing Business and Promotional Documents

Step-by-Step Projects with Screen Captures guide students to the desired outcome for each project part. Screen captures illustrate what the screen should look like at key points.

Magenta Text identifies material to type.

Check Your Work PDFs allow students to confirm they have completed the project activity correctly. These PDFs are accessed through links in the student ebook.

Multipart Projects provide a framework for instruction and practice on software feature. A project overview identifies tasks to accomplish and key features to use in completing the work

Key Terms and Definitions in the margins provide quick reference for chapter vocabulary.

A Chapter Summary reviews important concepts and features.

A Commands Review summarizes visually the main Word features covered in the chapter.

A **Workbook** note encourages students to go to the workbook pages of the ebook to access study tools and assessment activities.

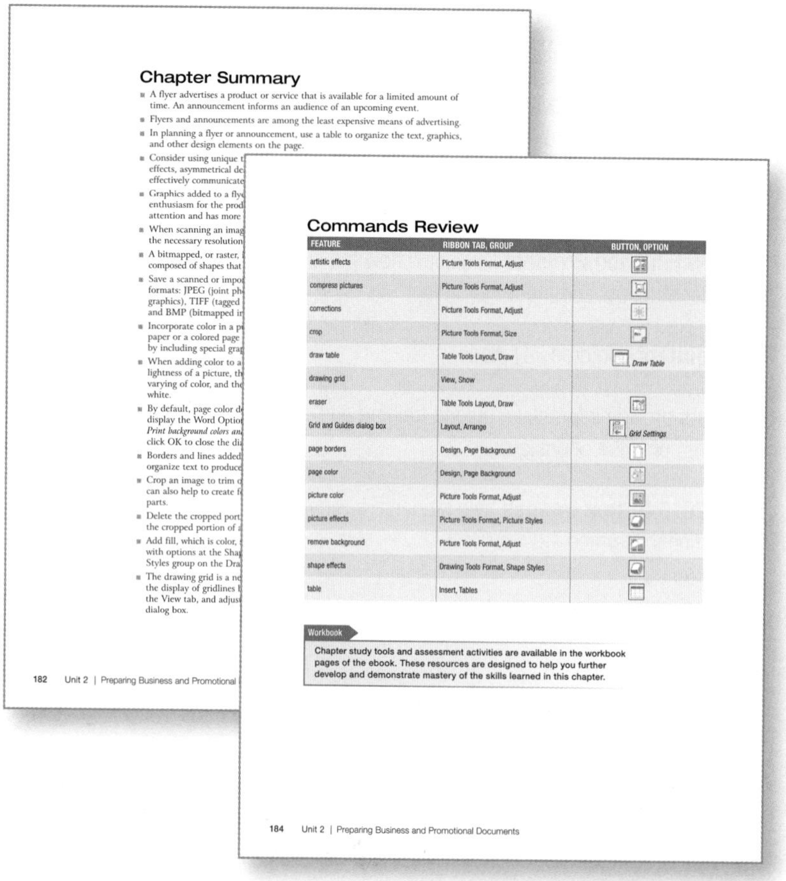

Chapter Summary

- A flyer advertises a product or service that is available for a limited amount of time. An announcement informs an audience of an upcoming event.
- Flyers and announcements are among the least expensive means of advertising.
- In planning a flyer or announcement, use a table to organize the text, graphics, and other design elements on the page.
- Consider using unique t… effects, asymmetrical de… effectively communicate…
- Graphics added to a flye… enthusiasm for the prod… attention and has more…
- When scanning an imag… the necessary resolution…
- A bitmapped, or raster, … composed of shapes that…
- Save a scanned or impo… formats: JPEG (joint ph… graphics), TIFF (tagged… and BMP (bitmapped i…
- Incorporate color in a p… paper or a colored page… by including special gra…
- When adding color to a… lightness of a picture, th… varying of color, and the… white.
- By default, page color d… display the Word Optio… *Print background colors an…* click OK to close the di…
- Borders and lines added… organize text to produce…
- Crop an image to trim … can also help to create f… parts.
- Delete the cropped port… the cropped portion of …
- Add fill, which is color, … with options at the Sha… Styles group on the Dra…
- The drawing grid is a ne… the display of gridlines … the View tab, and adjus… dialog box.

182 Unit 2 | Preparing Business and Promotional …

Commands Review

FEATURE	RIBBON TAB, GROUP	BUTTON, OPTION
artistic effects	Picture Tools Format, Adjust	
compress pictures	Picture Tools Format, Adjust	
corrections	Picture Tools Format, Adjust	
crop	Picture Tools Format, Size	
draw table	Table Tools Layout, Draw	*Draw Table*
drawing grid	View, Show	
eraser	Table Tools Layout, Draw	
Grid and Guides dialog box	Layout, Arrange	*Grid Settings*
page borders	Design, Page Background	
page color	Design, Page Background	
picture color	Picture Tools Format, Adjust	
picture effects	Picture Tools Format, Picture Styles	
remove background	Picture Tools Format, Adjust	
shape effects	Drawing Tools Format, Shape Styles	
table	Insert, Tables	

Workbook

Chapter study tools and assessment activities are available in the workbook pages of the ebook. These resources are designed to help you further develop and demonstrate mastery of the skills learned in this chapter.

184 Unit 2 | Preparing Business and Promotional Documents

Workbook Elements

Students access the *Workbook* ebook through the links menu in their ebook. The following elements are offered in the *Workbook* ebook, and in some cases in SNAP.

End-of-Chapter Elements

Study Tools include presentations with audio support and a glossary designed to help students review skills and concepts learned in the chapter. These tools are accessed through links in the ebook.

Concepts Check completion exercises allow students to assess their comprehension and recall of application features, terminology, and functions covered in the chapter. These exercises are accessed through SNAP and also through links in the ebook.

Recheck quizzes enable students to check how their skills have improved after completing chapter work. These quizzes are accessed through SNAP and also through links in the ebook.

Skills Assessment exercises ask students to practice what they have learned in the chapter with minimal screen captures and step-by-step instructions.

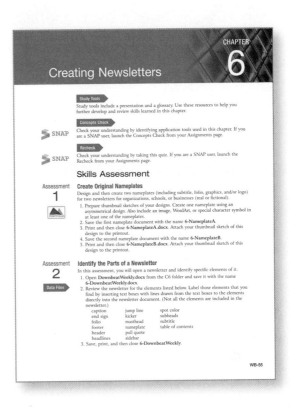

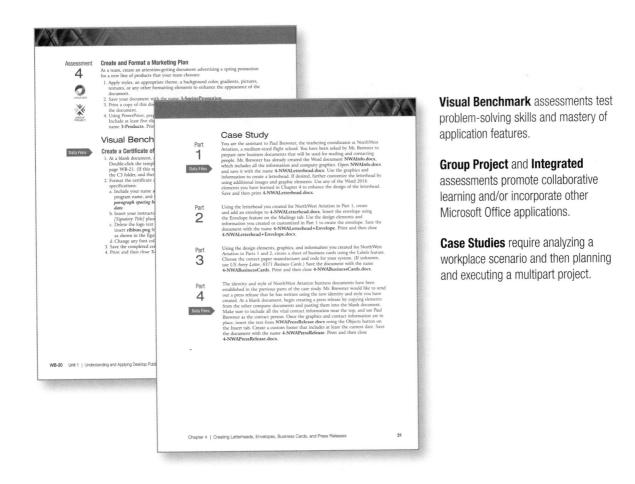

Visual Benchmark assessments test problem-solving skills and mastery of application features.

Group Project and **Integrated** assessments promote collaborative learning and/or incorporate other Microsoft Office applications.

Case Studies require analyzing a workplace scenario and then planning and executing a multipart project.

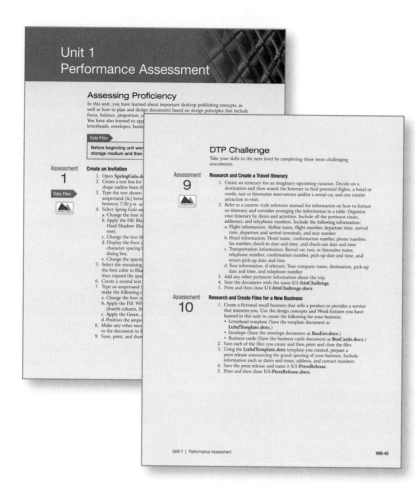

End-of-Unit Elements

Assessing Proficiency exercises
check mastery of features.

DTP Challenge assessments require
research, organization, and creativity as
students apply skills learned throughout
the unit.

SNAP Training and Assessment

SNAP

SNAP is a web-based training and assessment program and learning management
system (LMS) for learning Microsoft Office 2016. SNAP offers rich content, a
sophisticated grade book, and robust scheduling and analytics tools. SNAP courseware supports the *Benchmark Series* content and delivers live-in-the-application
assessments for students to demonstrate their skills mastery. Interactive tutorials increase skills-focused moments with guided training and measured practice.
SNAP provides automatic scoring and detailed feedback on the many activities, exercises, and quizzes to help identify areas where additional support is
needed, evaluating student performance at both individual and course levels. The
Benchmark Series SNAP course content is also available to export into any LMS
system that supports LTI tools.

Paradigm Education Solutions provides technical support for SNAP through
24-7 chat at ParadigmEducation.com. In addition, an online User Guide and other
SNAP training tools for using SNAP are available.

Student eBook and *Workbook* eBook

The student ebook and *Workbook* ebook, available through SNAP or online at ParadigmEducation.com/ebooks, provides access to the *Benchmark Series* content from any device (desktop, tablet, and smartphone), anywhere, through a live Internet connection. The versatile ebook platform features dynamic navigation tools including a linked table of contents and the ability to jump to specific pages, search for terms, bookmark, highlight, and take notes. The ebook offers live links to the interactive content and resources that support the print textbook, including the student data files, Precheck and Recheck quizzes, and interactive tutorials. The *Workbook* pages of the ebook also provide access to Study Tools such as chapter-based presentations with audio support. They also provide access to the end-of-chapter Concept Check, Skills Assessment, Visual Benchmark, Case Studies, and end-of-unit Performance Assessment activities.

Instructor eResources eBook

All instructor resources are available digitally through a web-based ebook at ParadigmEducation.com/ebooks. The instructor materials include these items:

- Planning resources, such as lesson plans, teaching hints, and sample course syllabi
- Presentation resources, such as PowerPoint slide shows with lecture notes
- Assessment resources, including live and annotated PDF model answers for chapter work and workbook activities, rubrics for evaluating student work, and chapter-based exam banks

About the Authors

Audrey Roggenkamp has been teaching courses in the Business Technology department at Pierce College Puyallup since 2005. Her courses have included keyboarding, skill building, and Microsoft Office program training. In addition to this title, she has coauthored *Benchmark Series: Microsoft® Office 2016, 2013, 2010,* and *2007; Marquee Series: Microsoft® Office 2016, 2013, 2010,* and *2007; Using Computers in the Medical Office: Microsoft® Word, Excel, and PowerPoint 2016, 2013, 2010, 2007,* and *2003; Signature Series: Microsoft Word 2013, 2010,* and *2007; Paradigm Keyboarding and Applications I: Using Microsoft® Word 2013, Sixth Edition, Sessions 1–60* and *Sessions 61–120; Paradigm Keyboarding and Applications I: Using Microsoft® Word 2016, Seventh Edition, Sessions 1–60* and *Sessions 61–120;* and *Computer and Internet Essentials: Preparing for IC³,* all for Paradigm Education Solutions.

Ian Rutkosky teaches business technology courses at Pierce College in Puyallup, Washington. In addition to this title, he has coauthored *Computer and Internet Essentials: Preparing for IC³; Benchmark Series: Microsoft® Office 2016, 2013; Marquee Series: Microsoft® Office 2016, 2013;* and *Using Computers in the Medical Office: Microsoft® Word, Excel, and PowerPoint 2013, 2010.* He is also a coauthor and consultant for Paradigm's SNAP training and assessment software.

Joanne (Marschke) Arford is originally from Berrien Springs, Michigan, lived in South Bend, Indiana, for several years, and has been residing in Naperville, Illinois, for the past 20 years. She and her husband, Frank, are the parents of three grown daughters, Rachel, Lisa, and Kaitlin. Joanne graduated from Western Michigan University in Kalamazoo, where she received her Bachelor's and Master's degrees in Business Education. Joanne is currently an adjunct faculty member at the College of DuPage in Glen Ellyn, Illinois. Her first desktop publishing textbook was co-authored with Nita Rutkosky and Judy Burnside. Since then she has written several editions of the Advanced Word Desktop Publishing textbook. Joanne is a member of the College of DuPage Adjuncts Association (CODAA) and has received the Illinois Business Education Association Writer's Hall of Fame awards for all of her textbooks.

Joanne enjoys reading, walking, and traveling. She has visited China, South Africa, Europe, and other destinations with her husband. Joanne also enjoys volunteering at the Loaves and Fishes Community Pantry in Naperville.

Acknowledgments

We would like to thank Nita Rutkosky and Brienna McWade for their continued support; Janet Blum of Fanshawe College in London, Ontario, and Traci J. H. Post for their important input as testers of projects and assessments and their help preparing supplemental materials.

Microsoft® Word Desktop Publishing

Unit 1

Understanding and Applying Desktop Publishing Concepts

Understanding Desktop Publishing

Performance Objectives

Precheck

Check your current skills to help focus your study.

Upon successful completion of Chapter 1, you will be able to:

1 Define desktop publishing

2 Initiate the desktop publishing process

3 Design the document

4 Evaluate documents using the Document Analysis Guide

5 Use Word 2016 in desktop publishing

6 Use online resources

Desktop Publishing Terms

⅓ - ⅔ rule	directional flow	reversed text
alignment	focus	rule of thirds
asymmetrical design	harmony	spread
balance	legibility	symmetrical design
consistency	proportion	thumbnail sketch
contrast	readability	white space
desktop publishing	resolution	Z pattern

Word Features Used

cover page	shapes	templates
crop	SmartArt	themes
online images	styles	WordArt
pictures	style sets	

Note: Comments on how to use this textbook and hints on the projects will appear in italicized bold type.

SNAP

If you are a SNAP user, launch the Precheck and Tutorials from your Assignments page.

Data Files

Before beginning chapter work, copy the C1 folder to your storage medium and then make C1 the active folder.

Project 1 **Evaluate a Flyer**   **1 Part**

You will open a predesigned flyer and use the Document Analysis Guide to determine if the flyer uses effective desktop publishing features and elements.

Defining Desktop Publishing

Since the 1970s, computers have been an integral part of the business environment. For many years, the three most popular types of software purchased for computers were word processing, spreadsheet, and database programs. The introduction of laser and inkjet printers, with their ability to produce high-quality documents in black and white as well as in color, led to the growing popularity of another category of programs called *desktop publishing software*.

Desktop publishing software allows the user to produce professional-looking documents for both office and home use. The term ***desktop publishing***, coined by Aldus Corporation president Paul Brainard in 1984, means that publishing can literally take place at your desk.

Desktop publishing may involve using dedicated software, such as Adobe InDesign, or an advanced word processing program with desktop publishing capabilities, such as Microsoft Word. For simpler desktop publishing projects, Word is a good choice; for more complex documents, high-end desktop publishing software may be more appropriate. Microsoft Publisher is a midrange desktop publishing program that comes with many professional-looking document templates. Adobe Illustrator and Photoshop are programs that may be used to supplement the desktop publishing process.

Until the mid-1980s, graphic design depended almost exclusively on design professionals. However, desktop publishing software changed that. Faster microprocessors; larger storage capacity; improved printer capabilities; an increased supply of clip art images and photos; the advent of CDs and DVDs, flash drives, and memory card readers; and access to the Internet have further expanded the role of desktop publishing. As illustrated in Figure 1.1, the past 50 years have seen an evolution from electric typewriters to personal computers to laptop computers as the most common desktop publishing tool. What will be next?

desktop publishing

Using specific desktop publishing software or high-end word processing software to produce professional-looking documents containing text and/or graphics

Figure 1.1 Producing Documents with a Typewriter, a Personal Computer, and a Laptop Computer

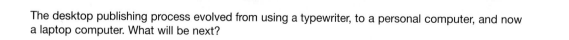

The desktop publishing process evolved from using a typewriter, to a personal computer, and now a laptop computer. What will be next?

In traditional publishing, several people may have been involved in completing a publication project, which naturally involved greater costs and time compared with today's desktop publishing. Using desktop publishing software, one person may be able to perform all the tasks necessary to complete a project and greatly reduce the costs of publishing documents. The two approaches, however, do have a great deal in common. Both processes involve planning the project, organizing content, analyzing the layout and design, arranging design elements, typesetting, printing, and distributing the project.

Desktop publishing can be used as the sole method for creating a publication, or it can be used in combination with traditional publishing. When carried out from start to finish by an individual or a group of people, desktop publishing produces results quickly and provides the ability to control the production from the initial layout and design to the final printing and distribution. However, desktop publishing and traditional publishing work well together. A project may begin on a desktop, where the document is designed and created, but an illustrator may be commissioned to create some artwork, and the piece may be sent to a commercial printer for printing and binding.

Using the results-oriented interface of Microsoft Office 2016, applying the enhanced desktop features found in Word 2016 and Publisher 2016, and integrating PowerPoint 2016, Excel 2016, and Access 2016, professional-looking publications are easy to create, contribute to, manage, review, edit, customize, print, and publish. The availability of OpenType fonts in Office 2016 also promotes cross-platform sharing between Apple computers and PCs.

DTP POINTER〉

Use OpenType fonts for cross-platform compatibility.

Projects that used to be outsourced can now be controlled and completed in-house by using desktop applications with publishing and data merge capabilities. Word 2016 and Publisher 2016, along with application-independent file formats (such as Portable Document Format [PDF], Extensive Markup Language [XML], and XML Paper Specification [XPS]), allow for cross-platform sharing regardless of the type of computer and applications the audience is using. In addition, it is more efficient to prepare and send publications to professional printers accustomed to working with PDF and XML file formats. Shared document technology, the Internet, and email provide opportunities to collaborate with others outside the home and office, even on the go.

Initiating the Desktop Publishing Process

The process of creating a publication begins with two steps: planning the publication and creating the content. During the planning process, the desktop publisher must decide on the purpose of the publication and identify the intended audience. When creating the content, the desktop publisher must make sure that readers will understand the intended message of the publication.

Planning the Publication

Initial planning is one of the most important steps in the desktop publishing process. During this stage, complete the following tasks:

- Clearly identify the purpose of your communication. Are you providing information? Are you selling a product? Are you announcing an event? Distinctly defining your goal will make it easier to organize your material in a way that helps you achieve that goal.

- Assess the target audience. Who will read the publication? Are they employees, coworkers, clients, friends, or family? What will the target audience expect from the publication? Will they expect a serious, conservative approach or an informal, humorous approach? Make sure to keep their needs and desires in mind in creating the content.

- Determine in what form the intended audience will be exposed to the message. Will the message be in a brochure as part of a packet of presentation materials for a company seminar? Or will the message take the form of a newspaper advertisement, surrounded by other advertisements? Will the message be in the form of a business card distributed when making sales calls? Or will the message be tacked on to a bulletin board? Understanding the method of delivery will help to refine the content of the publication.

- Decide what readers are to do after reading the message. Should they ask for more information? Should they respond in some way? Should they be able to contact someone in person, by telephone, or via email? Remember to include any necessary contact information based on your response to this step.

- Determine the budget for the entire project. Costs may include paper expenses based on quality, weight, and size; trimming, folding, and binding expenses; number of copies needed; delivery method used; and printing method used (color or black and white).

- Collect examples of effective designs. Create a folder of design ideas, and put copies of impressive designs into this folder. These designs may include flyers, promotional documents, newsletters, graphics, interesting type arrangements, and the like. Look through the design ideas folder before beginning a new project. Let favorite designs serve as a catalyst for developing personal ideas.

Creating the Content

The most important goal in desktop publishing is to communicate the message. Design is important because it increases the visual appeal of the document, but content is still the most important element. Create a document that clearly conveys the intended message to the intended audience.

To determine the message, identify the purpose and start organizing material. Establish a hierarchy of importance among the items in the communication. Consider what items will be most important to the reader, what will attract the reader's attention, and what will spark enough interest to retain the reader's focus. Think about what format or layout to follow. (Check the design ideas folder!) Clear and organized content combined with an attractive layout and design create an effective message.

Designing the Document

If the message is the most significant part of a communication, then worrying about the design may seem like a waste of time. However, a well-planned and relevant design sets the work apart from others and can help to focus the reader's attention on the message. Just as people may be judged by their appearance, a publication may be judged by its design. Taking a little more time to design a publication such as a business flyer, letterhead, or newsletter will make the document more convincing, attractive, and professional.

As with planning the content of a publication, when planning the design, consider the purpose of the document, the target audience, and the method of distribution. In addition, think about the following factors:

- What feeling should the document elicit?
- What is the most important information, and how can it be emphasized so the reader can easily identify the purpose of the document?
- What different types of information will be presented, and how can these elements be distinguished yet kept internally consistent?
- How much space is available?

An important first step in planning a design and layout is to prepare a thumbnail sketch. A ***thumbnail sketch*** is a miniature draft of the document being created, and preparing it is also known as *thinking on paper*. As shown in Figure 1.2, thumbnail sketches can be used to experiment with alternative locations for elements such as graphics, rules (horizontal and vertical lines), columns, and borders.

A good designer continually asks questions, pays attention to details, and makes thoughtful decisions that enhance the content of the publication. Consider examples A and B in Figure 1.3. Which document attracts the reader's attention, entices him or her to read on, looks convincing, and encourages him or her to take action?

Overdesigning is one of the most common tendencies of beginning desktop publishers. The temptation to use as many desktop publishing features as possible in one document is often difficult to resist. However, design elements should be used to communicate, not decorate. To create a visually appealing publication, start with the same classic design concepts used by professional designers. These concepts include focus, balance, proportion, contrast, directional flow, consistency, and color.

thumbnail sketch

A rough sketch used in planning a layout and design

DTP POINTER

Use design elements to communicate, not decorate.

Figure 1.2 Preparing Thumbnail Sketches: Thinking on Paper

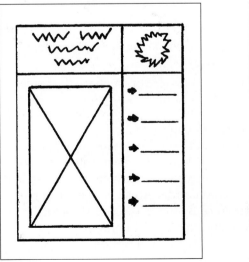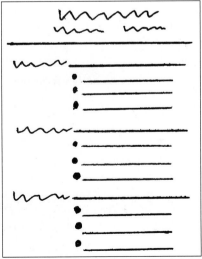

Figure 1.3 Using Design to Enhance Content

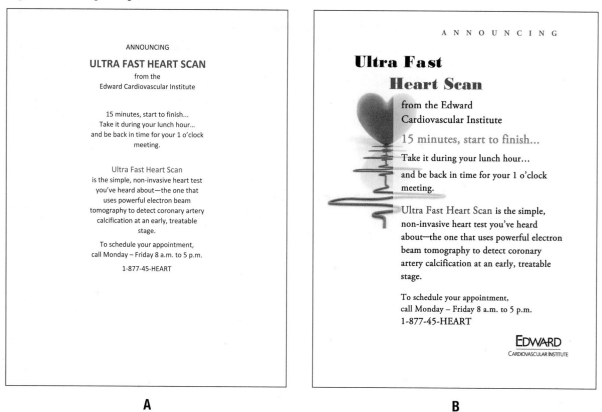

A

B

Creating Focus

The *focus*, or focal point, on a page is an element that draws the reader's attention. Elements that tend to draw focus are large, dense, unusual, and/or surrounded by white space.

Create focus in a document using these two elements:

- text created in larger, bolder, contrasting typefaces
- graphics, such as lines, clip art images, photographs, illustrations, watermarks, and logos

Whether focus is created through text or graphics, the reader will recognize it instantly.

Creating Focus with Text

In Word, OpenType fonts and TrueType fonts are available for text formatting. OpenType fonts were created jointly by Microsoft and Adobe in an effort to promote cross-platform compatibility between Macintosh and Windows. In some cases, a document created on a Macintosh computer might not print in the same way on a Windows-based computer. However, as OpenType fonts become more common, this difficulty may become less prevalent. OpenType fonts include exaggerated serifs and special ligatures for advanced users working with fine typographic controls (see Chapter 2 for more details). In addition, OpenType fonts can make it easier to set blocks of text that contain more than one language because they include multiple language character sets in each font.

In Word, the majority of fonts are OpenType fonts; however, a few TrueType fonts are still available. TrueType fonts were developed by Apple and Microsoft to replace the PostScript fonts used in earlier versions of Windows, but they are now being replaced with OpenType fonts.

Changing the weight, size, style, or letter spacing (tracking) of text and applying text effects (glow, shadow, reflection, or outline), color, rotation, shapes (WordArt), and even drop caps can effectively draw the reader's attention. Grouping blocks of similar text, using consistent alignment, and providing generous amounts of white space help to create focus using text. **White space** is empty background with no text or graphics (though it may not always be white). The amount of white space around a focal element can enhance its appearance and help to balance other design elements on the page. Use white space to emphasize the main message and give the reader's eyes a break from too much text. Consider using a guideline called the $^1/_3$ - $^2/_3$ **rule**, which says that one-third of a page should consist of white space if the remaining two-thirds contains text and other design elements.

Notice the use of text as a focal point in Figure 1.4B. The title "Kids at College" is formatted in Whimsy ICG Heavy, which is a youthful, energetic font. This formatting, along with a generous amount of white space, is much more effective at creating focus than the text in Figure 1.4A. Also notice the impact that the **reversed text** (white type on a black background) has on creating focus for the school name and the list of courses.

white space

Background space with no text or graphics

$^1/_3$ - $^2/_3$ *rule*

If two-thirds of a page contains text, graphics, and other content, then one-third should be white space

reversed text

Light type on a colored background

Figure 1.4 Creating Focus with Text

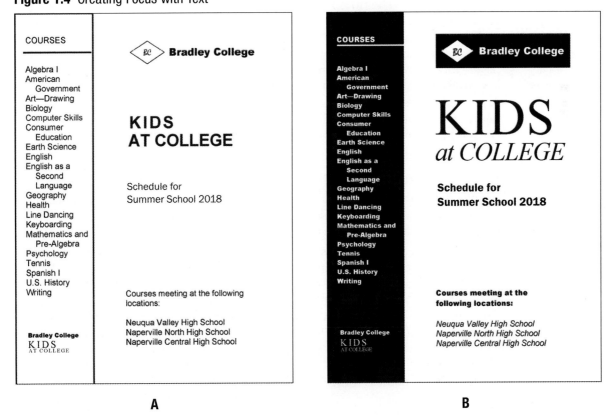

A

B

Creating Focus with Titles, Headlines, and Subheadings

When creating titles, headlines, and subheadings in reports, procedure manuals, newsletters, term papers, and tables of contents, use large or bold type surrounded by enough white space to contrast with the main text. In addition, keep the following points in mind:

- State the title or headline using precise, easily understood language.
- Select easy-to-read typefaces. **Legibility** is of utmost importance. Readers must be able to clearly see and read the individual letters in the title or headline.
- Size the title or headline in proportion to its importance relative to the surrounding text.
- Keep the line length of a headline fairly short, set the headline in a larger point size than the body type, and include enough white space around it so that it is clearly visible to the reader. This helps to improve **readability**, or the ease with which the reader's eyes move throughout text.

In any type of communication—semiannual report, office procedures manual, company newsletter, advertising flyer, or brochure—subheads may provide a secondary focal element. While the headline attracts the reader's attention, the subheads may be the key to maintaining it. Subheads provide order to text and give the reader further clues about the content of the publication. Make sure subheads are set in legible fonts and with appropriate line length, line spacing, and alignment.

Look at document A in Figure 1.5. Does any particular location on the page attract attention? The titles in document A may create a slight focus on the page. Now look at document B in the same figure. The bolded titles provide more focus and attention than the nonbolded titles. In document C, the title is the primary focus and the headings, set in reversed text, provide secondary focal points on the page. Notice how using the same font for all the headings makes the document organization readily apparent to the reader. Also notice that more white space appears above the headings than below them. This spacing connects the headings to the text that follows. Consistent formatting and font colors and sizes were created by applying styles, a style set, and a theme. These features will be discussed later in the chapter.

Creating Focus with Graphics

Graphics can be used to create focus on a page and can enhance the overall appearance of a publication. Many Word features may be used to add visual elements to publications, as shown in Figures 1.6 through 1.9 on page 12.

A SmartArt graphic is a visual representation of information that can quickly and easily be created, choosing from many different layouts, to effectively communicate the message. SmartArt—which can be inserted using the SmartArt button in the Illustrations group on the Insert tab and edited using the SmartArt Tools contextual tabs—uses text, shape, and color to create a focal point in a document, as shown in Figure 1.6. WordArt, images, clip art, watermarks, shapes, lines, and text boxes with fill effects are other graphic Word features and are shown in Figures 1.7, 1.8, and 1.9. Look at the document in each figure, and determine where the focal point is. Consider which design elements draw the reader into the document.

Figure 1.5 Creating Focus with Titles and Subheadings

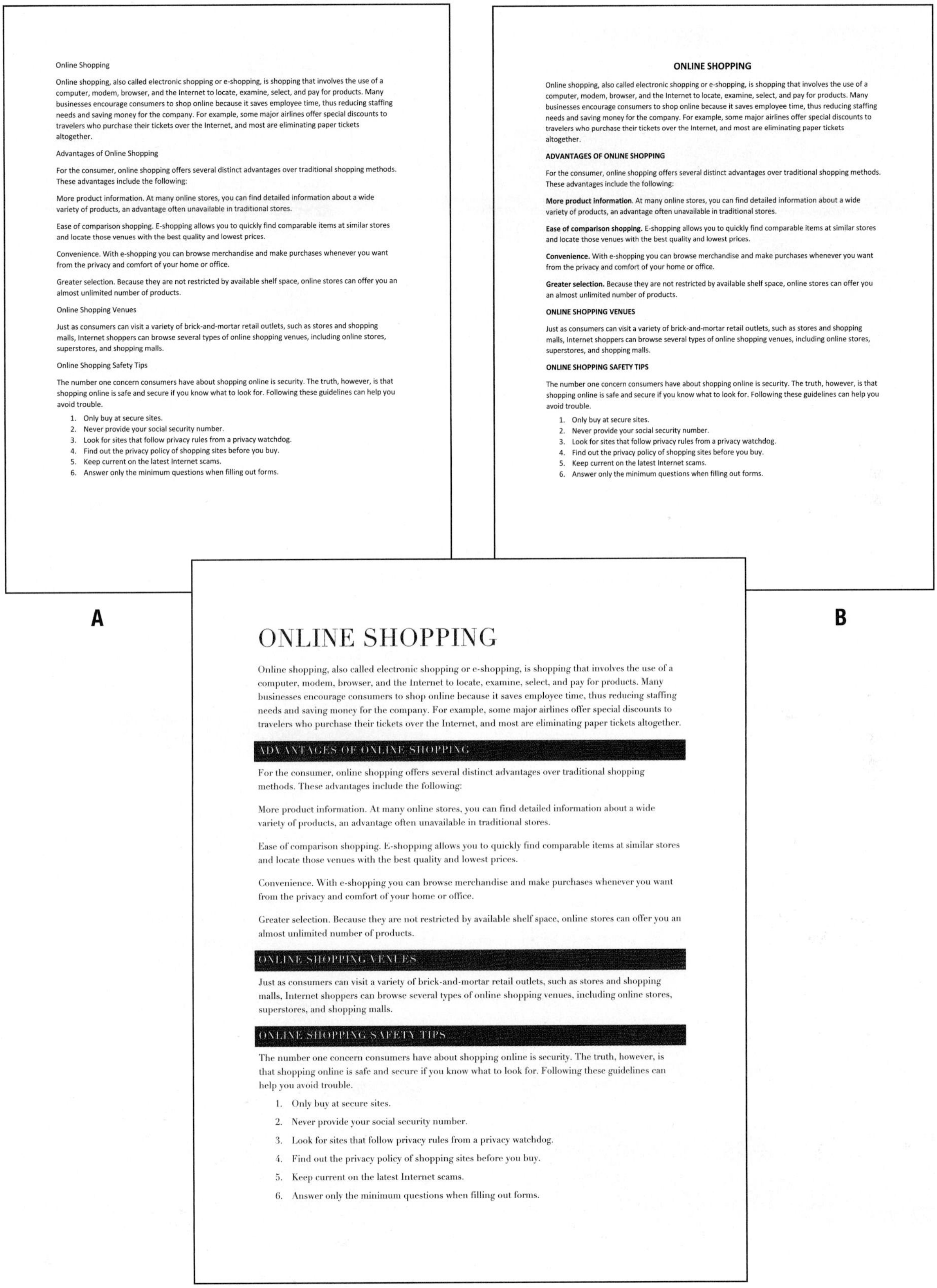

A

Online Shopping

Online shopping, also called electronic shopping or e-shopping, is shopping that involves the use of a computer, modem, browser, and the Internet to locate, examine, select, and pay for products. Many businesses encourage consumers to shop online because it saves employee time, thus reducing staffing needs and saving money for the company. For example, some major airlines offer special discounts to travelers who purchase their tickets over the Internet, and most are eliminating paper tickets altogether.

Advantages of Online Shopping

For the consumer, online shopping offers several distinct advantages over traditional shopping methods. These advantages include the following:

More product information. At many online stores, you can find detailed information about a wide variety of products, an advantage often unavailable in traditional stores.

Ease of comparison shopping. E-shopping allows you to quickly find comparable items at similar stores and locate those venues with the best quality and lowest prices.

Convenience. With e-shopping you can browse merchandise and make purchases whenever you want from the privacy and comfort of your home or office.

Greater selection. Because they are not restricted by available shelf space, online stores can offer you an almost unlimited number of products.

Online Shopping Venues

Just as consumers can visit a variety of brick-and-mortar retail outlets, such as stores and shopping malls, Internet shoppers can browse several types of online shopping venues, including online stores, superstores, and shopping malls.

Online Shopping Safety Tips

The number one concern consumers have about shopping online is security. The truth, however, is that shopping online is safe and secure if you know what to look for. Following these guidelines can help you avoid trouble.

1. Only buy at secure sites.
2. Never provide your social security number.
3. Look for sites that follow privacy rules from a privacy watchdog.
4. Find out the privacy policy of shopping sites before you buy.
5. Keep current on the latest Internet scams.
6. Answer only the minimum questions when filling out forms.

B

ONLINE SHOPPING

Online shopping, also called electronic shopping or e-shopping, is shopping that involves the use of a computer, modem, browser, and the Internet to locate, examine, select, and pay for products. Many businesses encourage consumers to shop online because it saves employee time, thus reducing staffing needs and saving money for the company. For example, some major airlines offer special discounts to travelers who purchase their tickets over the Internet, and most are eliminating paper tickets altogether.

ADVANTAGES OF ONLINE SHOPPING

For the consumer, online shopping offers several distinct advantages over traditional shopping methods. These advantages include the following:

More product information. At many online stores, you can find detailed information about a wide variety of products, an advantage often unavailable in traditional stores.

Ease of comparison shopping. E-shopping allows you to quickly find comparable items at similar stores and locate those venues with the best quality and lowest prices.

Convenience. With e-shopping you can browse merchandise and make purchases whenever you want from the privacy and comfort of your home or office.

Greater selection. Because they are not restricted by available shelf space, online stores can offer you an almost unlimited number of products.

ONLINE SHOPPING VENUES

Just as consumers can visit a variety of brick-and-mortar retail outlets, such as stores and shopping malls, Internet shoppers can browse several types of online shopping venues, including online stores, superstores, and shopping malls.

ONLINE SHOPPING SAFETY TIPS

The number one concern consumers have about shopping online is security. The truth, however, is that shopping online is safe and secure if you know what to look for. Following these guidelines can help you avoid trouble.

1. Only buy at secure sites.
2. Never provide your social security number.
3. Look for sites that follow privacy rules from a privacy watchdog.
4. Find out the privacy policy of shopping sites before you buy.
5. Keep current on the latest Internet scams.
6. Answer only the minimum questions when filling out forms.

C

ONLINE SHOPPING

Online shopping, also called electronic shopping or e-shopping, is shopping that involves the use of a computer, modem, browser, and the Internet to locate, examine, select, and pay for products. Many businesses encourage consumers to shop online because it saves employee time, thus reducing staffing needs and saving money for the company. For example, some major airlines offer special discounts to travelers who purchase their tickets over the Internet, and most are eliminating paper tickets altogether.

ADVANTAGES OF ONLINE SHOPPING

For the consumer, online shopping offers several distinct advantages over traditional shopping methods. These advantages include the following:

More product information. At many online stores, you can find detailed information about a wide variety of products, an advantage often unavailable in traditional stores.

Ease of comparison shopping. E-shopping allows you to quickly find comparable items at similar stores and locate those venues with the best quality and lowest prices.

Convenience. With e-shopping you can browse merchandise and make purchases whenever you want from the privacy and comfort of your home or office.

Greater selection. Because they are not restricted by available shelf space, online stores can offer you an almost unlimited number of products.

ONLINE SHOPPING VENUES

Just as consumers can visit a variety of brick-and-mortar retail outlets, such as stores and shopping malls, Internet shoppers can browse several types of online shopping venues, including online stores, superstores, and shopping malls.

ONLINE SHOPPING SAFETY TIPS

The number one concern consumers have about shopping online is security. The truth, however, is that shopping online is safe and secure if you know what to look for. Following these guidelines can help you avoid trouble.

1. Only buy at secure sites.
2. Never provide your social security number.
3. Look for sites that follow privacy rules from a privacy watchdog.
4. Find out the privacy policy of shopping sites before you buy.
5. Keep current on the latest Internet scams.
6. Answer only the minimum questions when filling out forms.

Figure 1.6 Using a SmartArt Graphic for Focus

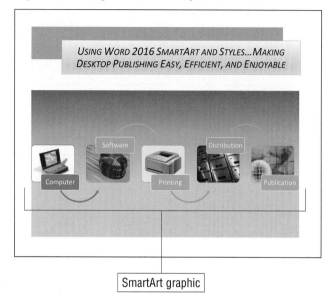

SmartArt graphic

Figure 1.7 Using Photos for Focus

photographs

Figure 1.8 Using an Online Image for Focus

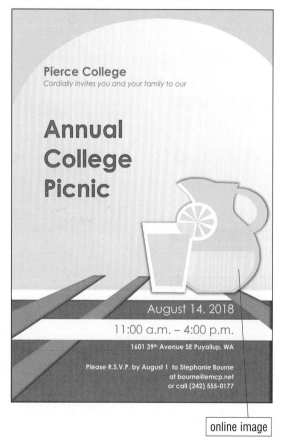

online image

Figure 1.9 Using a Watermark for Focus

watermark

When considering a graphic element as a focal point, remember the following points:

- Legibility is just as important with graphics as it is with titles and subheads. Graphics should support the message in the text and not interfere with its readability in any way.

DTP POINTER

Graphics should be relevant to the intended message.

- Communicate rather than decorate. Let the message dictate the use of graphic elements. Does the graphic enhance the message, or does it overshadow the message? Is it relevant, meaningful, and appropriate? If not, it is probably best to leave out the graphic.

- Less is best; keep it simple. One larger, well-chosen image will provide more impact than several smaller images. Too many images create visual confusion for the reader.

DTP POINTER

Keep the design simple.

- Crop an image if necessary to increase its impact. Crop to eliminate unnecessary elements and zoom in on the key parts of an image, or crop in unexpected ways to draw attention to the image. See Figure 1.10 for cropping examples. (Cropping will be covered in Chapter 5.)

DTP POINTER

Graphics should face the text.

- Position the graphic to face the text. A graphic facing away from the text draws the reader's eyes away from the most important part of the document—the content. Compare documents A and B in Figure 1.11. The graphic in document B creates a focal point that leads the reader's eye toward the text rather than away from it (as in document A).

If all other factors are equal, publications containing graphic elements are noticed and perused before text-only publications. In Figure 1.12, announcement A is not as effective as announcement B. The sun graphic/watermark in announcement B creates a major focal point that draws in the reader. "Good Morning Naperville" is also easier to read in announcement B, immediately giving the reader an idea of the content he or she can expect to find in the document. Varying the type size and type style helps to organize the remaining information and provide minor focal points on the page.

Figure 1.10 Cropping an Image to Increase Impact

A	**B**	**C**	**D**
Original Image	Cropping Using Aspect Ratio in Portrait at 4:5	Cropping Using the Crop Tool	Cropping to a Shape

Figure 1.11 Positioning Graphics to Face the Text

A

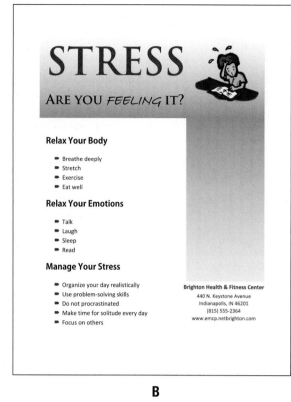

B

Figure 1.12 Using Graphics to Create Interest

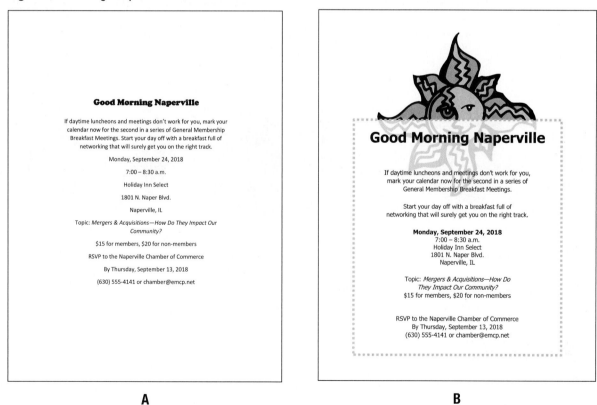

A   B

Creating Balance

balance

The equal distribution of design elements on a page

Attain **balance** by equally distributing the visual weight of various elements on the page, such as blocks of text, graphics, headings, ruled lines, and white space. Balance is either symmetrical or asymmetrical.

Creating Symmetrical Balance

symmetrical design

A layout that positions similar elements equally on both sides of a page to achieve balance

A **symmetrical design** contains similar elements of equal proportion or weight on the left and right sides and the top and bottom of the page. Symmetrical balance is easy to achieve because all the elements are centered on the page. When a symmetrically designed document is folded in half vertically (in other words, along its vertical line of symmetry), both halves of the document contain the same elements.

To better visualize the concept of symmetrical balance, look at the shapes in the top half of Figure 1.13. The squares, representing identical graphics, are positioned on the left and right sides of the page. The rectangle, representing a block of text, is centered between the two squares. Notice the dotted line, representing the vertical line of symmetry, splits the design in half. It is easy to see that the elements on both sides of the dotted line are equal in weight and proportion because they are the same. Now look at the example of a symmetrically designed letterhead in the bottom half of Figure 1.13. If the same line of symmetry is extended down through the sample letterhead, the design elements will be equally distributed on both sides of the page.

Creating Asymmetrical Balance

asymmetrical design

A layout that positions contrasting elements on a page to achieve balance

Symmetrical balance is easy to identify and to create. However, contemporary design favors asymmetrical balance. An **asymmetrical design** uses different design elements of varying weights and/or proportions to achieve balance on a page. Asymmetrical design is more flexible and visually stimulating than symmetrical design. Look at the shapes in the top half of Figure 1.14. Notice the dotted line (the line of vertical symmetry) that divides the page in half. Even without the dotted line, it is evident that the two sides do not match. Therefore, this is not a symmetrical design. However, just because the design is not symmetrical does not automatically mean that it is asymmetrically balanced.

The key to an effective asymmetrical design is achieving a visual balance on the page by using dissimilar or contrasting elements. Look again at the shapes and the white space in Figure 1.14. Is visual balance achieved on the page, even though the shapes are not the same and are not centered? The darker, denser square and its surrounding white space on the left half of the page are balanced by the longer, less dense rectangle and its surrounding white space on the right half of the page. Now look at how those same shapes are converted into the design elements used in the sample letterhead in the bottom half of Figure 1.14. The dissimilar design elements balance each other, resulting in an effective asymmetrical design.

spread

Two pages facing each other

Multiple-page documents add another dimension to the challenge of achieving balance. In the case of a multiple-page publication, it is essential to evaluate the balance of type and graphics in terms of each two-page unit, or **spread**, which is two pages facing each other, as shown in document B in Figure 1.15. Notice that the layout of document A is symmetrical, and the layout of document B is asymmetrical.

Figure 1.13 Creating Symmetrical Balance

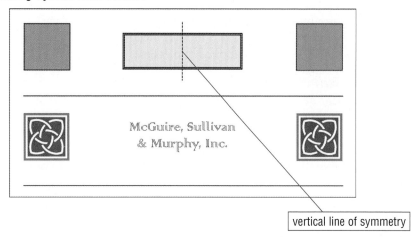

vertical line of symmetry

Figure 1.14 Creating Asymmetrical Balance

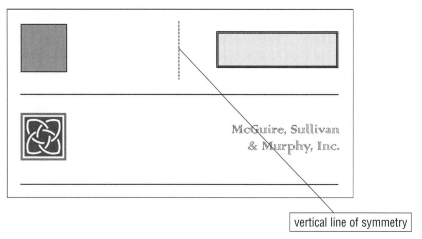

vertical line of symmetry

Figure 1.15 Comparing Symmetrical and Asymmetrical Newsletters

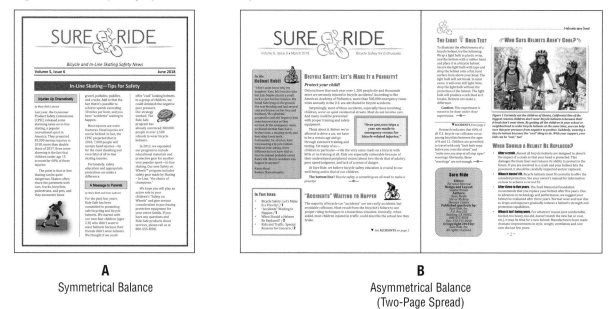

A
Symmetrical Balance

B
Asymmetrical Balance
(Two-Page Spread)

Using the Rule of Thirds

Strive to maintain *harmony* on each page or spread, regardless of the design balance. Harmony means that all the elements work together to create a page that is interesting to look at and easy to read. One way to promote design harmony is to apply a design guideline called the *rule of thirds*. This rule states that pages should be arranged in thirds, rather than halves or fourths. Studies indicate that this division of sections is more appealing to the eye than any other design. Figure 1.16 illustrates a document that is not in harmony (document A) and one that is in harmony (document B).

Creating Proportion

When designing a document, think about all the individual parts as they relate to the document as a whole. Readers tend to view larger elements as more important. Readers also are more likely to read a page where all the elements are in *proportion* to one another. When incorporating the concept of proportion into your documents, consider the following points:

- Size design elements, whether text or graphics, according to their relative importance to the message.
- Strive for variety. Try not to make all design elements the same size.
- Text, graphics, and other design elements should take up two-thirds of the document, and at least one-third of the document should be left for white space.

Decide which elements in the document are the most important in conveying your message. Next, decide which elements are the second most important, and so on. Once this hierarchy has been created, proportionally size the visual elements in the publication according to each element's priority. Proportional sizing ensures that the reader sees the most important information first. The typefaces and type sizes selected for headlines, subheads, and body text can set the proportional standards for a document.

Figure 1.16 Applying the Rule of Thirds to Create Harmony in a Document

A
Without Harmony

B
With Harmony

Evaluating Proportion between Heading, Subheading, and Body Text

When viewing the documents in Figure 1.17, look at the headline size in proportion to the body text. Think about this relationship when selecting the type size for the title or headline and the body text. When selecting the type size for the subhead, consider how the subhead relates proportionally to the headline and to the body text.

Sizing Graphics to Achieve Proportion

Sizing graphics is also important in maintaining proportion among all the design elements on a page. For instance, look at Figure 1.18A. The size of the image visually tells the reader that it is the most important item on the page. But should it be? As discussed earlier in this chapter, the intended message should always take priority. The image in document A may be relevant, but it is overpowering the message rather than supporting it. The image is out of proportion to its relative importance in the message.

Now look at Figure 1.18B. The musical image is too small to be effective. Looking at the document as a whole, the image is out of proportion to the surrounding elements. Look at the individual elements in Figure 1.18C as they relate to the whole document. All the design elements appear to be in proportion to each other and to their ranking of importance in the intended message.

Figure 1.17 Evaluating Headline Proportions

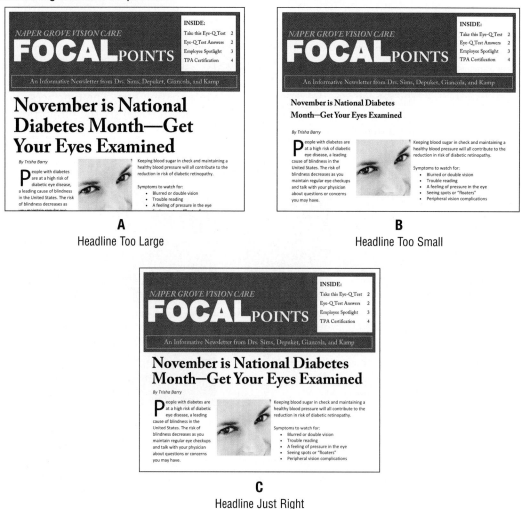

A
Headline Too Large

B
Headline Too Small

C
Headline Just Right

Figure 1.18 Sizing Graphics in Appropriate Proportion

| **A** | **B** | **C** |
| Image Too Large | Image Too Small | Image Just Right |

Using White Space Proportionally

White space must also be considered when evaluating proportion in a document. Keep the following pointers in mind:

- Narrow margins can make lines too long to read easily.
- Too much white space between columns makes the line length look choppy.
- Too little space between columns makes the text look squished and is harder to read.
- Excess white space between lines of text creates gaps that look out of proportion to the type size.
- Too little white space between lines of text reduces legibility.

Apply proportion consistently throughout an entire project. An integrated, unified look is established when elements are in proportion to one another.

Creating Contrast

contrast

Difference in degrees of lightness and darkness

Contrast is the difference between degrees of lightness and darkness on the page. Text with a low level of contrast gives an overall appearance of gray. Consider using strong contrast to achieve some emphasis or focus on the page. A high level of contrast is more visually stimulating and helps to draw the audience into the document. Use contrast as an organizational aid to help the reader move through the document and follow the flow of information. Headlines and subheads set in larger and denser type help to create contrast on an otherwise gray page, as shown in Figure 1.19.

DTP POINTER ➤

Add contrast by setting headings and subheads in larger, denser type.

In Figure 1.20A, notice that the contrast achieved by using a larger type size for the word *London* and reversed, bold text helps to grab attention. A black image against a solid white background produces a sharp contrast, as illustrated by the Tower Bridge graphic in Figure 1.20A. In addition, look at the program cover in Figure 1.20B. A sharp contrast exists between the black background and the white text and piano image, and a less sharp contrast exists between the light gray text and the watermark of musical notes in the background of the cover.

Figure 1.19 Using Contrast in Headlines and Text

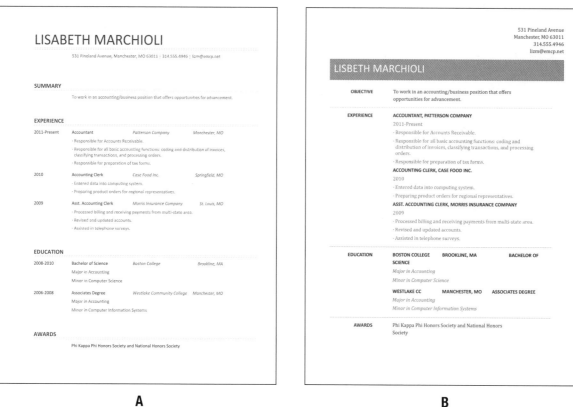

A
Resume with Little Visual Contrast

B
Resume with Strong Visual Contrast

Figure 1.20 Creating Contrast with Black-and-White Graphics and Text

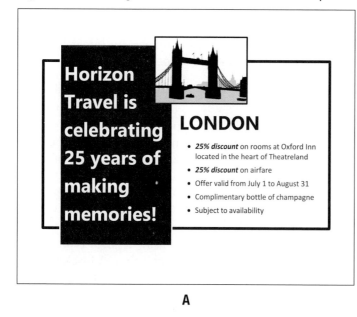

A

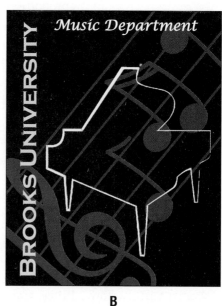

B

Achieving Contrast with Text

DTP POINTER ❯

Make contrasting elements strong enough to be noticed.

Text contrast can be accomplished by changing text direction and by mixing serif and sans serif fonts, large and small font sizes, uppercase and lowercase, roman and italics, thick fonts and thin fonts, and drop caps and normal text. See Figure 1.21 for examples. Avoid pairing fonts that are only slightly different from one another, such as Times New Roman and Bell MT. Instead, choose fonts with obvious differences, such as Arial Black (sans serif) and Invitation (serif). Word 2016 theme fonts take some of the guesswork out of choosing contrasting yet complementary fonts. The drop-down gallery in Figure 1.22 shows the theme font's name, such as *Office*, followed by the heading font, such as *Calibri Light*, and the body font, such as *Calibri*. These theme fonts are determined by the theme applied to the document.

Figure 1.21 Illustrating Contrasting Font Pairs

Figure 1.22 Selecting Fonts at the Theme Fonts Button Drop-down Gallery

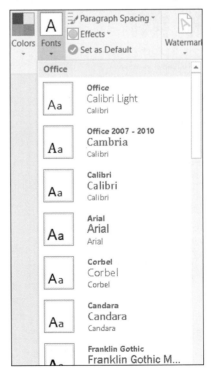

In addition to predesigned theme fonts, custom font pairs can be created. Do this by clicking the Design tab, clicking the Theme Fonts button in the Document Formatting group, clicking *Customize Fonts* at the drop-down gallery, and then saving the font pairs with a name.

DTP POINTER

Use bullets to organize information and add visual contrast.

Special characters can be used as bullets to define a list of important points, such as 👪, ⛵, 👁, 🏛, 🔔, 🍽, 🏫, and 🖋. These characters not only serve as organizational tools but also contribute visual contrast to a page. Formatting these special characters in a bolder and larger type size provides a higher level of contrast. Notice the family symbol and the pen bullets used in Figure 1.23A.

Achieving Contrast with White Space

DTP POINTER

Use plenty of white space to convey an open, lighter feeling.

White space is an important tool in achieving contrast. Use more white space on a page to project a more open, lighter feeling. When white space is limited, a more closed, darker feeling is projected. Think of white space as the floor space in a room. The more furniture and accessories in the room, the more crowded the room becomes. Rearranging or removing some of the furniture can provide more floor space, which produces an open, lighter feeling. A page, like a room, may need to be rearranged or pared down to create some contrasting white space. Too many design elements are crowding the page in Figure 1.23A. Notice how eliminating and rearranging some of the design elements to create more white space makes for a more open and lighter design in Figure 1.23B.

Figure 1.23 Adding White Space

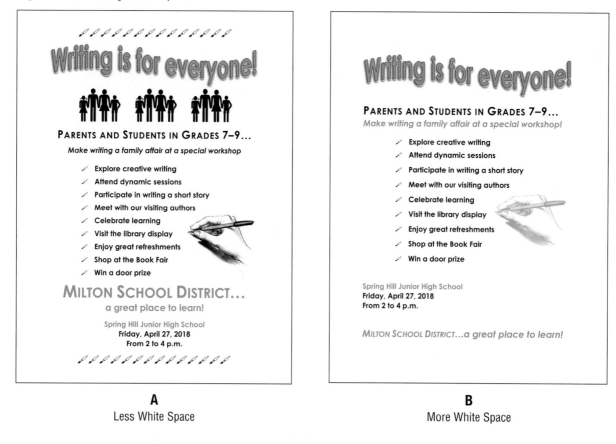

A
Less White Space

B
More White Space

Figure 1.24 Using Contrast to Improve Legibility

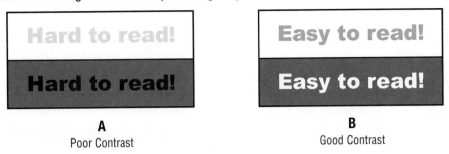

A
Poor Contrast

B
Good Contrast

Achieving Contrast with Color

The use of color in a heading, logo, graphic, or line or as a background can also create contrast on a page. When using more than one color, select colors that provide a pleasing sense of variety, not colors that create an unpleasant conflict. In addition, consider whether the color(s) used increases or decreases the legibility of a document. Color may look nice, but it will confuse the reader if there is not enough contrast in the text. In Figure 1.24A, the color of the text and the color of the background are too similar, making the text barely legible. The stark contrast between the color of the text and the color of the background in Figure 1.24B makes the text easy to read. Use high contrast to maximize legibility.

Creating Directional Flow

directional flow

Positioning elements to draw the reader's eyes through the document

Establish smooth *directional flow* in a document by organizing and positioning elements in such a way that the reader's eyes scan the text and find particular words or images that you wish to emphasize. Graphics and display type (larger than 14 points) act as focal elements that attract the eye as it scans a page. Focal elements may include a well-designed headline, subheads, logo, graphics, lines, shapes with text inside, charts, reversed text, or a shaded background. When establishing the directional flow of a document, complete the following:

DTP POINTER ❯

Rank information according to its importance in conveying the intended message.

- Organize information into groups of closely related items and then rank the groups in order of importance.
- Decide how to emphasize the most important information.
- Position elements so that the reader is drawn into the document and then directed through it.
- Use left or right alignment to establish a stronger visual connection between all the elements on the page.

While all of these elements are important to creating directional flow in a document, organizing information into groups should be a priority. Once information is organized into groups, enhancing directional flow with other design choices will be easier.

Organizing Your Information Visually

DTP POINTER ❯

Position related items close to each other on the page.

Organize information by grouping related items. Place the related items close to each other so the reader views them as one unit rather than as separate pieces. For example, a subheading should be close to the paragraph that follows it so that the reader recognizes the relationship between the two. Dates, times, and locations are also frequently positioned close together because they provide related information.

What happens when the information in a document has little or no organization? Look at Figure 1.25A. Not only is the document boring and uninviting to read, but it is difficult to determine what the document is about. Now look at Figure 1.25B. What has changed to make the document so much more appealing? The arrow shapes filled with relevant graphics point toward the document content. Therefore, the directional flow directs the reader's eyes from the left side (focal point) to the right side, where related content is grouped in a logical, easy-to-read manner. The italicized word *point* reinforces the right-pointing arrow shapes, and the slant of the text gives a feeling of movement.

Use color to organize a document, but remember that the chosen colors should reflect the nature of the business. Someone in an artistic line of work may use bolder, splashier colors than someone creating documents for a financial institution.

Headers and footers—text that appears repetitively at the top and bottom of each page respectively—also contribute to directional flow and visual organization in a publication. Chapter name, chapter number, report title, and page number are common items included in headers and footers. These page identifiers direct the reader to specific locations in a document.

Figure 1.25 Grouping Related Items and Creating Strong Directional Flow

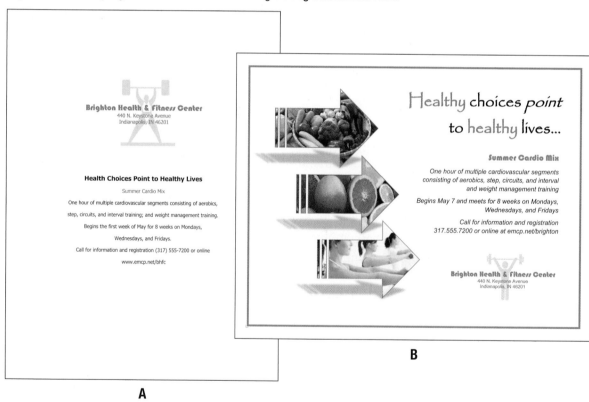

A

B

One of the easiest and most effective ways to visually organize a document is to apply a unified, preformatted design theme. When a design theme is applied to a document, elements of the theme can be inserted in the document. For example, if the Facet theme is applied to a document, a cover page can be inserted along with coordinating headers and footers, as shown in Figure 1.26.

Figure 1.26 Using a Coordinated Cover Page, Header, and Footer

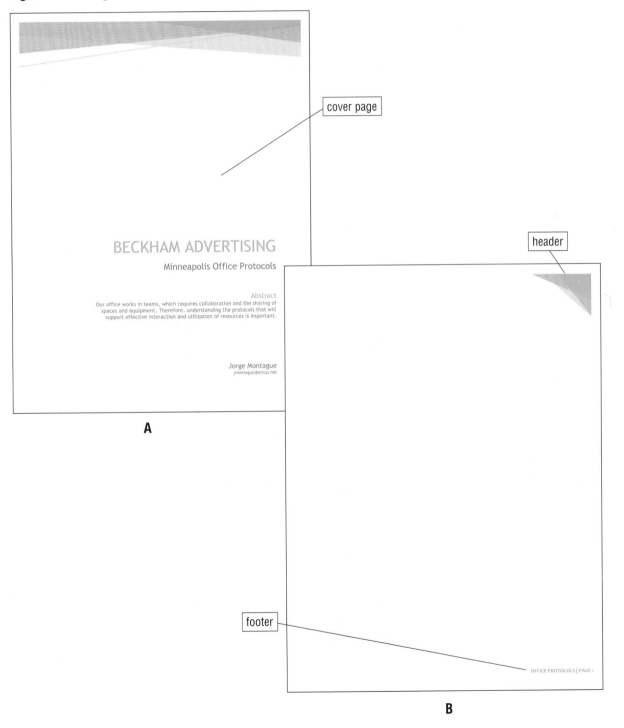

cover page

header

BECKHAM ADVERTISING

Minneapolis Office Protocols

Abstract
Our office works in teams, which requires collaboration and the sharing of spaces and equipment. Therefore, understanding the protocols that will support effective interaction and utilization of resources is important.

Jorge Montague
jmontague@emcp.net

A

OFFICE PROTOCOLS | PAGE 1

B

Emphasizing Elements

After organizing information into groups of related items, decide which information is most important in conveying the message and then emphasize that information. For example, the purpose of the flyer in Figure 1.27 is to inform readers of the class schedules for the Kids at College program. The courses and locations offered are important facts. Reversed text and larger font sizes emphasize these facts. The gradient fill adds to the overall appeal of the flyer.

Recognizing the Z Pattern

Z pattern

A pattern for organizing content and creating a dynamic directional flow that follows natural eye movement across a page

Directional flow in a strictly symmetrical design (all elements centered) is limited to movement down the visual center of the page, producing a static design. Conversely, an asymmetrical design creates a dynamic directional flow. When scanning a page, the eyes tend to move in a *Z pattern*: they begin at the upper left corner of the page, move to the right corner, then drop down to the lower left corner, and finally end up in the lower right corner of the page. In text-intensive publications such as magazines, newspapers, and books, visual landmarks are frequently set in these positions so that the reader will notice them. In an advertisement, the company name, address, and phone number often appear in the lower right corner.

Figure 1.28 helps demonstrate the Z pattern in a document. Remember that placing content according to the Z pattern is only a guideline. Some designs may use modified versions of the Z pattern, or they may not use it at all.

Figure 1.27 Emphasizing Important Information

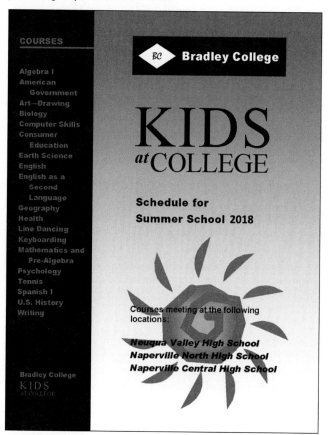

Figure 1.28 Recognizing Z-Pattern Directional Flow

Choosing Alignment

The method for positioning text and graphics on a page greatly influences the directional flow in a document. One of the keys to creating dynamic directional flow and producing professional-looking documents is *alignment*, or the linear arrangement of items on a page. Center alignment is fine when attempting to achieve a more formal look, as in a wedding invitation, but tends to be dull and boring in other types of documents. Break away from the center-alignment habit! Experiment with using a strong left or right alignment to visually connect elements on the page.

In Figure 1.29A, the varied alignment of all the elements causes them to appear disconnected, and the reader's eyes tend to jump from one corner to another. The business card in Figure 1.29B uses strong right alignment, grouped text, and bold formatting to lead the eyes from the top to the bottom.

alignment

Linear arrangement of items on a page

DTP POINTER ❯

Use a strong left or right alignment to visually connect elements on a page.

Figure 1.29 Analyzing the Importance of Visual Alignment

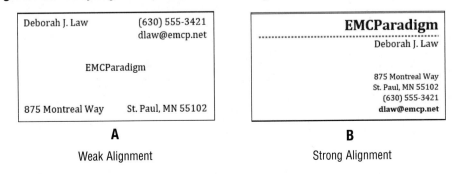

A

Weak Alignment

B

Strong Alignment

Establishing Consistency

consistency

Uniformity among design elements

Uniformity among specific design elements establishes a pattern of **consistency** in a document. Inconsistency can confuse and frustrate readers and can lead to a reduction in comprehension. To avoid this, design elements such as margins, columns, typefaces, type sizes, spacing, alignment, and color should remain consistent throughout a document. In any document, whether single-page or multiple-page, using consistent elements helps to integrate all the individual parts into a whole unit. Repetitive, consistent elements can lend identity to a set of documents and provide the reader with a sense of familiarity.

Consistent elements are evident in many of the figures in this chapter. Consider, for example, the flyer in Figure 1.28 on page 27. Consistency is achieved by using the same color of blue in the heading, the bullets, the sky in the sailboat image, the title of the event, and the phone number. Additional consistent elements in the flyer include the left alignment, the flag bullets, the spacing between the bullets, the typeface used for the text, and the margins.

DTP POINTER

Use consistent elements to unify different business documents created for the same company or person.

Use consistent elements when designing separate business documents for the same company or person, such as business cards, letterhead, and envelopes. In Figure 1.30, the consistent elements (the company name, logo, and colors) included in each document are obvious. The reader knows immediately that all three documents are associated with the same company, which serves to reinforce the brand and identity of that organization.

Evaluating Consistency

Consistency establishes unity not only *within* a section or chapter (or newsletter or advertisement) but also *among* the sections or chapters (or a series of newsletters or advertisements). Notice how the consistent elements used in the pages in Figure 1.31 contribute to the unified appearance of the document. The blue color scheme is carried throughout the pages of the manual, including the cover page. The same typeface appears on the cover and in the headers, section headings, and subheadings. A different typeface is used for the body text and remains consistent throughout the document. Additionally, a thin, horizontal line appears in the header on every page except the cover.

Figure 1.30 Creating Consistency among Documents

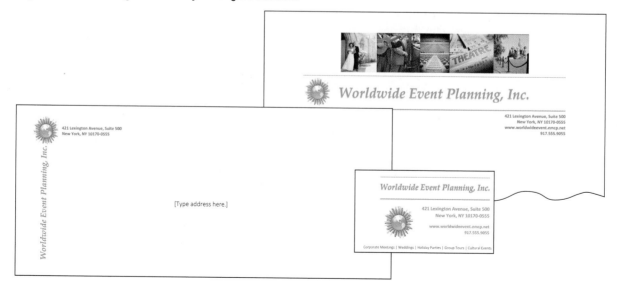

Figure 1.31 Applying Consistent Formatting and Color

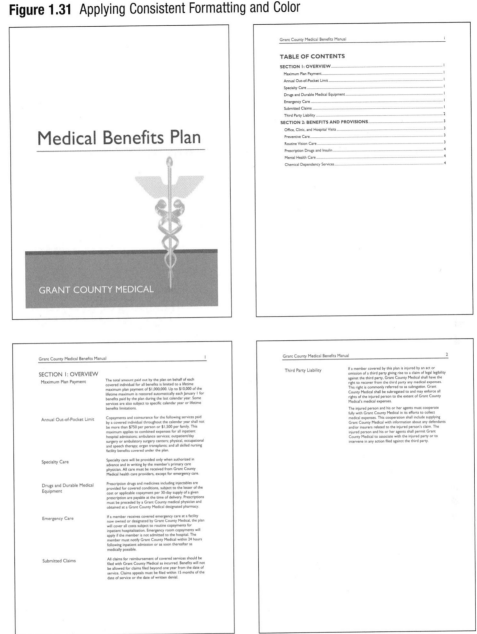

DTP POINTER

Do not distract the reader by overusing graphics.

If an image is inserted in a document, use the image for ideas on creating design consistency. For example, in Figure 1.32, the postmarked stamp image on the postcard provided the basis for the color scheme. The image is used on both sides of the postcard, and the blue box used for the return address on the front of the postcard inspired the use of the blue box on the back of the postcard. When designing a document, remember that consistent elements are repetitive, so keep it simple and distinct. Too much of a good thing can be distracting.

Figure 1.32 Using a Graphic to Create Consistency

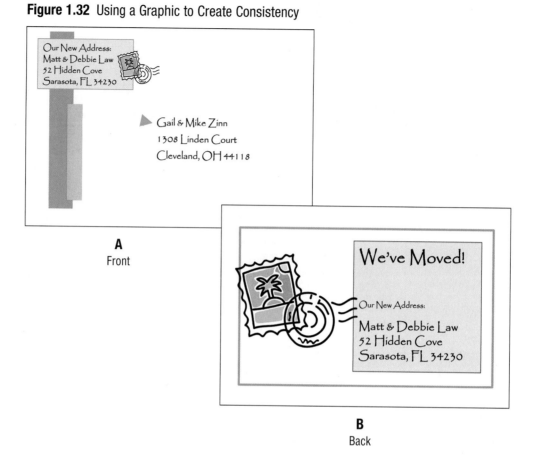

A
Front

B
Back

Applying Styles for Consistency within a Document

One way to ensure consistent formatting throughout a document is to apply styles. Word 2016 provides a gallery of professionally designed styles for titles, headings, subheadings, and body text, among other design elements. These styles include preselected combinations of fonts, font sizes, colors, and spacing. Apply a style by clicking in the text to be formatted and then clicking a style thumbnail in the Styles group on the Home tab. The formatting applied by a style will vary depending on the style set. Style sets—such as Basic (Stylish), Casual, Centered, Lines (Simple), and Shaded—can be applied by clicking one of the thumbnails in the Document Formatting group on the Design tab. Using styles and style sets greatly simplifies the process of applying and adjusting formatting in a document.

DTP POINTER ❯

The formatting applied by each style depends on the active style set in the document.

Applying Themes for Consistency among Documents

Just as styles reinforce consistency within a document, themes help to promote consistency among different files created in Word, Excel, Access, and/or PowerPoint. Because the same themes are available in all the programs in the Office 2016 suite, a design theme can be applied to a group of related documents to give them a cohesive and professional look. Each theme contains a set of formatting choices that includes colors, fonts (including heading and body text fonts), and effects (including lines and fill effects). Look at the examples in Figure 1.33, which have all been formatted using the Quotable theme. Although they are different types of documents, they still convey a united appearance, making it clear that they are related. Apply a theme by clicking the Design tab, clicking the Themes button, and then clicking one of the options at the drop-down gallery.

DTP POINTER ❯

A theme is a set of formatting characteristics that includes colors, fonts, and effects.

 Themes

Figure 1.33 Using the Quotable Theme in Word, PowerPoint, and Excel

A
Word Document

B
PowerPoint Slide

C
Excel Worksheet

Using Color

When designing a document, the use of color is a powerful tool to help create focus and communicate the message. Always identify the target audience in planning a document, and think about the impact color will have on the audience. Someone who is trying to attract the attention of a youthful audience may use bolder, splashier colors than someone creating documents for an accounting business. In addition, men and women often respond differently to the same color. Color can even elicit an emotional response from the reader; keep in mind cultural differences and how other cultures interpret uses of color. For example, in Western cultures, orange represents autumn, harvest, warmth, and high visibility. In Eastern cultures, orange represents compassion, joy, humility, and good health.

The colors in the fall leaves in Figure 1.34 reinforce the subject of the text, which is a list of courses offered during the fall semester at a college. Color can help organize ideas and highlight important facts. When used appropriately, color can enhance the professional look of a document.

Figure 1.34 Using Color to Communicate

Applying Guidelines for Using Color

Follow these guidelines when using color in documents:

DTP POINTER

Use color sparingly.

- Use color sparingly—less is best! Limit your use of colors to two or three, including the color of the paper.

- Use color to identify a consistently recurring element.

- Do not let color overpower content. Color can add emphasis and style, but the message is most important!

- Remember the importance of contrast. If the background of your document is white or light-colored, do not set the text in a light color; it will be too difficult to read. Black text is still the easiest to read. Conversely, do not set the text in black if the background of your document is dark.

- Avoid changing all the text to one color, such as red. It is harder to read and defeats the purpose of using color to create focus and emphasis.

- Use light colors for shaded backgrounds and watermarks.

Using Color in Graphics and Text Elements

Word provides many ways of inserting color into a document. Use predesigned graphics, borders, page colors, bullets, and lines. Also, create custom-colored shapes, lines, borders, text boxes, and text. For instance, the event invitation in Figure 1.35 uses WordArt to emphasize the event name and an attention-getting zebra border to reinforce the safari theme. The zebra facing the grouped text also reinforces the invitation theme, and the green gradient fill in the text boxes on the front and back side of the invitation make the reader feel like he or she is with the animals on a green savanna in Africa.

Using Colored Paper

If a color printer is not available, consider using colored paper to add interest to a publication. Colored paper can match the tone or mood created in the document. Orange paper used for a Halloween flyer, as shown in Figure 1.36B on page 34, is an inexpensive alternative to color graphics and text like the ones shown in Figure 1.36A on page 34. The audience will recognize the theme of the flyer by associating the paper color with the event. The colored paper provides contrast and adds vitality and life to the publication.

Using Preprinted Stationery

Turn plain white documents into colorful, attention-grabbing documents by purchasing preprinted stationery, envelopes, brochures, or presentation packets from paper supply companies or your local office supply store. Achieve color, emphasis, and contrast through an assortment of colorful page borders, patterned and solid-colored papers, as well as gradient, marbleized, and speckled papers. Many paper suppliers provide free catalogs and offer inexpensive sample paper packets.

DTP POINTER

Conduct an Internet search to find information on providers of specialty papers in the area.

Figure 1.37A on page 35 shows a certificate created in Word, and Figure 1.37B illustrates that same certificate printed on paper with a preexisting star design. The gray fill and blue border applied in Word reinforce the colors in the paper. When printing on predesigned paper, make sure to place the elements in a document appropriately so that they will print in the right locations. (Experiment with plain paper first!)

Figure 1.35 Using Color Graphics and WordArt

A
Front

B
Back

Choosing Printing Options

Even though laser printers have become more affordable, color laser printers (and color laser printer cartridges) remain rather expensive. A less expensive but still good alternative is an inkjet color printer. An inkjet printer uses color ink cartridges to produce color. (The paper may be slightly damp when first removed from the printer.) Improve the *resolution* of the printed document by using specially designed inkjet paper. Some inkjet printers are capable of achieving near-photographic quality with a resolution of 5,760 × 1,440 or higher. Learn more about a printer's settings by accessing the Print backstage area and clicking the Printer Properties link.

Another option for printing documents in color is to send a formatted copy to a commercial printer. A commercial printer can print in almost any color, but adding color can add significant costs to the project. Always check prices and the budget first.

resolution

The fineness of detail in an image or text produced by a monitor or printer

Figure 1.36 Comparing Color Graphics and Colored Paper

Figure 1.37 Using Preprinted Paper

A
Layout and Text Created in Word

B
Printed on a Paper Style Called *Star Gala* by Paper Direct

Evaluating Documents Using the Document Analysis Guide

Up to this point, the importance of carefully planning and designing a publication according to the desktop publishing concepts of focus, balance, proportion, contrast, directional flow, consistency, and color has been covered. In Project 1, the document will be evaluated using the Document Analysis Guide, which can be printed from the C1 folder on your storage medium. The Document Analysis Guide is a tool used to evaluate design concepts in selected documents.

A Document Evaluation Checklist may also be printed from the C1 folder on your storage medium. This tool provides a way to evaluate progress during the planning and creation of a document and is directed toward the finished product. The Document Evaluation Checklist will be used in both units in this book. Both forms will be used to analyze your own documents, existing commercial publications, and/or other students' desktop publications.

DTP POINTER

Save documents often.

Creating desktop published documents involves many steps and often a lot of experimentation. Save documents frequently to ensure having a recent version to fall back on and to avoid losing work if a power or system failure occurs. Word automatically saves a document recovery file every 10 minutes. Change this setting at the Word Options dialog box with *Save* selected in the left panel. Display the Word Options dialog box by clicking the File tab and then clicking *Options*.

Project 1 Evaluating a Document
Part 1 of 1

Evaluate the flyer illustrated in Figure 1.38 by completing the following steps:
1. Open **DocumentAnalysisGuide.docx** from the C1 folder.
2. Save the document with the name **1-Evaluate**.
3. View Figure 1.38.
4. Complete an analysis of the flyer in Figure 1.38 by typing short answers to the questions in the Document Analysis Guide.
5. Save, print, and then close **1-Evaluate.docx**.

Figure 1.38 Flyer to Be Evaluated in Project 1

Using Word in Desktop Publishing

Microsoft Word 2016 is a visual word processing application that provides an efficient means of editing and manipulating text and graphics to produce professional-looking documents. Word is linear in nature, in that every character, picture, and object is part of a line of text. However, Word also contains many features and options that allow linear objects to be changed to floating objects that can be moved around the document.

DTP POINTER ▶

Experiment with different layouts and designs.

Become familiarized with design principles by studying well-designed publications and by experimenting with personal publications. Analyze what makes a specific design and layout visually appealing and unique, and try using the same principles or variations of them in personal publications. Take advantage of the special design and layout features that Word 2016 has to offer. Make sure to allow time for trial and error. Creating a quality publication requires a lengthy process of revising, refining, and making adjustments. Above all else, experiment! View each document in terms of focus, balance, proportion, contrast, directional flow, consistency, and use of color. Ask others' opinions of a document and listen to their feedback. The final judge is the reader, so always try to look at a document from the reader's perspective.

The remaining chapters in this book cover the steps for creating specific personal and business desktop publishing products, such as letterheads, business cards, newsletters, flyers, brochures, postcards, online and hard-copy forms, and posters. In addition to step-by-step directions for completing the products using Word 2016, each project will introduce guidelines relevant to that document type and reinforce the design concepts introduced in this chapter. Remember these key points:

- Take the time to design!
- Communicate, rather than decorate!
- Less is always best!
- Readability is the key!

Project 2 Create a Portfolio   1 Part

You will learn how to build a portfolio while completing the projects and assessments in this book.

Project 2 Creating a Portfolio   Part 1 of 1

Begin a job-hunting portfolio of the documents you will create in the assessments throughout the workbook. Workbook assessments marked with the portfolio icon should be included in your portfolio. These documents have been chosen to show a prospective employer a wide range of your desktop publishing skills. You may also include any additional documents from the chapter projects and unit assessments. Because the assessments are less structured than the projects, your creativity can really shine! Your instructor will determine a due date and any other specific requirements for your portfolio. If possible, purchase plastic sheet protectors for your documents and a binder to hold them. You may also want to create a title page and/or a table of contents for your portfolio. Figure 1.39 shows several sample portfolios. Open **PortfolioRequirements.docx** located in the C1 folder and then print a copy of the document.

As an alternative, your instructor may request that you prepare an electronic version of your portfolio by saving your cover, divider pages, and a select number of publications in PDF format and then sending them to him or her as an email attachment. These pages may also be posted to your blog, if you have one, or uploaded to OneDrive. You might also consider preparing your portfolio as a PowerPoint presentation and sending it to your instructor electronically.

Figure 1.39 Comparing Photos of Sample Portfolios

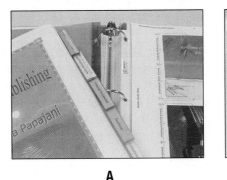

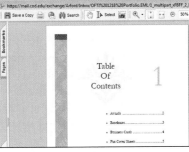

A
Hard-Copy Portfolio

B
Electronic Portfolio

You will create an invitation using an online template and insert an image into the invitation. You will also use the Windows Snipping Tool to capture a screenshot of an image.

Preview Finished Project

Using Online Resources

The Internet can provide a wealth of information on desktop publishing as well as resources such as templates and images that can be downloaded from websites. In a preferred browser or search engine, type *desktop publishing* in the search box. The search results will provide access to websites on various aspects of the desktop publishing field, which may include reviews on the newest books; definitions of common terms; discussions of graphics, layout, and design; and facts on career opportunities. Links to free clip art, fonts, photos, and templates can also be found on the Internet. Search using other keywords—such as *clip art*, *free clip art*, *fonts*, *graphics*, *graphic designers*, *Microsoft Word*, *word processing*, *web design*, *logos*, *digital cameras*, and *scanning*—to learn about different techniques and approaches to producing professional-looking documents.

Search engines that provide image results include Google, Bing, and Yahoo. Be sure to read the copyright information associated with each image collection. Many images are free to use privately, but permission may be needed if the images are used for a profit-making endeavor.

Most graphics on the Web can be downloaded by right-clicking the image and then clicking the *Save picture as* option at the shortcut menu that displays. The file name and location (such as a USB drive) can be changed at the regular Save As dialog box. Again, be sure to abide by the copyright of downloaded materials! Most images are copyrighted.

Using Online Templates

Tutorial

Creating a Document Using a Template

Microsoft Word 2016 provides access to online templates. To access these templates, click the File tab and then click the *New* option. Microsoft has collaborated with various content experts to provide hundreds of professionally designed templates for Word, Excel, Access, Publisher, PowerPoint, Visio, and OneNote. Initiate a search to find a template and then double-click the template thumbnail to open a document based on the template. Fine-tune a template by tailoring it to the needs of the document. Many templates reinforce integration of the Office programs by using a common theme.

Occasionally, the words *Compatibility Mode* will display in the Title bar next to the document name. This indicates that some new features are disabled to prevent problems when working with previous versions of Office. Converting the document to the newer version will enable these features but may result in layout changes. To convert the document to Word 2016 format, click the File tab and then click the Convert button at the Info backstage area.

1. At a blank document, search for a template and open a new document by completing the following steps:
   a. Click the File tab and then click the *New* option.
   b. At the New backstage area, type company picnic in the search text box and then press the Enter key.
   c. Double-click the first *Company picnic invitation flyer* thumbnail (the one with the orange graphic at the bottom). ***Note: If this template is no longer available, open CollegePicnicTemplate.docx from the C1 folder.***
2. Click the *[Company Name]* placeholder and then type the name of your college.
3. Click in the placeholder text *Annual Company Picnic* and then type Annual College Picnic.
4. Click the *[Date]* placeholder under the pitcher of lemonade and then type August 18, 2018.
5. Click the first *[Time]* placeholder and then type 11:00 a.m.
6. Click the second *[Time]* placeholder and then type 4:00 p.m.
7. Click the *[Address | City, ST]* placeholder and then type the address of your college.
8. Click the *[Date]* placeholder right of the text *Please R.S.V.P. by* and then type August 1.
9. Click the *[Name]* placeholder and then type Stephanie Bourne.
10. Click the *[Email]* placeholder and then type bourne@emcp.net.
11. Click the *[Phone]* placeholder and then type (242) 555-0177.
12. Save the document by completing the following steps:
    a. Click the File tab and then click the *Save As* option.
    b. At the Save As backstage area, click the *Browse* option.
    c. Navigate to your C1 folder and double-click the folder to open it.
    d. Type 1-CollegeInvitation in the *File name* text box.
    e. Click the Save button and leave the file open for the next project.

Check Your Work

Figure 1.40 Reviewing Image Results at the Insert Pictures Window

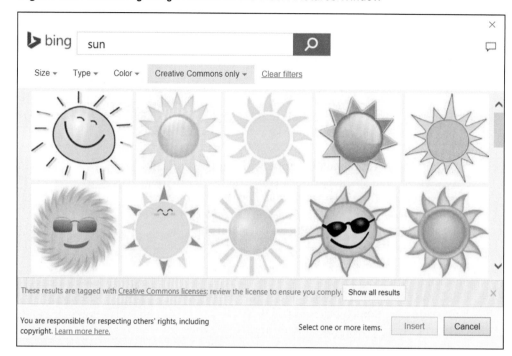

Using Bing Images

Tutorial

Inserting, Sizing, and Positioning an Image

Online Pictures

In addition to the image files available in some of the student data file folders, more image files, such as clip art and photographs, are available at the Insert Pictures window. Search for images at the Insert Pictures window by clicking in the *Bing Image Search* text box, typing a search word or phrase, and then pressing the Enter key. For example, search for images using the word *sun*, and images will display in the Insert Pictures window similar to what is shown in Figure 1.40.

Project 3b Inserting an Online Image   Part 2 of 3

1. With **1-CollegeInvitation.docx** open, add a sun clip art image by completing the following steps:
   a. Press Ctrl + Home to move the insertion point to the beginning of the document.
   b. Click the Insert tab and then click the Online Pictures button in the Illustrations group.

c. At the Insert Pictures window, click in the *Bing Image Search* text box, type sun, and then press the Enter key.

d. Click the sun clip art image shown below and then click the Insert button. ***Note: If this image is not available, use sun.png located in the C1 folder.***

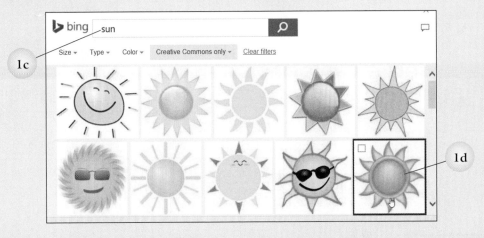

2. With the clip art image still selected, format the image by completing the following steps:

a. Adjust the size of the image by clicking in the *Shape Height* measurement box in the Size group on the Picture Tools Format tab, typing 2, and then pressing the Enter key.

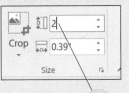

b. Change the text wrapping by clicking the Wrap Text button in the Arrange group and then clicking *Behind Text* at the drop-down list.

c. Drag the selected image to the location indicated in the image below (see also Figure 1.41).

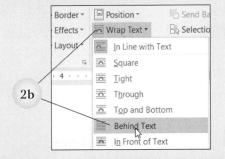
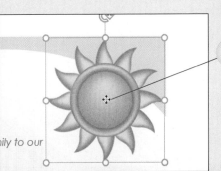

3. Click the Save button on the Quick Access Toolbar.

4. Print the document by clicking the File tab, clicking the *Print* option, and then clicking the Print button. (Leave the document open for the next exercise.)

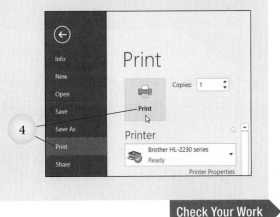

Check Your Work

Figure 1.41 Invitation Created in Projects 3a and 3b

Figure 1.42 Using the Snipping Tool

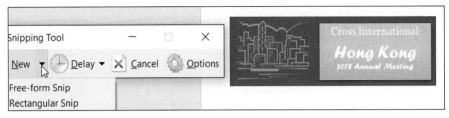

Using the Windows 10 Snipping Tool

In addition to all the Office 2016 components, an assortment of office tools is included with most editions of Microsoft Windows. One of the tools you may want to become familiar with is the Snipping Tool. Use the Snipping Tool to capture a screenshot, or a snip, of any object on the screen and then annotate, save, or share the image. After the image is saved, it may be inserted into a document from the Insert Pictures dialog box. Figure 1.42 illustrates the Snipping Tool window next to a logo that can be captured and reused in a variety of documents.

Insert Pictures

Project 3c Using the Windows 10 Snipping Tool   **Part 3 of 3**

1. With **1-CollegeInvitation.docx** open, scroll down the document to display the lemonade glass and pitcher image.
2. Display the Start menu by clicking the Start button.
3. At the Start menu, type snip.
4. Click the Snipping Tool app in the results list.
5. At the Snipping Tool dialog box, click the New button arrow and then click *Free-form Snip* at the drop-down list.
6. With the scissors tool, draw a free-form shape around the lemonade glass and pitcher image.
7. Click the Save Snip button and then save the picture as **1-Lemonade.png** in the C1 folder. *Hint: This image has now been saved in a graphic format and may later be inserted into a document.*

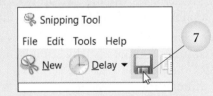

8. Close the Snipping Tool window.
9. Save and then close **1-CollegeInvitation.docx**.

Chapter Summary

- Use desktop publishing software to produce professional-looking documents for office and home use. For simple desktop publishing projects, use Microsoft Word; for more complex projects, use a high-end desktop publishing application.

- When planning a publication, clearly define the purpose, assess the target audience, decide the form in which the audience will see the message, decide what outcome is expected after readers receive the message, determine the budget, and collect examples of effective design.

- Effective design involves planning and organizing content. Decide what items are most important to the reader. Design concepts such as focus, balance, proportion, contrast, directional flow, consistency, and color are essential to creating a visually attractive publication that presents information in a logical, organized manner.

- Focus can be created by using text created in larger, bolder, contrasting typefaces, such as for titles and subheads and by using graphics, such as lines, clip art, and photographs.

- White space is the empty background with no text or graphics. Use white space to emphasize the main message and give the reader's eyes a break from too much text.

- Balance on a page is created by equally distributing the visual weight of elements on a page in either a symmetrical or asymmetrical manner. Symmetrical design, in which all elements are centered, contains similar elements of equal weight or proportion on the left and right sides and the top and bottom of the page. Asymmetrical design uses contrasting elements of various proportions and weights to achieve balance on the page.

- Design harmony may be accomplished by applying a design guideline called the *rule of thirds*. This rule states that pages should be arranged in thirds rather than in halves or fourths. Studies indicate that this basic grid is more appealing to the eye than any other design.

- In establishing a proportional relationship among the elements on a page, think about all the parts as they relate to the document as a whole. Proportionally size the visual elements in a publication according to their relative importance to the intended message and try not to make all design elements the same size.

- Text, graphics, and other design elements should take up two-thirds of the document, and one-third of a publication should consist of white space.

- Contrast is the difference between varying degrees of lightness and darkness on the page. A high level of contrast is more visually stimulating and helps to draw the audience into the document. Contrast also serves as an organizational aid to help the reader move through the document and easily follow the flow of information.

- Directional flow can be produced by grouping related elements and placing them close to each other on the page, by using consistent alignment to establish a strong visual connection between the elements on a page, and by positioning elements in such a way that the reader is drawn through the text and to particular words or images that the designer wishes to emphasize.

- Consistent elements—such as margins, columns, typefaces, type sizes, spacing, alignment, and color—help to integrate all the individual parts of a document and provide a sense of unity. Repetitive, consistent elements can also lend identity to a set of documents.

- Modify fonts, colors, margins, table formatting, and other elements by choosing different style formats from the Styles group on the Home tab. Also apply different style sets with options in the Document Formatting group on the Design tab.
- The use of style sets and document themes in Word help to make formatting efficient and consistent for any publication or group of similarly designed publications.
- A theme is a set of formatting characteristics that includes colors, fonts (including heading and body text fonts), and effects (including lines and fill effects).
- Use color on a page to help organize ideas; emphasize important information; provide focus, contrast, directional flow, and consistency; and establish or reinforce an identity.
- Evaluate and analyze well-designed documents to determine how the message is communicated, how elements are incorporated into the design, and so on.
- A wealth of information and resources are available on the Internet, including free clip art, photographs, templates, and helpful newsletters.
- Access online templates through Word 2016 by clicking the File tab and then clicking the *New* option. At the New backstage area, search for a template by entering a search phrase and then pressing the Enter key.
- Access images online by clicking the Insert tab and then clicking the Online Pictures button. Use the *Bing Image Search* text box to search for images using a search phrase.
- Use the Snipping Tool to capture a screenshot, or snip, of any object on the screen, and then annotate, save, or share the image.

Commands Review

FEATURE	RIBBON TAB, GROUP	BUTTON
Insert Picture dialog box	Insert, Illustrations	
Insert Pictures window	Insert, Illustrations	
SmartArt	Insert, Illustrations	
styles	Home, Styles	
templates	File, *New*	
themes	Design, Document Formatting	

Workbook

Chapter study tools and assessment activities are available in the workbook pages of the ebook. These resources are designed to help you further develop and demonstrate mastery of the skills learned in this chapter.

Applying and Modifying Fonts

Performance Objectives

Upon successful completion of Chapter 2, you will be able to:

1 Define typography terms

2 Apply desktop publishing guidelines

3 Use fonts in Windows 10

4 Apply and modify font color

5 Add symbols and special characters

6 Apply advanced font formatting

7 Refine word and line spacing

Desktop Publishing Terms

ascender	leading	saturation
baseline	ligature	serif
cap height	line spacing	swash
descender	luminescence	tracking
em dash	monospaced	typeface
en dash	pitch	typestyle
font	point size	x-height
hue	proportional	
kerning	sans serif	

Word Features Used

font color	special characters
Format Painter	symbols
kerning	text effects
line spacing	

SNAP

If you are a SNAP user, launch the Precheck and Tutorials from your Assignments page.

Data Files

Before beginning chapter work, copy the C2 folder to your storage medium and then make C2 the active folder.

Project 1 **Apply Font Formatting to a Sign**   **2 Parts**

You will open a preformatted document, add additional text, and then format the document by modifying the font and font colors.

Preview Finished Project

Defining Typography Terms

typeface* or *font

A set of characters with a common design and shape

An important element in any type of document is the font used to format the text. Understanding basic typography and the terms used to describe it is useful when choosing a font for a document. As discussed in Chapter 1, when planning a document, consider the purpose of the document, the audience, the feeling the document is to elicit, and how to emphasize the most important information. Make sure the headlines, graphics, and typography work together to support the desired message.

baseline

An imaginary horizontal line upon which characters rest

Important desktop publishing terms and guidelines related to applying and modifying fonts will be introduced in this chapter. These concepts will be applied by creating documents such as a conference sign, a sales flyer, and a corporate invitation.

x-height

The height of the lowercase letter *x* of a font

Defining Typefaces

One of the most important considerations in establishing a particular mood or feeling in a document is choosing the right typeface. A ***typeface*** is a set of characters with a common design and shape. (Microsoft Word refers to a typeface as a ***font***.) For example, consider using a decorative typeface for invitations and menus, but use a simple block-style typeface for headlines and reports. Choose a typeface that reflects the content, the expectations of the audience, and the projected image.

cap height

The distance between the baseline and the top of a capital letter

ascender

The part of a lowercase character that rises above the x-height

Certain elements distinguish one typeface from another. The characters in a line of text rest on an imaginary horizontal line called the ***baseline***. Parts of certain characters may extend above and below this baseline. Figure 2.1 illustrates the various parts of type.

The ***x-height*** is the height of the main body of the lowercase characters in the typeface and is equivalent to the height of the lowercase letter *x*. The ***cap height*** is the distance between the baseline and the top of a capital letter. ***Ascenders*** are the parts of lowercase characters that rise above the x-height (for example, the upper part of a lowercase letter *h*), and ***descenders*** are the parts of lowercase characters

descender

The part of a lowercase character that extends below the baseline

Figure 2.1 Identifying the Parts of Type

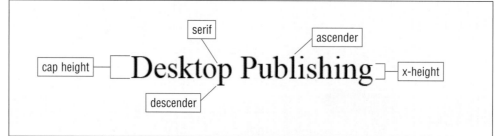

that extend below the baseline (for example, the swoop of a lowercase letter *j*). ***Serifs*** are the small strokes at the beginnings and ends of characters.

serif
A small stroke at the beginning or end of a character

monospaced
The same amount of horizontal space is allotted for each character in a typeface

proportional
A varying amount of horizontal space is allotted for each character in a typeface

A typeface is either ***monospaced*** or ***proportional***. A monospaced typeface allots the same amount of horizontal space for each character; professional publications rarely use this kind of typeface. Courier is an example of a monospaced typeface. Proportional typefaces allow a varying amount of space for each character. For example, the lowercase letter *i* takes up less space than the uppercase letter *M*. In addition, different proportional typefaces take up different amounts of horizontal space. For example, the same sentence takes up far more horizontal space when set in Century Gothic than in Times New Roman.

DTP POINTER
Use a serif font for a text-intensive document.

Typefaces fall into two main categories: serif and sans serif. Traditionally, serif typefaces are easier to read and are used with text-intensive documents, such as business letters, manuals, and reports. Serifs help move the reader's eyes across the page.

sans serif
Describes a typeface for which the characters do not have small strokes at the ends

The characters in a ***sans serif*** typeface do not have serifs. (*Sans* is French for *without*.) Sans serif typefaces are often used for headlines and advertisements because the characters are easier to recognize. In modern designs, sans serif typefaces may also be used for body text, but several practices should be avoided. For instance, lines should not contain more than seven or eight words, and bold, italics, outlining, and shadowing should not be applied. Figure 2.2 shows examples of serif, sans serif, and monospaced typefaces.

Microsoft Office 2016 includes many typefaces designed for extended on-screen reading, and they are integrated into the templates offered as part of Microsoft Office. These typefaces include the default, Calibri, as well as Cambria, Candara, Consolas, Constantia, and Corbel. Calibri, Candara, and Corbel are sans serif typefaces; Cambria and Constantia are serif typefaces; and Consolas is monospaced.

DTP POINTER
Use a sans serif font for headings.

Defining Type Sizes

pitch
The number of characters that can be printed in 1 horizontal inch

Type size (font size) is defined by two measurements: pitch and point size. ***Pitch*** is a measurement used for monospaced typefaces; it reflects the number of characters that can be printed in 1 horizontal inch. For some printers, pitch is referred to as *cpi*, or *characters per inch*. For example, the font Courier 10 cpi is the same as 10-pitch Courier.

DTP POINTER
Sans serif typefaces are more readable than serif typefaces when set in very small point sizes.

Figure 2.2 Comparing Serif, Sans Serif, and Monospaced Typefaces

Serif Typefaces	Sans Serif Typefaces	Monospaced Typefaces
Cambria	Calibri	Consolas
Constantia	Candara	Lucida Console
Times New Roman	Corbel	OCR A Extended
Bell MT	Agency FB	Courier New
Harrington	Arial	
Bookman Old Style	Tahoma	
Book Antiqua	Impact	

Figure 2.3 Comparing Point Sizes in Wide Latin and Arial Fonts

point size

A vertical character measurement; one point is approximately equal to ¹/₇₂ of an inch

Point size is a vertical character measurement. The characters in a proportional typeface are measured in units called *points* (measured vertically from the top of the ascenders to the bottom of the descenders). A point is approximately ¹/₇₂ of an inch. The higher the point size, the larger the characters. Figure 2.3 shows Wide Latin and Arial typefaces in a variety of point sizes. For each point size, the characters in the two typefaces vary greatly in width, but their heights are identical.

Defining Typestyles

typestyle

A variation of a typeface, such as regular or normal, bold, italic, or bold italic

A *typestyle* is a variation of a font that causes the text to appear thicker (bold) and/or slanted (italic). Within a typeface, characters may have various typestyles. Typestyles are divided into four main categories: normal (also known as light, black, regular, or roman), bold, italic, and bold italic. Apply a typestyle to text by selecting the text and then clicking the Bold button and/or the Italic button in the Font group on the Home tab. Alternatively, click the Font group dialog box launcher to display the Font dialog box and then select a typestyle to apply regular, italic, bold, or bold italic formatting to a font.

Applying Desktop Publishing Guidelines

Desktop publishing includes general guidelines, or conventions, that provide a starting point for designing documents. For instance, use moderation in choosing typefaces and type sizes; two fonts and three font sizes are usually adequate for most publications. Too many typefaces give the document a disorderly appearance, confuse the reader, and take away from the content. Remember that serif fonts are more formal and are the standard for long blocks of text. Sans serif typefaces are cleaner and more contemporary in form and thus are favored for large text and headlines. Line length and line spacing are also factors to consider in choosing appropriate typefaces.

DTP POINTER

To read an overview on topics related to typography and free fonts, go to https://www.microsoft.com/Typography.

Using OpenType Fonts

OpenType is a font format that was developed jointly by Microsoft and Adobe. OpenType fonts can potentially contain many thousands of characters. This means that an OpenType font may contain multiple alphabets (such as Latin, Greek, Japanese, and more). This font format provides several advantages over older font technologies, such as TrueType. OpenType fonts have better support for international character sets, cross-platform support between Windows and Macintosh computers, support for Postscript and TrueType fonts, and support for advanced typographic features, which include special ligatures (combined characters) and *swashes* (exaggerated serifs).

swash

An exaggerated serif

Using Fonts to Save Ink

In addition to reinforcing the message of a document, the right font can also help save money on printing. The amount of ink used in printing is determined by the thickness of the font. Choosing a font with *narrow* or *light* in its name is usually more ink efficient than using a font with *bold* or *black* in its name. Also, sans serif fonts tend to use less ink than serif fonts.

DTP POINTER ▶

Choose ink-efficient fonts to reduce printing costs.

The following fonts are listed in order from most to least ink efficient: Century Gothic, Times New Roman, Calibri, Verdana, Arial, Trebuchet, Tahoma, and Franklin Gothic Medium. However, note that Century Gothic is a wider font and may extend the text to an additional page, which means that it could be less paper efficient.

Using Fonts to Enhance Design

The fonts chosen for a document can greatly affect the feeling the document elicits in the reader, thus contributing to or detracting from its effectiveness. The combination of fonts may create a harmonious, contrasting, or conflicting design, as shown in Figure 2.4. The harmonious and contrasting designs shown in documents A and B are desirable, whereas the conflicting design shown in document C is not.

Figure 2.4 Comparing Harmonious, Contrasting, and Conflicting Designs

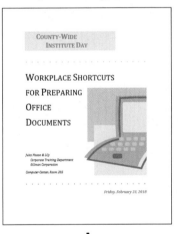

A
Harmonious Design

B
Contrasting Design

C
Conflicting Design

DTP POINTER

Contrasting fonts create interest in a document.

A harmonious design is calm and comfortable, although not particularly exciting. This makes it well suited for traditional documents, such as formal invitations. A harmonious design is created using one font and applying different effects to it. Other design elements (borders, graphics, and symbols) with the same qualities as the chosen font may also be used to enhance the design.

A contrasting design is created by using fonts that are very different from one another but still complementary. Achieve a contrasting design by using font pairs that are thick and thin, dark and light, sans serif and serif, or plain and ornate or that are set in two colors or sizes, as shown in Figure 2.5. Using a contrasting design helps to create a bold, interesting look, which draws the reader in and holds his or her interest.

A conflicting design is created when two or more fonts that look too similar are used in a document. The fonts are different but not different enough to easily tell them apart. Avoid creating conflicting designs in documents.

Additionally, remember to use fonts that complement the message of the document. Figure 2.6 shows examples of unique fonts that may be well suited to particular applications.

Figure 2.5 Creating Interesting Designs with Fonts

Figure 2.6 Matching the Font to the Message

Sample	Font Name
Alleycat Seafood Restaurant	Alleycat
CARIBBEAN CRUISE	BERMUDA SOLID
South of the Border	Chilada ICG Uno
Wedding Invitation	Calligrapher
Casper the Ghost	Chiller
Kids on Campus	Curlz MT
Certificate of Completion	Diploma
COMPUTER SEMINAR	NEWTRON ICG
LINE DANCING CLASS	COTTONWOOD
RED PAPERCLIPS	PAPERCLIP
Camp Sandy Feet	KidTYPEPaint
Four Corners Art Gallery	Matura MT Script Capitals

Using Fonts in Windows 10

When software is loaded on a computer, any fonts associated with that software are loaded into Windows 10. View all the fonts that have been loaded into a Windows 10 computer by displaying the Control Panel, clicking the *Appearance and Personalization* category, and then clicking the *Fonts* option.

DTP POINTER

Substitute a different font if a particular font is not supported by the printer.

If the printer connected to the computer does not support a font or font size used to format text, Word may substitute the closest possible font or font size. View the substituted fonts in the Font Substitution dialog box (shown in Figure 2.7) by displaying the Word Options dialog box, clicking the *Advanced* option in the left panel, and then clicking the Font Substitution button in the *Show document content* section. **Note: If a project in this textbook calls for a particular font that is not available on the computer, simply substitute another font.**

Figure 2.7 Viewing the Font Substitution Dialog Box

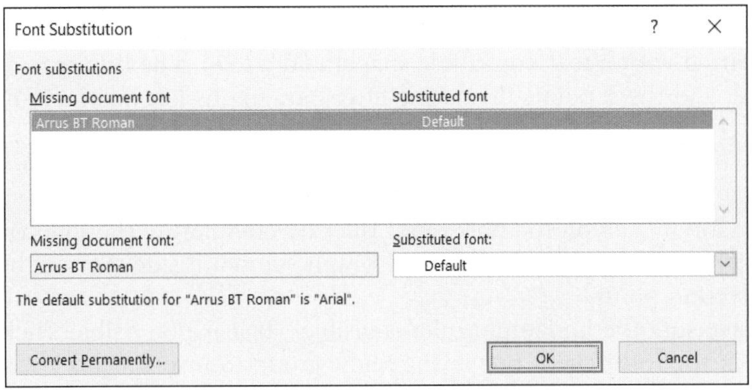

Embedding Fonts in Word

Embedding fonts in a Word document is a good way to make sure that they will look the same when viewed on other computers. Embedding a font attaches the associated font file to the document so the font will display on computers that do not have that particular font file. To embed fonts in Word, display the Word Options dialog box, click the *Save* option in the left panel, insert a check mark in the *Embed fonts in the file* check box, and then insert a check mark in the desired embedding option, as shown in Figure 2.8. Note that embedding fonts can increase the document's file size and may not work for some commercially restricted fonts.

Changing Default Font Formatting

Word documents are based on a template that applies default formatting. For Word 2016, this default formatting includes 11-point Calibri, 1.08 line spacing, and 8 points of spacing after each paragraph (inserted each time the Enter key is pressed).

To change the default font, click the Font group dialog box launcher to display the Font dialog box. At the Font dialog box, select a font to use as the default and then click the Set As Default button in the lower left corner of the dialog box. At the dialog box that displays, determine whether to set the new default font for just the current document or for all documents created based on the Normal.dotm template and then click OK. Font selections made within a document through the Font dialog box will override the default font settings for the current document only.

Figure 2.8 Embedding Fonts in a Word Document

Project 1a Applying Font Formatting to a Conference Sign
Part 1 of 2

1. Open **Sign.docx** from the C2 folder on your storage medium. (The document has been formatted with a text box, a line shape, and a logo. The line spacing has been changed to single, and the 8 points of spacing after paragraphs has been removed.)
2. Save the document with the name **2-Sign**.
3. Click the Show/Hide ¶ button in the Paragraph group on the Home tab to turn on the display of nonprinting characters.
4. Insert a right tab on the horizontal ruler by completing the following steps:
   a. Click immediately left of the paragraph symbol inside the text box to position the insertion point.
   b. Make sure the horizontal ruler is visible. (If it is not visible, click the View tab and then click the *Ruler* check box in the Show group to insert a check mark.)

c. Click the Alignment button at the left side of the ruler until the right tab symbol displays.
d. Position the arrow pointer on the 8.25-inch mark on the horizontal ruler and then click the left mouse button.

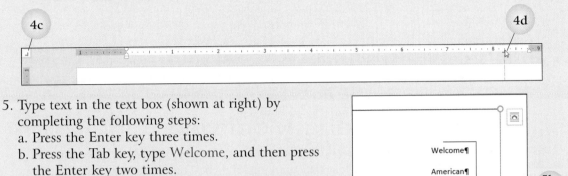

5. Type text in the text box (shown at right) by completing the following steps:
   a. Press the Enter key three times.
   b. Press the Tab key, type Welcome, and then press the Enter key two times.
   c. Press the Tab key, type American, and then press the Enter key.
   d. Press the Tab key, type Society, and then press the Enter key.
   e. Press the Tab key, type of Public, and then press the Enter key. (The text will appear behind the red line, which will be adjusted later in the project. You may need to change the *o* in *of* back to lowercase.)
   f. Press the Tab key, type Accountants, and then press the Enter key two times.
   g. Press the Tab key, type June 18 through June 22, and then press the Enter key two times.
6. Apply font formatting to the text by completing the following steps:
   a. Select the word *Welcome*. (Do not select the paragraph symbol.)
   b. Change the font to 48-point Cambria and then apply bold and italic formatting.
   c. Select the text *June 18 through June 22*.
   d. Change the font to 14-point Cambria and then apply bold and italic formatting.
   e. Select the text *American Society of Public Accountants*.
   f. Change the font to 66-point Franklin Gothic Demi. ***Hint: Type the value in the Font Size option text box.***
7. With the text *American Society of Public Accountants* still selected, change the line spacing by completing the following steps:
   a. Click the Paragraph group dialog box launcher.
   b. At the Paragraph dialog box, click the *Line spacing* option box arrow and then click *Exactly* at the drop-down list.
   c. Select the current measurement in the *At* measurement box and then type 66.
   d. Click OK.
8. Copy the red horizontal line by completing the following steps:
   a. Select the red horizontal line below *Welcome*.
   b. Press Ctrl + C to create a copy of the line.

c. Press Ctrl + V to paste the copy of the line.

d. With the new copy of the line selected, drag the line so it is positioned below *Accountants*, as shown in Figure 2.10 (page 59). You will make further formatting changes to this file in Project 1b.

9. Click the Show/Hide ¶ button in the Paragraph group on the Home tab to turn off the display of nonprinting characters.

10. Save **2-Sign.docx**.

Check Your Work

Applying and Modifying Font Color

Tutorial

Applying Font Formatting Using the Font Group

 Font Color

hue

The color itself

saturation

The intensity of a color

luminescence

The brightness of a color

Modify text formatted in the default font by applying color. Apply font colors to text by selecting the text and then clicking the Font Color button in the Font group on the Home tab. The Font Color button drop-down gallery displays two groups of colors (*Theme Colors* and *Standard Colors*), but a wider variety of colors can be accessed by clicking the *More Colors* option to display the Colors dialog box. At the Colors dialog box, click the Standard tab to display 127 colors and 15 shades of gray. ***Hint: Choosing*** **Automatic** ***at the Font Color button drop-down gallery and then changing the background of the document to black causes the text color to change automatically to white.***

At the Colors dialog box with the Custom tab selected, customize font colors with any of 16 million colors. Create custom colors by choosing the RGB (red, green, blue) or HSL (hue, saturation, luminescence) color models, as shown in Figure 2.9. To create a custom color using the RGB model, adjust the values in the *Red*, *Green*, and *Blue* measurement boxes by entering values between 0 and 255 or by using the measurement box up and down arrows. Adjust colors in the HSL model using three factors: ***hue***, which is the color itself; ***saturation***, which is the color's intensity; and ***luminescence***, which is the brightness of the color. Adjust the values similarly to how the values are adjusted in the RGB model. If the document contains an object or text with a desired color, copy the color from one object to another using Format Painter.

Figure 2.9 Customizing Colors Using Color Models

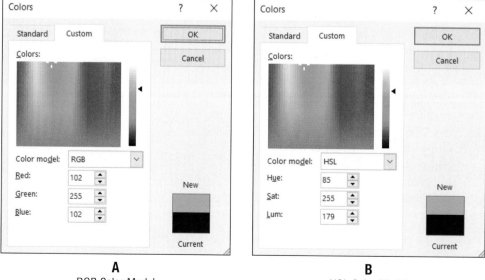

A
RGB Color Model

B
HSL Color Model

1. With **2-Sign.docx** open, change the font color by completing the following steps:
   a. Select the text *Welcome*.
   b. Click the Font Color button arrow.
   c. Click the *White, Background 1, Darker 50%* color (first column, last row in the *Theme Colors* section).
   d. Select the text *June 18 through June 22* and then press the F4 function key. (This applies the same gray color that was applied to *Welcome*.)
2. Change the font color at the Colors dialog box by completing the following steps:
   a. Select the text *American Society of Public Accountants*.
   b. Click the Font Color button arrow.
   c. Click *More Colors* at the drop-down gallery.
   d. At the Colors dialog box, click the Custom tab.
   e. Select the current number in the *Red* measurement box and then type 30.
   f. Press the Tab key (this selects the current number in the *Green* measurement box) and then type 90.
   g. Press the Tab key (this selects the current number in the *Blue* measurement box) and then type 160.
   h. Click OK.
3. Apply text effects and change the font color by completing the following steps:
   a. Select the word *of*.
   b. Change the font to 54-point Cambria and then apply italic formatting.
   c. Click the Text Effects and Typography button in the Font group on the Home tab and then click the *Gradient Fill, Gray* option (first column, second row).
   d. Click the Text Effects and Typography button, point to *Shadow* at the drop-down gallery, and then click the *Offset: Right* option (first column, second row in the *Outer* section).
   e. Click the Font Color button arrow and then click *More Colors* at the drop-down gallery.
   f. At the Colors dialog box, click the Standard tab.

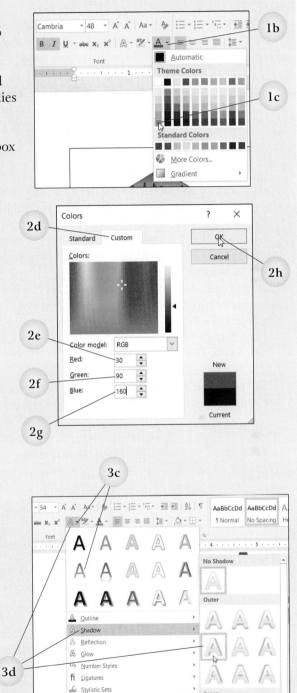

g. Click the third red color from the right in the bottom row of the honeycomb.

h. Click OK.

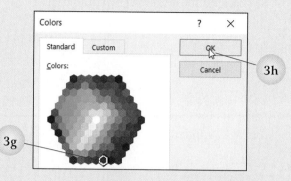

4. Click the Show/Hide ¶ button to turn on the display of nonprinting characters, position the insertion point immediately left of the second paragraph mark under the text *June 18 through June 22*, and then complete the following steps:

a. Set a left tab at the 0.5-inch mark on the horizontal ruler.

b. Press the Tab key, type Sponsored by, and then press the Enter key.

c. Press the Tab key and then type Banks&Wells. (Do not add a space before or after the & symbol.)

5. Select the text *Sponsored by* and then change the font to 12-point Cambria, apply bold italic formatting, and change the font color to White, Background 1, Darker 50%.

6. Select the text *Banks&Wells* and then make the following changes:

a. Change the font to 12-point Franklin Gothic Demi.

b. Apply the Blue, Accent 1, Darker 50% font color.

7. Select the & symbol in the text *Banks&Wells* and then make the following changes:

a. Click the Shading button arrow in the Paragraph group on the Home tab and then click the *Blue, Accent 1, Darker 50%* option at the drop-down gallery.

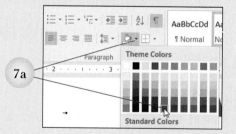

b. Click the Font Color button arrow and then click the *White, Background 1* color.

8. Apply a red border and a texture to the text box by completing the following steps:

a. Click the border of the text box to select it. (The border will turn to a solid line when it has been selected.)

b. Click the Drawing Tools Format tab.

c. Click the Shape Outline button arrow in the Shape Styles group and then click the *Dark Red* color (first option in the *Standard Colors* section).

d. Click the Shape Outline button arrow, point to *Weight*, and then click *1½ pt* at the drop-down gallery.

e. Click the Shape Fill button arrow, point to *Texture*, and then click the *Recycled paper* option (second column, fourth row).

f. Click the Home tab and then click the Show/Hide ¶ button to turn off the display of nonprinting characters.

9. Compare your document to the document shown in Figure 2.10 and make any changes needed for the two documents to be the same.

10. Save, print, and then close **2-Sign.docx**.

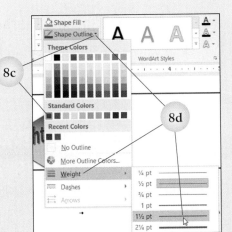

Check Your Work

Figure 2.10 Conference Sign Created in Projects 1a and 1b

Preview Finished Project

Adding Symbols and Special Characters

Symbols and special characters add interest and originality to documents. Sometimes, it is the small touches that make a difference, such as adding a symbol (❖) at the end of an article in a newsletter, enlarging a symbol (ϒ) and using it as a graphic on a page, or adding a special character (™) to clarify text. Interesting symbols are found in such fonts as (normal text), Wingdings, Wingdings 2, Wingdings 3, and Webdings. Examples of special characters include an em dash (—), en dash (–), copyright symbol (©), registered trademark symbol (®), ellipsis (. . .), and nonbreaking hyphen (-).

To insert a symbol, click the Symbol button in the Symbols group on the Insert tab and then click one of the symbols in the drop-down list or click *More Symbols* at the bottom of the drop-down list to display the Symbol dialog box. At the Symbol dialog box, shown in Figure 2.11, select the Symbols tab, select the desired font, and then double-click the symbol or click the symbol once, click the Insert button, and then click the Close button (or press the Esc key). To insert a special character at the Symbol dialog box, click the Special Characters tab and then insert the character in the document using one of the methods just described.

Recently used symbols display on the Symbol button drop-down list and also appear toward the bottom of the Symbol dialog box for easy access. Another way to quickly access a frequently used symbol is to write down the character code for that symbol and then enter that number in the *Character code* text box near the bottom of the Symbol dialog box with the Symbols tab selected.

Figure 2.11 Inserting a Symbol at the Symbol Dialog Box

Click this option box arrow to display a list of fonts. Choose the font that contains the desired symbol.

Recently used symbols appear in this section of the dialog box.

The *Character code* text box identifies the number of the symbol used. Type the character code for the symbol in this text box.

Creating Em and En Dashes

em dash

A dash that indicates a pause in speech; it is as wide as the uppercase letter *M* of the typeface

en dash

A dash that indicates a continuation; it is as wide as the lowercase letter *n* of the typeface

An *em dash* (—) is used to indicate a pause in speech, and an *en dash* (–) is used to indicate a continuation, as in the ranges *116–133* and *January–March*. An em dash is generally the width of the uppercase letter *M* in the typeface, and an en dash is the width of the lowercase letter *n*. Both em and en dashes can be inserted at the Symbol dialog box with the Special Characters tab selected. In addition, an em dash can be inserted from the keyboard by pressing Alt + Ctrl + Num - (minus key on the numeric keypad), and an en dash can be inserted by pressing Ctrl + Num - . Do not include spaces before or after en dashes and em dashes. Additionally, the AutoCorrect feature includes an option that will automatically create em dashes. To create an em dash, type a word, type two hyphens, type the next word, and then press the spacebar or press the Enter key. When the spacebar or the Enter key is pressed, AutoCorrect automatically converts the two hyphens into an em dash.

Using Smart Quotes

DTP POINTER

Use straight quotation marks to indicate inches and feet.

In typesetting, the tail of an open quotation mark (") extends upward and the tail of a close quotation mark (") extends downward. Straight quotes are typically used to indicate inches (") and feet ('). Word's Smart Quotes feature, which is active by default, will automatically choose the quote style that is appropriate.

To turn the Smart Quotes feature on or off, click the File tab, click *Options*, click *Proofing* in the left panel, click the AutoCorrect Options button, click the AutoFormat As You Type tab, and then click the "*Straight quotes*" with "*smart quotes*" check box to insert or remove the check mark. In addition, symbols and special characters may be added to the AutoCorrect feature, which will automatically insert a specific symbol when using the corresponding keyboard command. For example, type *(c)* and AutoCorrect will automatically change the three characters to the © special character. Symbols may also be copied to the Clipboard and pasted into the text when needed.

Project 2 **Formatting a Sales Flyer with Special Characters** Part 1 of 1

1. Open **CCarpet.docx** and then save it with the name **2-CCarpet**.
2. Click in the text box in the upper left corner of the document and then type Create a comfortable, warm, and inviting home with an Adana area rug.
3. Insert a registered trademark symbol after *Adana* by completing the following steps:
   a. Position the insertion point after the word *Adana*.
   b. Click the Insert tab.
   c. Click the Symbol button in the Symbols group and then click *More Symbols* at the drop-down list.
   d. At the Symbol dialog box, click the Special Characters tab.
   e. Double-click the *Registered* option in the *Character* list box.
   f. Click the Close button to close the dialog box.

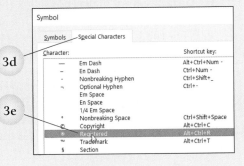

---

4. Delete the *o* in *Camino* and then insert the *ó* symbol (the letter *o* with an acute accent) by completing the following steps:
   a. Select the *o* in *Camino* in the text box at the bottom of the document and then press the Delete key.
   b. Click the Symbol button in the Symbols group and then click *More Symbols* at the drop-down list.
   c. At the Symbol dialog box, make sure that *(normal text)* is selected in the *Font* option box. If *(normal text)* is not selected, click the *Font* option box arrow and then click *(normal text)* at the drop-down list.
   d. Scroll down to approximately the eleventh row in the *Symbols* list box and then double-click the *ó* symbol (Character code 00F3).
   e. Click the Close button.

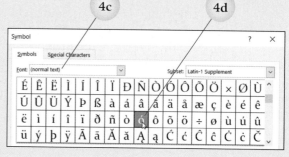

5. Turn off smart quotes by completing the following steps:
   a. Click the File tab and then click *Options*.
   b. At the Word Options dialog box, click *Proofing* in the left panel.
   c. Click the AutoCorrect Options button.
   d. At the AutoCorrect dialog box, click the AutoFormat As You Type tab.
   e. Click the "*Straight quotes*" with "*smart quotes*" check box to remove the check mark.
   f. Click OK.
   g. Click OK to close the Word Options dialog box.

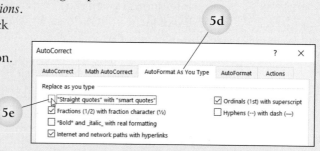

6. Click right of the first bullet below the heading *Rectangle sizes:* and then type 4' x 6'.
7. Click right of the second bullet below the heading *Rectangle sizes:* and then type 6' x 8'6".
8. Click right of the third bullet below the heading *Rectangle sizes:* and then type 8' x 9'6".

9. Replace the hyphen between *10 a.m.* and *5 p.m.* with an en dash by completing the following steps:
   a. Select the hyphen between *10 a.m.* and *5 p.m.* below the heading *Store hours:*
   b. Click the Symbol button and then click *More Symbols* at the drop-down list.
   c. At the Symbol dialog box, click the Special Characters tab.
   d. Double-click the *En Dash* option in the *Character* list box.
   e. Click the Close button.
10. Select the hyphen between *9 a.m.* and *6 p.m.* and then replace it with an en dash.
11. Select the hyphen between *Mon.* and *Fri.* and then replace it with an en dash.
12. Turn smart quotes back on by completing Steps 5a to 5d, inserting a check mark in the "*Straight quotes*" with "*smart quotes*" check box at the AutoCorrect dialog box, and then clicking OK two times.
13. Save, print, and then close **2-CCarpet.docx**.

Check Your Work

Project 3 Apply Advanced Font Formatting to an Invitation **2 Parts**

You will open a preformatted invitation and apply advanced font, word, and line spacing options to it.

Preview Finished Project

Applying Advanced Font Formatting

Word 2016 offers advanced font formatting features that can improve the appearance of text. Access advanced font formatting options at the Font dialog box with the Advanced tab selected. Use options at this dialog box to specify character spacing for text, apply OpenType features, and apply text effects to selected text.

Adjusting Character Spacing

DTP POINTER

Be cautious when adjusting character spacing. Such adjustments can reduce the readability of the text.

Each typeface is designed with a specific amount of space between characters. This character spacing may be changed with options at the Font dialog box with the Advanced tab selected, as shown in Figure 2.12. Use the *Scale* option in the *Character Spacing* section to stretch or compress text horizontally as a percentage of the current size (from 1% to 600%). Expand or condense the spacing between characters with the *Spacing* option. Choose either the *Expanded* or *Condensed* option and then enter the specific point amount in the *By* measurement box. Raise or lower selected text in relation to the baseline with the *Position* option. Choose either the *Raised* or *Lowered* option and then enter the point amount in the *By* measurement box.

Kerning Character Pairs

kerning

Decreasing or increasing the horizontal space between specific character pairs

Adjust the spacing between certain character pairs (referred to as **kerning**) by selecting the text and then inserting a check mark in the *Kerning for fonts* check box at the Font dialog box with the Advanced tab selected. Kerning moves certain character combinations closer together to improve readability and help the eye move along the text. Generally, the horizontal spacing of a typeface is designed to optimize the body text, which is usually between 9 and 13 points. At larger sizes, the same relative horizontal space can appear loose, especially when uppercase and lowercase letters are combined. Kerning visually equalizes the space between specific characters and is usually used in headlines and other blocks of large type (14 points and larger). Figure 2.13 illustrates common character pairs that are

Figure 2.12 Adjusting Character Spacing on the Advanced Tab of the Font Dialog Box

Use the *Scale* option to stretch or compress text horizontally as a percentage of the current size.

Use the *Position* option to raise or lower selected text in relation to the baseline.

Turn on kerning to adjust spacing between character pairs.

Use the *Spacing* option to expand or condense spacing between characters.

Figure 2.13 Comparing Examples of Character Pairs Kerned and Not Kerned

WA (kerned)   Ta (kerned)
WA (not kerned)   Ta (not kerned)

Ty (kerned)   Vi (kerned)
Ty (not kerned)   Vi (not kerned)

affected by using the kerning feature. In Word, kerning can be accomplished automatically or character pairs can be selected and kerned manually.

Using Automatic Kerning

When automatic kerning is turned on, Word adjusts the space between certain character pairs above a specific point size. Not all character pairs are affected with automatic kerning. Some common character pairs that may be automatically kerned are *Ta, To, Ty, Vi,* and *WA*. The amount of space that is adjusted for a specific character pair is defined in a kerning table, which is part of the printer definition. The printer definition is a preprogrammed set of instructions that tells the printer how to perform various features.

To turn on automatic kerning, display the Font dialog box with the Advanced tab selected. Click the *Kerning for fonts* check box to insert a check mark. In the *Points and above* measurement box, type a value or use the up and down arrows to specify the minimum point size for kerning to take effect.

Using Manual Kerning

Use manual kerning to specify which character pairs to kern. Manual kerning is especially helpful when increasing or decreasing space between characters to improve legibility, to create a special effect, or to fit text in a specific amount of space.

To manually kern a character pair, select the characters and then display the Font dialog box with the Advanced tab selected. Click the *Spacing* option box arrow and then click the *Expanded* option (to increase the spacing between the selected character pair) or the *Condensed* option (to decrease the spacing). In the *By* measurement box, use the up and down arrows to specify the amount by which the space between letters in the selected character pair should be increased or decreased.

Applying OpenType Features

Word 2016 offers advanced OpenType features at the Font dialog box with the Advanced tab selected (see Figure 2.14) that can be used to enhance the visual appeal of text. Available OpenType features include ligatures, number spacing, number forms, and stylistic sets.

Figure 2.14 Applying OpenType Features on the Advanced Tab of the Font Dialog Box

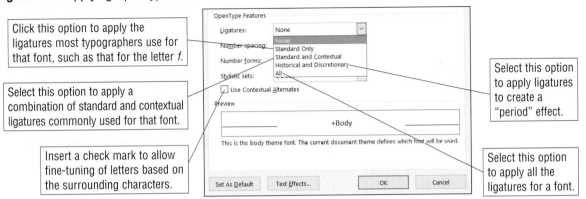

Click this option to apply the ligatures most typographers use for that font, such as that for the letter *f*.

Select this option to apply a combination of standard and contextual ligatures commonly used for that font.

Insert a check mark to allow fine-tuning of letters based on the surrounding characters.

Select this option to apply ligatures to create a "period" effect.

Select this option to apply all the ligatures for a font.

Applying Ligatures

ligature

A single character created from combined characters

A ***ligature*** is a combination of characters joined into a single character. OpenType fonts support four ligature options:

- Standard Only: Standard ligatures are designed to enhance readability. For example, if the Candara font is used, the standard ligatures *fi, ff,* and *fl* appear, as shown in the first image in Figure 2.15.

- Standard and Contextual: These ligatures are designed to enhance readability by better joining the characters that make up a ligature, as shown in the second image in Figure 2.15.

- Historical and Discretionary: These ligatures are designed to be ornamental and are not meant to improve readability. Historical and discretionary ligatures are not commonly used but are available to create a historical or "period" effect, as shown in the third image in Figure 2.15.

- All Ligatures: All the ligature combinations will be applied to the selected text, as shown in the bottom image in Figure 2.15.

Figure 2.15 Comparing Text with and without Ligatures

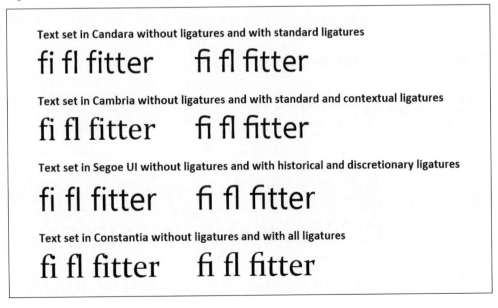

Text set in Candara without ligatures and with standard ligatures

fi fl fitter   fi fl fitter

Text set in Cambria without ligatures and with standard and contextual ligatures

fi fl fitter   fi fl fitter

Text set in Segoe UI without ligatures and with historical and discretionary ligatures

fi fl fitter   fi fl fitter

Text set in Constantia without ligatures and with all ligatures

fi fl fitter   fi fl fitter

Adjusting Number Spacing

The *Number spacing* option in the *OpenType Features* section of the Font dialog box with the Advanced tab selected is set at *Default*, which means the spacing between numbers has been determined by the font designer. Choosing the *Proportional* option allows a different amount of space before and after each specific number. For example, the space before and after *1* is narrower than the space before and after *5*, as shown in Figure 2.16A. Three Microsoft fonts—Candara, Constantia, and Corbel—use proportional number spacing by default. Use the *Tabular* option to allot the same amount of space before and after each specific number, as shown in Figure 2.16B. This is recommended for numbers in columns to make them align vertically. The Cambria, Calibri, and Consolas fonts use tabular spacing by default.

Adjusting Number Forms

The *Number forms* option is also set at *Default*. Change this to *Lining* for all numbers to be the same height and not extend below the baseline, as shown in Figure 2.16C. This is recommended for numbers in tables and forms. The Cambria, Calibri, and Consolas fonts use the *Lining* option by default. Choose the *Old-style* option to extend numbers above and below the baseline, as shown in Figure 2.16D. Three fonts that use the *Old-style* option are Candara, Constantia, and Corbel.

Applying Stylistic Sets

In addition to the previously mentioned OpenType features, stylistic sets can be used to apply formatting to text. Apply a stylistic set to change the appearance of text with a font applied, as shown at the top of Figure 2.17. Use the Text Effects and Typography button drop-down gallery or the Font dialog box with the Advanced tab selected to change the stylistic set.

Another adjustment that may be applied to fine-tune text is the *Use Contextual Alternates* option in the *OpenType Features* section of the Font dialog box with the Advanced tab selected. Use this feature to give a script font a more natural and flowing appearance, as shown at the bottom of Figure 2.17. Notice the slight differences in letters such as *t, n, s,* and *h*.

Keep in mind that not all fonts have ligature combinations, number spacing and forms, stylistic sets, and contextual alternates. Experiment with fonts to find the ones that provide these features.

Figure 2.16 Using Number Spacing Options

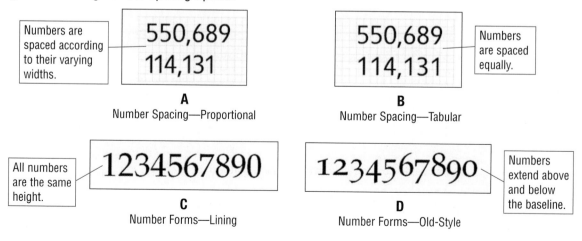

Numbers are spaced according to their varying widths.

550,689
114,131

A
Number Spacing—Proportional

Numbers are spaced equally.

550,689
114,131

B
Number Spacing—Tabular

All numbers are the same height.

1234567890

C
Number Forms—Lining

1234567890

Numbers extend above and below the baseline.

D
Number Forms—Old-Style

Figure 2.17 Applying Stylistic Sets and Contextual Alternates to Text

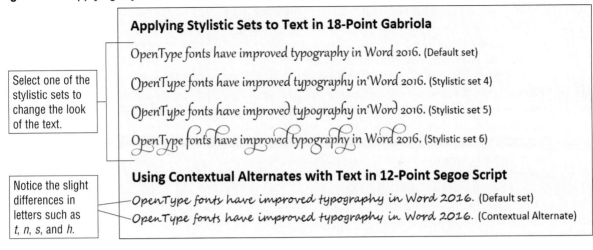

Select one of the stylistic sets to change the look of the text.

Applying Stylistic Sets to Text in 18-Point Gabriola

OpenType fonts have improved typography in Word 2016. (Default set)

OpenType fonts have improved typography in Word 2016. (Stylistic set 4)

OpenType fonts have improved typography in Word 2016. (Stylistic set 5)

OpenType fonts have improved typography in Word 2016. (Stylistic set 6)

Notice the slight differences in letters such as *t, n, s,* and *h.*

Using Contextual Alternates with Text in 12-Point Segoe Script

OpenType fonts have improved typography in Word 2016. (Default set)

OpenType fonts have improved typography in Word 2016. (Contextual Alternate)

Project 3a Formatting a Corporate Event Invitation   Part 1 of 2

1. Open **ORInvitation.docx** and then save it with the name **2-ORInvitation**.
2. Change the theme colors by completing the following steps:
   a. Click the Design tab.
   b. Click the Theme Colors button in the Document Formatting group.
   c. Click the *Red Violet* option at the drop-down gallery.
3. Select the first two lines of text (*Europe, Middle East,* and *Africa Regional Dinner*) and then make the following changes:
   a. Click the Home tab and then click the Font group dialog box launcher.
   b. At the Font dialog box with the Font tab selected, scroll down the *Font* list box and then click *Gabriola.* (You can also select the *+Body* text that displays in the option box at the top of the list box, type the letter g to display fonts that begin with *g,* and then click *Gabriola* in the list box.)
   c. Select the current measurement in the *Size* measurement box and then type 42.
   d. Click the Advanced tab.
   e. Click the *Scale* option box arrow and then click *90%* at the drop-down list.
   f. Click the *Spacing* option box arrow and then click *Condensed* at the drop-down list.
   g. Click in the *Kerning for fonts* check box to insert a check mark.
   h. Select the current number in the measurement box right of the *Kerning for fonts* option and then type 14.
   i. Click the *Stylistic sets* option box arrow, scroll down the drop-down list and then click 6.
   j. Click OK to close the dialog box.

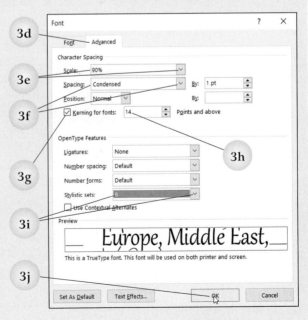

k. With the two lines of text still selected, click the Text Effects and Typography button in the Font group on the Home tab.

l. Click the *Fill: Pink, Accent color 1; Shadow* option at the drop-down gallery (second column, first row).

4. Select all the text except the last two lines (the text from *Europe, Middle East* through *Sea of Marmara before dinner*) and then click the Center button in the Paragraph group on the Home tab.

5. Select the last two lines of text (*Elvan Basaran* and *Managing Partner*) and then click the Align Right button in the Paragraph group.

6. Select the lines of text beginning with *You are invited to join* through *Managing Partner* and then change the font to 16-point Papyrus.

7. Compare your document with the document shown in Figure 2.18.

8. Save **2-ORInvitation.docx**.

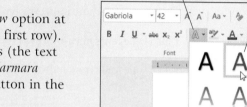

Check Your Work

Figure 2.18 Invitation Created in Project 3a

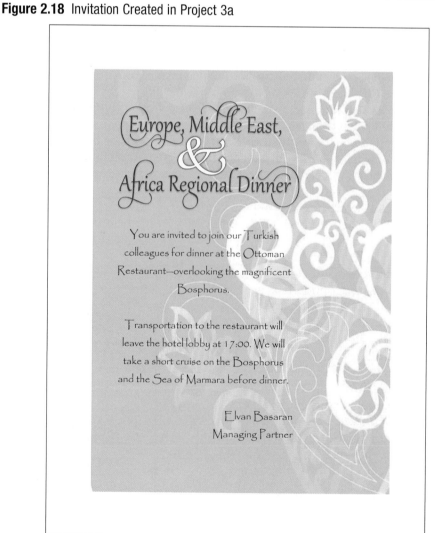

Refining Word and Line Spacing

Tutorial

Changing Line
Spacing

In addition to character formatting, refining word and line spacing can help make a document look more polished and professional. Refine word spacing by adjusting the tracking in a document, and refine line spacing by adjusting the leading.

Tracking Text

tracking

Equally reducing or increasing the horizontal spaces between all the characters in a selected block of text

In traditional typesetting, equally reducing or increasing the horizontal spaces between all the characters in a block of text is called **tracking**. Tracking affects all characters, whereas kerning affects only specific character pairs. However, the purpose of tracking is the same as that of kerning: to produce more attractive, easy-to-read type. In addition, tracking can be used to create unusual spacing for a specific design effect or to fit text into a certain amount of space.

In Word, tracking is virtually the same as manual kerning: both processes involve condensing or expanding character spacing at the Font dialog box. Whereas manually kerning involves adjusting the spacing of selected character pairs, tracking involves adjusting the character spacing of a selected block of text, such as a heading, a subheading, or a phrase. Adjust tracking by selecting the text and then expanding or condensing it at the Font dialog box with the Advanced tab selected. Refer to Figure 2.19 to see how adjusting the tracking affects the text.

Setting Line Spacing

line spacing

The vertical spacing between lines; expressed in points or as a percentage of the line height

leading

The amount of white space between lines

☰ ▾ Line
Spacing

Line spacing is the vertical spacing of the lines within a paragraph and is expressed as a fixed amount in points or as a percentage of the line height. Line spacing includes **leading** (pronounced *ledd-ing*), which is the amount of white space between lines. The height of the characters plus the leading equals the line spacing; however, some word processing programs refer to leading as line spacing and consider the line spacing measured from baseline to baseline. By clicking the Line Spacing button in the Paragraph group on the Home tab, line spacing can be set at 1.0, 1.15, 1.5, 2.0, 2.5, or 3.0. The default setting for body text is 1.08 line spacing with 8 points of spacing after paragraphs. The leading depends on the font size selected; the larger the font size, the larger the amount of leading between the lines. Most leading is set at 20 percent of the size of the font. That means that there will be 2 points of leading between text that is set at 10 points and 2.4 points of leading if the font is set for 12 points.

Figure 2.19 Comparing Tracking (Normal, Condensed, and Expanded Character Spacing)

22-point font size with normal character spacing — *Desktop Publishing Using Word 2016*

22-point font size condensed by 1.5 points — *Desktop Publishing Using Word 2016*

22-point font size expanded by 2 points — *Desktop Publishing Using Word 2016*

Setting Leading

Leading cannot be specifically set in Word. However, the *At least* and *Exactly* options at the *Line spacing* option box in the Paragraph dialog box, as shown in Figure 2.20, come close to setting leading. Both of these settings refer to the number of points measured from baseline to baseline between lines. For instance, set the *Exactly* setting to 16 points for a paragraph containing 12-point text, which will result in 4 points of leading between lines. If the same setting is used with 20-point text, there will be no leading, and the tops of the larger letters will be cut off. Experiment with the *At least* and *Exactly* options to get a better feel for using them. Any extra space added to a line of text is added below the text. Table 2.1 explains all the options at the *Line spacing* option box.

Setting Spacing Before or After a Paragraph

One way to add space before or after a paragraph is to choose the *Add Space Before Paragraph* option or the *Remove Space After Paragraph* option at the Line and Paragraph Spacing button drop-down list in the Paragraph group on the Home tab. The Layout tab also contains *Before* and *After* measurement boxes that work like their counterparts in the Paragraph dialog box. Of course, space can be added between paragraphs by pressing the Enter key. However, each press of the Enter key is considered a paragraph in itself, which can make things difficult when trying to apply styles to paragraphs of text. By adding line spacing before or after a paragraph, the line spacing becomes a part of that paragraph.

Paragraph spacing can also be adjusted by clicking the Paragraph Spacing button in the Document Formatting group on the Design tab. At the drop-down list that displays, click one of these options: *No Paragraph Space, Compact, Tight, Open, Relaxed, Double,* or *Custom Paragraph Spacing.*

Figure 2.20 Adjusting Line Spacing in the *Line Spacing* Option Box

Choose the *At least* option or the *Exactly* option at this drop-down list to set specific line spacing.

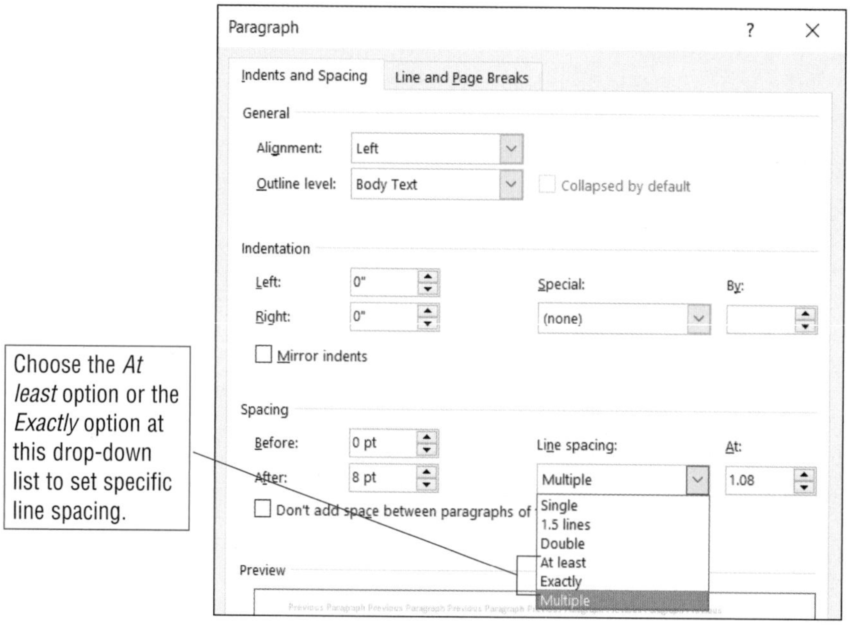

Table 2.1 Line Spacing Options Available at the Paragraph Dialog Box

Option	Effect on Text
Single	No extra space between lines in the paragraph
1.5 Lines	An extra half-height blank line below each line of the paragraph
Double	An extra blank line below each line of the paragraph
At Least	A minimum height for each line in the paragraph; specified in points
Exactly	A specific height for each line in the paragraph; specified in points (If the size specified is smaller than the largest font size used in the paragraph, the large letter will be cut off on top)
Multiple	The line height times any value from 0 to 132, in decimal increments of 0.01

Project 3b Changing the Word and Line Spacing in an Invitation

Part 2 of 2

1. With **2-ORInvitation.docx** open, select the lines of text beginning with *You are invited to join* through *Managing Partner* and then make the following changes:
   a. Click the Font group dialog box launcher.
   b. At the Font dialog box, click the Advanced tab, if necessary.
   c. Click the *Spacing* option box arrow and then click *Condensed* at the drop-down list.
   d. Make sure *1 pt* displays in the *By* measurement box right of the *Spacing* option box and then click OK to close the Font dialog box.
2. With the text still selected, click the Line Spacing button in the Paragraph group on the Home tab and then click *Line Spacing Options* at the drop-down list.
3. Click the *Line spacing* option box arrow in the *Spacing* section and then click *Exactly* at the drop-down list.
4. Click the *At* measurement box down arrow four times. (This will display *8 pt* in the measurement box.)
5. Click OK to close the dialog box. Notice that the spacing between the selected lines of text is significantly decreased and the lines of text merge together.
6. With the text still selected, click the Paragraph group dialog box launcher.
7. Click the *Line spacing* option box arrow in the *Spacing* section and then click *At least* at the drop-down list.
8. Click the *At* measurement box up arrow four times. (This will display *16 pt* in the measurement box.)
9. Click OK to close the dialog box.
10. Save, print, and then close **2-ORInvitation.docx**.

Check Your Work

Chapter Summary

- A *typeface* is a set of characters with a common design and shape.
- Characteristics that distinguish one typeface from another include x-height, cap height, height of ascenders, depth of descenders, and serifs.
- A *serif* is a small stroke on the end of a character. A sans serif typeface does not have serifs.
- Typefaces are either monospaced or proportional. A monospaced typeface allots the same amount of horizontal space to each character, while a proportional typeface allots a varying amount to each character.
- Point size is a vertical character measurement; one point is approximately $1/72$ of an inch. The larger the point size, the larger the characters.
- A typestyle is a variation of a font that causes the text to display thicker or slanted. Apply a typestyle to text by selecting the text and then clicking the Bold or Italic button in the Font group on the Home tab. Use options at the Font dialog box to also apply typestyles to selected text.
- OpenType fonts support international character sets, cross-platform support between Windows and Macintosh computers, support for Postscript and TrueType fonts, and support for advanced typographic features, such as special ligatures (combined characters) and swashes (exaggerated serifs).
- Choose narrow or lighter fonts, such as Century Gothic, Times New Roman, Calibri, and Verdana, to decrease the amount of ink used to print a document.
- Embed a font in a document to attach the associated font file to the document and ensure that the font will appear the same on computers without that particular font file.
- Change the default font of a document at the Font dialog box. Select a new default font, click the Set As Default button, and then click OK at the message that displays.
- At the Colors dialog box, click the Standard tab to display 127 font colors and 15 shades of gray; customize font colors with the Custom tab selected.
- At the Colors dialog box with the Custom tab selected, change the *hue*, which is the color itself; the *saturation*, which is the color intensity; and the *luminescence*, which is the brightness of the color. The values of *Red*, *Green*, and *Blue* can also be changed.
- Insert a special symbol in a document by clicking the Symbol button in the Symbols group on the Insert tab, clicking the *More Symbols* option, and then clicking the Symbols tab or the Special Characters tab at the Symbol dialog box.
- An em dash (—) is used to indicate a pause in speech and is generally the width of an uppercase letter *M* of a typeface.
- An en dash (–) indicates a continuation, such as *116–133* or *January–March*, and is the width of a lowercase letter *n* of a typeface.
- In typesetting, the tail of the open quotation mark curves upward (") and the tail of the close quotation mark curves downward ("). Straight quotes are typically used to indicate inches (") and feet (').
- Use options in the *Character Spacing* section of the Font dialog box with the Advanced tab selected to adjust character spacing and turn on kerning.

- *Kerning* involves decreasing or increasing the horizontal space between specific character pairs. To kern character pairs automatically, insert a check mark in the *Kerning for fonts* check box at the Font dialog box with the Advanced tab selected. To kern a character pair, select the character pair and then use the *Spacing* option box at the Font dialog box with the Advanced tab selected to expand or condense the space between them.

- The *OpenType Features* section of the Font dialog box with the Advanced tab selected provides options for choosing a ligature style, specifying number spacing and form, and applying stylistic sets.

- In traditional typesetting, equally reducing or increasing the horizontal space between all the characters in a block of text is called *tracking*. Tracking affects all the characters, while kerning affects only specific pairs.

- Adjust line spacing by clicking the Line Spacing button in the Paragraph group on the Home tab and then selecting an option at the drop-down gallery. Adjust the line spacing, including the leading, by using the *At least* or *Exactly* option at the *Line spacing* option box drop-down list at the Paragraph dialog box with the Indents and Spacing tab selected.

- Spacing adjustments can be made by adding points of space before or after paragraphs of text. Do this with options at the Line and Paragraph Spacing button drop-down list in the Paragraph group on the Home tab, the *Before* and *After* measurement boxes on the Layout tab, or the Paragraph Spacing button drop-down gallery in the Document Formatting group on the Design tab.

Commands Review

FEATURE	RIBBON TAB, GROUP	BUTTON	KEYBOARD SHORTCUT
font color	Home, Font		
Font dialog box	Home, Font		Ctrl + D
line spacing	Home, Paragraph		
symbol	Insert, Symbols		

Workbook

Chapter study tools and assessment activities are available in the workbook pages of the ebook. These resources are designed to help you further develop and demonstrate mastery of the skills learned in this chapter.

Creating Personal Documents and Templates

Performance Objectives

Upon successful completion of Chapter 3, you will be able to:

1 Use Word to create personal documents
2 Create a personal calendar
3 Arrange drawing objects to enhance personal documents
4 Create personal return address labels
5 Create a template and insert content controls
6 Create a resume using a template

Precheck

Check your current skills to help focus your study.

Desktop Publishing Terms

grouping	nudging	stacking

Word Features Used

bring forward	images	shape styles
content controls	quick parts	tables
Design mode	rotate	templates
drawing canvas	send backward	text wrapping
forms	shape fill	ungroup
form fields	shape outline	
group	shapes	

Data Files

Before beginning chapter work, copy the C3 folder to your storage medium and then make C3 the active folder.

SNAP

If you are a SNAP user, launch the Precheck and Tutorials from your Assignments page.

You will create a personal calendar using a calendar template, and the calendar will include a background image, a formatted image, and a shape.

Preview Finished Project

Using Word to Create Personal Documents

This chapter covers producing personal documents using Word's features such as tables, text boxes, and labels, to produce calendars, address labels, certificates, resumes, change-of-address postcards, and hanging name tags. This chapter also introduces how to apply basic desktop publishing concepts, such as planning and designing document content, maintaining consistency, and achieving balance.

While creating the documents in this chapter, consider how to apply what has been discussed in previous chapters to create other personal documents. Several examples of personal documents are shown in Figure 3.1.

Figure 3.1 Creating Personal Documents

Personalized Calendar

Personal Note Cards

Graduation Invitation

Nutrition Log

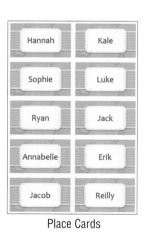

Place Cards

Gift Tags

Birthday Party Invitation

Change-of-Address Card

Recipe Card

Creating a Personal Calendar

A calendar can be one of the most basic tools of organization in everyday life. Although electronic calendars are becoming increasingly prevalent both at work and at home, many people still prefer the at-a-glance convenience of using a printed calendar to schedule appointments, plan activities, and serve as a reminder of important dates and events.

In addition to these personal applications, a calendar also can be used as a marketing tool in promoting a service, product, or program. For example, a schedule of upcoming events may be typed on a calendar as a reminder to all the volunteers working for a charitable organization, or the calendar can be sent to prospective donors as a daily reminder of the organization. Numerous predesigned calendar templates are available in Office 2016. Search for these templates at the New backstage area. In addition, Publisher, PowerPoint, and Excel also include professionally prepared calendar designs, as shown in Figure 3.2.

Figure 3.2 Illustrating Sample Online Calendar Templates

A
Word Calendar Template

B
Publisher Calendar Template

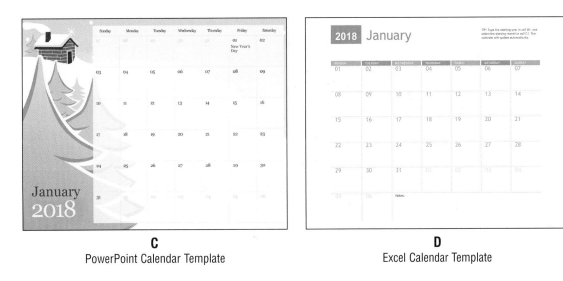

C
PowerPoint Calendar Template

D
Excel Calendar Template

Inserting Calendar Building Blocks

Tutorial

Inserting and
Sorting Building
Blocks

 Quick Parts

Building blocks are reusable pieces of content and other document parts that are stored in galleries. *Calendar 1*, in the Building Blocks Organizer dialog box shown in Figure 3.3, is an example of a calendar building block. Display the Building Blocks Organizer by clicking the Quick Parts button in the Text group on the Insert tab and then clicking *Building Blocks Organizer* at the drop-down list. Click the building block name and then click the Insert button to insert it into a document.

Table

Predesigned calendar building blocks also can be inserted into a Word document by clicking the Table button in the Tables group on the Insert tab, pointing to *Quick Tables*, and then clicking the calendar in the *Built-In* section at the side menu, as shown in Figure 3.4. Consider inserting a calendar building block into a newsletter, travel itinerary, flyer, pamphlet, or other business or personal document.

Editing an Image in a Calendar

Many calendar templates include an image placeholder. Delete the placeholder or replace the image by clicking the Pictures button or the Online Pictures button in the Illustrations group on the Insert tab.

Color

Images inserted into a calendar can be edited using tools in Word. For example, to turn an image into a watermark, click the Color button in the Adjust group on the Picture Tools Format tab and then click *Washout* in the *Recolor* section (see Figure 3.5). Next, click the Wrap Text button in the Arrange group and then click *Behind Text* at the drop-down gallery.

Figure 3.3 Using Calendar Building Blocks

Click *Name* to sort the building blocks alphabetically by name. This will display all the calendar options together.

Figure 3.4 Inserting Quick Tables from the Table Button Drop-down List

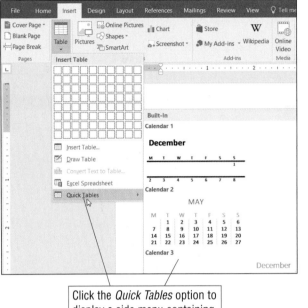

Click the *Quick Tables* option to display a side menu containing predesigned calendar options.

Figure 3.5 Using the *Recolor* Section of the Color Button Drop-down Gallery

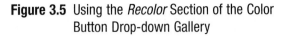
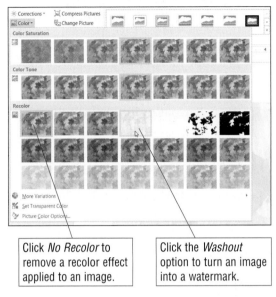

Click *No Recolor* to remove a recolor effect applied to an image.

Click the *Washout* option to turn an image into a watermark.

The Color button in the Adjust group on the Picture Tools Format tab provides many options for design creativity. The following are some helpful tips for working with recoloring options:

- Before clicking an effect option, hover the mouse pointer over it. The live preview feature will show what the image will look like with that effect applied.

- Access additional colors by clicking *More Variations* at the Color button drop-down gallery. If the desired color cannot be found in the *Theme Colors* or *Standard Colors* sections, click *More Colors* to display the Colors dialog box.

- Remove a recolor effect but keep any other changes made to an image by clicking the *No Recolor* option (first option in the *Recolor* section).

Adding a Shape to a Calendar

Another way to add interest to a calendar is to insert a predesigned shape as an attention-getter. Insert a shape by clicking the Insert tab, clicking the Shapes button in the Illustrations group, clicking the specific shape at the drop-down list, and then clicking or dragging in the document. A shape may include text, color, and other special effects. Add text to a shape by selecting the shape and then typing the text or by selecting a shape, right-clicking it, and then clicking *Add Text* at the shortcut menu. This positions the insertion point inside the shape.

1. At a blank document, click the Insert tab, click the Pictures button, navigate to the C3 folder on your storage medium, and then double-click *leaves.png* at the Insert Picture dialog box.

2. With the image selected, click the Size group dialog box launcher on the Picture Tools Format tab.

3. At the Layout dialog box with the Size tab selected, remove the check mark from the *Lock aspect ratio* check box in the *Scale* section, type 9.5 in the *Absolute* measurement box in the *Height* section, type 7 in the *Absolute* measurement box in the *Width* section, and then click OK.

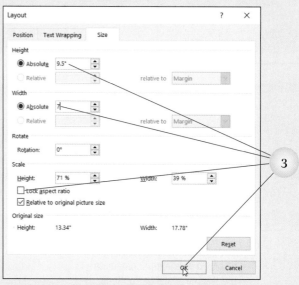

4. With the image still selected, customize the image by completing the following steps:

   a. Click the Color button in the Adjust group and then click the *Washout* option in the *Recolor* section.

   b. Click the Position button in the Arrange group and then click the *Position in Middle Center with Square Text Wrapping* option.

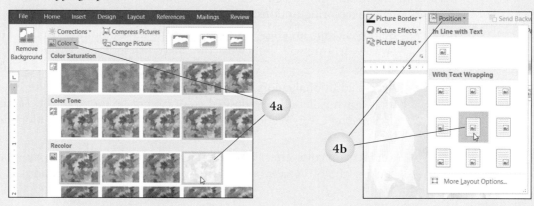

5. Insert and customize the image of the school bus as shown in Figure 3.6 on page 83 by completing the following steps:

   a. Click the Insert tab, click the Pictures button, navigate to the C3 folder, and then double-click *schoolbus.png* at the Insert Picture dialog box. Part of the school bus image will display below the leaves image.

   b. With the school bus image selected, click the Wrap Text button in the Arrange group on the Picture Tools Format tab and then click the *In Front of Text* option.

   c. Change the width of the school bus image to 6.2 inches.

   d. Drag the image so it is positioned as shown in Figure 3.6.

6. Save the document with the name **3-Calendar**. Keep the document open.

7. Insert a predesigned calendar below the school bus image by completing the following steps:

   a. Click the File tab and then click the *New* option.

   b. At the New backstage area, type banner calendar in the search text box and then press the Enter key.

   c. Double-click the *Banner calendar* option (similar to the one shown at the right).

   d. At the Select Calendar Dates dialog box, click the *Month* option box arrow and then click *September* at the drop-down list. Click the *Year* option box arrow, click *2019* at the drop-down list, and then click OK to close the dialog box.

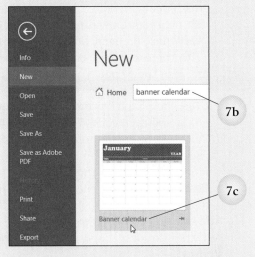

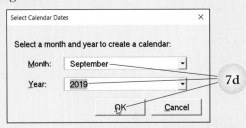

   e. Click OK at the Word Calendar dialog box.

8. Format the calendar by completing the following steps:

   a. With the insertion point positioned in the top table (contains the cells with the green shading), click the Table Tools Layout tab, click the Delete button in the Rows & Columns group, and then click *Delete Table* at the drop-down list.

   b. With the insertion point positioned in the first cell in the table (contains the word *Sunday*), click the Insert Above button in the Rows & Columns group, click the Merge Cells button in the Merge group, and then type September.

   c. Select the last two rows in the table, click the Delete button in the Rows & Columns group, and then click *Delete Rows* at the drop-down list.

   d. Select the entire table. On the Table Tools Layout tab, click the Properties button in the Table group. At the Table Properties dialog box, click the Table tab, if necessary, change the *Measure in* option to *Inches*, change the value in the *Preferred width* measurement box to *6* inches, and then click OK.

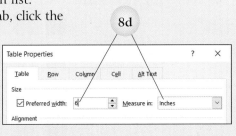

   e. Click the Table Tools Design tab and then click the *Header Row* check box in the Table Style Options group to remove the check mark.

   f. Select the first row and then change the font size to 18 points.

   g. Select the second row, change the font size to 9 points, and then apply the White, Background 1, Darker 15% shading color.

   h. Select rows 3 through 12 and then change the font size to 9 points.

   i. Select the entire calendar (table) and then click the Copy button in the Clipboard group on the Home tab.

   j. Make **3-Calendar.docx** the active document.

9. Create and format a text box for the calendar table by completing the following steps:
   a. With **3-Calendar.docx** the active document, click the Insert tab, click the Text Box button in the Text group, and then click *Draw Text Box* at the drop-down list. Position the crosshairs below the school bus photo and then drag to create a text box with a height of 4.8 inches and a width of 6.2 inches. (Size the text box using the *Shape Height* and *Shape Width* measurement boxes in the Size group on the Drawing Tools Format tab.)
   b. With the text box selected, click the Shape Fill button arrow in the Shape Styles group and then click the *Gold, Accent 4, Lighter 60%* color.

   c. Click the Shape Outline button arrow in the Shape Styles group and then click *No Outline* at the drop-down gallery.
   d. With the insertion point positioned inside the text box, click the Paste button in the Clipboard group on the Home tab to paste the calendar.
   e. Position the school bus image and the calendar as shown in Figure 3.6.
10. Add the text to the dates as shown in Figure 3.6.
11. Add the starburst shape to the calendar as shown in Figure 3.6 by completing the following steps:
   a. Click the Insert tab, click the Shapes button in the Illustrations group, and then click the *Explosion: 8 Points* option in the *Stars and Banners* section.
   b. In the top right corner of the school bus image, draw a star that is approximately 2 inches high and 1.5 inches wide.
   c. With the star shape selected, click the More Shape Styles button in the Shape Styles group and then click the *Intense Effect - Gold, Accent 4* option (fifth column, sixth row in the *Theme Styles* section).

   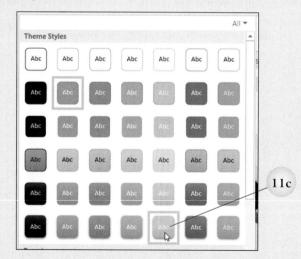

   d. With the star still selected, change the font to 12-point Berlin Sans FB; change the font color to Black, Text 1; change the alignment to center; and then type Welcome back to school! Resize and position the star if necessary.
12. Save, print, and then close **3-Calendar.docx**.
13. Close the calendar template document without saving changes.

Check Your Work

Figure 3.6 Calendar Created in Project 1

Arranging Drawing Objects to Enhance Personal Documents

Drawing objects include shapes, diagrams, flow charts, and WordArt. Enhance these objects with colors, patterns, text borders, and other effects. Use layers in a document to move, position, and stack objects and images.

Using Layers in Documents

An image or text can be inserted in a document and then layered in front of, behind, or in the same layer as the text. A Word document contains three layers—the foreground layer (or drawing layer), the text layer, and the background layer—as illustrated in Figure 3.7.

 Wrap Text

The text layer is the one that people are the most accustomed to working with if they use Word mainly for word processing. When an image is inserted in a document, the default text wrapping In Line With Text is applied to the image and the image is anchored to a paragraph in the text layer. In some situations, the text wrapping may need to be changed so the image can be moved within the document. This is accomplished by clicking the Wrap Text button in the Arrange group on the Picture Tools Format tab and then clicking one of the following options: Square, Tight, Through, Top and Bottom, Behind Text, or In Front of Text. By default, shapes—such as lines, ovals, and arrows—display in the foreground layer, above the text layer. Text or graphics created in the Header and Footer panes display in the background layer, below the text layer. Figure 3.8 illustrates objects and text in the various layers of a document.

Moving and Positioning Objects Precisely

To move a drawing object, start by selecting the object. To move multiple drawing objects at the same time, select the first object, press and hold down the Shift key while selecting the additional objects, and then drag the drawing objects to the new location.

nudging

Using the arrow keys to move an object in small increments and in specific directions across the document screen

Move a selected drawing object in small increments in a specific direction by pressing the Up Arrow, Down Arrow, Right Arrow, or Left Arrow key. This is called ***nudging***, and it allows for positioning an object more precisely than by dragging it. To nudge an object, make sure the text wrapping for the object has been changed to any setting other than In Line with Text. Another way to align a drawing object or group of objects is to select the object or objects, click the Align button in the Arrange group on the Drawing Tools Format tab, and then click an option to position the object or group of objects precisely on the page or precisely in relation to each other.

Align

Figure 3.7 Understanding Layers in Word

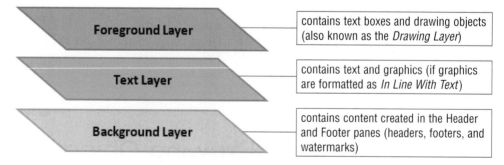

Figure 3.8 Understanding the Contents of the Layers in a Document

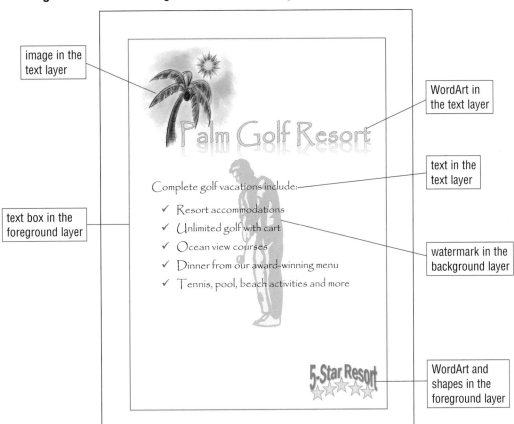

image in the text layer

WordArt in the text layer

text in the text layer

text box in the foreground layer

watermark in the background layer

WordArt and shapes in the foreground layer

Palm Golf Resort

Complete golf vacations include:

✓ Resort accommodations
✓ Unlimited golf with cart
✓ Ocean view courses
✓ Dinner from our award-winning menu
✓ Tennis, pool, beach activities and more

5-Star Resort

Using a Drawing Canvas to Align Drawing Objects

DTP POINTER

Using the drawing canvas helps keep the objects in a drawing together.

DTP POINTER

Duplicate an object and align the original and duplicate objects at the same time by pressing and holding down the Shift key and the Ctrl key and dragging and dropping the image.

When a drawing object is inserted in a Word document, it can be placed in a drawing canvas. A drawing canvas helps to arrange a drawing in a document and provides a framelike boundary between the drawing and the rest of the document. By default, the canvas has no border or background, but formatting can be applied to the drawing canvas as to any drawing object. Using this feature also helps to keep parts of the drawing together, which is especially helpful if the drawing consists of several objects. The best practice is to insert a drawing canvas when including more than one shape in a drawing. For example, to create a flow chart, start by inserting a drawing canvas and then add the shapes and lines for the chart.

To insert a drawing canvas, click in the document where the drawing will be created, click the Insert tab, click the Shapes button in the Illustrations group, and then click *New Drawing Canvas* at the bottom of the drop-down list. A drawing canvas, in which shapes can be drawn, is inserted in the document.

After inserting shapes in the drawing canvas, right-click on the drawing canvas border and then click *Fit, Expand,* or *Scale Drawing* at the shortcut menu. Click the *Fit* option to reduce the area around the drawing objects, as shown in Figure 3.9. Notice that the drawing canvas adjusts to fit all three objects into one tight area. If the wrapping style of the drawing canvas is changed to In Front of Text and the canvas is dragged to another location in the document, all three items will move with it. Click *Expand* at the shortcut menu to expand the drawing canvas, and click *Scale Drawing* to turn on the scaling feature, which changes the size of objects as the borders of the drawing canvas are changed.

Figure 3.9 Adjusting the Drawing Canvas to Fit the Contents

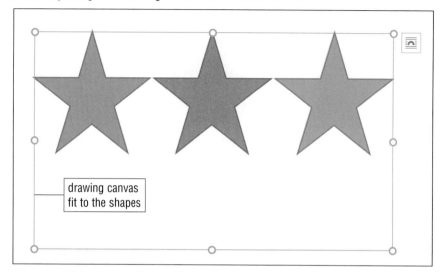

drawing canvas
fit to the shapes

Stacking Objects

stacking

Drawing one object on top of another

Drawing one object on top of another is known as **stacking**. Objects automatically stack in individual layers as they are added to a document. The stacking order is visible when objects overlap. The top object covers portions of the objects beneath it.

DTP POINTER

Stacking drawn shapes works only when *not* using a drawing canvas.

 Bring Forward

Send Backward

 Selection Pane

Stack as many drawing objects as needed and then rearrange them by selecting an object, clicking the Bring Forward button arrow in the Arrange group on the Drawing Tools Format tab, and then clicking *Bring Forward, Bring to Front,* or *Bring in Front of Text*, as shown in Figure 3.10. Alternatively, send the object backward by clicking the Send Backward button arrow in the Arrange group and then clicking *Send Backward, Send to Back,* or *Send Behind Text*, as shown in Figure 3.11. Use the Selection pane to select individual objects and change their order and visibility. Display the Selection pane by clicking the Selection Pane button in the Arrange group on the Drawing Tools Format tab or Picture Tools Format tab.

Figure 3.10 Rearranging Objects with the Bring Forward Button on the Drawing Tools Format Tab

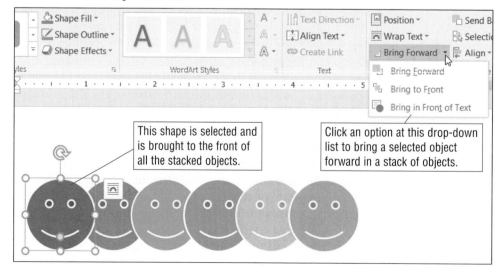

This shape is selected and is brought to the front of all the stacked objects.

Click an option at this drop-down list to bring a selected object forward in a stack of objects.

Figure 3.11 Rearranging Objects with the Send Backward Button on the Drawing Tools Format Tab

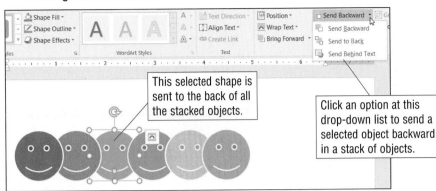

This selected shape is sent to the back of all the stacked objects.

Click an option at this drop-down list to send a selected object backward in a stack of objects.

Grouping Objects

grouping

Combining objects as a single unit

 Group

DTP POINTER ❯

If the group feature does not work properly, change the text-wrapping option for the object or use the drawing canvas to group the objects as one unit.

 Rotate

DTP POINTER ❯

Generally, position graphics facing the document text.

Grouping objects combines multiple drawing objects as a single unit. To group drawing objects, press and hold down the Shift key and click each object. With the objects selected, click the Group button in the Arrange group on the Drawing Tools Format tab and then click *Group* at the drop-down list, as shown in Figure 3.12. When the objects have been grouped, sizing handles should appear around the new unit rather than each individual object, but selecting individual objects within a group is still possible. If an object is lost in a stack that has been grouped, select the group and then press the Tab key to cycle forward or press Shift + Tab to cycle backward through the objects until the specific object is selected. Ungroup drawing objects by selecting the grouped object, clicking the Group button in the Arrange group, and then clicking *Ungroup* at the drop-down list.

Rotating and Flipping Objects

To rotate or flip an object or group of objects, select it, click the Rotate button in the Arrange group on the Drawing Tools Format tab, and then click the option that corresponds with the direction to turn the object or group of objects, as shown in Figure 3.13. Click *More Rotation Options* at the bottom of the Rotate button drop-down gallery to display the Layout dialog box with the Size tab selected. Rotate an object in more precise increments using the *Rotation* measurement box in the *Rotate* section of the Layout dialog box. Another method for rotating an object is to use the rotation handle on the selected object, as shown in Figure 3.14.

Figure 3.12 Grouping Objects

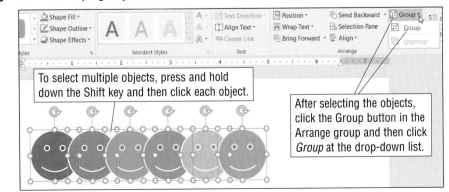

To select multiple objects, press and hold down the Shift key and then click each object.

After selecting the objects, click the Group button in the Arrange group and then click *Group* at the drop-down list.

Figure 3.13 Rotating an Object Using the Rotate Button

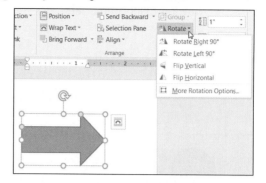

Figure 3.14 Rotating an Object Using the Rotation Handle

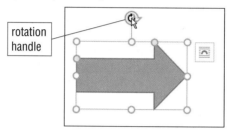

rotation handle

Creating Personal Return Address Labels

Tutorial

Creating Mailing Labels with the Same Name and Address and an Image

Preprinted return address labels are convenient and cost-effective to use at home and at the office. For paying bills, addressing holiday cards, or mailing a large number of PTA newsletters, the convenience of having preprinted return address labels is worth the time it takes to create them. Create personal labels using the labels feature in Word. Word includes a variety of predefined label formats that coordinate with the sizes of labels that can be purchased at office supply stores.

When purchasing labels, be careful to select the appropriate labels for a specific printer. Labels are available in sheets for laser and inkjet printers. Carefully follow the printer's directions and any directions on the label packaging to be sure the sheets are properly inserted into the printer.

The labels feature is used in Project 2 to create Avery 5160 labels that include an image. These labels measure 1 inch by 2.63 inches. Use smaller labels for personal return address labels, such as Avery 8167 labels, which measure 0.5 inch by 1.75 inches.

 Labels

DTP POINTER

View information on how to use labels and access additional templates at www.averylabels.com.

The personal address label design created in Project 2 can be saved to the Quick Part gallery so it can be used again, if necessary. Recall that the Quick Part gallery contains pieces of content that can be reused in various documents. To save content to the Quick Part gallery, select the content (which can include text and objects), click the Insert tab, click the Quick Parts button in the Text group, and then click *Save Selection to Quick Part Gallery* at the drop-down list. This displays the Create New Building Block dialog box with *Quick Parts* specified in the *Gallery* option box. Type a name for the building block, type a description (if desired), and then click OK. To insert content saved to the Quick Part gallery into a document, click the Quick Parts button on the Insert tab and then click the quick part at the drop-down list.

1. At a blank document, click the Mailings tab and then click the Labels button in the Create group.
2. At the Envelopes and Labels dialog box with the Labels tab selected, click the Options button.
3. At the Label Options dialog box, if necessary, change the *Label vendors* option to *Avery US Letter*, click *5160 Easy Peel Address Labels* in the *Product number* list box, and then click OK.

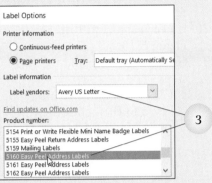

4. At the Envelopes and Labels dialog box, click the New Document button.
5. If the gridlines of the labels (cells) do not display, click the Table Tools Layout tab and then click the View Gridlines button in the Table group.
6. With the insertion point positioned in the first cell, click the Insert tab and then click the Pictures button in the Illustrations group. Navigate to the C3 folder and then double-click *palmtree.jpg*. *Note: You may insert an image of your own choosing and insert your own name and address instead of the name and address given in the following steps.*
7. With the image selected, click the Color button in the Adjust group on the Picture Tools Format tab, click *Set Transparent Color* at the drop-down gallery, and then click in the gray background of the palm tree image to remove the background color.
8. Click the Rotate button in the Arrange group on the Picture Tools Format tab and then click *Flip Horizontal* at the drop-down list.

9. Change the height of the image to 0.9 inch. (The width will automatically adjust to 0.9 inch.)
10. Apply Square text wrapping to the image and then position it at the left edge of the first cell, vertically centered between the top and bottom borders of the cell.
11. Draw a text box that measures 0.7 inch in height and 1.7 inches in width and then position it at the right of the palm tree image. Verify the sizes in the *Shape Height* and *Shape Width* measurement boxes in the Size group on the Drawing Tools Format tab.
12. With the text box selected, click the Shape Styles group task pane launcher.
13. At the Format Shape task pane, make sure *Shape Options* is selected, click the Layout & Properties icon, click *Text Box*, change all the margins to 0 inches, and then close the task pane.

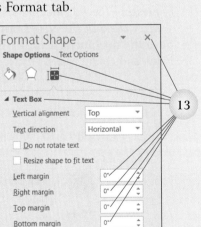

14. Remove the text box shape fill and shape outline.
15. Position the insertion point inside the text box and then click the Align Right button in the Paragraph group on the Home tab.
16. Change the font to 11-point Constantia and then type the following (you may substitute your own name and address):

> Joan & John Kane (Press Shift + Enter.)
> 55 Pine Island Road (Press Shift + Enter.)
> Myrtle Beach, SC 29472

17. Select *Joan & John Kane*, apply bold formatting, and then change the font size to 13 points.

18. With the names still selected, click the Font Color button arrow, and then click *More Colors* at the drop-down list. At the Colors dialog box with the Standard tab selected, click the dark-orange color (third from the left in the bottom row), as shown at the right, and then click OK.

19. Select the text box containing the name and address and then apply Square text wrapping.

20. If necessary, adjust the text box so it is positioned as shown in Figure 3.15.

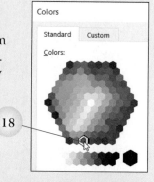

21. Group the image and the text box by completing the following steps:

   a. Click the palm tree image, press and hold down the Shift key, and then click the text box containing the name and address. Make sure the image and the text box both have a solid border around them, indicating that they are selected.

   b. Click the Drawing Tools Format tab, click the Group button in the Arrange group, and then click *Group* at the drop-down list.

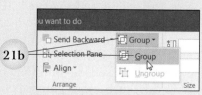

22. Save the contents of the label to the Quick Part gallery by completing the following steps:

   a. With the grouped object selected in the first label, click the Insert tab, click the Quick Parts button in the Text group, and then click *Save Selection to Quick Part Gallery* at the drop-down list.

   b. Type address in the *Name* text box at the Create New Building Block dialog box and then click OK. Close the document without saving the changes.

23. Create a new sheet of labels using the quick part you created in Step 22 by completing the following steps:

   a. At a blank document, click the Mailings tab, click the Labels button in the Create group, and then make sure the product listed in the *Label* section on the Labels tab is *Avery US Letter, 5160 Easy Peel Address Labels*.

   b. With the Labels tab selected in the Envelopes and Labels dialog box, position the insertion point in the *Address* text box, type address, press the F3 function key, and then click the New Document button. ***Note: The Address text box will appear blank after pressing the F3 function key, but the address labels will appear after clicking the New Document button.***

24. Save the document with the name **3-Address**.

25. Print and then close **3-Address.docx**.

Check Your Work

Figure 3.15 Personal Return Address Labels Created in Project 2

You will create an award certificate using a Word template that includes text and date content controls, and then you will create an award based on the template.

Preview Finished Project

Creating a Template and Inserting Content Controls

Whether creating a client survey form for the marketing and research department of a company or creating an award certificate for volunteers at a local hospital, using a template that contains content controls will save time and effort.

Creating a Form Template

DTP POINTER

If content controls are not available on the Developer tab, the open document may have been created in an older version of Word. Convert the file by clicking the File tab, clicking the Convert button, and then clicking OK.

In Word, a form is a protected document that includes fields in which information is entered. A form document contains content controls that can be added and customized. For example, many online forms are designed with a drop-down list content control that provides a restricted set of choices. Content controls can provide instructional text for users and can be set to disappear when users type in their own text. Content controls are located on the Developer tab, as shown in Figure 3.16.

Complete the following steps to add the Developer tab to the ribbon:

1. Click the File tab and then click *Options*.
2. At the Word Options dialog box, click *Customize Ribbon* in the left panel.
3. In the *Customize the Ribbon* section, click the *Developer* check box to insert a check mark and then click OK.

Complete the following steps to create a form template:

1. Design the form by sketching a layout, or use an existing form as a guide and then enter the text into a document that will appear in the form template.
2. At the document containing the form text, add content controls and instructional text prompting the user to insert information at the keyboard.
3. Save the document as a protected template.

Figure 3.16 Using the Developer Tab

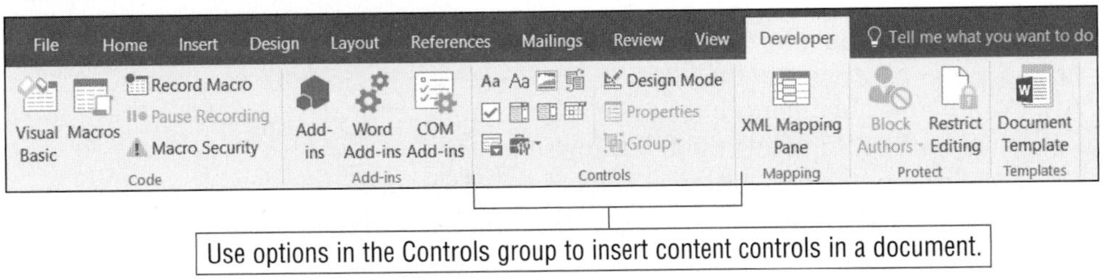

Use options in the Controls group to insert content controls in a document.

Inserting a Date Picker Content Control

Date Picker Content Control

The certificate in Project 3 will be saved as a template to be used over and over. A date picker content control will be added to the document so that the user can enter the date. A date picker content control contains a pop-up calendar that appears when the user clicks the down-pointing arrow at the right side of the content control. Using a date picker content control helps prevent users from making errors when entering the date. Insert a date picker content control into a document by positioning the insertion point at the desired location in the document and then clicking the Date Picker Content Control button in the Controls group on the Developer tab.

Adding Instructional Text to a Content Control

Adding placeholder text can be helpful to instruct the user on how to fill in a particular content control included in the template. The instructions are replaced by content when the user fills in the template.

Design Mode

To add instructional text to a content control, complete the following steps:

1. Click the Design Mode button in the Controls group on the Developer tab.
2. With the content control selected, click the Properties button in the Controls group, type the instructional text in the *Title* text box in the *General* section of the Content Control Properties dialog box, and then click OK.
3. Click the Design Mode button to exit Design mode.

Creating a Certificate Using a Template

Certificates are usually created to recognize or commemorate an award or achievement. Examples of these types of documents include diplomas, volunteer recognition awards, and program completion certificates. Some other uses for certificates include coupons, warranties, and special-offer documents. If many versions of the same certificate will be created, saving the certificate as a template can save time.

Certificates can be created in both Word and PowerPoint using online templates. These templates are available at http://office.microsoft.com/en-us/templates /default.aspx. A custom certificate template can also be created.

When printing a certificate, consider using high-quality uncoated bond stock or parchment paper in a conservative color, such as natural, cream, off-white, light gray, or any light marbleized color. In addition, consider using certificates with preprinted borders, ribbons, seals, and jackets, which are generally available through many mail order catalogs and office supply stores.

Project 3 Creating an Award Certificate   Part 1 of 1

1. At a blank document, begin creating a template for the certificate shown in Figure 3.17 on page 96 by completing the following steps:
   a. Click the File tab and then click the *Export* option.
   b. At the Export backstage area, click *Change File Type* in the middle panel, click *Template (*.dotx)* in the *Document File Types* section, and then click the Save As button in the *Change File Type* section.
   c. At the Save As dialog box, navigate to the C3 folder, type 3-AwardTemplate in the *File name* text box, verify that *Word Template (*.dotx)* displays in the *Save as type* option box, and then click the Save button.

d. Change the page orientation to landscape.

e. Change the top, bottom, left, and right margins to 0.75 inch.

f. Click the Design tab, click the Page Borders button in the Page Background group, click the *Art* option box arrow at the Borders and Shading dialog box with the Page Border tab selected, scroll down the drop-down list, and then click the diamond-shape border, as shown at the right.

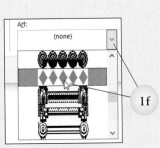

1f

g. Click the Options button at the Borders and Shading dialog box.

h. At the Border and Shading Options dialog box, click the *Measure from* option box arrow and then click *Text*. Type 4 in each of the four margin measurement boxes and then click OK two times.

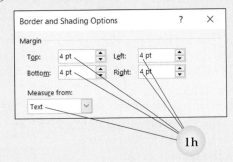

1h

i. Create a text box inside the border in a position similar to that shown in Figure 3.17 on page 96 that measures 6.67 inches in height and 5.86 inches in width.

j. With the text box selected, click the More Shape Styles button in the Shape Styles group on the Drawing Tools Format tab and then click the *Subtle Effect - Blue, Accent 1* option (second column, fourth row in the *Theme Styles* section).

k. With the text box still selected, click the Shape Fill button arrow in the Shape Styles group, point to *Gradient*, and then click the *From Center* option (second column, second row in the *Variations* section).

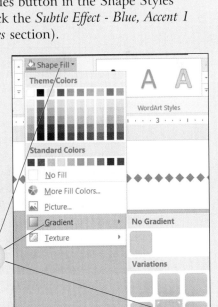

1k

l. Click the Shape Outline button arrow in the Shape Styles group and then the click *Blue, Accent 1, Lighter 60%* color (fifth column, third row in the *Theme Colors* section).

m. With the insertion point positioned inside the text box, click the Insert tab, click the Object button arrow in the Text group, click *Text from File* at the drop-down list, navigate to the C3 folder, and then double-click ***Award.docx***.

2. Display the Developer tab on the ribbon by completing the following steps (skip to Step 3 if the Developer tab is already available on the ribbon):

a. Click the File tab and then click *Options*.

b. At the Word Options dialog box, click *Customize Ribbon* in the left panel.

c. In the *Customize the Ribbon* section of the Word Options dialog box, click the *Developer* check box to insert a check mark and then click OK.

3. Insert and modify content controls in the template by completing the following steps:
   a. Click the Show/Hide ¶ button in the Paragraph group on the Home tab to turn on the display of nonprinting characters.
   b. Position the insertion point at the third paragraph symbol below *Awarded to* and then click the Developer tab.
   c. Click the Design Mode button in the Controls group (this toggles the feature on) and then click the Plain Text Content Control button in the Controls group.

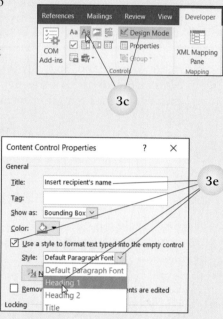

   d. With the insertion point positioned in the plain text content control, click the Properties button in the Controls group.
   e. At the Content Control Properties dialog box, type Insert recipient's name in the *Title* text box and then click the check box left of the *Use a style to format text typed into the empty control* option to insert a check mark. Click the *Style* option box arrow and then click *Heading 1* at the drop-down list. Click OK to close the dialog box.
   f. Position the insertion point on the blank line (left of the tab symbol) below *Ameeta Singh, M.D.*, and then click the Date Picker Content Control button in the Controls group on the Developer tab.

   g. With the insertion point positioned in the date picker content control, click the Properties button in the Controls group.
   h. At the Content Control Properties dialog box, type Select award date in the *Title* text box, click the third date format in the *Display the date like this* list box in the *Date Picker Properties* section, and then click OK.

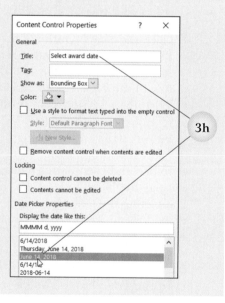

   i. To insert a date content control below *Diane Gohlke, R.N.*, position the insertion point in front of the paragraph symbol at the end of the line below the name and then repeat steps 3f through 3h.
   Alternative: You can drag and drop a copy of the date picker content control by clicking the control, pressing and holding down the Ctrl key, dragging the pointer to the desired position, and then releasing the mouse and the Ctrl key.
   j. Click the Design Mode button to turn off the feature.
   k. Select the text *Community Service Award* and then change the font to 32-point Broadway.

l. With the text still selected, click the Text Effects and Typography button, point to *Shadow* at the drop-down list, scroll down the side menu, and then click the *Perspective: Upper Left* option (first column, first row in the *Perspective* section).

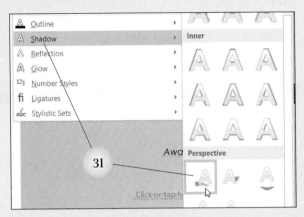

m. Click the Show/Hide ¶ button to turn off the display of nonprinting characters.

4. Draw the signature lines in the award by completing the following steps:

a. Click the Insert tab.

b. Click the Shapes button in the Illustrations group and then click the *Line* option in the *Lines* section.

c. Press and hold down the Shift key as you drag the crosshairs to draw a line above *Ameeta Singh, M.D.* The line should be 2.5 inches wide. ***Hint: Select the line and then verify the correct width at the* Shape Width *measurement box in the Size group on the Drawing Tools Format tab.***

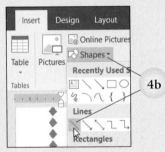

d. With the line selected, click the Drawing Tools Format tab, click the Shape Outline button arrow in the Shape Styles group, and then click the *Black, Text 1* color (second column, first row in the *Theme Colors* section).

e. With the line still selected, press and hold down the Ctrl key as you drag and drop a copy of the line above *Diane Gohlke, R.N.*, as shown in Figure 3.17.

5. Insert a picture and a logo by completing the following steps:

a. Position the insertion point in the upper left corner of the document, near the gray diamond border. Click the Insert tab and then click the Pictures button in the Illustrations group.

b. At the Insert Picture dialog box, navigate to the C3 folder and then double-click ***healthcare.png***.

c. With the image selected, click the Wrap Text button in the Arrange group on the Picture Tools Format tab and then click *In Front of Text* at the drop-down list.

d. Position the image as shown in Figure 3.17.

e. Insert the logo by clicking the Insert tab, clicking the Pictures button in the Illustrations group, navigating to the C3 folder, and then double-clicking ***EdwardCardio.png***.

f. With the logo selected, click the Wrap Text button and then click *In Front of Text* at the drop-down list.

g. Size and position the image as shown in Figure 3.17.

6. Save and then close **3-AwardTemplate.dotx**.

7. Open the award template and then create a document based on the template by completing the following steps:
   a. Open File Explorer.
   b. Navigate to the C3 folder.
   c. Double-click *3-AwardTemplate.dotx*.
8. Click the placeholder text *Click or tap here to enter text.* and then type Kathleen Sinnamon. Press the Tab key, click the date picker content control arrow, and then click the current date. Press the Tab key and then click the current date again.
9. Save the document with the name **3-CompletedAward**.
10. Print and then close **3-CompletedAward.docx**.

Check Your Work

Figure 3.17 Certificate Created in Project 3

Creating a Resume Using a Template

A resume is a document that provides a person's educational background, work history, volunteer experience, and awards and/or certificates. A resume is generally submitted to a potential employer when applying for a job. A resume should be short (one to three pages), be visually appealing to the reader, contain keywords that employers look for in an applicant's information, and be updated on a regular basis.

There are three common resume formats: chronological, which lists a candidate's work experience in chronological order, usually beginning with the current job; functional, which emphasizes the skills of the candidate and his or her achievements; and hybrid, which is a combination of the chronological and functional resumes.

Word includes several resume templates at the New backstage area. Type *resume* in the search text box or click the *Resume* option at the New backstage area to display all the available resume templates.

Project 4 Creating a Resume   Part 1 of 1

1. At a blank document, create the resume shown in Figure 3.18 by completing the following steps:
   a. Click the File tab and then click the *New* option.
   b. At the New backstage area, click in the search text box, type resume, and then press the Enter key.
   c. Double-click the first resume option, *Resume*, as shown at the right.
2. Select the name that displays in the *[Author]* placeholder at the beginning of the document and then type Erik Karlsen.
3. Click in the *[Address, City, ST ZIP Code]* placeholder and then type 4431 Alder Avenue, Salem, OR 97304.
4. Click in the *[Telephone]* placeholder and then type (971) 555-2815.
5. Click in the *[Email]* placeholder and then type ekarlsen@emcp.net.

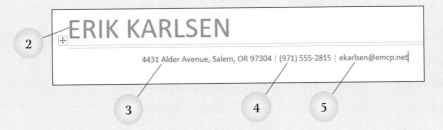

ERIK KARLSEN

4431 Alder Avenue, Salem, OR 97304 | (971) 555-2815 | ekarlsen@emcp.net

6. Continue filling in all the placeholders as shown in Figure 3.18. Delete the extra table row in the *COMPUTER SKILLS* section.
7. Select the entire document and then change the font color to Black, Text 1.
8. Save the document with the name **3-Resume**.
9. Print and then close **3-Resume.docx**.

Check Your Work

Figure 3.18 Resume Created in Project 4

ERIK KARLSEN

4431 Alder Avenue, Salem, OR 97304 | (971) 555-2815 | ekarlsen@emcp.net

SUMMARY

I seek to launch a career as a civil engineer in the public sector to further develop and use my scientific and computer knowledge.

COMPUTER SKILLS

Software

· MS Word

· MS Excel

· MS PowerPoint

· AutoCAD

· Civil3D

· ArcGIS

EXPERIENCE

2016 to present   Intern, *Polk County Public Works & Utilities, Surface Water Management Division*

· assist civil engineer with project design, drafting, specifications, and plan preparations

· help with surveying, gathering field data, collecting GPS data, and mapping

· use of Geographic Information System (GIS)

2014 to 2016   Survey Assistant, *Evergreen Surveying Company*

· determine property boundaries

· prepare maps, reports, and legal descriptions

· calculate shape, contour, location, and elevation of land and land features

EDUCATION

2014 to 2017   Bachelor of Science in Civil Engineering, *University of Oregon*

2013 to 2014   Associate of Science in Mathematics, *Salem Community College*

Chapter Summary

- Use Word templates to create personal documents, such as calendars, address labels, certificates, resumes, change-of-address postcards, and hanging name tags.

- Templates contain various placeholders in the form of text boxes containing formatted sample text or images; drawing objects in specific sizes, shapes, and colors; and sample images.

- A calendar is a basic organizational tool that also can be used as a marketing tool to promote a service, product, or program. Create a calendar from scratch, insert a predesigned calendar building block, or use a predesigned online template to create a calendar.

- Add interest to a calendar by inserting a predesigned shape. A shape may include text, color, and other special effects.

- Edit images inserted in a calendar with options on the Picture Tools Format tab.

- Text and images in Word are arranged in layers. Each document includes a foreground layer, a text layer, and a background layer. The foreground layer contains text boxes and drawing objects, the text layer contains text and graphics that are formatted in the In Line With Text text wrapping style, and the background layer contains content created in the Header and Footer panes (including watermarks).

- Move multiple drawing objects at the same time by selecting the first object, pressing and holding down the Shift key, clicking any additional objects, and then dragging the drawing objects to the desired location.

- Move selected objects in small increments in a specific direction (called *nudging*) by pressing the Up Arrow, Down Arrow, Right Arrow, or Left Arrow key on the keyboard. A drawing object or group of objects can also be aligned with options at the Align button drop-down list.

- A drawing canvas helps arrange a drawing in a document. To insert a drawing canvas, click the Shapes button in the Illustrations group on the Insert tab and then click *New Drawing Canvas* at the bottom of the drop-down list.

- Objects automatically stack in individual layers as they are added to a document. The stacking order is visible when objects overlap; the top object covers portions of the objects beneath it. Rearrange stacked drawing objects by selecting an object and then clicking the Bring Forward button or the Send Backward button in the Arrange group on the Drawing Tools Format tab.

- Grouping objects combines multiple drawing objects into a single unit. Group and ungroup selected objects with options at the Group button drop-down gallery in the Arrange group on the Drawing Tools Format tab.

- Objects can be flipped or rotated with options at the Rotate button drop-down gallery. The Rotate button is located in the Arrange group on the Drawing Tools Format tab.

- Select a predefined label at the Envelopes and Labels dialog box to create personal return labels, shipping labels, address labels, place cards, tent cards, and many more useful labels.

- Return address labels can be duplicated on a sheet of labels by saving a formatted label as a building block to the Quick Part gallery, where it can be named, saved, and reused.

- Create a form, which is a protected document that includes fields in which information is entered, to save the time of re-creating the same document.

- Content controls can be added to documents or templates to provide instructional text for users and allow users to efficiently insert data into templates, forms, and documents.
- A date picker content control can be added to the document so that the user can select a date from a pop-up calendar.
- Certificate templates are available at the New backstage area.
- A resume is a document that lists a job applicant's work experience, educational background, volunteer work, and certificates and/or awards. The three most common resume formats are chronological, functional, and hybrid.
- Resume templates are available at the New backstage area.

Commands Review

FEATURE	RIBBON TAB, GROUP	BUTTON
align	Drawing Tools Format, Arrange; Layout, Arrange	
bring forward	Drawing Tools Format, Arrange; Layout, Arrange	
color	Picture Tools Format, Adjust	
date picker content control	Developer, Controls	
group	Drawing Tools Format, Arrange	
labels	Mailings, Create	
plain text content control	Developer, Controls	Aa
quick parts	Insert, Text	
rotate	Drawing Tools Format, Arrange	
Send Backward	Drawing Tools Format, Arrange; Layout, Arrange	
shapes	Insert, Illustrations	
tables	Insert, Tables	

Workbook

Chapter study tools and assessment activities are available in the workbook pages of the ebook. These resources are designed to help you further develop and demonstrate mastery of the skills learned in this chapter.

Creating Letterheads, Envelopes, Business Cards, and Press Releases

CHAPTER 4

Performance Objectives

Upon successful completion of Chapter 4, you will be able to:

1   Identify the purposes of letterheads
2   Use letterhead templates
3   Create custom letterheads
4   Use text boxes in design
5   Create horizontal and vertical-ruled lines
6   Create envelopes
7   Create business cards
8   Create a press release

Desktop Publishing Terms

logo
pixel

press release
ruled line

Word Features Used

anchors
borders and shading
Click and Type
envelopes
kerning
labels

line spacing
quick parts
shapes
text boxes
text wrapping

Precheck

Check your current skills to help focus your study.

Data Files

Before beginning chapter work, copy the C4 folder to your storage medium and then make C4 the active folder.

SNAP

If you are a SNAP user, launch the Precheck and Tutorials from your Assignments page.

You will create a letterhead from a template. You will also create a custom letterhead with text boxes, grouped objects, and ruled lines.

Preview Finished Project

Understanding the Purposes of Letterheads

DTP POINTER

A letterhead conveys specific information, establishes an identity, and projects an image.

In planning a letterhead design, think about the purpose of a letterhead. While the content of a letter may vary, the purposes of any letterhead are generally the same: to convey specific information, to establish an identity, and to project an image.

Conveying Information

Consider all the necessary information a letterhead should include. Also consider what items readers expect to find in a letterhead. Although the information provided may vary, a letterhead commonly contains the following:

- Name of company or organization
- Logo
- Address
- Shipping or mailing address, if different from street address
- Telephone numbers, including area codes (Include an all-number version of any phone number that incorporates a spelled-out word or phrase; also include any extra phone numbers, such as a local number and/or a toll-free number.)
- Fax number, including area code
- Email address
- Web address
- Marketing statement or company slogan

The information in a letterhead tells the reader how to contact the person or business by phone, by email, by regular mail, or in person. Omitting an important component in a letterhead projects a careless attitude and can negatively affect a business.

Establishing an Identity

A business relationship is often initiated through written communication. For example, a buyer from one company may write to a sales representative at another company inquiring about a certain product or asking for a price list; a real estate agent may send out a letter to residents in surrounding communities explaining his or her services; or a volunteer organization may send letters to local businesses soliciting their support. Whatever the reason for the letter, a letterhead with a specific design and layout helps to establish the identity of the organization. When readers are exposed to the same pattern of consistent elements in a letterhead over a period of time, they soon begin to establish a certain level of familiarity with the organization name, logo, colors, and so forth. Therefore, a letterhead should be immediately recognizable and identifiable.

Further emphasize the identity of an organization by using some of the design elements from the letterhead in other business documents. Many direct-mail paper suppliers offer lines of attractively designed color letterheads, along with coordinating envelopes, business cards, fax cover sheets, press release forms, brochures, postcards, note cards, disc labels, and more. Plan the layout of the letterhead text to complement the existing design and then print the text on the predesigned paper. Purchasing a coordinating line of predesigned paper saves on the high costs of professional designing and printing. It also provides a quick, convenient way to establish an identity among readers.

Projecting an Image

Along with establishing an identity, a letterhead helps to project an image. Assess the target audience when determining the image to be projected. Who are they? What is their background, education, age, and so on? What image should readers form in their minds about the company, business, or organization? What does their experience tell them to expect?

Look at the two Financial Consultation letterheads in Figure 4.1. What image of the business comes to mind when viewing each letterhead? The top letterhead projects a fun, casual, not-so-professional image, while the bottom letterhead conveys a more serious, businesslike attitude. Even though these images may not be accurate representations of the business, they affect the way readers think about the business. However, giving readers exactly what they expect can sometimes lead to boredom. The challenge is to create a design that gives readers what they expect and at the same time sets the letterhead apart from the rest.

DTP POINTER

Printing on high-quality paper presents a professional image.

Printing a letterhead on high-quality paper can add to the cost, but it certainly presents a more professional image. Purchase this kind of paper at a commercial printer. Many print shops will sell paper by the sheet, along with matching envelopes.

Figure 4.1 Comparing Letterhead Designs

Using Letterhead Templates

DTP POINTER
Use coordinating templates to establish identity and consistency among internal and external business documents.

Word includes a variety of predesigned online template documents, including letterheads. Search for letterhead templates by clicking the File tab and then clicking the *New* option. At the New backstage area, type *letterhead* in the search text box and then press the Enter key. Two sample letterhead templates are shown in Figure 4.2.

The descriptive names of the letterhead templates coordinate with the descriptive names for the memo, fax, report, and resume templates provided by Microsoft Office. Using coordinating templates is an easy way for a business to establish identity and consistency among its internal and external documents.

Customizing a Logo Used in a Template

logo
An image or symbol designed to represent a company or brand

A ***logo*** is an image or symbol designed to represent a company or brand. In Project 1a, a logo in a Word letterhead template will be customized as a group of drawing objects. A group of objects needs to be ungrouped before individual objects can be customized. Once the ungrouped objects are customized, regroup the objects.

Figure 4.2 Using Word Templates for Letterheads

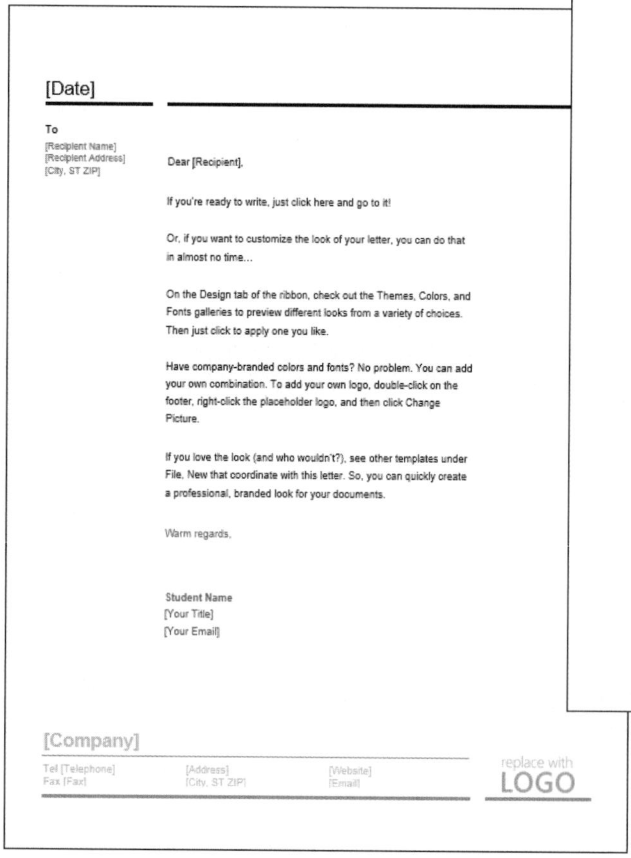
[Date]

To
[Recipient Name]
[Recipient Address]
[City, ST ZIP]

Dear [Recipient],

If you're ready to write, just click here and go to it!

Or, if you want to customize the look of your letter, you can do that in almost no time...

On the Design tab of the ribbon, check out the Themes, Colors, and Fonts galleries to preview different looks from a variety of choices. Then just click to apply one you like.

Have company-branded colors and fonts? No problem. You can add your own combination. To add your own logo, double-click on the footer, right-click the placeholder logo, and then click Change Picture.

If you love the look (and who wouldn't?), see other templates under File, New that coordinate with this letter. So, you can quickly create a professional, branded look for your documents.

Warm regards,

Student Name
[Your Title]
[Your Email]

[Company]
Tel [Telephone] Fax [Fax] [Address] [City, ST ZIP] [Website] [Email]
replace with LOGO

Letterhead (Red and Black Design)

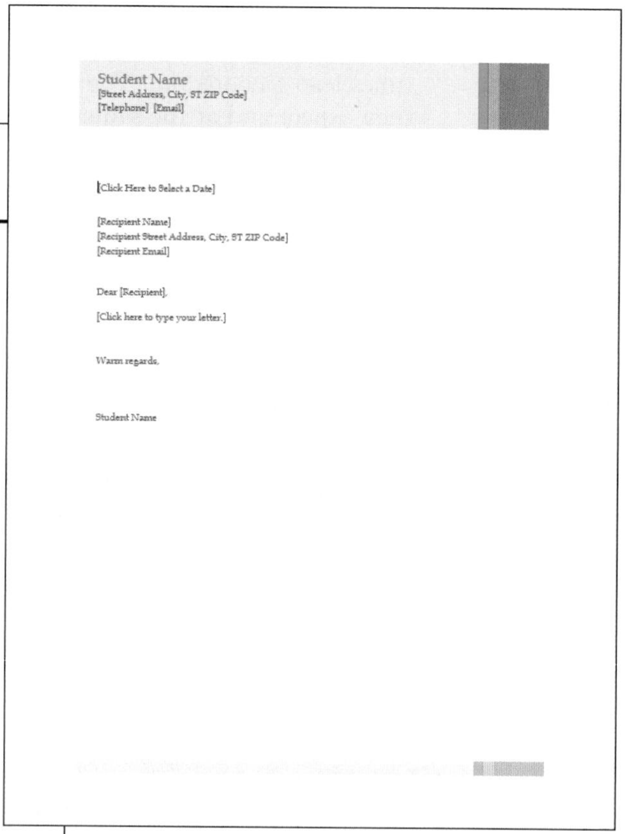
Student Name
[Street Address, City, ST ZIP Code]
[Telephone] [Email]

[Click Here to Select a Date]

[Recipient Name]
[Recipient Street Address, City, ST ZIP Code]
[Recipient Email]

Dear [Recipient],

[Click here to type your letter.]

Warm regards,

Student Name

Business letter (Sales Stripes Design)

To ungroup and then regroup a group of drawing objects, complete the following steps:

Group

1. With the group of objects selected, click the Group button in the Arrange group on the Drawing Tools Format tab or Picture Tools Format tab and then click *Ungroup* at the drop-down list.
2. Click in a blank area of the document to deselect any objects. If a prompt displays to convert the picture to a drawing object, click Yes.
3. Customize an individual component of the object by clicking the component and then making changes with the options on the Drawing Tools Format tab or the Picture Tools Format tab.
4. To regroup the components of the object, click in the object, click the Home tab, click the Select button in the Editing group, and then click *Select All* at the drop-down list.
5. With all the components in the object selected, click the Drawing Tools Format tab, click the Group button in the Arrange group, and then click *Group* at the drop-down list.

Select

Using the Selection Pane

Word provides the Selection pane to make working with layers a little easier. The Selection pane lists each item separately and custom effects can be applied to just one item, without having to click through the layers on the page. To access this feature, click the Select button in the Editing group on the Home tab and then click *Selection Pane* at the drop-down list. Figure 4.3 shows a document with the Selection pane active.

The Selection pane offers a couple of options that make working with layers easier. For example, a layer can be moved within the order of all the layers. To move a layer in front of or behind other layers, first select the layer and then use the Bring Forward or Send Backward button to adjust the layer's order in the list. Alternatively, click a layer and click and hold down the left mouse button, drag the layer to the new location in the list of layers, and then release the mouse button. The Selection pane also includes an option to show or hide a layer. Toggle whether a layer is visible by clicking the eye icon ([👁]) at the right side of the layer.

Figure 4.3 Using the Selection Pane

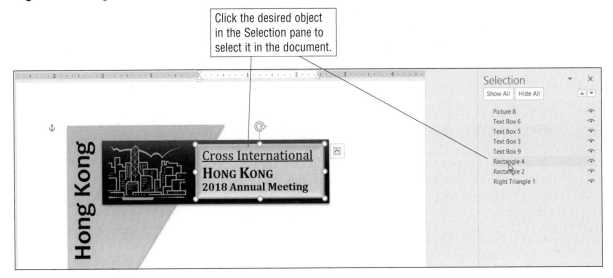

1. In Word, open **GraphicEdgeTemplate.dotx** from the C4 folder and then save it as a template with the name **4-GraphicEdgeTemplate**. Make sure *Word Template (*.dotx)* displays in the *Save as type* option box.
2. Display the Selection pane by clicking the Select button in the Editing group on the Home tab and then clicking *Selection Pane* at the drop-down list. Notice the list of objects contained in the document that displays in the Selection pane.
3. Customize the logo graphic as shown in Figure 4.4 on page 108 by completing the following steps:
   a. Click *Picture 5* in the Selection pane to select the logo graphic.
   b. Click the Picture Tools Format tab.
   c. Click the Group button in the Arrange group and then click *Ungroup* at the drop-down list.
   d. At the message asking if you want to convert the imported picture to a Microsoft Office drawing object, click the Yes button.
   e. Drag the object back to its original position.
   f. Click outside the object to deselect it and then click the red shape (left shape) of the logo.
   g. Click the Drawing Tools Format tab.
   h. Click the Shape Fill button arrow in the Shape Styles group and then click the *Light Green* color (fifth color in the *Standard Colors* section).
   i. Select all of the objects, click the Group button in the Arrange group, and then click *Group* at the drop-down list.
4. Close the Selection pane by clicking the Close button in the upper right corner of the pane.
5. Format the text *Financial Consultation* and the text box containing it by completing the following steps:
   a. Select the text *Financial Consultation* and then type Graphic Edge.
   b. Select *Graphic Edge* and then change the font to 15-point Castellar.
   c. Select the text box containing *Graphic Edge* by clicking the border of the text box.
   d. With the text box selected, click the Drawing Tools Format tab.
   e. Click the Shape Outline button arrow in the Shape Styles group, point to *Dashes* at the drop-down gallery, and then click the fourth option at the side menu.
   f. Change the color of the dashed line by clicking the Shape Outline button arrow and then clicking the *Light Green* color (fifth option in the *Standard Colors* section).

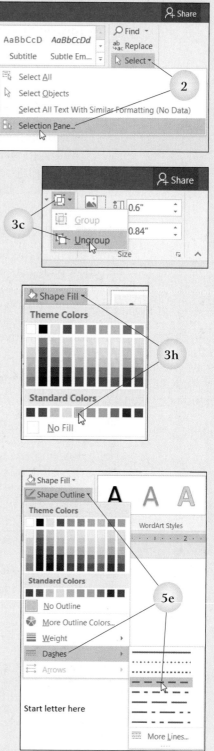

6. Replace the text in the text box in the bottom right corner of the template with the text shown in Figure 4.4 (the company address, telephone numbers, and email address).
7. Add an orange gradient fill and change the shape of the text box containing the address by completing the following steps:
   a. Select the text box containing the address information.
   b. Click the Drawing Tools Format tab if necessary to make it active.
   c. Click the More Shape Styles button in the Shape Styles group.
   d. Click the *Subtle Effect - Orange, Accent 2* shape style (third column, fourth row).
   e. Click the Edit Shape button in the Insert Shapes group, point to *Change Shape* at the drop-down list, and then click the *Flowchart: Manual Input* option in the *Flowchart* section.

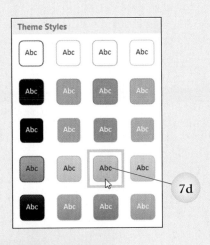

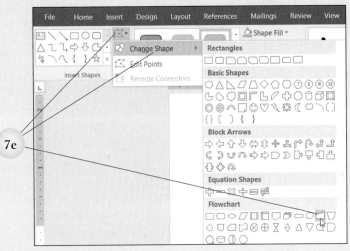

8. Save and then close **4-GraphicEdgeTemplate.dotx**.
9. Open File Explorer, navigate to the C4 folder, and then double-click **4-GraphicEdgeTemplate.dotx**. (This opens a document based on the template.)
10. Select the text *Start letter here* (the text is inside a text box) and then insert a document by completing the following steps:
    a. Click the Insert tab.
    b. Click the Object button arrow in the Text group and then click *Text from File* at the drop-down list.
    c. At the Insert File dialog box, navigate to the C4 folder and then double-click **GraphicText.docx**.
11. Save the document with the name **4-GELetter**.
12. Print and then close **4-GELetter.docx**.

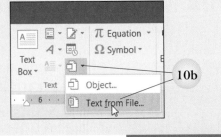

Check Your Work

Figure 4.4 Letterhead Created in Project 1a

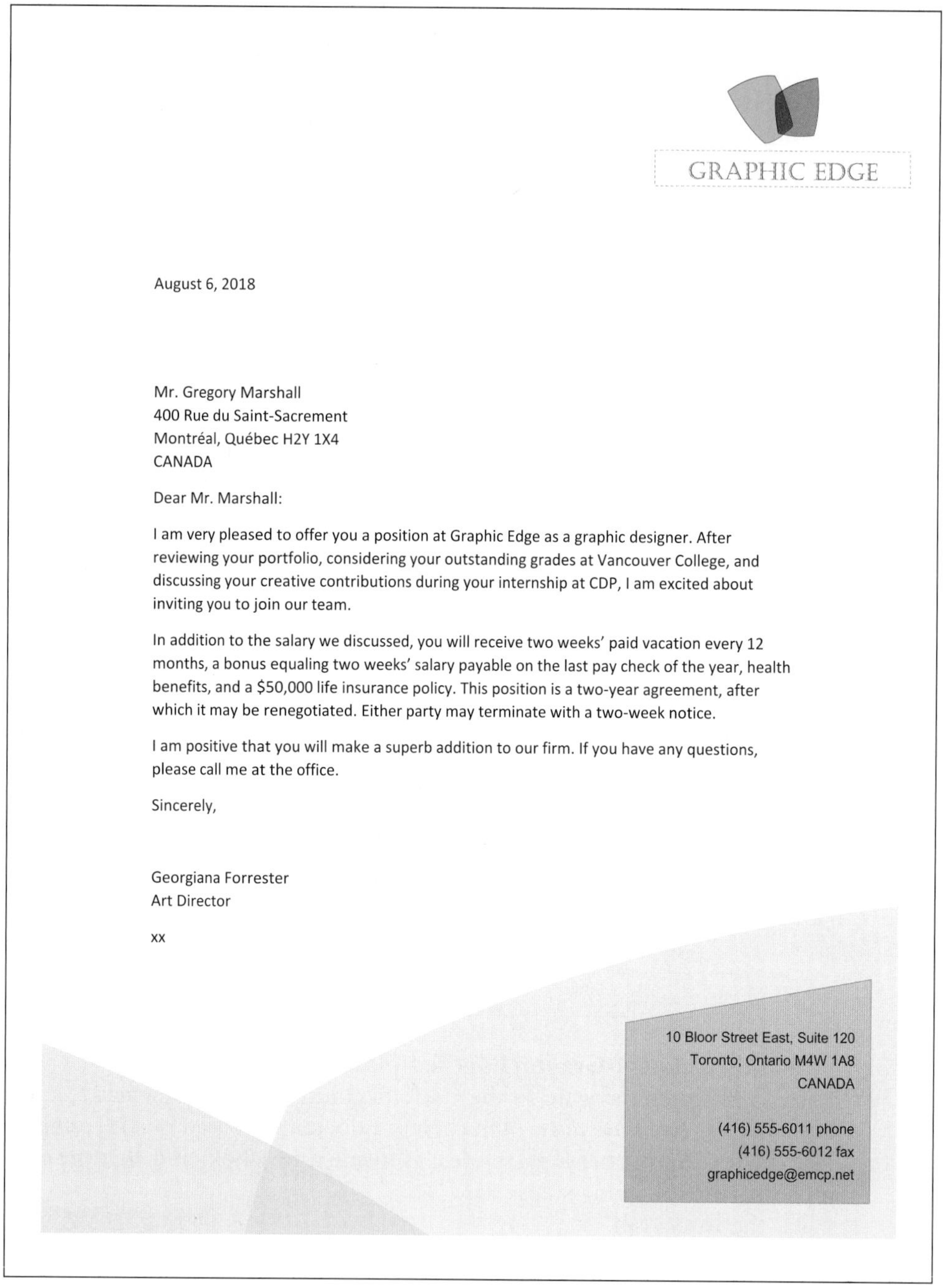

August 6, 2018

Mr. Gregory Marshall
400 Rue du Saint-Sacrement
Montréal, Québec H2Y 1X4
CANADA

Dear Mr. Marshall:

I am very pleased to offer you a position at Graphic Edge as a graphic designer. After reviewing your portfolio, considering your outstanding grades at Vancouver College, and discussing your creative contributions during your internship at CDP, I am excited about inviting you to join our team.

In addition to the salary we discussed, you will receive two weeks' paid vacation every 12 months, a bonus equaling two weeks' salary payable on the last pay check of the year, health benefits, and a $50,000 life insurance policy. This position is a two-year agreement, after which it may be renegotiated. Either party may terminate with a two-week notice.

I am positive that you will make a superb addition to our firm. If you have any questions, please call me at the office.

Sincerely,

Georgiana Forrester
Art Director

xx

GRAPHIC EDGE

10 Bloor Street East, Suite 120
Toronto, Ontario M4W 1A8
CANADA

(416) 555-6011 phone
(416) 555-6012 fax
graphicedge@emcp.net

Creating Custom Letterheads

Designing and creating a custom letterhead creates a unique identity and saves time and money. A letterhead that has been created by a commercial printer may be used by more than one business because it saves the printer time to reuse designs. Contracting a graphic designer to create a custom letterhead is expensive and not a very viable option for individuals and small businesses.

Incorporating Design Concepts in Letterheads

When designing a letterhead, it is a good idea to start by creating thumbnail sketches to try out ideas. While working on the sketches and ultimately when creating the letterhead, consider the following design concepts:

- Focus: Create a focal point in the letterhead to draw in the audience.
- Balance: Use a symmetrical layout, in which similar elements are distributed evenly on the page, or use an asymmetrical layout, in which dissimilar elements are distributed unevenly on the page in such a way as to balance one another.
- Proportion: Design elements sized in proportion to their relative importance to the intended message. A letterhead should not take up any more than 2 inches at the top of the page—preferably less.
- Contrast: Use enough contrast to make it noticeable, and make sure there is enough white space surrounding darker elements on the page.
- Directional flow: Group related items close to each other, and establish a visual connection between items on the page by using strong alignment.
- Consistency: Use one typeface but vary the type size, typestyle, or color. Repeat elements that tie the letterhead to subsequent pages, such as a ruled horizontal line that is repeated as a footer on each page.
- Color: Use color sparingly to provide emphasis and contrast, and use a color that meets readers' expectations for the mood, tone, and image of the organization and message.

Using the Click and Type Feature

Tutorial

Using Click and Type

The Click and Type feature can be used to insert text, graphics, tables, and other items into a blank area of a Word document. In Print Layout view, drag the mouse pointer across the document to view the Click and Type pointer with different alignment options, as shown in Figure 4.5. Double-click to move the insertion point to the location of the mouse pointer. Word will automatically change the paragraph alignment. Once the insertion point is in the desired location, begin typing or insert a graphic or other item.

If the Click and Type feature does not work, check to see that it is enabled by displaying the Word Options dialog box, clicking *Advanced* in the left panel, and then making sure a check mark displays in the *Enable click and type* check box in the *Editing options* section.

Figure 4.5 Using Click and Type Alignment

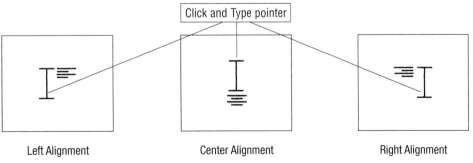

| Left Alignment | Center Alignment | Right Alignment |

Figure 4.6 Using Vertical Page Position

Customize Status Bar	
Formatted Page Number	1
Section	1
✓ Page Number	Page 1 of 1
Vertical Page Position	1"
Line Number	1
Column	1
✓ Word Count	0 words
✓ Spelling and Grammar Check	
✓ Language	

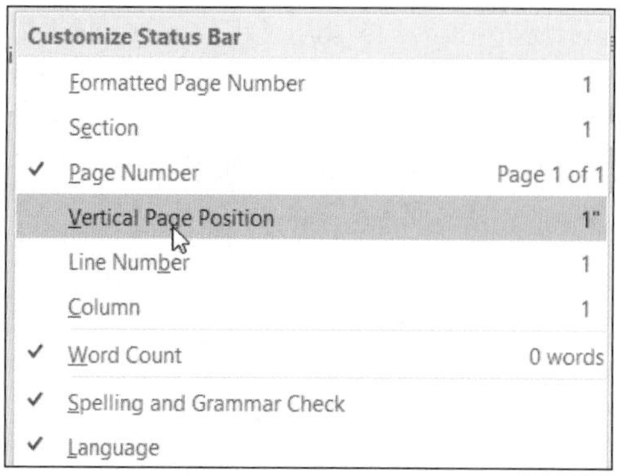

Using the Vertical Page Position Feature

DTP POINTER

Turn on the Vertical Page Position feature to view the exact location of the insertion point relative to the top of the document.

To add the vertical location of the insertion point to the items displayed on the Status bar, right-click the Status bar and then click the *Vertical Page Position* option at the Customize Status Bar pop-up menu, as shown in Figure 4.6. Use this feature to position text at an exact distance from the top of the page. For example, set the text 2 inches from the top of the page to make room for the preprinted letterhead.

Using Text Boxes in Design

Text boxes are useful in desktop publishing because they can be moved to any position on the page by dragging with the mouse or by specifying exact horizontal and vertical locations at the Layout dialog box. Another important feature of text boxes is that they are created in the drawing (foreground) layer and considered drawing objects. Like any other object in Word, a text box can be placed above or below the text layer in a Word document. Text can be wrapped around a text box in a variety of ways, the direction of the text within a text box can be changed, and text boxes can be linked.

Additionally, like other Word objects, text boxes can be formatted with options on the Drawing Tools Format tab, as shown in Figure 4.7. Attributes such as shape fill, outline, and effects can be used to customize a text box.

Setting Text Box Margins

By default, a text box has left and right internal margins of 0.1 inch and top and bottom internal margins of 0.05 inch. To adjust these margins, click the desired text box to access the Drawing Tools Format tab and then click the Shape Styles group task pane launcher. When the Format Shape task pane displays, click the Layout & Properties icon and then click the *Text Box* option. Adjust the values in the measurement boxes for the internal margins, as shown in Figure 4.8.

Figure 4.7 Formatting Options on the Drawing Tools Format Tab

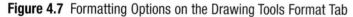

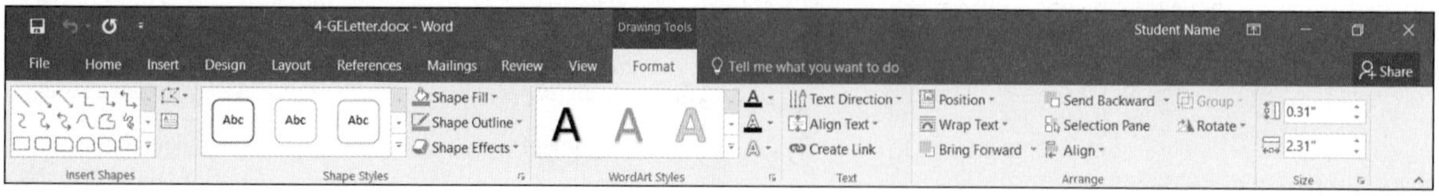

Figure 4.8 Adjusting Text Box Properties in the Format Shape Task Pane

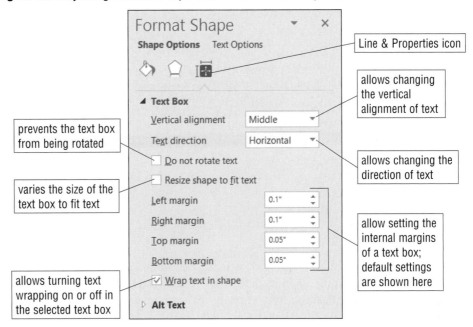

Line & Properties icon

allows changing the vertical alignment of text

prevents the text box from being rotated

allows changing the direction of text

varies the size of the text box to fit text

allow setting the internal margins of a text box; default settings are shown here

allows turning text wrapping on or off in the selected text box

Positioning a Text Box

One of the biggest advantages to using a text box is being able to position it anywhere on the page. Word provides several ways of positioning text boxes: using the move handle on the text box, using the keyboard, using the Position button in the Arrange group on the Drawing Tools Format tab, and using options at the Layout dialog box with the Position tab selected. To move a text box using the move handle (four-headed arrow), click the outline of the text box, click and hold down the mouse button, drag the outline of the text box to the new location, and then release the mouse button.

 Position

To move a text box using the keyboard, click the outline of the text box and then use the arrow keys to nudge the text box in small increments across the document page. When the text box is nudged, it moves one space over on the drawing grid, which is a set of intersecting lines used to align objects. The drawing grid is not visible in the document, and the lines do not print. To view the gridlines, click the View tab and then insert a check mark in the *Gridlines* check box in the Show group. Move a text box one pixel at a time by pressing and holding down the Ctrl key while an arrow key is pressed. A *pixel* is a single unit of measurement that a computer monitor uses to paint images on the screen. These units, which often appear as tiny dots, compose the pictures displayed by the monitor.

pixel

A single unit of measurement that a computer monitor uses to paint images on the screen

Additionally, a text box can be positioned using the Position button in the Arrange group on the Drawing Tools Format tab. Click the outline of the text box to select it, click the Position button, and then choose the desired location for the text box, as shown in Figure 4.9. Each option in the drop-down gallery depicts how the document text will wrap around the text box.

Position a text box precisely on a page using the options at the Layout dialog box with the Position tab selected. To do this, click the outline of the text box and

Figure 4.9 Positioning a Text Box Using the Position Button Drop-down Gallery

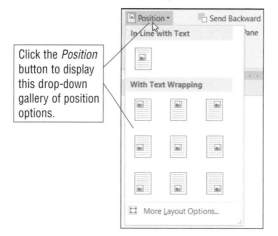

Click the *Position* button to display this drop-down gallery of position options.

then click the Size group dialog box launcher on the Drawing Tools Format tab to open the Layout dialog box. Alternatively, open the Layout dialog box by clicking the Position button in the Arrange group on the Layout tab or the Wrap Text button on the Drawing Tools Format tab and then clicking *More Layout Options* at the drop-down list. At the Layout dialog box, shown in Figure 4.10, click the Position tab. In the *Horizontal* section, make sure *Absolute position* is selected and then type the desired measurement in the corresponding measurement box. In the *to the right of* option box, select the point (*Margin, Page, Column, Character, Left Margin, Right Margin, Inside Margin,* or *Outside Margin*) from which the selected text box can be horizontally positioned. Follow the same process in the *Vertical* section. Using this method provides precise control over the placement of the text box.

4.10 Using the Layout Dialog Box to Precisely Position a Text Box Horizontally and Vertically

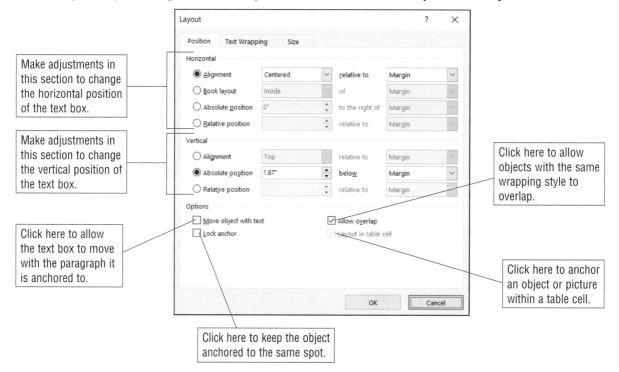

Make adjustments in this section to change the horizontal position of the text box.

Make adjustments in this section to change the vertical position of the text box.

Click here to allow the text box to move with the paragraph it is anchored to.

Click here to allow objects with the same wrapping style to overlap.

Click here to anchor an object or picture within a table cell.

Click here to keep the object anchored to the same spot.

Copying a Text Box

In some situations, an exact copy of a text box may need to be created and placed in a different location in the document. To do this, position the insertion point on the text box outline until the I-beam turns into a pointer with a four-headed arrow attached. Press and hold down the Ctrl key and the left mouse button, drag the copy of the text box to the desired location, and then release the Ctrl key and mouse button.

Anchoring a Text Box

Every object, including a text box, is automatically anchored, or attached, to the paragraph closest to it. To see the paragraphs that objects are anchored to, the display of object anchors feature must be enabled. To turn on the display of object anchors, click the File tab, click *Options*, click *Display* in the left panel of the Word Options dialog box, click the *Object anchors* check box to insert a check mark, and then click OK to close the dialog box. Figure 4.11 shows a paragraph and text box with the object anchor displayed.

When a text box is repositioned, the anchor moves to the paragraph closest to the new position of the text box. The following points provide more information about object anchors in Word:

DTP POINTER

To prevent a text box from moving with the paragraph it is anchored to, click the *Move object with text* check box at the Layout dialog box with the Position tab selected to remove the check mark.

- A text box always appears on the same page as the paragraph that it is anchored to. By default, the text box moves with the paragraph it is anchored to, but the paragraph will not move with the text box.

- Move a text box independently of the paragraph that it is anchored to by clicking the outline of the text box to select it, displaying the Layout dialog box, clicking the Position tab, and then removing the check mark from the *Move object with text* check box.

- To keep the text box on the same page as the paragraph that it is anchored to, click the *Lock anchor* check box to insert a check mark. If the paragraph is moved to another page, the text box will be moved to that page as well.

- To make an object stay at a specific location on a page regardless of the text that surrounds it, display the Layout dialog box and click the Position tab. Enter specific measurements at the *Absolute position* measurement box in the *Horizontal* section and in the *Vertical* section, and make selections in the *to the right of* and *below* option boxes. Lastly, remove the check mark from the *Move object with text* check box.

Figure 4.11 Viewing an Object Anchor

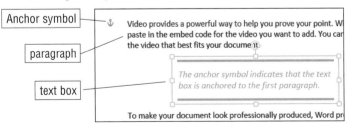

Anchor symbol

paragraph

text box

Video provides a powerful way to help you prove your point. W paste in the embed code for the video you want to add. You car the video that best fits your document.

The anchor symbol indicates that the text box is anchored to the first paragraph.

To make your document look professionally produced, Word pr

Wrapping Text around a Text Box

By default, a text box displays in the layer above (or in front of) the text. To wrap text around, behind, or in front of a text box, select the text box, display the Drawing Tools Format tab, and then click the Wrap Text button in the Arrange group. Several wrapping options are available, and the way a text box appears with each option applied is illustrated in Figure 4.12. The wrapping styles available at the Wrap Text button drop-down list are summarized in Table 4.1.

At the Layout dialog box with the Text Wrapping tab selected, use the *Wrap text* section to modify the way text wraps around a text box. The options available in the *Wrap text* section are described in Table 4.2.

Figure 4.12 Comparing Text-Wrapping Styles

In Line with Text

On the Insert tab, the galleries include items that are designed to coordinate with the overall look of your document. You can use these galleries to insert tables, headers, footers, lists, cover pages, and other document building blocks. When you create pictures, charts Square or diagrams, Tight they also coordinate with your current document look. You can easily change the formatting of selected text in the document by using the Font group or selecting a style from the Styles

Behind Text

Top and Bottom

group on the Home tab. You can also format text by using the other buttons and options on the Home tab. Most controls offer a choice of using the look from the current theme or Through using a format Edit Wrap Points ou specify In Front of Text nge the overall look of your document, cho tab. To change the styles in the Styles elements on the Design gallery, change the style set at the Design tab. Both the Themes gallery and Styles gallery provide reset commands so that you can always restore the look of your document to the original theme or styles.

Table 4.1 Text-Wrapping Styles Available at the Wrap Text Button Drop-down Gallery

Wrapping Style	Description	Button
In Line with Text	The object is placed in the text layer at the insertion point in a line of text.	
Square	Text wraps around all four sides of the selected text box or object.	
Tight	Text wraps tightly around the shape of an object, rather than the box holding the object. (This style is more apparent when applied to a shape other than a square or rectangle.)	

continues

Table 4.1 Text-Wrapping Styles Available at the Wrap Text Button Drop-down Gallery—*Continued*

Wrapping Style	Description	Button
Through	This option is similar to *Tight*. Text not only wraps around the shape of an object, but it also flows through any open areas of the object box. This option may produce a visible change with certain graphics, but no changes will occur when applied to a text box.	
Top and Bottom	Text wraps around the top and bottom of the text box (object) but not on both sides. Text stops at the top of the text box (object) and restarts on the line below the object.	
Behind Text	Text wrapping is removed, and the text box or object is placed behind the text layer in the document.	
In Front of Text	Text wrapping is removed, and the text box or object is placed in front of the text. This is the default setting.	
Edit Wrap Points	This option allows wrapping text more closely to the object.	

Table 4.2 Advanced Wrapping Styles Available on the Text-Wrapping Tab of the Layout Dialog Box

Wrapping Style	Description
Both sides	Text wraps on both sides of the text box.
Left only	Text wraps along the left side of the text box but not the right side.
Right only	Text wraps along the right side of the text box but not the left side.
Largest only	Text wraps along the longest side of the object. This does not produce any changes when applied to a text box.

Customizing Text Boxes

By default, a text box has a black single-line outline around all the sides and contains a white background fill. However, a text box can be customized in a variety of ways, including changing the outline style and color and changing the background fill color.

Changing Text Box Outlines and Effects

The following methods, along with some creativity, can be used to customize the outline of a text box (or other object).

Shape
Outline

To add, remove, or change the color, weight, or style of a text box outline, select the text box and then click the Shape Outline button arrow in the Shape Styles group on the Drawing Tools Format tab. At the Shape Outline button drop-down gallery, click a color in the *Theme Colors* or *Standard Colors* section or click the *More Outline Colors* option to pick from an extended selection of standard colors or to create custom colors. Click *Weight* or *Dashes* to change the thickness or style of the text box outline. Click *No Outline* to remove the outline from around the text box. A colored outline can also be applied to a text box by clicking one of the shape style thumbnails in the Shape Styles group. Click the Shape Styles group task pane launcher to access outline options at the Format Shape task pane. Three examples of outlines are shown in Figure 4.13.

Shape Effects

To add shape effects to a text box, select the text box; click the Shape Effects button in the Shape Styles group; point to *Preset, Shadow, Reflection, Glow, Soft Edges, Bevel,* or *3-D Rotation*; and then click an option at the side menu. Figure 4.14 illustrates examples of these shape effects.

Changing Text Box Fill

Shape Fill

Customize the text box fill with the Shape Fill button in the Shape Styles group on the Drawing Tools Format tab. Click the Shape Fill button arrow and then choose a fill color in the *Theme Colors* or *Standard Colors* section of the drop-down gallery or choose from the *No Fill, More Fill Colors, Picture, Gradient,* and *Texture* options, as shown in Figure 4.15. Fill colors can also be added to a text box with the second through sixth rows of shape styles that are available by clicking the More Shape Styles button at the right side of the shape style thumbnails in the Shape Styles group.

Add a transparent effect to the text box fill color by clicking the Shape Fill button arrow, clicking the *More Fill Colors* option, and then dragging the slider in the *Transparency* section of the Colors dialog box, as shown in Figure 4.16. The transparency can also be changed by adjusting the percentage in the measurement box at the right side of the *Transparency* section.

Figure 4.13 Changing Text Box Outlines

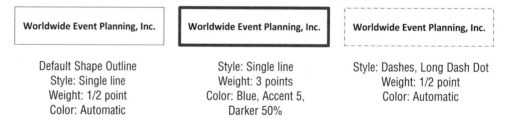

| Worldwide Event Planning, Inc. | Worldwide Event Planning, Inc. | Worldwide Event Planning, Inc. |

| Default Shape Outline
Style: Single line
Weight: 1/2 point
Color: Automatic | Style: Single line
Weight: 3 points
Color: Blue, Accent 5,
Darker 50% | Style: Dashes, Long Dash Dot
Weight: 1/2 point
Color: Automatic |

Figure 4.14 Changing Text Box Effects

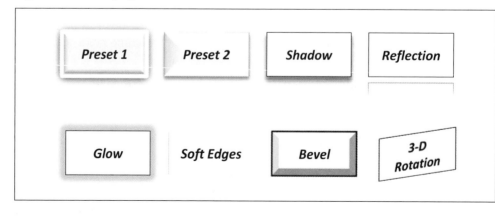

Preset 1   *Preset 2*   *Shadow*   *Reflection*

Glow   *Soft Edges*   *Bevel*   *3-D Rotation*

Figure 4.15 Changing Shape Fill

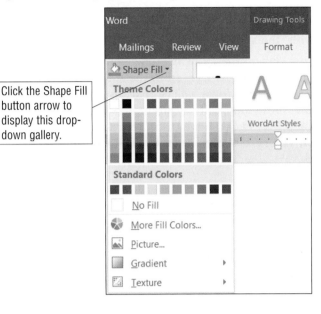

Click the Shape Fill button arrow to display this drop-down gallery.

Figure 4.16 Adding Transparency to a Color

Transparency slider

Transparency measurement box

Creating Horizontal and Vertical Ruled Lines

Horizontal and vertical lines can be drawn in a document by using line options at the Shapes button drop-down list or by using paragraph borders. As with text boxes, the weight, length, position, color, and shading of the lines can be adjusted. In typesetting, these horizontal and vertical lines are called *ruled lines* (also known as *rules* or *ruling lines*) to distinguish them from lines of type.

Horizontal- and vertical-ruled lines are used to guide a reader's eyes across and down the page, to separate sections or columns of text, to add visual interest, and to act as boundaries to the surrounding text. A thicker line serves as a stronger visual barrier than a thinner line. Make sure the ruled lines in a document are consistent in both purpose and appearance.

ruled line

A horizontal or vertical line

DTP POINTER

Ruled lines act as boundaries to surrounding text.

 Shapes

Drawing Horizontal and Vertical Lines

To insert a horizontal or vertical line, click the Insert tab, click the Shapes button in the Illustrations group, click the desired line option in the *Lines* section of the drop-down list, and then click and drag in the document to create the line. Create a straight horizontal, vertical, or diagonal line by pressing and holding down the Shift key while dragging to draw the line.

Sizing and Formatting Lines

Sizing a drawn line is similar to sizing a text box. Select the line to be sized and then position the mouse pointer on either sizing handle until it turns into cross-hairs. (Press and hold down the Shift key to make sure the line retains its shape and direction.) Drag the crosshairs in the appropriate direction until the line is the desired length and then release the mouse button. For a precise measurement, select the line and then enter a measurement in the *Shape Width* measurement box in the Size group on the Drawing Tools Format tab.

Format a drawn line with options on the Drawing Tools Format tab. Select different weights, such as those shown in Figure 4.17, from the side menu that displays when pointing to *Weight* at the drop-down gallery that displays after clicking the Shape Outline button arrow in the Shape Styles group. Choose colors, such as those shown in the figure, by selecting options in the *Theme Colors* or *Standard Colors* section of the drop-down gallery. Use the *Dashes* or *Arrows* option to change the shape of the line.

Positioning Horizontal and Vertical Lines

Horizontal and vertical lines are positioned in the same way a text box is positioned. Select the line and then reposition it using the mouse, the arrow keys on the keyboard, options on the Drawing Tools Format tab, or options at the Layout dialog box with the Position tab selected.

Creating Horizontal Lines Using Paragraph Borders

Every paragraph created in Word is surrounded by an invisible frame. (Remember that a paragraph may contain text or consist of only a hard return.) To add a border to the top, the bottom, or one or both sides of a paragraph, use the options at the Borders button drop-down gallery in the Paragraph group on the Home tab. To change the position of the border, click the Borders button arrow and then click the desired border location at the drop-down gallery.

 Borders

Border lines can be created and customized with options at the Borders and Shading dialog box with the Borders tab selected, as shown in Figure 4.18. Display this dialog box by clicking the Borders button arrow and then clicking *Borders and Shading* at the drop-down gallery. The dialog box contains options for changing the border settings, line style, line color, line width, and location and the distance between the borders and text.

Figure 4.17 Customizing Line Weights and Colors

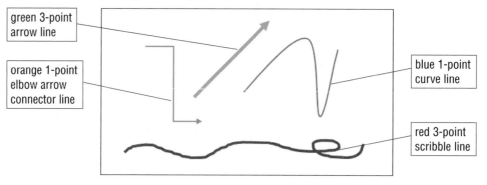

Figure 4.18 Customizing in the Borders and Shading Dialog Box with the Borders Tab Selected

Click the right side, left side, top, or bottom of this preview area to insert or remove a border.

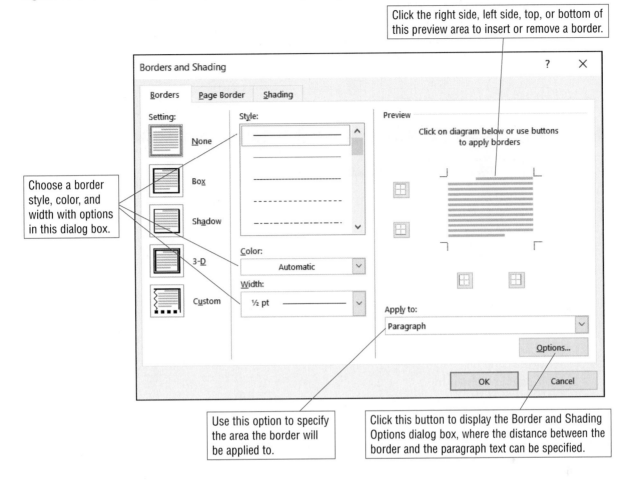

Choose a border style, color, and width with options in this dialog box.

Use this option to specify the area the border will be applied to.

Click this button to display the Border and Shading Options dialog box, where the distance between the border and the paragraph text can be specified.

Project 1b Creating a Letterhead with Text Boxes, Grouped Objects, and Ruled Lines   Part 2 of 2

1. Open **WEPLetterhead.docx** and then save the document with the name **4-WEPLetterhead**.
2. Arrange the pictures to create the letterhead as shown in Figure 4.19 on page 123 by completing the following steps:
   a. Click each picture and then drag each image to form a straight, tight line of pictures. *Hint: The images have already been sized appropriately and their text wrapping has been changed to Tight. To get a better view for aligning the picture objects, zoom in.*

2a

b. Once the images have been positioned appropriately, press and hold down the Shift key and then click each image.

c. With all five images selected (their sizing handles should be displayed), click the Picture Tools Format tab, click the Align button in the Arrange group, and then click *Align Top* at the drop-down list.

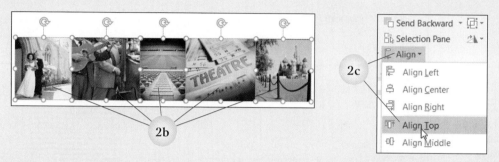

d. With the images still selected, click the Group button in the Arrange group and then click *Group* at the drop-down list.

3. Position the grouped image by completing the following steps:

a. With the grouped image selected, click the Position button in the Arrange group on the Picture Tools Format tab and then click *More Layout Options* at the drop-down list.

b. Click the *Alignment* option in the *Horizontal* section of the Layout dialog box.

c. Click the down-pointing arrow right of the option box containing the word *Left* and then click *Centered* at the drop-down list.

d. Click the *relative to* option box arrow in the *Horizontal* section and then click *Page* at the drop-down list.

e. Make sure the *Absolute position* option in the *Vertical* section is selected.

f. Select the current measurement in the *Absolute position* measurement box and then type 0.5.

g. Click the *below* option box arrow and then click *Page* at the drop-down list.

h. Click OK.

4. Draw the blue horizontal line shown below the grouped image in Figure 4.19 on page 123 by completing the following steps:

a. Click the Insert tab, click the Shapes button in the Illustrations group, and then click the *Line* option (first option in the *Lines* section).

b. Press and hold down the Shift key and then click and drag in the document to create a horizontal line.

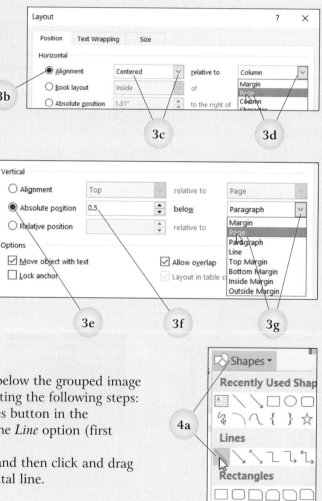

c. With the line selected, click the More Shape Styles button in the Shape Styles group on the Drawing Tools Format tab and then click the *Subtle Line - Accent 5* style (sixth column, first row).

d. Click in the *Shape Width* measurement box in the Size group, type 6.5, and then press the Enter key.

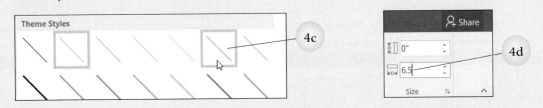

e. Drag the line so it is positioned under the grouped image, as shown in Figure 4.19 on page 123.

f. With the line selected, click the Position button in the Arrange group and then click *More Layout Options* at the drop-down list.

g. At the Layout dialog box, click the *Alignment* option in the *Horizontal* section and then change the alignment to centered relative to the page by selecting the options *Centered* and *Page* (see image at right).

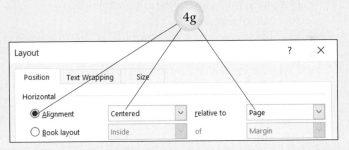

h. Click OK to close the dialog box.

5. Insert the globe image by completing the following steps:

a. Turn on the display of nonprinting characters, position the insertion point left of the fifth paragraph symbol from the top, and then turn off the display of nonprinting characters.

b. Click the Insert tab and then click the Pictures button in the Illustrations group.

c. At the Insert Picture dialog box, navigate to the C4 folder and then double-click ***globesun.png***.

d. With the image selected, click in the *Shape Height* measurement box in the Size group on the Picture Tools Format tab, type 0.7, and then press the Enter key. (Word will automatically change the shape width to 0.7 inch.)

e. Click the Wrap Text button in the Arrange group and then click *In Front of Text* at the drop-down list.

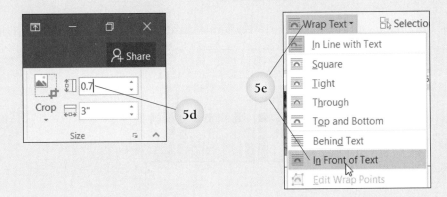

f. Drag the image so it is positioned as shown in Figure 4.19.

6. Create the *Worldwide Event Planning, Inc.* text by completing the following steps:
   a. Click the Insert tab, click the Text Box button in the Text group, and then click *Draw Text Box* at the drop-down list.
   b. Click and drag in the document to create a rectangular text box that is approximately 5.0 inches wide and 0.6 inch tall.
   c. Type Worldwide Event Planning, Inc.
   d. Select the text, click the Home tab, click the Text Effects and Typography button in the Font group, and then click the *Fill: Blue, Accent color 1; Shadow* option (second column, first row).
   e. Change the font to 24-point Palatino Linotype and then apply bold and italic formatting.
   f. Display the Font dialog box with the Advanced tab selected, turn on kerning at 24 points and above, and then click OK to close the dialog box.

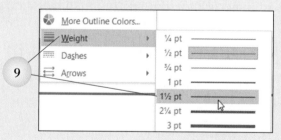

7. Customize the text box by completing the following steps:
   a. Click to select the text box border.
   b. Click the Drawing Tools Format tab.
   c. Click the Shape Fill button arrow in the Shape Styles group and then click *No Fill* at the drop-down gallery.
   d. Click the Shape Outline button arrow and then click *No Outline* at the drop-down gallery.
   e. Drag the text box so it is positioned as shown in Figure 4.19.
8. Select the blue line you previously created. Press and hold down the Ctrl key and the mouse button and drag a copy of the line below the text *Worldwide Event Planning, Inc.*
9. With the line selected, click the Drawing Tools Format tab, click the Shape Outline button arrow, point to *Weight*, and then click *1¹/₂ pt* at the side menu.

10. Click the Shape Outline button arrow again and then click the *Green, Accent 6* option.

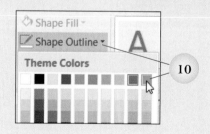

11. Drag the line so it is positioned as shown in Figure 4.19. *Hint: With the line selected, use the arrow keys on the keyboard to nudge it into the correct position.*
12. Select the text box containing the address and then position it as shown in Figure 4.19.
13. Save, print, and then close **4-WEPLetterhead.docx**.

Check Your Work

Figure 4.19 Letterhead Created in Project 1b

Worldwide Event Planning, Inc.

421 Lexington Avenue, Suite 500
New York, NY 10170-0555
www.worldwideevent.emcp.net
917.555.9055

You will use the envelope feature to create an envelope based on the letterhead you created in the previous project.

Preview Finished Project

Creating Envelopes

DTP POINTER

Use a company letterhead as the starting point for the designs of all the business documents.

Use a company letterhead as the starting point for the designs of the other business documents. Using an envelope designed in coordination with a letterhead is another way of projecting a professional image and establishing an identity with the target audience. Using some of the same design elements in both the letterhead and the envelope contributes to continuity and consistency among the documents. The same elements can be carried over into memo and fax templates, business cards, invoices, and brochures.

Designing an Envelope

DTP POINTER

Use consistent elements to establish a visual connection between an envelope and letterhead.

When planning an envelope design, remember that the envelope does not have to be an exact replica of the letterhead. Rather, select common elements to establish a visual link between the two documents. Keep in mind that the design area of an envelope is smaller and shaped differently than that of a letterhead. Using the same typeface and typestyles in a smaller type size and repeating a graphic may be just enough to establish that link.

Changing the Text Direction

DTP POINTER

Consider the actual size of the design area.

Text Direction

One effective method of utilizing the generally small design area of an envelope is to change the direction of the text. Changing the direction of the text makes use of space that would otherwise be wasted. Change the direction of the text within a text box by clicking the Text Direction button in the Text group on the Drawing Tools Format tab. Rotating the text can add focus and contrast to text. Figure 4.20 shows the options available at the Text Direction button drop-down list.

Figure 4.20 Using the Text Direction Button Drop-down List

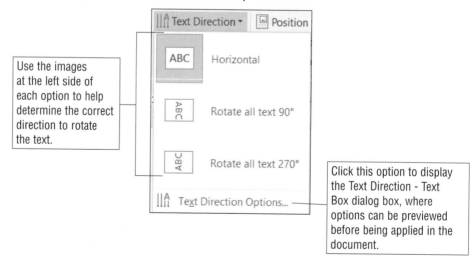

Use the images at the left side of each option to help determine the correct direction to rotate the text.

Click this option to display the Text Direction - Text Box dialog box, where options can be previewed before being applied in the document.

Using the Envelope Feature

Word's envelope feature makes creating professional-looking envelopes easy and inexpensive. This feature displays in the document screen a blank envelope that already contains the appropriate formatting for the margins and a text box in the mailing address position.

To create a customized envelope for a particular document and insert a logo in the envelope, complete the following steps:

1. Open the document the envelope will be based on and then click the Mailings tab.
2. Click the Envelopes button in the Create group.
3. At the Envelopes and Labels dialog box with the Envelopes tab selected, click the Options button.
4. At the Envelope Options dialog box, make sure the desired envelope size displays in the *Envelope size* option box. If it does not, select the desired size. (If the desired size is not listed, click *Custom size* at the drop-down list and then enter the dimensions of the envelope.)
5. Select a font for the delivery address and the return address.
6. Click the Printing Options tab in the Envelope Options dialog box, select the feed method required by the printer, and then click OK.
7. At the Envelopes and Labels dialog box with the Envelopes tab selected, click the Add to Document button to display the envelope at the top of the document window.
8. Position the insertion point inside the envelope, insert a logo, and then drag to position the logo.

Word adds the envelope to the beginning of the current document and numbers the envelope as page 1 and the first page of the document as page 2. To print just the envelope (without the rest of the document), select page 1 in the preview pane at the Print backstage area, click *Print Current Page* in the *Settings* section, and then click the Print button.

Envelopes

Checking Envelope Printing Options

To determine the best way to feed an envelope into the printer, display the Envelopes and Labels dialog box with the Envelopes tab selected and then view the information. If the feed method displayed in the *Feed* section of the Envelopes and Labels dialog box does not work for the printer, click the Options button and then choose the correct options in the *Feed method* section and the *Feed from* option box at the Envelope Options dialog box with the Printing Options tab selected. Feed methods are visually displayed at this dialog box, as shown in Figure 4.21.

Figure 4.21 Selecting Feed Methods at the Envelope Options Dialog Box

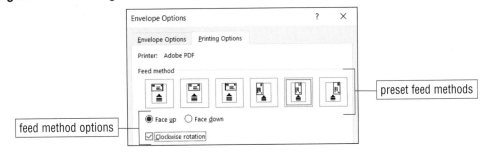

1. Create an envelope design to coordinate with the Worldwide Event Planning letterhead created in Project 1b by completing the following steps:
   a. Open **4-WEPLetterhead.docx** from the C4 folder.
   b. Click the Mailings tab and then click the Envelopes button in the Create group.
   c. At the Envelopes and Labels dialog box with the Envelopes tab selected, delete any text that appears in the *Delivery address* text box. If a default address appears in the *Return address* text box, click the *Omit* check box to insert a check mark.
   d. Click the Options button, make sure *Size 10* displays in the *Envelope size* option box, and then click OK.
   e. Click the Add to Document button to insert a blank envelope in your document.

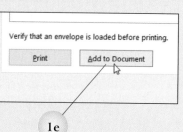

1e

2. Scroll down, select the text box in the letterhead containing the text *Worldwide Event Planning, Inc.*, and then copy it by pressing Ctrl + C.
3. Scroll back up, click in the upper left corner of the envelope, and then press Ctrl + V to paste the text box in the envelope.
4. Customize the text box in the envelope by completing the following steps:
   a. With the text box selected, click the Drawing Tools Format tab.
   b. Rotate the text box by clicking the Rotate button in the Arrange group and then clicking *Rotate Left 90°* at the drop-down list.

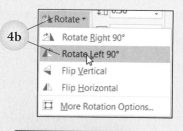

4b

   c. Click in the *Shape Height* measurement box in the Size group and then type 0.5.
   d. Click in the *Shape Width* measurement box, type 3.0, and then press the Enter key.
   e. Change the font size to 14 points.
   f. Move the text box to the left side of the envelope, as shown in Figure 4.22.

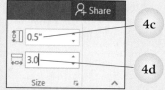

4c

4d

5. Copy the globe image from the letterhead and then paste it into the envelope.
6. Size and position the image in the envelope as shown in Figure 4.22.
7. Copy the text box containing the address in the letterhead and then paste it into the envelope.
8. Select the address text and then change the paragraph alignment to left.
9. Delete the website and phone number from the address.
10. Drag the return address text box to the location shown in Figure 4.22.
11. Position the insertion point in the text box in the middle of the envelope and then type [Type address here.].
12. Save your envelope and letterhead as a template by completing the following steps:
    a. Press the F12 function key to display the Save As dialog box.
    b. At the Save As dialog box, click the *Save as type* option box and then click *Word Template (*.dotx)* at the drop-down list.
    c. Type 4-WEPLetterhead+Envelope in the *File name* text box.
    d. Navigate to the C4 folder and then click the Save button.
13. Close **4-WEPLetterhead+Envelope.dotx**.

Check Your Work

Figure 4.22 Letterhead with Envelope Created in Project 2

Using the labels feature, you will create business cards based on the letterhead you created in Project 1b and the envelope you created in Project 2.

Preview Finished Project

Creating Business Cards

A business card generally includes a name, title, company or organization name, address, telephone number, fax number, email address, and web address. A business card can also include a one-sentence description of a business, a business philosophy, or a slogan. Handing someone a business card is one of the best personal marketing opportunities, so it is important to design it thoughtfully.

Designing Business Cards

DTP POINTER

Keep a business card design simple and elegant.

To establish an identity and to be consistent with other business documents, such as letterheads and envelopes, include the company logo on the business card. Most business cards are created with a sans serif typeface because the characters are easier to read. The type sizes may vary from 12 to 14 points for important words, such as a name and title, and from 8 to 10 points for telephone and fax numbers. Create variety by using bold, italic, small caps, or text effects. Figure 4.23 illustrates two similar business cards that include all the necessary information but are slightly different in design. The card on the right is the best choice, as it reinforces a consistently strong right alignment. The photograph in the right-hand card adds a more updated, professional feel than the clip art image used in the left-hand example.

DTP POINTER

For better printing results, make sure images are at least 300 dpi.

DTP POINTER

Use a search engine to locate an online printing source for documents.

Business cards should be printed on high-quality cover stock paper. Specially designed full-color papers and forms for creating business cards more easily and professionally are available at office supply stores and paper companies. Printing business cards at home saves the expense of having to place a large minimum order with an outside printer. This is especially helpful to a new small business. Alternatively, create a custom business card and then take it to a professional printer to be printed in a large quantity or contact an online printing source for convenient, efficient printing. Be sure to contact the printer first to confirm whether a Word file saved in PDF format will be acceptable.

Figure 4.23 Evaluating Business Card Design

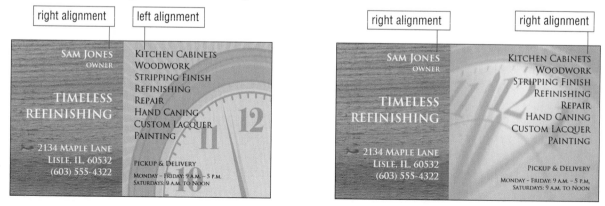

Using the Labels Feature to Create Business Cards

 Labels

Use Word's labels feature and a business card label option to create business cards similar to the ones shown in Figure 4.24. The business card label option can also be used to create membership cards, name tags, coupons, placeholders, and friendly reminder cards. Most label options will produce 10 business cards—two columns of labels with five rows in each column. The columns and rows are set up automatically in a Word table, and each label (business card) appears in a cell in the table.

DTP POINTER

Do not use more than two or three fonts in a business card design; one font is preferable. Create interest by changing the font size and adding other font effects.

When creating business cards, use the label option that matches the labels that have been purchased. Common business card label options are Avery 5371 and 8371 Business Cards. The only difference between these two label product numbers is the paper type. Label 5371 is made to be used in a laser printer, and label 8371 is made to be used in an inkjet printer. In both cases, the business cards will be 2 inches by 3.5 inches and the sheet containing the business cards will be 8.5 inches by 11 inches.

One method of creating business cards with the labels feature is to insert blank labels in the document, create the first label, and then save the elements of the label to the Quick Part gallery. Display the Envelopes and Labels dialog box with the Labels tab selected, type the quick part name in the *Address* text box, press the F3 function key, and then click the New Document button.

Quick Parts

Using Online Templates to Create Business Cards

DTP POINTER

Use a generous amount of white space in a business card.

As an alternative to designing personal business cards, view and download an array of professionally designed online business card templates. Figure 4.25 illustrates some of the business card templates available online.

To download an online business card template, click the File tab and then click the *New* option. At the New backstage area, type *business cards* in the search text box and then press the Enter key. Double-click to download the desired business card template.

Figure 4.24 Creating Business Cards

Figure 4.25 Using Online Business Card Templates

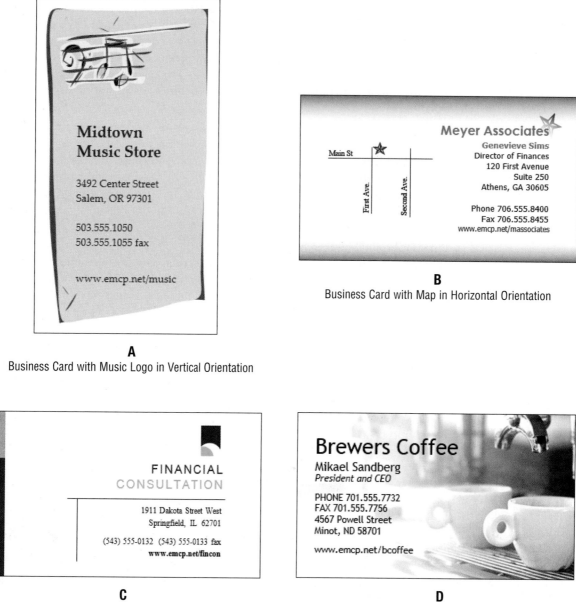

A
Business Card with Music Logo in Vertical Orientation

B
Business Card with Map in Horizontal Orientation

C
Business Card for Professional Services Company

D
Business Card for Small Business

Project 3 Creating Business Cards Using the Labels Feature and Quick Part Gallery　　　Part 1 of 1

1. At a blank document, create the business cards shown in Figure 4.26 on page 134 by completing the following steps:
   a. Click the Mailings tab.
   b. Click the Labels button in the Create group.
   c. At the Envelopes and Labels dialog box with the Labels tab selected, click the Options button.

d. At the Label Options dialog box, change the option in the *Label vendors* option box to *Avery US Letter*, if necessary, select *8371 Business Cards* in the *Product number* list box, and then click OK.

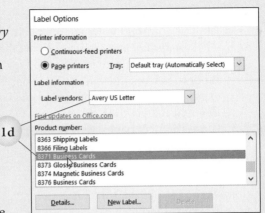

e. Delete any text that may appear in the *Address* list box and then click the New Document button.

f. If the table gridlines do not display, click the Table Tools Layout tab and then click the View Gridlines button in the Table group.

2. Create the blue line that appears at the top of the business card by completing the following steps:
   a. Click the Insert tab.
   b. With the insertion point positioned in the first cell of the table in the document, click the Shapes button in the Illustrations group and then click the first line shape in the *Lines* section of the drop-down list.

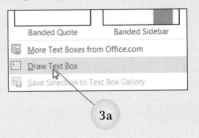

   c. Press and hold down the Shift key while dragging the crosshairs to draw a horizontal line that is 2.75 inches in length. With the line selected, verify the length using the *Shape Width* measurement box in the Size group on the Drawing Tools Format tab.
   d. With the line still selected, apply the Subtle Line - Accent 5 style from the Shape Styles gallery (sixth column, first row).

   e. Position the line as shown in Figure 4.26 on page 134.
3. Create a text box that will contain the company name by completing the following steps:
   a. Click the Insert tab, click the Text Box button in the Text group, and then click *Draw Text Box* at the drop-down list.

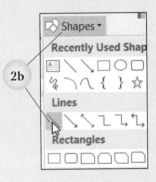

   b. Position the crosshairs in the first label (cell) and then draw a text box that is approximately the same size and in the same location as the *Worldwide Event Planning, Inc.* text box shown in Figure 4.26.
   c. With the text box selected, change the height to 0.4 inch and the width to 3 inches.
   d. Remove the shape outline and the shape fill.
   e. Change the font to 14-point Palatino Linotype, apply bold and italic formatting, and then apply the Fill: Blue, Accent color 1; Shadow style using the Text Effects and Typography button drop-down gallery (second column, first row).
   f. Type Worldwide Event Planning, Inc. and then right-align the text within the text box.

g. Display the Format Shape task pane by clicking the Shape Styles group task pane launcher on the Drawing Tools Format tab.

h. Click *Shape Options* in the Format Shape task pane, if necessary, click the Layout & Properties icon, click *Text Box* (if necessary to expand the list of options), and then change the right margin to 0 inches.

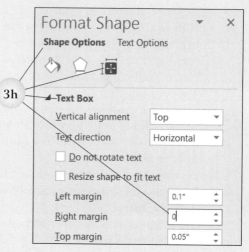

i. Close the task pane.

j. Select the text in the text box and then display the Font dialog box with the Advanced tab selected.

k. At the dialog box, turn on kerning at 12 points and above, select *Standard and Contextual* in the *Ligatures* option box drop-down list, and then click OK to close the dialog box.

4. Make a copy of the blue line and then format it by completing the following steps:

a. Select the blue line, press and hold down the Ctrl key, and then drag a copy of the line below the text box containing the text *Worldwide Event Planning, Inc.*

b. With the new line selected, use the Shape Outline button on the Drawing Tools Format tab to change the color of the line to Green, Accent 6, (last column, first row in the *Theme Colors* section) and to change the weight to $1^1/_2$ pt.

5. Create another text box to contain the address text by completing the following steps:

a. Draw a text box that measures 1 inch high by 2.75 inches wide.

b. Remove the shape outline and the shape fill.

c. With the insertion point positioned inside the text box, press Ctrl + R to change to right alignment.

d. Display the Format Shape task pane, change the right margin to 0 inches (refer to Step 3h), and then close the task pane.

e. Type the following text:

421 Lexington Avenue, Suite 500 (Press Shift + Enter)
New York, NY 10170-0555 (Press Enter)
www.worldwideevent.emcp.net (Press Shift + Enter)
917.555.9055

f. Remove the hyperlink from the website text by right-clicking the website address and then clicking *Remove Hyperlink* at the shortcut menu.

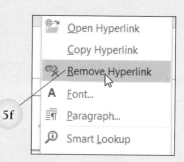

g. Select the text in the text box you just typed, change the font size to 9 points, apply bold formatting, and then apply the Green, Accent 6 font color.

h. Select the web address and telephone number and then change the font size to 8 points.

i. Position the text box as shown in Figure 4.26 on page 134.

6. Create another text box to contain the text *Corporate Meetings...*, as shown in Figure 4.26, by completing the following steps:

a. Draw a text box that measures 0.25 inch high by 3.5 inches wide.

b. Remove the shape outline and the shape fill.

c. Position the insertion point inside the text box and then press Ctrl + E to change to center alignment.

d. Change the font size to 7 points, change the font color to Blue, Accent 1, Darker 25%, and then type the following text:
Corporate Meetings | Weddings | Holiday Parties | Group Tours | Cultural Events
(Press the spacebar before and after each bar character.)
e. Position the text box as shown in Figure 4.26.

7. Position the insertion point in the upper left corner of the table cell (not in a text box) and then insert the globe sun clip art image. (You can copy it from the letterhead or insert it from the C4 folder.)

8. Change the height of the globe sun image to 0.8 inch, change the text wrapping to In Front of Text, and then position the image as shown in Figure 4.26.

9. Group the objects in the business card and then save the grouped object as a quick part by completing the following steps:
a. Select the two lines.
b. Press and hold down the Shift key and then select the remaining text boxes and globe sun image. (All six objects should be selected.)
c. Click the Drawing Tools Format tab.
d. Click the Group button in the Arrange group and then click *Group* at the drop-down list.
e. Click the Insert tab.
f. Click the Quick Parts button in the Text group and then click *Save Selection to Quick Part Gallery* at the drop-down list.
g. At the Create New Building Block dialog box, type XX-Worldwide in the *Name* text box (type your initials in place of the *XX*) and then click OK.

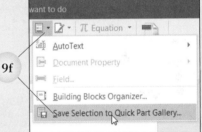

10. Create a full sheet of business cards using your quick part by completing the following steps:
a. Click the Mailings tab and then click the Labels button in the Create group.
b. At the Envelopes and Labels dialog box with the Labels tab selected, click the Options button.
c. At the Label Options dialog box, make sure that *Avery US Letter* is selected in the *Label vendors* option box and that *8371 Business Cards* is selected in the *Product number* list box and then click OK to close the dialog box.
d. At the Envelopes and Labels dialog box with the Labels tab selected, delete any text that may appear in the *Address* list box, type XX-Worldwide (type your initials in place of the *XX*), and then press the F3 function key.
e. At the same dialog box, make sure that *Full page of the same label* is selected and then click the New Document button. (A full sheet of business cards will display on your screen.)

11. Save the full sheet of business cards with the name **4-WEPBusinessCards**.
12. Print and then close **4-WEPBusinessCards.docx**. Printing the business cards on thick cardstock made especially for your type of printer is preferable. If you print the business cards on plain paper, you may want to print the table gridlines as shown in Figure 4.26 so you can see the business card borders and use them for trimming. (To print the gridlines, display the Table Tools Design tab and then click the *Table Grid* option in the Table Styles gallery.)
13. Close the document that you used for creating the sample label without saving it.

Check Your Work

Figure 4.26 Business Cards Created in Project 3

You will create a press release using WordArt and other features taught earlier in the chapter. You will create custom colors and fill an object with a picture.

Preview Finished Project

Creating a Press Release

press release

A written or recorded communication directed to the news media for the purpose of announcing something newsworthy

Many businesses use a document called a **press release**, which is a written or recorded communication directed to the news media for the purpose of announcing something newsworthy. Typically, a press release is mailed, faxed, or emailed to newspapers, radio stations, and television stations, but it may also be posted on the Internet. Press releases can announce a range of news items, such as scheduled events, personal promotions, awards, new products and services, sales and other financial data, accomplishments, and new office or store openings.

Project 4 Creating a Press Release with WordArt   Part 1 of 1

1. Open **4-WEPLetterhead.docx**, which was created in Project 1b.
2. Save the grouped image in the letterhead as a graphic file in PNG format by completing the following steps:
   a. Display the Start menu.
   b. At the Start menu, type snip.
   c. Click the Snipping Tool tile in the search results.
   d. Click the New button arrow at the Snipping Tool window and then click the *Rectangular Snip* option.
   e. Drag the crosshairs to create a box around the grouped images in the letterhead.

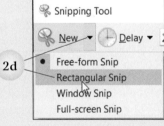

   f. At the Snipping Tool window, click the Save Snip button.
   g. At the Save As dialog box, type 4-WEPGraphic in the *File name* text box.
   h. Click the down-pointing arrow right of the *Save as type* option box and then click *Portable Network Graphic file (PNG) (*.PNG)* at the drop-down list.
   i. Navigate to the C4 folder and then click the Save button.
   j. Close the Snipping Tool window.
   k. Close **4-WEPLetterhead.docx**.
3. Open **PressRelease.docx** from the C4 folder and then save the document with the name **4-PressRelease**.
4. Select the text in the upper left cell of the table and then apply the following formatting:
   a. Change the font to 7.5-point Century Gothic.
   b. Change the line spacing to 1.15.
   c. Select the text *Contact: Margo Hamel* and then apply bold formatting.

5. Insert WordArt with a graphic background in the upper right cell by completing the following steps:

a. Position the insertion point in the upper right cell of the table and then click the Insert tab.

b. Click the WordArt button in the Text group and then click the *Fill: White; Outline: Blue, Accent color 5; Shadow* option (fourth column, first row).

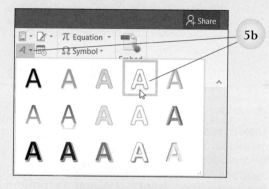

c. Type Worldwide Event Planning, Inc.

d. Select the text you just typed and then change the font to 18-point Bookman Old Style and, if necessary, apply bold formatting.

e. With the text still selected, display the Font dialog box with the Advanced tab selected.

f. Turn on kerning for fonts 12 points and above, select *Standard and Contextual* at the *Ligatures* option box drop-down list, and then click OK to close the dialog box.

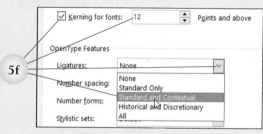

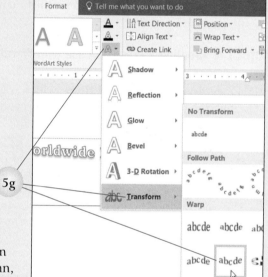

g. With the text in the top right cell still selected, click the Text Effects button in the WordArt Styles group on the Drawing Tools Format tab, point to *Transform*, and then click the *Chevron: Down* option (second column, second row in the *Warp* section).

h. Click the Text Outline button arrow in the WordArt Styles group and then click *Dark Blue* (ninth color in the *Standard Colors* section).

i. Using the mouse, drag the corner sizing handles to increase the size of the WordArt object to fill the cell.

j. With the WordArt object selected (the outline on the object will be a solid line and the sizing and rotation handles will be visible), click the Shape Fill button arrow in the Shape Styles group and then click the *Picture* option at the drop-down gallery.

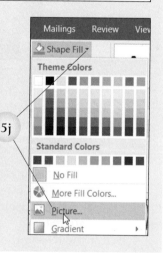

k. At the Insert Pictures window, click the Browse button that displays to the right of *From a file*.

l. At the Insert Picture dialog box, navigate to the C4 folder and then double-click *4-WEPGraphic.png*.

6. Press Ctrl + End to position the insertion point below the table, type PRESS RELEASE, and then press the Enter key.

7. Select the text *PRESS RELEASE* and then apply the following formatting:
   a. Change the font to 42-point Century Gothic.
   b. Click the Font Color button arrow in the Font group on the Home tab and then click the *More Colors* option.
   c. At the Colors dialog box, click the Custom tab.
   d. Make sure that *RGB* is selected in the *Color model* option box and then type 42 in the *Red* measurement box, 90 in the *Green* measurement box, and 120 in the *Blue* measurement box.

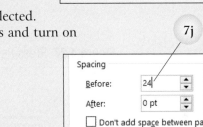

   e. Click OK to close the dialog box.
   f. Display the Font dialog box with the Advanced tab selected.
   g. Change the *Spacing* option to *Condensed* by 0.25 points and turn on kerning for type 14 points and above.
   h. Click OK to close the dialog box.
   i. Display the Paragraph dialog box.
   j. In the *Spacing* section, change the value in the *Before* measurement box to *24*.
   k. Click OK to close the dialog box.

8. Press Ctrl + End and then press the Enter key.

9. Change the font to 14-point Century Gothic and then apply the blue color used in Step 7d to the text.

10. Type Worldwide Event Planning, Inc. Announces Global Expansion and then press Shift + Enter.

11. Type London will serve Eastern European region. and then press the Enter key two times.

12. Select the text *London will serve Eastern European region.*, change the font size to 11 points, and then apply italic formatting.

13. Press Ctrl + End, change the font to 10-point Century Gothic, and then change the font color to Black, Text 1.

14. Type the three paragraphs of text shown in the press release in Figure 4.27. Apply bold formatting to the location, date, and colon in the first sentence of the first paragraph. For the fourth paragraph, type three # symbols with spaces after the first and second symbols and then center the paragraph.

15. Select the three paragraphs of text you typed, display the Paragraph dialog box, and then apply the following formatting:
    a. Change the line spacing to *Single*.
    b. In the *Spacing* section, change the value in the *After* measurement box to 18 points.
    c. Click OK to close the dialog box.

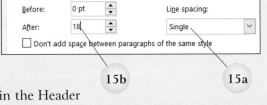

16. Replace the text in the footer as shown in Figure 4.27 by completing the following steps:
    a. Click the Insert tab, click the Footer button in the Header & Footer group, and then click *Edit Footer* at the drop-down list.
    b. Select the text *Type release date and time here* and then type For release 9 a.m. EST, July 23, 2018, USA – 14:00, U.K.
    c. Select the text you just typed and then change the font to 10-point Century Gothic.

d. Click the date picker content control that displays in the left margin.

e. Click the date picker down-pointing arrow and then click the *July 23, 2018* option in the calendar. (You will need to navigate to the year 2018 and the month of July.)

f. Double-click in the document to close the Footer pane.

17. Save, print, and then close **4-PressRelease.docx**.

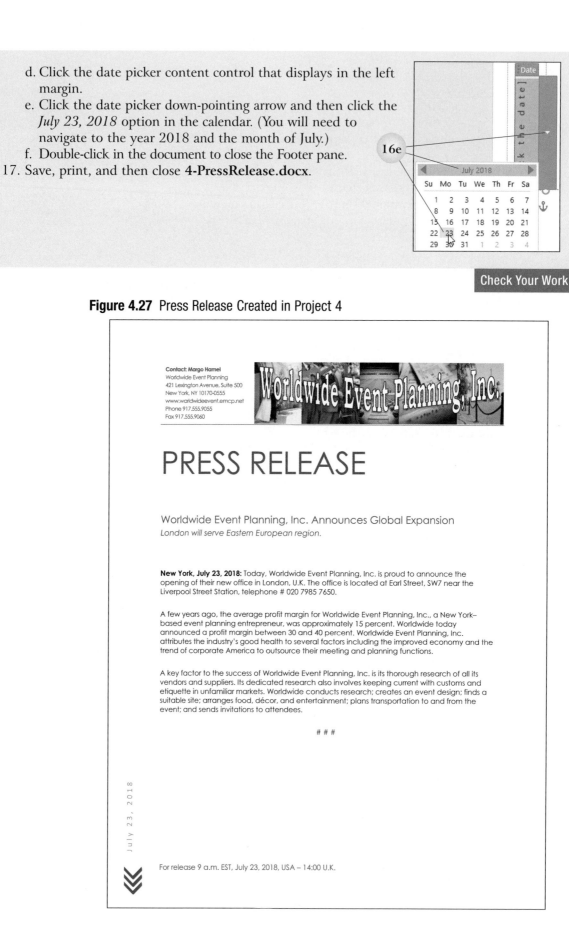

Check Your Work

Figure 4.27 Press Release Created in Project 4

Chapter Summary

- In planning the design of a letterhead, think about its purposes: to convey specific information, to establish an identity, and to project an image for a business.

- A number of predesigned online letterhead templates are available for download and can be customized by adding a logo to represent a company or brand.

- Objects can be grouped, ungrouped, and regrouped. Group objects by selecting each object and then clicking the Group button in the Arrange group on the Drawing Tools Format tab or the Picture Tools Format tab.

- The Selection pane lists each item in a document. Display the Selection pane by clicking the Select button in the Editing group on the Home tab and then clicking *Selection Pane* at the drop-down list.

- Designing and producing a custom letterhead can be a less costly alternative to having one produced by a professional designer and printer.

- When designing a letterhead, consider the following design concepts: focus, balance, proportion, contrast, directional flow, consistency, and color.

- Use the Click and Type feature to insert text, graphics, tables, and other items into a blank area of a document.

- To add the vertical location of the insertion point to the items displayed on the Status bar, right click the Status bar and then click the *Vertical Page Position* option at the Customize Status Bar pop-up menu.

- Text boxes are extremely useful in desktop publishing because text and graphics can be placed at exact horizontal and vertical locations on the page. They can also be customized with options such as shape fill, outline, and effects.

- Adjust text box margins with options at the Format Shape task pane with the Layout & Properties icon selected and the Text Box options expanded.

- Position a text box precisely on a page using options at the Layout dialog box with the Position tab selected.

- Quickly copy a text box by pressing and holding down the Ctrl key, clicking the border of the source text box and holding down the left mouse button, dragging the new text box to a desired location, and then releasing the Ctrl key and mouse button.

- A pixel is a single unit of measurement that a monitor uses to paint images on a screen.

- Every object, including a text box, is automatically anchored, or attached, to the paragraph closest to it. Turn on the display of object anchors by clicking the File tab, clicking *Options*, clicking *Display* in the left panel of the Word Options dialog box, clicking the *Object anchors* check box to insert a check mark, and then clicking OK.

- Specify whether text should wrap around, behind, or in front of a text box with options at the Wrap Text button drop-down gallery.

- Customize a text box using buttons and options at the Drawing Tools Format tab or the Format Shape task pane. Click the Shape Styles group launcher to display the Format Shape task pane.

- Ruled lines act as boundaries to the surrounding text. Ruled lines can be used in a document to create a focal point, draw the eye across or down the page, separate columns and sections, or add visual appeal.

- Horizontal and vertical lines can be drawn using options at the Shapes button in the Illustrations group on the Insert tab. Create a straight line by holding down the Shift key and then dragging. Format a drawn line with buttons and options on the Drawing Tools Format tab.

- Horizontal and vertical lines are positioned in the same way shapes are positioned. Select the line and then reposition it using the mouse, the arrow keys on the keyboard, options on the Drawing Tools Format tab, or options at the Layout dialog box with the Position tab selected.

- To add lines around one or all the sides of a paragraph, use options at the Borders button drop-down gallery in the Paragraph group on the Home tab. Move a border by clicking the Borders button arrow and then clicking the desired location at the drop-down gallery.

- When creating the design for an envelope, select common elements from the letterhead to establish a link between the two documents.

- Change the direction of text to make use of space. Change the direction of the text within a text box by clicking the Text Direction button in the Text group on the Drawing Tools Format tab.

- Create an envelope by clicking the Mailings tab, clicking the Envelopes button in the Create group, and then clicking the Add to Document button. Customize an envelope and check printing options using tabs at the Envelope Options dialog box. Display this dialog box by clicking the Options button at the Envelopes and Labels dialog box with the Envelopes tab selected.

- With the Envelopes and Labels dialog box displayed, click the Options button to display envelope and printing options. Customize the printing options to match the printer and paper manufacturer being used.

- Business cards provide another way to establish an identity among a target audience. Establish an identity and stay consistent with other business documents, such as envelopes and letterheads, by including the company logo on the business card.

- Use Word's labels feature and a business card label option to create business cards. Save the elements of the label to the Quick Part gallery. Choose a business card label at the Envelopes and Labels dialog box with the Labels tab selected. Choose a label vendor and product number at the Label Options dialog box.

- Search for business card templates online by clicking the File tab, clicking the *New* option, typing a search phrase in the *Search for online templates* text box, and then pressing the Enter key.

- With the WordArt feature, distort or modify text to conform to a variety of shapes. Use options in the WordArt Styles group on the Drawing Tools Format tab to customize WordArt text.

- A press release is a written or recorded communication directed to the news media to announce something newsworthy. Create a press release to inform the public of scheduled events, personal promotions, awards, new products and services, sales and other financial data, accomplishments, and new office or store openings.

Commands Review

FEATURE	RIBBON TAB, GROUP	BUTTON
borders	Home, Paragraph	
envelopes	Mailings, Create	
group	Drawing Tools Format, Arrange; Layout, Arrange; Picture Tools Format, Arrange	
labels	Mailings, Create	
position	Drawing Tools Format, Arrange	
quick parts	Insert, Text	
select	Home, Editing	
shape effects	Drawing Tools Format, Shape Styles	
shape fill	Drawing Tools Format, Shape Styles	
shape outline	Drawing Tools Format, Shape Styles	
shapes	Insert, Illustrations	
templates	File, *New*	
text direction	Drawing Tools Format, Text	
view table gridlines	Table Tools Layout, Table	
wrap	Drawing Tools Format, Arrange	

> **Workbook**
>
> Chapter study tools and assessment activities are available in the workbook pages of the ebook. These resources are designed to help you further develop and demonstrate mastery of the skills learned in this chapter.
>
> Unit assessment activities are also available in the workbook pages of the ebook. These activities are designed to help you demonstrate mastery of the skills learned in this unit.

Microsoft® Word Desktop Publishing

Unit 2

Preparing Business and Promotional Documents

Creating Flyers and Announcements

Performance Objectives

Upon successful completion of Chapter 5, you will be able to:

1 Plan and design flyers and announcements

2 Insert images from a scanner or digital camera

3 Use color to enhance promotional documents

4 Show document content

5 Modify document elements to enhance promotional materials

6 Adjust images

Desktop Publishing Terms

announcement	crop marks	HSL
bitmapped graphic	dpi	nonprinting area
bleed	fill	raster graphic
brightness	flyer	RGB
CMYK	gradient	transparent
color tone	grayscale	vector graphic
crop		

Word Features Used

artistic effects	page color	shape fill
brightness	picture effects	shape outline
contrast	picture styles	shape styles
corrections	position	tables
crop	recolor	text wrapping
drawing grid	remove background	ungroup
gradient	rotate	WordArt
group	shape effects	

Project 1 **Create an Announcement on Workshops**   **3 Parts**

You will create the layout of an announcement with a table and then add images, text, and page color to the announcement.

Preview Finished Project

Planning and Designing Flyers and Announcements

flyer

A promotional document used to advertise a product or service that is available for a limited amount of time

Flyers and announcements are two types of promotional documents. A *flyer* generally advertises a product or service that is available for a limited amount of time. Flyers can be found stuffed into grocery bags; attached to mailboxes, door handles, and windshields; and stacked on a countertop in a store. The basic purpose of a flyer is to communicate a message at a glance, so the contents of a flyer should be brief and to the point. For a flyer to be effective, the basic layout and design should be free of clutter, without too much text or too many graphics. Use white space generously to set off an image or text and to help promote good directional flow.

announcement

A promotional document used to inform an audience of an upcoming event

An *announcement* informs an audience of an upcoming event. An announcement may create interest in an event but does not necessarily promote a product or service. For instance, an announcement might inform readers of new course offerings at a local community college or of an upcoming community gathering, sporting event, concert, race, contest, raffle, or store opening.

DTP POINTER

Preparing a thumbnail sketch is especially helpful when creating a flyer or announcement.

As with any other desktop publication, planning should be the first step in creating a flyer or announcement. Because a limited amount of space is available when creating either of these documents, preparing a thumbnail sketch is especially important. Doing so allows you to capture your thoughts on paper. Clearly define the purpose and assess the target audience. Consider the target audience even when making design decisions, such as choosing type sizes—for example, the older the audience, the larger the print might need to be. Remember to consider the budget as well. Generally, flyers and announcements are some of the least expensive means of advertising.

DTP POINTER

Consider the audience when choosing type sizes.

Successful promotional documents attract the reader's attention and keep it. Consider how to attract the reader's eyes by using interesting headlines, dynamic images, and pops of color for emphasis. Keep in mind that a reader generally looks at the images first, then the headline, and finally the company logo. The goal is to hold his or her attention long enough to see all three!

Using Tables for Page Layout

Tutorial

Creating a Table

Tutorial

Changing the Table Layout

After creating a thumbnail sketch for a flyer or announcement, draw a table in a Word document to block off areas of the page and reflect the layout sketched in the thumbnail. Figure 5.1 shows how a table can serve as a framework for creating an announcement.

Figure 5.1 Using a Table to Create an Announcement

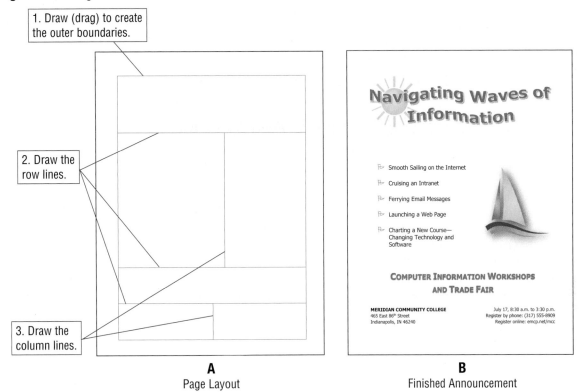

A
Page Layout

B
Finished Announcement

Tutorial

Changing the
Table Design

 Table

Draw Table

Eraser

To create a table layout like the one shown in Figure 5.1A, use the *Draw Table* option. To display this option, click the Insert tab, click the Table button in the Tables group, and then click *Draw Table* at the drop-down list. This causes the mouse pointer to display as a pen. Draw table lines in the document by clicking and holding down the left mouse button and then dragging in the document. After creating the table, click the Draw Table button in the Draw group on the Table Tools Layout tab to turn off the drawing feature. If lines from the table need to be removed, click the Eraser button in the Draw group. This causes the mouse pointer to display as an eraser. Drag the eraser along or click the lines to be removed.

Change the row height and column width within the table by using the measurement boxes in the Cell Size group on the Table Tools Layout tab. In addition, the row height can be changed by dragging the row border up or down and the column width can be changed by dragging the column border left or right.

The Table Tools Layout tab also contains many other buttons to adjust and format a table. Use these to customize table properties, insert and delete rows and columns, merge and split cells, specify text alignment within cells, and sort data in a table. The Table Tools Design tab is next to the Table Tools Layout tab and contains buttons and options to apply and customize a table style, apply shading and border lines to a table or cells, and customize table borders.

1. At a blank document, draw the table shown in Figure 5.1A on page 147 by completing the following steps:
    a. Click the Insert tab.
    b. Click the Table button in the Tables group and then click *Draw Table* at the drop-down list. (This causes the mouse pointer to display as a pen.)
    c. Create the outer boundary of the table by clicking and holding down the left mouse button, dragging in the document from approximately the upper left corner of the page to the lower right corner of the page, and then releasing the mouse button.
    d. Position the pen at the left boundary line approximately 2 inches below the top boundary line of the table and then drag to create a horizontal line from the left boundary line to the right boundary line.
    e. Position the pen at the left boundary line approximately 2.5 inches above the bottom boundary line and then drag to create a horizontal line from the left boundary line to the right boundary line.
    f. Position the pen at the left boundary line approximately 1.25 inches below the line you drew in Step 1e and then drag to create a horizontal line from the left boundary line to the right boundary line.
    g. In the second row, position the pen approximately 3 inches from the right boundary line and then drag down to create a vertical line.
    h. In the bottom row, position the pen at the approximate center of the row and then drag to create a vertical line.
    i. Click the Draw Table button in the Draw group on the Table Tools Layout tab to turn off the drawing feature.
2. Click the table move handle in the upper left corner of the table (a four-headed arrow inside a square) to select the entire table and then change the font to Tahoma.
3. With the table still selected, remove the border lines by clicking the Table Tools Design tab, clicking the Borders button arrow in the Borders group, and then clicking *No Border* at the drop-down gallery. (Dashed gridlines should display the table lines. If these gridlines are not visible, click the Table Tools Layout tab and then click the View Gridlines button in the Table group.)

4. Save the document with the name **5-Announcement**.

Using Text to Create Focus

DTP POINTER

White space creates a clean page that is easy to read.

To effectively communicate the message of a flyer or announcement, the text needs to stand out. Consider using unique (yet legible) typefaces, bold and italic formatting, WordArt, text effects, asymmetrical design, and plenty of white space to grab the reader's attention with text. Use color or white space to emphasize the most important text and direct readers to the information they need to know first. Keep in mind the concept of proportion discussed in Chapter 1, which says that one-third of the document should be white space if two-thirds are taken up with text and/or graphics. Do not use more than three fonts or three colors.

DTP POINTER

Remember this concept of proportion: one-third of the document should be white space and two-thirds should be text or graphics.

After finishing a document, look at it from a distance to make sure that the essential details are the most visible. Figure 5.2 illustrates a flyer that attracts attention by using varying fonts and font attributes.

Using Images for Emphasis

DTP POINTER

Choose images that relate to the message.

Images can add excitement to a publication and generate enthusiasm. Well-placed images can transform a plain page into a compelling visual document, as shown in Figure 5.3—however, using an image is effective only if the image enhances the subject of the document. For example, clip art illustrations tend to create a fun, playful, or whimsical appearance, whereas photographs convey a more professional, sophisticated, or serious tone. If choosing from among many images, select the simplest one. A simple image demands more attention and has more impact; an image that is too complicated can create clutter and confusion.

DTP POINTER

Leave plenty of white space around a graphic.

Use images to aid in directional flow, and use white space generously around images. Use the thumbnail sketch as a tool to help make decisions on the positions, sizes, and orientation of images.

Figure 5.2 Using Text to Create Focus in an Announcement

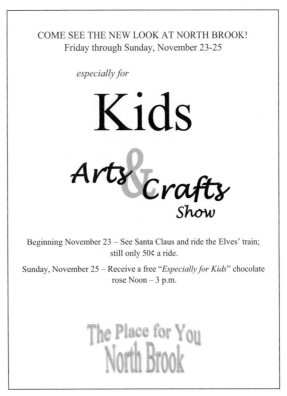

COME SEE THE NEW LOOK AT NORTH BROOK!
Friday through Sunday, November 23-25

especially for

Kids

Arts & *Crafts*
Show

Beginning November 23 – See Santa Claus and ride the Elves' train;
still only 50¢ a ride.

Sunday, November 25 – Receive a free *"Especially for Kids"* chocolate
rose Noon – 3 p.m.

The Place for You
North Brook

Figure 5.3 Using Images for Emphasis in a Flyer

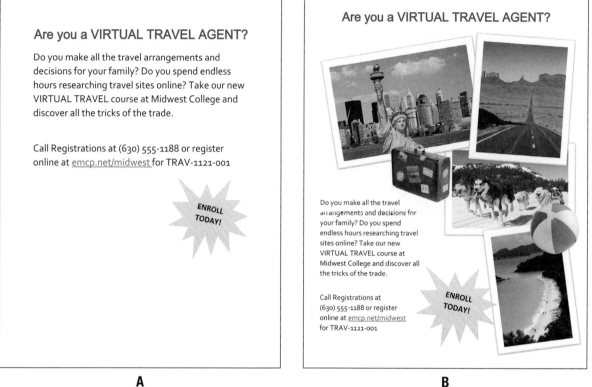

A
Flyer without Images

B
Flyer with Images

DTP POINTER ❯

Do not overuse clip art; use one main visual element per page.

Consider using clip art images and/or photographs to create personalized and unique graphics. For example, combine clip art images with other clip art images and then crop, size, or color different areas of the combined image. Alternatively, edit a photograph by using tools within Word, Paint, or, if possible, a photo-editing program such as Adobe Photoshop.

Project 1b Adding Text and Images to an Announcement

Part 2 of 3

1. With **5-Announcement.docx** from Project 1a open, click in the first cell in the table and then insert WordArt text in the cell by completing the following steps (refer to Figure 5.4 on page 152):
   a. Click the Insert tab, click the WordArt button in the Text group, and then click the *Fill: Blue, Accent color 5; Outline: White, Background color 1; Hard Shadow: Blue, Accent color 5* option (third column, bottom row).
   b. Type Navigating Waves of Information.

c. Click in the *Shape Height* measurement box in the Size group on the Drawing Tools Format tab, type 1.35, and then press the Enter key.

d. Click the Text Effects button in the WordArt Styles group, point to *Transform*, and then click the *Double Wave: Up-Down* option (last column, fifth row in the *Warp* section).

e. Click the Text Fill button arrow in the WordArt Styles group and then click the *Blue* option at the drop-down gallery (eighth color in the *Standard Colors* section).

f. Drag the WordArt text box so it is centered vertically and horizontally in the first cell.

2. Click in the first cell outside the WordArt text box and then insert the image of the sun as shown in Figure 5.4 by completing the following steps:

a. Click the Insert tab and then click the Online Pictures button in the Illustrations group.

b. At the Insert Pictures window, type sun in the *Bing Image Search* text box and then press the Enter key.

c. Scroll down the window, click the image shown at the right, and then click the Insert button. *Note: If this image is not available, use a similar image or use sun.png from the C5 folder.*

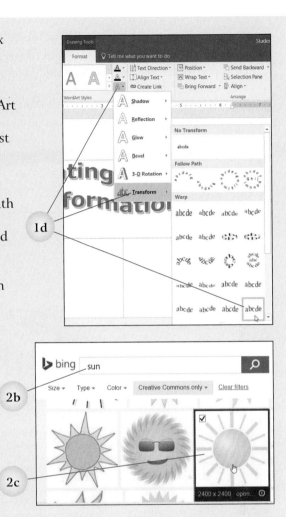

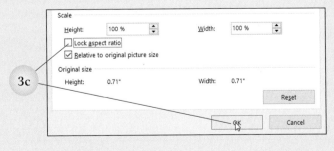

d. With the sun image selected, click in the *Shape Height* measurement box on the Picture Tools Format tab, type 1.7, and then press the Enter key.

3. Click in the second cell in the second row and then insert the image of the sailboat by completing the following steps:

a. Click the Insert tab and then click the Pictures button.

b. At the Insert Picture dialog box, navigate to the C5 folder and then double-click **sailboat.png**.

c. With the sailboat image selected, click the Size group dialog box launcher on the Picture Tools Format tab. At the Layout dialog box with the Size tab selected, click the *Lock aspect ratio* check box in the *Scale* section to remove the check mark and then click OK to close the dialog box.

d. Click in the *Shape Height* measurement box in the Size group and then type 3.6.

e. Click in the *Shape Width* measurement box, type 2.8, and then press the Enter key.

f. Apply the Drop Shadow Rectangle picture style (fourth option in the Picture Styles group).

g. Click the Wrap Text button and then click *Square* at the drop-down gallery.

h. Drag the sailboat image so it is centered horizontally and vertically in the cell.

4. Save **5-Announcement.docx**.

Check Your Work

Figure 5.4 Text and Graphics Added to the Announcement in Project 1b

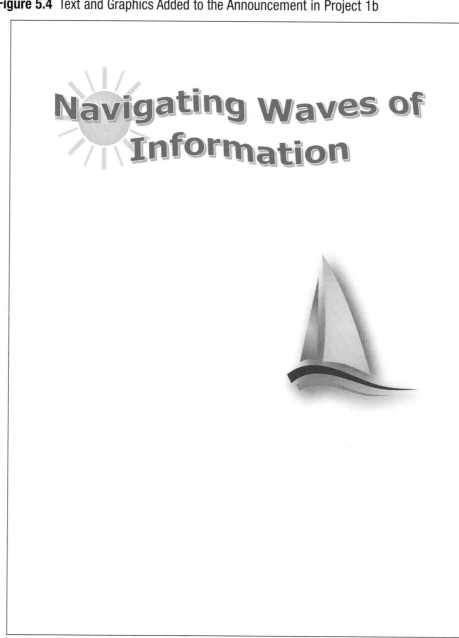

Inserting Images from a Scanner or Digital Camera

In addition to clip art and photographs, images from a scanner or digital camera can be inserted into a document in a manner similar to how an image from the computer can be inserted. If scanning an image, save the image to a folder on a computer or storage medium. To use an image from a digital camera, transfer the image file to a folder on a computer or storage medium. Once the image file has been placed in a folder on a computer or storage medium, insert the image by clicking the Pictures button on the Insert tab to display the Insert Picture dialog box. At the dialog box, navigate to the folder containing the image and then double-click the image to insert it in the document.

Understanding and Selecting Scanner Resolution

A scanner is a device that converts hard copies of text or images into digital form so they can be stored on a computer. Recall from Chapter 1 that the term *resolution* refers to the fineness of detail of an image. Resolution is measured in dots per inch, or *dpi*. The higher the dpi, the more finely detailed the image will be, so using higher-resolution images is usually more desirable.

dpi

Dots per inch; the unit of measurement for resolution

Despite the importance of having high resolution, one of the most common mistakes made when using a scanner is overscanning. Most scanners are capable of scanning up to 1,200 dpi or more, so it may be tempting to scan at the highest resolution. However, if a 5-by-7-inch image is scanned at 1,200 dpi, the resulting digital image will take up 140 MB of memory. A good rule of thumb is to scan images at 300 dpi. This is the resolution required for most print publications. If the image will be later used for a digital purpose, such as embedding it in an email or posting it on a website, save it down to 72 dpi so that it will take less time to load.

Understanding Graphic File Formats

There are two major types of graphics: bitmapped (or raster) graphics and vector graphics. **Bitmapped graphics**, or **raster graphics**, are composed of pixels in a grid. Remember from Chapter 4 that a pixel is an individual dot or square of color in a picture or graphic. Each pixel, or "bit," in the image contains information about the color to be displayed. A bitmapped graphic is a collection of individual pixels of color that can be edited one by one or as a group. Bitmapped images have a fixed resolution and cannot be resized without losing image quality. Enlarging a bitmapped image enlarges the size of the pixels used to create it and causes the image to appear jagged or blurry around the edges. A photograph is a kind of bitmapped image. Most bitmapped images can be converted easily to other bitmap-based formats.

bitmapped or *raster graphic*

An image composed of individual pixels of color that can be edited one by one or as a group

vector graphic

An image made up of mathematically defined lines and curves

Vector graphics are made up of shapes (lines and curves) that are mathematically defined. Resize a vector graphic by dragging the sizing handles surrounding the image; the edges will remain smooth because the shapes in the image resize accordingly. If a software program has the word *draw* or *illustrate* in its name, the images and drawings created in it will be vector graphics. Images imported using a scanner cannot typically be saved in a vector graphics file format.

Choosing Graphic File Formats

After an image has been scanned or imported from a digital camera, it can be saved in several different file formats. The most common formats are JPEG (joint photographic experts group), PNG (portable network graphics), TIFF (tagged image file format), GIF (graphics interchange format), and BMP (bitmap image). Choosing the right format depends on how the image will be used.

When choosing an image format, consider that the GIF format allows only 256 colors (8-bit), so it may not be as desirable as TIFF and JPEG formats, which allow for more colors. The PNG format is the successor to GIF, and it supports True Color (16 million colors). The PNG and GIF formats are typically used for online viewing. The general rule is to use JPEG for photographic images and GIF or PNG for images that have text, sharp lines, or large areas of solid colors.

Using Color to Enhance Promotional Documents

Tutorial

Applying Page Background Color

Color is a powerful tool in communicating information. Incorporate color into a document through text or images by using colored paper or a colored page background; by adding lines, shapes, or borders; and by including special graphics such as charts and graphs.

Understanding Color Terms Used in Desktop Publishing

brightness

The relative lightness of a picture

When working on desktop publishing projects in Word 2016 or any other program, some specialized terms may be used to explain color. The following is a list of some of these terms and their definitions, many of which have been defined in previous chapters:

CMYK

Stands for *cyan, magenta, yellow,* and *key (black)*—the colors that printers combine to create all other colors

- *Balance* is the amount of light and dark in a picture.
- **Brightness** or *value* is the amount of light in a color.
- **CMYK** is an acronym for *cyan, magenta, yellow,* and *key (black)*. A color printer combines these colors to create all other colors.
- *Contrast* is the amount of gray in a color.
- **Gradient** is an effect created by a gradual varying of color.
- **Grayscale** is a range of shades from black to white.
- *Hue* is a variation of a primary color, such as green-blue.
- *Luminescence* is the brightness of a color, that is, of the amount of black or white added to a color. The larger the luminescence number, the lighter the color.
- **RGB** is an acronym for *red, green,* and *blue.* Each pixel on a computer monitor is made up of some combination of these three colors.
- *Saturation* is the purity of a color. A color is completely pure, or saturated, when it is not diluted with white.

gradient

An effect created by a gradual varying of color

grayscale

A range of shades from black to white

RGB

Stands for the colors *red, green,* and *blue*—the colors that make up each pixel on a computer monitor

Adding and Printing Page Color

nonprinting area

The area along the edges of the page where text and images will not print

bleed

When elements are printed to the edge of the paper

DTP POINTER

Add approximately 0.125 inch (¹/₈ inch) to the margins of a document for the area that will be trimmed away to create a bleed.

DTP POINTER

Be careful that the text does not come too close to the edge of a page with a bleed; it may be in danger of being trimmed off.

crop marks

Marks that show where a page will be trimmed

Add page color to a Word document with the Page Color button in the Page Background group on the Design tab. Page color, by default, displays on the screen but does not print. To print the page color in a document, click the File tab and then click *Options*. At the Word Options dialog box, click *Display* in the left panel. In the *Printing options* section of the dialog box, click the *Print background colors and images* check box to insert a check mark and then click OK to close the dialog box.

When page color is applied to a document, the color will appear to extend to the edges of the page on the screen, but the page may print with a white border along the edges of the paper. This border is a limitation of the printer hardware known as the ***nonprinting area***, and it may measure approximately 0.25 inch. Most inkjet and laser printers do not allow printing to the edge of the page. To create the look of a ***bleed*** (elements are printed to the edge of the paper), print to a larger paper size and then trim to the desired size. Determine the nonprinting area of a desktop printer by setting the left, right, top, and bottom margins to 0. The margins will automatically reset to the minimum margin that is supported by the printer. Make note of the size of the printer's nonprinting area.

Showing Document Content

Options for turning on and off the display of certain content in a document are available in the *Show document content* section of the Word Options dialog box with *Advanced* selected in the left panel. To turn on an option, insert a check mark in the option's check box.

To view the margin boundaries in a document, insert a check mark in the *Show text boundaries* check box (see Figure 5.5). The boundaries that display in the document do not print. Use boundary lines to position design elements on the page.

Crop marks show where a publication page will be trimmed. In Word, these marks display on the screen when the *Show crop marks* option has been selected at the Word Options dialog box (see Figure 5.5). Crop marks show on a printed page only when the content has been printed to a paper size that is larger than the document page.

Figure 5.5 Showing Boundaries and Crop Marks at the Word Options Dialog Box

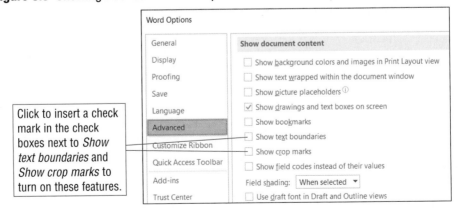

Click to insert a check mark in the check boxes next to *Show text boundaries* and *Show crop marks* to turn on these features.

1. With **5-Announcement.docx** open, insert the announcement text by completing the following steps:

   a. Position the insertion point in the first cell of the second row of the table and then use the Object button in the Text group on the Insert tab to insert **Sailing.docx** from the C5 folder.

   b. Position the insertion point in the cell in the third row of the table and then insert **TradeFair.docx** from the C5 folder. Press the Backspace key one time to delete the extra line after the inserted text. Make sure that the text is horizontally centered. Resize the row if necessary.

   c. Position the insertion point in the first cell in the fourth row and insert **Meridian.docx** from the C5 folder. Press the Backspace key one time to delete the extra line after the inserted text.

   d. Position the insertion point in the second cell in the fourth row and insert **Register.docx** from the C5 folder. Press the Backspace key one time to delete the extra line after the inserted text.

   e. With the insertion point positioned in the second cell in the fourth row, click the Align Top Right button in the Alignment group on the Table Tools Layout tab.

   f. Make sure that the table fits on one page. If not, make slight adjustments to row heights until the table fits on one page and the document does not have a second page.
   Hint: When you position the mouse pointer on a line in the table, the mouse pointer should display as a left-and-right-pointing arrow with two vertical lines in the middle or as an up-and-down-pointing arrow with two horizontal lines in the middle. Drag to move the line and then release the left mouse button when you are satisfied with the position.

2. Add a page color by clicking the Design tab, clicking the Page Color button in the Page Background group, and then clicking the *Gold, Accent 4, Lighter 80%* option (eighth column, second row in the *Theme Colors* section).

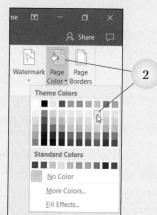

3. Turn on the printing of background colors and the display of crop marks by completing the following steps:

   a. Click the File tab and then click *Options*.

   b. At the Word Options dialog box, click *Display* in the left panel.

   c. Click the *Print background colors and images* check box to insert a check mark.

   d. Click *Advanced* in the left panel.

   e. Scroll down the dialog box to the *Show document content* section and then click the *Show crop marks* check box to insert a check mark.

   f. Click OK to close the dialog box.

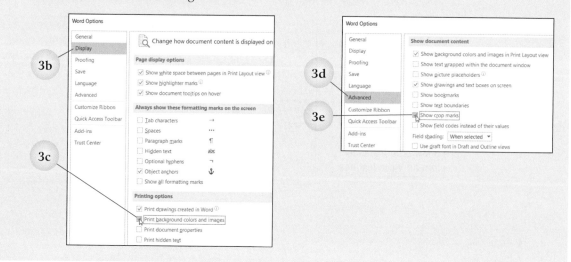

4. View the entire page by clicking the View tab and then clicking the One Page button in the Zoom group. If any item is not positioned as shown in Figure 5.6, drag any boundary line in the table to adjust the size of the cell. If the flyer displays too high or low on the page, change the top and/or bottom margins to center the flyer vertically on the page. Use the crop marks as a reference for aligning the flyer in the center of the page.
5. Change the view back to 100% by clicking the 100% button on the View tab.
6. Save, print, and then close **5-Announcement.docx**.
7. Open a blank document, display the Word Options dialog box with *Display* selected in the left panel, and then remove the check mark from the *Print background colors and images* option. Click *Advanced* in the left panel, remove the check mark from the *Show crop marks* check box, close the dialog box and then close the blank document without saving changes.

Check Your Work

Figure 5.6 Announcement Created in Project 1c

Create an Announcement on Exercise Classes

You will open a document containing only text, display the drawing grid, add shapes, and then add picture fills to the shapes. You will also insert an image and then crop the image to a shape.

Preview Finished Project

Modifying Document Elements to Enhance Promotional Materials

Word provides a variety of features that can be used to modify document elements to better support the message of an announcement or flyer. As discussed in Chapter 4, ruled lines can be used to create a focal point, draw the eye across or down the page, separate columns and sections, and add visual appeal. Borders can be used to frame text and graphics. Shading can be used to create visual interest in the background of a table, a paragraph, selected text, or a drawing object. Shape and picture effects can be added to graphics to create depth and movement. Examples of lines, borders, shading, and effects are displayed in Figure 5.7.

Figure 5.7 Illustrating Lines, Borders, Shading, Shadow, Bevel Effects, and Table Styles

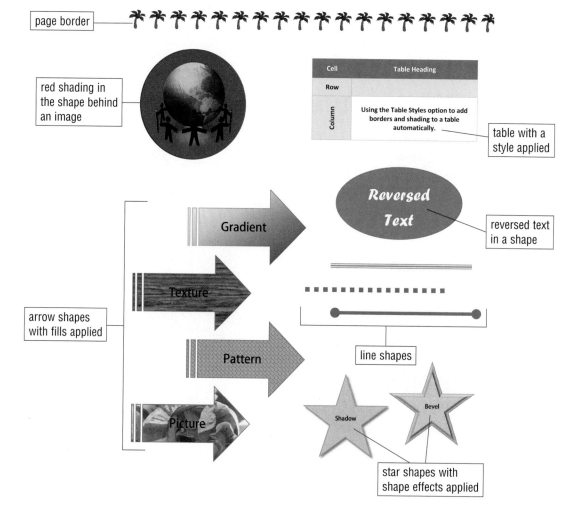

Cropping an Image

At times, an image may need to be resized and/or cropped to fit in a placeholder. While resizing means dragging the sizing handles around an image to make the entire image larger or smaller, *cropping* involves trimming off the edges of an image. For example, Figure 5.8A depicts a rectangular image that needs to fit in a larger square placeholder. To adjust the image to fit the placeholder, drag the corner sizing handles to resize the image to fit the width of the placeholder (see Figures 5.8B and 5.8C) and then crop off the top of the image to make it a square (see Figures 5.8D and 5.8E).

When cropping an image, crop only sections that distract the reader from the primary focus of the image. For example, in Figure 5.8, the primary focus of the image is the hand on the keyboard. Cropping from the bottom of the image would remove a portion of the hand, whereas cropping from the top of the image keeps the hand in the image as the primary focus.

Note that this is just one method of resizing and cropping an image to fit in a placeholder. In addition to adjusting images to fit in placeholders, cropping is also used to create focus on one part of an image and to remove unnecessary parts of an image.

Figure 5.8 Resizing and Cropping an Image

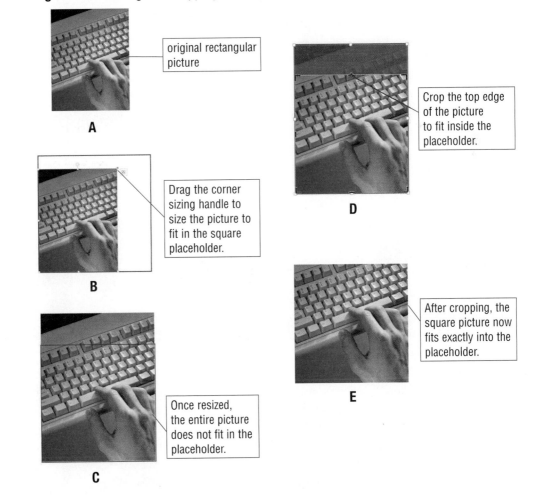

original rectangular
picture

A

Drag the corner
sizing handle to
size the picture to
fit in the square
placeholder.

B

Once resized,
the entire picture
does not fit in the
placeholder.

C

Crop the top edge
of the picture
to fit inside the
placeholder.

D

After cropping, the
square picture now
fits exactly into the
placeholder.

E

Using Cropping Options

 Crop

To display the cropping options shown in Figure 5.9, select the image, click the Crop button arrow in the Size group on the Picture Tools Format tab, and then click an option at the drop-down list. Consider these cropping suggestions:

- Crop one side by dragging the center cropping handle on the specific side inward.
- Crop equally on two sides at the same time by pressing and holding down the Ctrl key while dragging the center cropping handle on either side inward.
- Crop equally on all four sides at the same time by pressing and holding down the Ctrl key while dragging a corner cropping handle inward.
- Crop an image to exact dimensions by right-clicking the image and then clicking *Format Picture* at the shortcut menu that displays. At the Format Picture task pane, click the Picture icon, click *Crop*, and then adjust the values in the *Width* and *Height* measurement boxes in the *Crop position* section.

Figure 5.10 illustrates the results of applying various cropping options. Experiment with the available options to learn how they can be used to emphasize certain parts of your image.

Figure 5.9 Using Enhanced Cropping Options

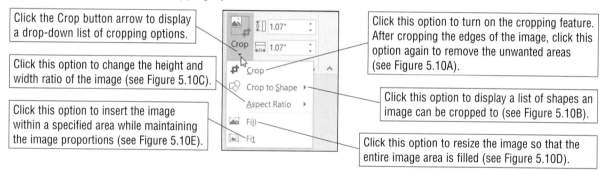

Click the Crop button arrow to display a drop-down list of cropping options.

Click this option to change the height and width ratio of the image (see Figure 5.10C).

Click this option to insert the image within a specified area while maintaining the image proportions (see Figure 5.10E).

Click this option to turn on the cropping feature. After cropping the edges of the image, click this option again to remove the unwanted areas (see Figure 5.10A).

Click this option to display a list of shapes an image can be cropped to (see Figure 5.10B).

Click this option to resize the image so that the entire image area is filled (see Figure 5.10D).

Figure 5.10 Applying Cropping Options to a Photograph

A
Cropping Using the *Crop* Option

B
Cropping Using the
Crop to Shape Option

Cropping Using the *Portrait 2:3* Option at the *Aspect Ratio* Side Menu

C

D
Cropping Using the *Fill* Option

E
Cropping Using the *Fit* Option

Deleting Cropped Areas of an Image

After an image is cropped, the cropped portions remain part of the image file. Reduce the file size by removing the cropped portions. Deleting the cropped portion of an image cannot be undone, so make sure no more changes are needed before deleting the cropped portions.

To delete the cropped areas from an image, complete the following steps:

1. Click the image.

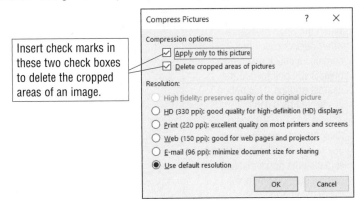
Compress
Pictures

2. Click the Compress Pictures button in the Adjust group on the Picture Tools Format tab.
3. Click the *Delete cropped areas of pictures* check box in the *Compression options* section to insert a check mark, as shown in Figure 5.11, and make sure that a check mark also displays in the *Apply only to this picture* check box.
4. Click OK to close the Compress Pictures dialog box.

Adding Fill to Document Elements

fill

Color, shading, or
other background
added inside a
drawing object

A background, or *fill*, can be added to tables, paragraphs, selected text, shapes, objects, and some images. Fill a drawing object with a solid color or a gradient, a pattern, a texture, or even a picture. A shape can be filled with a photograph or clip art to create an interesting focal point or to reinforce the theme of a document.

To add an image as fill, insert a shape, click the Shape Fill button arrow in the Shape Styles group on the Drawing Tools Format tab, and then click Picture at the drop-down gallery. At the Insert Pictures window, search for and then insert the desired image.

Another method for filling a shape with an image is to insert the image, make sure the image is selected, click the Crop button arrow in the Size group on the Picture Tools Format tab, point to *Crop to Shape* at the drop-down list, and then click the shape at the side menu. The image will conform to the design shape. This method is shown in Figure 5.12.

Figure 5.11 Using the Compress Pictures Dialog Box

Insert check marks in
these two check boxes
to delete the cropped
areas of an image.

Compress Pictures   ?   ✕

Compression options:
☑ Apply only to this picture
☑ Delete cropped areas of pictures

Resolution:
○ High fidelity: preserves quality of the original picture
○ HD (330 ppi): good quality for high-definition (HD) displays
○ Print (220 ppi): excellent quality on most printers and screens
○ Web (150 ppi): good for web pages and projectors
○ E-mail (96 ppi): minimize document size for sharing
◉ Use default resolution

OK   Cancel

Figure 5.12 Adding a Picture Fill to a Shape

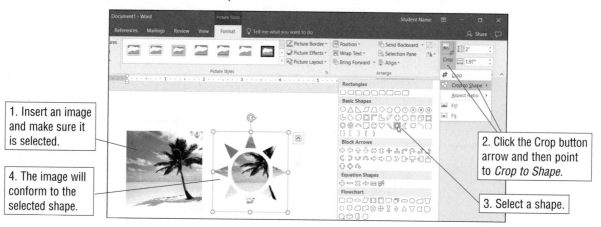

1. Insert an image and make sure it is selected.

4. The image will conform to the selected shape.

2. Click the Crop button arrow and then point to *Crop to Shape*.

3. Select a shape.

Using the Drawing Grid

The Word drawing grid is a network of lines that help to align drawing objects, such as shapes, text boxes, clip art, and pictures. As an object is drawn, Word pulls it into alignment with the nearest intersection of gridlines. By default, the gridlines of the drawing grid are not visible. To display the gridlines, click the View tab and then click the *Gridlines* check box in the Show group to insert a check mark. Adjust settings for the drawing grid at the Grid and Guides dialog box, shown in Figure 5.13. Display this dialog box by clicking the Layout tab, clicking the Align button in the Arrange group, and then clicking *Grid Settings* at the drop-down list.

Align

The horizontal and vertical spacing between the gridlines defaults to 0.13 inch. Change this vertical spacing with options in the *Grid settings* section of the Grid and Guides dialog box. The dialog box also contains options for specifying the types of gridlines to display and how often the gridlines show on the screen. To temporarily move an object without it snapping to a gridline, press the Alt key while moving the object.

Figure 5.13 Customizing the Drawing Grid at the Grid and Guides Dialog Box

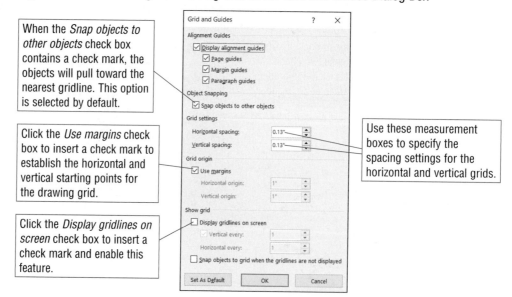

When the *Snap objects to other objects* check box contains a check mark, the objects will pull toward the nearest gridline. This option is selected by default.

Click the *Use margins* check box to insert a check mark to establish the horizontal and vertical starting points for the drawing grid.

Click the *Display gridlines on screen* check box to insert a check mark and enable this feature.

Use these measurement boxes to specify the spacing settings for the horizontal and vertical grids.

1. Open **Health.docx** and save it with the name **5-Health**.
2. Click the Show/Hide ¶ button in the Paragraph group on the Home tab to turn on the display of nonprinting characters.
3. Apply formatting to the text by completing the following steps (refer to Figure 5.14 on page 167):
   a. Select the text *Healthy choices point to healthy lives....*
   b. Change the font to 36-point Papyrus and apply bold formatting.
   c. Press and hold down the Ctrl key, and then select the text *healthy*.
   d. Apply the Green, Accent 6, Darker 25% font color.
   e. Select the word *point* and then apply italic formatting.
4. Position the insertion point in the text box below *Healthy choices...* and then insert **Cardio.docx** from the C5 folder.
5. Apply formatting to the text in the text box by completing the following steps:
   a. Select all the text you just inserted in the text box.
   b. Change the font to 14-point Arial, apply italic formatting, and then change the paragraph alignment to right.
   c. Select *Summer Cardio Mix*, remove the italic formatting, change the font to 18-point Bauhaus 93, and then apply the Green, Accent 6, Darker 25% font color.
   d. Click the text box border to select the text box and then remove the shape fill and shape outline.
6. Apply formatting to the text in the *Brighton Health* text box by completing the following steps:
   a. Select all the text in the text box and then change the paragraph alignment to center.
   b. Select *Brighton Health & Fitness Center* and then change the font to 16-point Bauhaus 93 and apply the Green, Accent 6, Darker 25% font color.
   c. Select both lines of the address and then change the font to 10-point Arial and apply the Green, Accent 6, Darker 25% font color.
   d. Select the text box containing the text you just formatted and then remove the shape fill and shape outline.
7. Position the insertion point in the text box behind the *Brighton* text and then insert the symbol (logo) as shown in Figure 5.14 by completing the following steps:
   a. Click the Insert tab, click the Symbol button in the Symbols group, and then click *More Symbols* at the drop-down list.
   b. At the Symbol dialog box with the Symbols tab selected, change the font to Webdings.
   c. Click the symbol shown at the right (approximately the seventh row).
      Hint: Type 134 *in the* **Character code** *text box to locate the symbol.*
   d. Click the Insert button and then click the Close button.
   e. Select the symbol, change the font size to 115 points, and then apply the White, Background 1, Darker 15% font color.

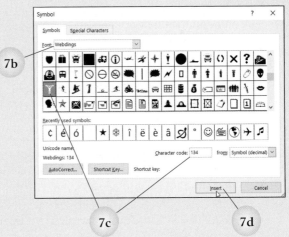

f. Center the symbol in the text box and then, if necessary, position the text box as shown in Figure 5.14 on page 167.

g. Remove the shape fill and shape outline from the text box.

8. Insert an image and then crop the image into an arrow shape by completing the following steps:

a. Press Ctrl + Home to move the insertion point to the beginning of the document.

b. Click the Insert tab, click the Pictures button in the Illustrations group, navigate to the C5 folder at the Insert Picture dialog box, and then double-click *vegetables.jpg*.

c. With the image selected, change the text wrapping to Tight and then move the image to the left margin of the document.

d. With the image still selected, click the Crop button arrow in the Size group on the Picture Tools Format tab and then point to *Crop to Shape* at the drop-down list.

e. At the side menu, click the *Arrow: Striped Right* option in the *Block Arrows* section.

f. Change the height of the arrow to 2.3 inches and, if necessary, the width to 3.15 inches.

g. Click the Picture Effects button in the Picture Styles group on the Picture Tools Format tab, point to *Shadow*, scroll down the side menu, and then click the *Perspective: Upper Left* option (first option in the *Perspective* section).

h. Position the arrow as shown in Figure 5.14.

9. Turn on the display of the drawing grid to help align the arrow shapes shown in Figure 5.14 by completing the following steps:

a. Click the Layout tab, click the Align button in the Arrange group, and then click *Grid Settings* at the drop-down list.

b. At the Grid and Guides dialog box, make sure that a check mark appears in the *Snap objects to other objects* check box.

c. Select the current measurement in the *Horizontal spacing* measurement box in the *Grid settings* section and then type 0.22.

d. Select the current measurement in the *Vertical spacing* measurement box in the *Grid settings* section and then type 0.22.

e. Make sure that a check mark appears in the *Use margins* check box in the *Grid origin* section.

f. Click the *Display gridlines on screen* check box in the *Show grid* section to insert a check mark.

g. Select the current number in the *Vertical every* measurement box and then type 2.

h. Select the current number in the *Horizontal every* measurement box, type 2, and then click OK to close the dialog box.

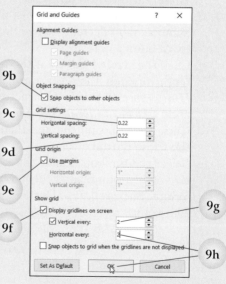

10. Create the middle arrow by completing the following steps:
   a. Click the Insert tab, click the Shapes button in the Illustrations group, and then click the *Arrow: Striped Right* option in the *Block Arrows* section.
   b. Drag the crosshairs to create an arrow similar to the one at the right and to the middle arrow shown in Figure 5.14 on page 167. Use the gridlines to make the arrow approximately the same size as the top arrow in the figure.
   c. Change the height of the arrow to 2.3 inches and the width to 3.15 inches.
   d. Click the Shape Effects button in the Shape Styles group, point to *Shadow*, scroll down the side menu, and then click the *Perspective: Upper Left* option (first option in the *Perspective* section).
   e. Position the arrow as shown in Figure 5.14.

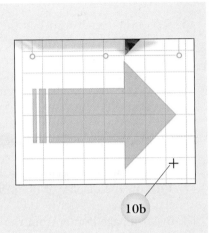

10b

11. With the arrow selected, copy it by pressing and holding down the Ctrl key and then dragging the copy of the arrow below the middle arrow, as shown at right.

12. Insert a picture fill in the middle arrow by completing the following steps:
   a. Click the middle arrow to select it.
   b. Click the Drawing Tools Format tab if necessary to make it active.
   c. Click the Shape Fill button arrow in the Shape Styles group and then click *Picture* at the drop-down gallery.

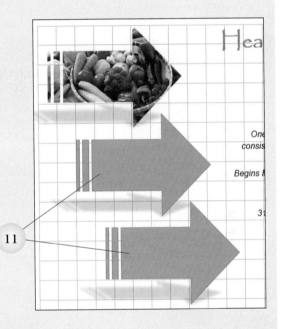

11

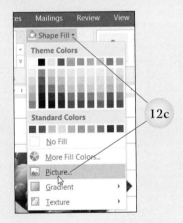

12c

   d. At the Insert Pictures window, click the *Browse* option.
   e. At the Insert Picture dialog box, navigate to the C5 folder and then double-click *fruit.jpg*.
13. Complete steps similar to those in Step 12 to insert the image **exercise.jpg** in the bottom arrow (see Figure 5.14).
14. Select the three arrows, change the shape outline to Green, Accent 6, Darker 25% (last column, fifth row in the *Theme Colors* section), and then deselect the arrows.

15. Select the top arrow, click the Picture Tools Format tab, click the Picture Border button arrow in the Picture Styles group, point to *Weight*, and then click *1 pt* at the side menu. Click anywhere in the document to deselect the arrow.

16. Turn off the display of the drawing grid by clicking the View tab and then clicking the *Gridlines* check box in the Show group to remove the check mark.

17. Turn off the display of nonprinting characters.

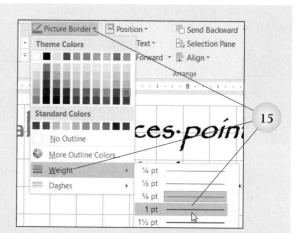

18. Insert a page border from the *Art* option box by completing the following steps:

   a. Click the Design tab and then click the Page Borders button in the Page Background group.

   b. At the Borders and Shading dialog box with the Page Border tab selected, click the *Art* option box arrow.

   c. Scroll to the end of the drop-down list, scroll back up the list, and then click the fifteenth page border from the bottom (a thin-thick line). Verify that you have chosen the correct line by comparing its appearance in the *Preview* section of the dialog box with the preview image shown below.

   d. Click the *Color* option box arrow and then click the *Green, Accent 6, Darker 25%* option (last column, fifth row in the *Theme Colors* section).

   e. Click OK to close the dialog box.

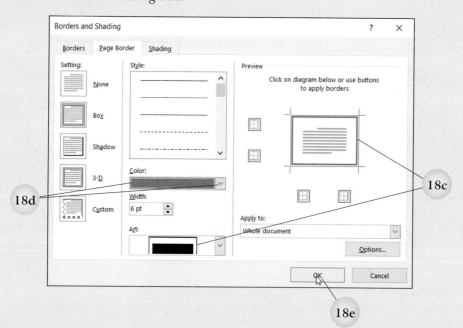

19. Make any necessary adjustments to the arrows so they appear similar to those shown in Figure 5.14.

20. Save, print, and then close **5-Health.docx**.

Check Your Work

Figure 5.14 Announcement Created in Project 2

Project 3 Create a Flyer on Home and Office Design   1 Part

You will create a flyer with matching colors and an image with a picture border and text effects.

Preview Finished Project

Matching Colors within a Document

To make a flyer or announcement look even more professional, select a font color by matching a color from an image used in the document, as shown in Figure 5.15. To do this, start by ungrouping the image. Images saved in the PNG, JPG, or GIF file format cannot be ungrouped. If an image can be ungrouped, the Group button on the Picture Tools Format tab will be active.

HSL

Stands for *hue, saturation,* and *luminescence*

Select a segment of the ungrouped image that contains the desired color, display the Colors dialog box with the Custom tab selected, click the *More Fill Colors* option at the drop-down gallery, and then write down the values from the *Red, Green,* and *Blue* measurement boxes. Alternatively, click the *Color model* option box arrow on the Custom tab in the Colors dialog box, click *HSL* at the drop-down list, and then record the **HSL** values in the *Hue, Saturation,* and *Luminescence measurement boxes*. Use the same values to apply color to selected fonts and drawing objects.

Figure 5.15 Matching Colors from an Ungrouped Image

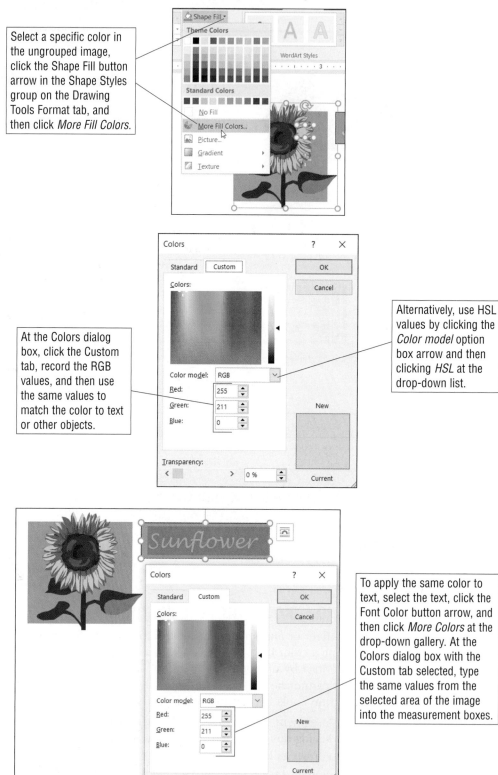

Select a specific color in the ungrouped image, click the Shape Fill button arrow in the Shape Styles group on the Drawing Tools Format tab, and then click *More Fill Colors*.

At the Colors dialog box, click the Custom tab, record the RGB values, and then use the same values to match the color to text or other objects.

Alternatively, use HSL values by clicking the *Color model* option box arrow and then clicking *HSL* at the drop-down list.

To apply the same color to text, select the text, click the Font Color button arrow, and then click *More Colors* at the drop-down gallery. At the Colors dialog box with the Custom tab selected, type the same values from the selected area of the image into the measurement boxes.

Applying Shape and Picture Effects

Tutorial

Formatting a
Shape and Line

Shape
Effects

Picture
Effects

Add depth to lines, text boxes, drawing objects, and photographs using either shape effects or picture effects, as shown in Figure 5.16. Display shape effects by selecting the drawing object and then clicking the Shape Effects button in the Shape Styles group on the Drawing Tools Format tab. Display picture effects by selecting the picture object and then clicking the Picture Effects button in the Picture Styles group on the Picture Tools Format tab.

Effects are also available at the Format Shape task pane, as shown in Figure 5.17A. Display this task pane by selecting the drawing object and then clicking the Shape Styles group task pane launcher on the Drawing Tools Format tab. Picture effects are available at the Format Picture task pane, as shown in Figure 5.17B. Display this task pane by selecting the picture object and then clicking the Picture Styles group task pane launcher on the Picture Tools Format tab.

Figure 5.16 Adding Interest with Picture Effects

Preset: *Preset 4*

Shadow: *Offset: Top*

Reflection: *Tight
Reflection: Touching*

Glow: *8 point; Blue,
Accent color 1*

Soft Edges:
25 Point

Bevel: *Divot*

3-D Rotation: *Perspective:
Contrasting Left*

Figure 5.17 Using the Format Shape Task Pane and Format Picture Task Pane

A
Format Shape Task Pane

B
Format Picture Task Pane

1. At a blank document, change the theme colors to Violet II by clicking the Design tab, clicking the Theme Colors button in the Document Formatting group, and then clicking *Violet II* at the drop-down gallery.
2. Insert a flower border as shown in Figure 5.18 on page 172 by completing the following steps:
   a. Click the Insert tab and then click the Pictures button in the Illustrations group.
   b. At the Insert Picture dialog box, navigate to the C5 folder and then double-click **FlowerBorder.wmf**.
3. Customize the flower border by completing the following steps:
   a. With the flower border selected, right-click the border image and then click *Edit Picture* at the shortcut menu.
   b. Click each segment of the flowers and apply a variation of the purple color in the *Theme Colors* section of the Shape Fill button drop-down gallery. Use Figure 5.18 as a guide but feel free to make your own choices.
   c. Select the flower border image (not a segment of the image), click the Position button in the Arrange group on the Drawing Tools Format tab, and then click the *Position in Middle Center with Square Text Wrapping* option at the drop-down gallery.

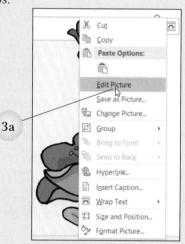

4. Create a text box inside the graphic border and then insert text by completing the following steps:
   a. Click the Insert tab, click the Text Box button in the Text group, and then click *Draw Text Box* at the drop-down list.
   b. Drag the crosshairs to draw a box inside the graphic border.
   c. Remove the shape fill and shape outline from the text box.
   d. With the insertion point positioned inside the text box, insert **Design.docx** from the C5 folder.
   e. Select all the text and then change the font to Tempus Sans ITC.
5. Select *Details by Design* in the text box and then apply the following formatting:
   a. Change the font to 48-point Gabriola.
   b. Apply the Purple, Accent 2, Darker 25% font color.
   c. Display the Font dialog box with the Advanced tab selected. Expand the character spacing by 0.5 points, choose *Standard and Contextual* from the *Ligatures* option box drop-down list, choose *6* from the *Stylistic sets* option box drop-down list, and then click OK to close the dialog box.

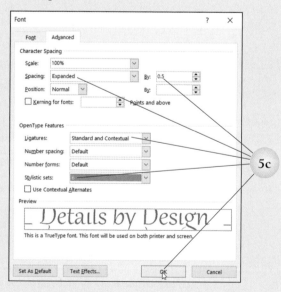

6. Position the insertion point in front of *RESIDENTIAL AND*, then press the Tab key.

7. Position the insertion point in front of *COMMERCIAL DESIGN* and then press the Tab key two times.
8. Select *RESIDENTIAL AND COMMERCIAL DESIGN* and then make the following changes:
   a. Click the Text Effects and Typography button in the Font group on the Home tab and then click the *Gradient Fill: Blue, Accent color 5; Reflection* option (second column, second row).

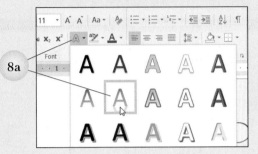

   b. Change the font size to 16 points.
   c. Apply bold formatting.
   d. Change the font color to a green that matches some of the leaves by clicking the Font Color button arrow and then clicking *More Colors* at the drop-down gallery. At the Colors dialog box, click the Custom tab. Type 51 in the *Red* measurement box, 153 in the *Green* measurement box, and 102 in the *Blue* measurement box and then click OK.

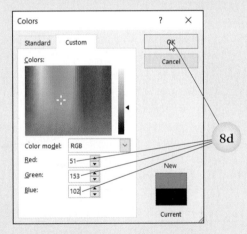

9. Position the insertion point in front of *Think spring!*, press Ctrl + Shift + End to select the text from the insertion point to the end of the text in the text box, and then click the Center button in the Paragraph group on the Home tab. (If necessary, resize the text box border to ensure that the text fits inside the picture border, similar to how it appears in Figure 5.18.)
10. Select *Think spring!*, change the font size to 26 points, apply bold formatting, and then apply the Purple, Accent 2, Darker 25% font color.
11. Select the text from the paragraph that begins *Plan a new look* through the end of the text box, apply bold formatting, and then change the font color to the green color you applied in Step 8d. (The green color you previously applied will display in the *Recent Colors* section of the drop-down gallery.)
12. Resize the text box and make any other needed adjustments so your document appears similar to the flyer shown in Figure 5.18.
13. Save the document with the name **5-Design**.
14. Print and then close **5-Design.docx**.

Check Your Work

Figure 5.18 Flyer Created in Project 3

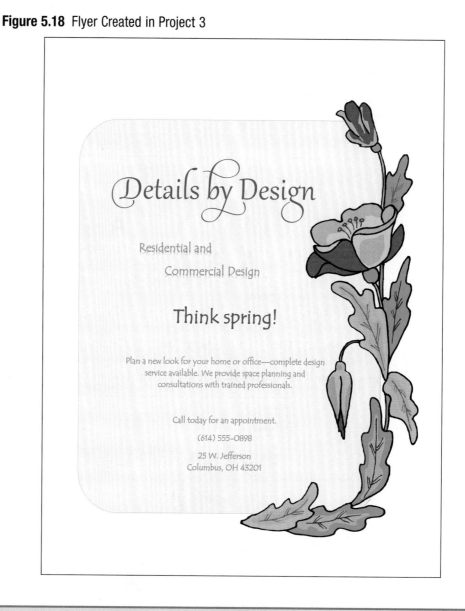

Project 4 **Create an Announcement for a Safari Ball**   **1 Part**

You will open a document containing a border, make changes to the border, add a text box and text, add WordArt, and then add and format an image. You will then create the back side of the announcement, which will contain a text box, WordArt, and images.

Preview Finished Project

Adjusting Images

The Picture Tools Format tab contains numerous options for customizing images, including adjusting the brightness or contrast of an image, applying distinctive styles with depth and dimension, and selecting unique effects. The creative opportunities are boundless.

Adjusting Brightness, Contrast, Sharpness, and Softness

![Corrections icon] Corrections

Adjust the brightness, or relative lightness, of an image; the contrast (difference between the darkest and lightest areas of an image); and the sharpness or softness of an image with options at the Corrections button drop-down gallery in the Adjust group on the Picture Tools Format tab. Figure 5.19A shows an original image of two penguins. Figure 5.19B shows the same image with the brightness increased by 20 percent and the contrast decreased by 20 percent. Notice the lighter overall color of the image and the way the foreground and background images blend together. Figure 5.19C shows the image with the brightness decreased by 20 percent and the contrast increased by 20 percent. This image is darker than images A and B, and the penguins' dark heads clearly stand out against the lighter background.

To enhance the finer details in an image or blur any slight imperfections, adjust the image clarity in the *Sharpen/Soften* section of the Corrections button drop-down gallery. Figure 5.20 depicts an original image (A), one that has been sharpened by 50 percent (B), and one that has been softened by 50 percent (C).

Figure 5.19 Adjusting Brightness and Contrast

A	**B**	**C**
Original Picture	Brightness: +20% Contrast: -20%	Brightness: -20% Contrast: +20%

Figure 5.20 Sharpening and Softening an Image

A	**B**	**C**
Original Picture	Sharpen: 50%	Soften: 50%

Adjusting Color Saturation, Color Tone, and Recolor

 Color

Adjust the three image qualities—saturation, color tone, and recolor—with options at the Color button drop-down gallery in the Adjust group on the Picture Tools Format tab. Recall from Chapter 2 that saturation is the purity or intensity of a color. Increasing the saturation makes an image appear more vivid, while reducing the saturation makes the image appear more dull. (For example, selecting 0 percent saturation makes a colored image appear black and white.) Figure 5.21B depicts an image in which the saturation has been increased by 300 percent, and Figure 5.21C shows an image in which the saturation has been decreased by 33 percent.

color tone

The overall color temperature of an image, where reds and yellows are warm and blues and greens are cool

Color tone refers to the overall color of an image and is also referred to as *color temperature*. The original color tone of an image is created by the light source used when the picture is taken, but this value can be adjusted to achieve a particular look in the image. The options in the *Color Tone* section of the Color button drop-down gallery are labeled with temperatures ranging from *4700K* to *11200K*, where *K* stands for *kelvin*. Blue and green tones are considered cool, or lower in temperature, and red and yellow are considered warm, or higher in temperature. For example, selecting the *11200K* option gives an image an overall red/yellow tone, as shown in Figure 5.21D.

Apply an overall color to an image with options in the *Recolor* section of the Color button drop-down gallery. The image in Figure 5.21E has been recolored using the *Green, Accent color 6 Dark* option.

Figure 5.21 Adjusting Saturation, Color Tone, and Recolor at the Color Gallery

A
Original Picture

B
Saturation: 300%

C
Saturation: 33%

D
Color Tone: 11200K

E
Recolor: Green,
Accent color 6 Dark

Using the Format Picture Task Pane

Tutorial

Formatting an Image at the Format Picture Task Pane

Images can be adjusted in many ways using options at the Corrections button drop-down gallery and the Color button drop-down gallery in the Adjust group on the Picture Tools Format tab. Adjustments to images can also be made that are not provided by these predesigned options.

To make customized adjustments, display the Format Picture task pane by clicking *Picture Corrections Options* at the bottom of the Corrections button drop-down gallery or *Picture Color Options* at the bottom of the Color button drop-down gallery. The *Picture Corrections* and *Picture Color* sections of the Format Picture task pane provide sliders and measurement boxes for adjusting values more precisely. Each of these sections also contains a Presets button that can be clicked to view and choose from popular adjustment options, as shown in Figure 5.22.

Making a Color Transparent

transparent

See-through or clear; containing no color

Consider making one color in an image ***transparent***, or see-through, to better show any text that is layered on top of it, to layer images on top of each other, or to remove or hide parts of an image. To make a color in an image transparent, select the image, click the Color button in the Adjust group on the Picture Tools Format tab, and then click the *Set Transparent Color* option. The mouse pointer changes to an eraser with an arrow at the end. Point the arrow at the color in the image to be made transparent and then click the left mouse button.

Word will make only one color in an image transparent. If more than one color needs to be removed, do so in another image-editing program and then insert the image into the Word document. See Figure 5.23 for an example of the transparency feature.

Figure 5.22 Choosing from the Most Common Preset Color Saturation and Color Tone Options

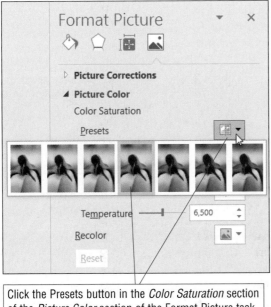

Click the Presets button in the *Color Saturation* section of the *Picture Color* section of the Format Picture task pane to display these thumbnails.

Click the Presets button in the *Color Tone* section of the *Picture Color* section of the Format Picture task pane to display these thumbnails.

Figure 5.23 Setting Transparent Color

A
Original Graphic

B
Graphic with Transparency Applied
to the Light-Green Background Color

Applying Artistic Effects

Artistic
Effects

Use the Artistic Effects button in the Adjust group on the Picture Tools Format tab to make an image look like a sketch, drawing, or painting. Note that only one artistic effect can be applied at a time to an image, so applying a new artistic effect will remove the previously applied artistic effect. Figure 5.24 shows the effects of applying the Photocopy effect and the Pencil Grayscale effect to an image.

Compressing Pictures

One way to reduce the file size of an image is to compress it. To do this, select the image and then click the Compress Pictures button in the Adjust group on the Picture Tools Format tab. Make the desired selections at the dialog box and then click OK. As discussed earlier in this chapter, compressing a picture after cropping can be especially helpful, as it removes the unwanted areas of the picture from the file.

Compressing a picture can change the amount of detail retained in the original picture. This means that after compression, the image may look different than it did before compression. Compress a picture and save the file before applying any adjustments or artistic effects.

Figure 5.24 Applying Artistic Effects

A
Original Graphic

B
Photocopy Effect

C
Pencil Grayscale Effect

Figure 5.25 Removing the Background of an Image

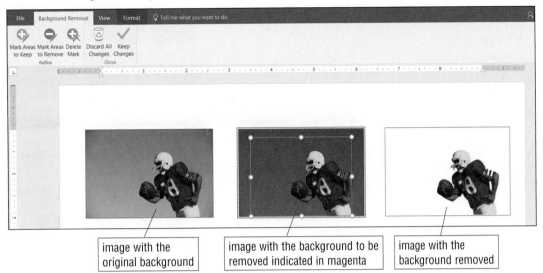

image with the original background

image with the background to be removed indicated in magenta

image with the background removed

Removing the Background of an Image

Remove Background

Use the Remove Background button in the Adjust group on the Picture Tools Format tab to remove unwanted portions of an image. Select an image and then click the Remove Background button to display the Background Removal tab with three options in the Refine group and two options in the Close group, as shown in Figure 5.25. The background area that will be removed displays in a magenta color. Click the Mark Areas to Keep button to draw lines that mark areas to keep in the image. Click the Mark Areas to Remove button to draw lines that mark areas to remove from the image. Use the Delete Mark button to delete lines drawn to mark areas to keep or remove. Use the Discard all Changes button to close the Background Removal tab and discard all the changes. Finally, click the Keep Changes button to close the Background Removal tab and keep all the changes.

Using Pictures Styles

Approximately 30 borders and effects can be added to enhance the appeal of an image. Picture styles are available in the Picture Styles group on the Picture Tools Format tab. The options in the Picture Styles gallery are enabled with the live preview feature, so simply hover the mouse over each effect to see how it will look when applied to the image.

Project 4 Creating the Front and Back Sides of an Announcement with a Border, a Text Box, WordArt, and an Image

Part 1 of 1

1. Open **SafariBall.docx** and save it with the name **5-SafariBall**.
2. Customize the zebra border by completing the following steps:
   a. Click the zebra border to select it.
   b. Click the Picture Tools Format tab.
   c. Change the height of the image to 5.1 inches and the width to 7.1 inches.

d. Click the Rotate button in the Arrange group and then click *Rotate Right 90°* at the drop-down gallery.

e. Click the Position button in the Arrange group and then click the *Position in Middle Center with Square Text Wrapping* option.

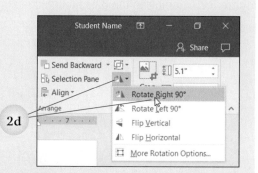

3. Create a text box containing the document text as shown in Figure 5.26A on page 181 by completing the following steps:

a. Draw a text box in the document.

b. Change the height of the text box to 5.5 inches and the width to 3.5 inches.

c. Click the Position button and then click the *Position in Middle with Square Text Wrapping* option.

d. With the insertion point positioned in the text box, insert **SafariText.docx** from the C5 folder.

e. With the insertion point still positioned in the text box, apply the Facet theme.

f. Click the Drawing Tools Format tab, click the More Shape Styles button in the Shape Styles group, and then click the *Subtle Effect - Green, Accent 1* option (second column, fourth row in the *Theme Styles* section).

4. Insert WordArt in the text box as shown in Figure 5.26A by completing the following steps:

a. Position the insertion point in the first blank line below the text *Please join us for the*.

b. Click the Insert tab, click the WordArt button in the Text group, and then click the *Gradient Fill: Red, Accent color 5; Reflection* option (second column, second row).

c. Type SIXTH ANNUAL, press Shift + Enter, and then type SAFARI BALL.

d. Click the border of the WordArt text box to select it.

e. Click the Text Fill button arrow in the WordArt Styles group on the Drawing Tools Format tab and then click the *Dark Green, Accent 2, Darker 25%* option (sixth column, fifth row in the *Theme Colors* section).

f. Change the font size of the WordArt text to 28 points.

g. Drag the WordArt so it is positioned as shown in Figure 5.26A.

h. Click outside the WordArt text box to deselect it.

5. Insert the zebra picture shown in Figure 5.26A by completing the following steps:

a. With the insertion point still positioned outside the WordArt text box, click the Insert tab and then click the Pictures button in the Illustrations group.

b. At the Insert Picture dialog box, navigate to the C5 folder and then double-click *zebra.png*.

c. With the zebra image selected, click the Wrap Text button in the Arrange group and then click the *In Front of Text* option at the drop-down gallery.

d. Make sure that the entire zebra image is visible. If not, adjust the position of the image.

e. Click the Remove Background button in the Adjust group on the Picture Tools Format tab.

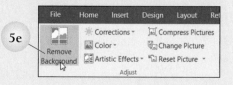

f. Position the mouse pointer on the bottom middle sizing handle of the zebra image background and then drag the bottom border of the background down to the bottom of the image.

g. Drag the left middle sizing handle until the left border of the background is just left of the zebra's left ear.

h. Drag the top middle sizing handle up until the top border of the background is just above the zebra's ears.

i. Drag the right middle sizing handle until the right border of the background is at the right border of the image. (Make sure the parts of the image that remain match what you see in the image to the right and in Figure 5.26A on page 181. You may need to continue to adjust the borders or use the Mark Areas to Keep button to ensure that the background has been completely removed and the desired parts of the image display.)

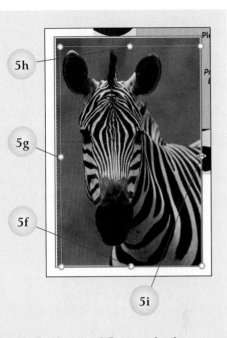

j. Click the Keep Changes button in the Close group on the Background Removal tab.

k. Change the height of the zebra image to 1.8 inches.

l. Drag the zebra image so it is positioned as shown in Figure 5.26A.

6. Save, print, and then close **5-SafariBall.docx**.

7. Display a new blank document, insert a text box, and then modify it by completing the following steps:

a. Change the height of the text box to 7.1 inches and the width to 5.1 inches.

b. Change the position to Position in Middle Center with Square Text Wrapping.

c. Apply the Facet theme.

d. Make the Drawing Tools Format tab active, click the More Shape Styles button in the Shape Styles group, and then click the *Subtle Effect - Green, Accent 1* option (second column, fourth row in the *Theme Styles* section).

e. With the insertion point positioned in the text box, insert **SafariAuction.docx** from the C5 folder.

8. Insert and modify the WordArt as shown in Figure 5.26B by completing the following steps:

a. Click the Insert tab if necessary to make it active, click the WordArt button in the Text group, and then click the *Gradient Fill: Red, Accent color 5; Reflection* option (second column, second row).

b. Type LIVE AUCTION ITEMS:.

c. Click the border of the WordArt text box to select it.

d. Click the Text Fill button arrow in the WordArt Styles group on the Drawing Tools Format tab and then click the *Dark Green, Accent 2, Darker 25%* option (sixth column, fifth row in the *Theme Colors* section).

e. Change the font size of the WordArt to 26 points.

f. Position the WordArt as shown in Figure 5.26B.

g. Click outside the WordArt text box to deselect it.

9. Insert and modify the image of the leopard by completing the following steps:

a. Click in the upper left corner of the document, outside the announcement text box, and then insert **leopard.png** from the C5 folder using the Insert Picture dialog box. *Hint: Make sure the insertion point is not positioned inside the text box.*

b. Change the height of the image to 2 inches.

c. Apply Tight text wrapping.

d. Apply the Drop Shadow Rectangle picture style (fourth option in the Picture Styles group).

e. Position the leopard image as shown in Figure 5.26B.

10. Click in the upper left corner of the document, outside the announcement text box, and then insert and modify the image of the lion by completing the following steps:

a. Insert **lion.png** from the C5 folder using the Insert Picture dialog box.

b. Change the height of the image to 2 inches.

c. Apply Tight text wrapping.

d. Apply the Center Shadow Rectangle picture style (fourth option in the Picture Styles group).

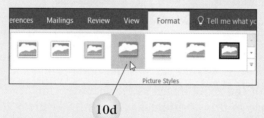

10d

e. Click the Send Backward button in the Arrange group on the Picture Tools Format tab.

f. Position the lion image as shown in Figure 5.26B.

11. Insert the image of the paw prints by completing the following steps:

a. Click in the upper left corner of the document, outside the announcement text box, and then insert **paws.png** from the C5 folder using the Insert Picture dialog box.

b. Change the text wrapping for the image to In Front of Text.

c. Apply the Orange, Accent color 4 Dark color (fifth column, second row in the *Recolor* section of the Color button drop-down gallery).

d. Move the paws image to the bottom of the text box, as shown in Figure 5.26B.

12. Save the document with the name **5-SafariBallBack**.

13. Print the document on the back of **5-SafariBall.docx**. Trim the page to 5 inches by 7 inches.

14. Close **5-SafariBallBack.docx**.

Check Your Work

Figure 5.26 Front and Back of the Announcement Created in Project 4

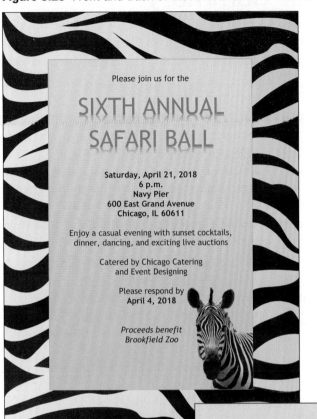

A

B

Chapter Summary

- A flyer advertises a product or service that is available for a limited amount of time. An announcement informs an audience of an upcoming event.

- Flyers and announcements are among the least expensive means of advertising.

- In planning a flyer or announcement, use a table to organize the text, graphics, and other design elements on the page.

- Consider using unique typefaces, bold and italic formatting, WordArt, text effects, asymmetrical design, and white space to grab the reader's attention and effectively communicate the message of the flyer.

- Graphics added to a flyer or announcement can create excitement and generate enthusiasm for the product, service, or event. A simple graphic demands more attention and has more impact than a complex one.

- When scanning an image, consider the destination where it will be saved and the necessary resolution and file format.

- A bitmapped, or raster, image is composed of pixels of color. A vector graphic is composed of shapes that are mathematically defined.

- Save a scanned or imported image from a camera in these commonly used file formats: JPEG (joint photographic experts group), PNG (portable network graphics), TIFF (tagged image file format), GIF (graphics interchange format), and BMP (bitmapped image).

- Incorporate color in a publication through text and images by using colored paper or a colored page background; by adding lines, shapes, and borders; and by including special graphics, such as charts and graphs.

- When adding color to a document, consider the brightness, which is the relative lightness of a picture, the gradient, which is an effect created by a gradual varying of color, and the grayscale, which is a range of shades from black to white.

- By default, page color does not print. To print the page color in a document, display the Word Options dialog box, click *Display* in the left panel, click the *Print background colors and images* check box to insert a check mark, and then click OK to close the dialog box.

- Borders and lines added to a document aid directional flow, add color, and organize text to produce professional-looking results.

- Crop an image to trim off the edges and make it fit in a placeholder. Cropping can also help to create focus on part of an image and to remove unnecessary parts.

- Delete the cropped portions of an image to reduce the size of the file. Deleting the cropped portion of an image cannot be undone.

- Add fill, which is color, shading, or other background, inside a drawing object with options at the Shape Fill button drop-down gallery located in the Shape Styles group on the Drawing Tools Format tab.

- The drawing grid is a network of lines that help align drawing objects. Turn on the display of gridlines by clicking the *Gridlines* check box in the Show group on the View tab, and adjust gridline settings with options at the Grid and Guides dialog box.

- Selecting a font color that matches one of the colors from an image in a document is a good way to create unity. Ungroup the image, select the portion that contains the desired color, display the Colors dialog box to discover the color formula, and then apply that color to the selected fonts.

- Apply effects to lines, text boxes, and shapes with options on the Drawing Tools Format tab and the Format Shape task pane. Apply effects to images, such as pictures and clip art, with options on the Picture Tools Format tab and the Format Picture task pane.

- Use options at the Corrections button drop-down gallery in the Adjust group on the Picture Tools Format tab to adjust the brightness, lightness, contrast, sharpness, and softness of an image. The correction of an image can also be adjusted with options in the Format Picture task pane.

- Use options at the Color button drop-down gallery in the Adjust group on the Picture Tools Format tab to adjust the saturation, color tone, and recolor of an image.

- Color tone is the overall color temperature of an image, where reds and yellows are warm and blues and greens are cool. The color of an image can also be adjusted with options in the Format Picture task pane.

- Make an image transparent to better show any text that is layered on top of it, to layer images on top of each other, or to remove or hide parts of an image.

- Use options at the Artistic Effects button drop-down gallery in the Adjust group on the Picture Tools Format tab or in the Format Picture task pane to make an image look like a sketch, drawing, or painting.

- Compress a picture to reduce the size of the file and to permanently remove any cropped areas.

- Use the Remove Background button on the Picture Tools Format tab to remove unwanted portions of a picture.

- Apply creative borders and effects to a picture with picture styles, which are available on the Picture Tools Format tab.

Commands Review

FEATURE	RIBBON TAB, GROUP	BUTTON, OPTION
artistic effects	Picture Tools Format, Adjust	
compress pictures	Picture Tools Format, Adjust	
corrections	Picture Tools Format, Adjust	
crop	Picture Tools Format, Size	
draw table	Table Tools Layout, Draw	, Draw Table
drawing grid	View, Show	
eraser	Table Tools Layout, Draw	
Grid and Guides dialog box	Layout, Arrange	, Grid Settings
page borders	Design, Page Background	
page color	Design, Page Background	
picture color	Picture Tools Format, Adjust	
picture effects	Picture Tools Format, Picture Styles	
remove background	Picture Tools Format, Adjust	
shape effects	Drawing Tools Format, Shape Styles	
table	Insert, Tables	

Workbook

Chapter study tools and assessment activities are available in the workbook pages of the ebook. These resources are designed to help you further develop and demonstrate mastery of the skills learned in this chapter.

Creating Newsletters

Performance Objectives

Upon successful completion of Chapter 6, you will be able to:

1   Plan and understand the basic elements of a newsletter

2   Design the page layout of a newsletter

3   Create a newsletter with elements such as a nameplate, folio, subtitle, headline, byline, body text, subhead, and images

4   Distribute a newsletter via the mail, email, and the web

5   Save a newsletter as a template

6   Understand newsletter design and formatting techniques

7   Add design elements to a newsletter, including headers and footer, spot color, sidebars, a table of contents, pull quotes, kickers, end signs, linked text boxes, captions, and a masthead

Desktop Publishing Terms

body text	folio	MHTML	sidebar
byline	graphic	mirror margins	spot color
caption	gutter	nameplate	subhead
column	headline	orphan	subtitle
copyfitting	HTML	pull quote	table of contents
drop cap	jump line	river	tombstoning
em space	kicker	screening	widow
end sign	masthead	self-mailer	

Word Features Used

borders and shading	headers and footers	page numbers	styles
building blocks	linked text boxes	pictures	symbols
captions	mail merge	quick parts	templates
column breaks	margins	save as template	text boxes
columns	page borders	section break	Widow/Orphan control

Data Files

Before beginning chapter work, copy the C6 folder to your storage medium and then make C6 the active folder.

You will create a newsletter that contains a nameplate, subtitle, headline, subhead, byline, image, logo, folio, and body text. You will also learn how to distribute the newsletter via mail, email, and the web.

Preview Finished Project

Planning a Newsletter

A newsletter is used to communicate information to a group of people, such as members of a club or employees within an organization. Before beginning a newsletter, first create a plan. Deciding on what content to include in a newsletter is easier once the audience and the purpose for the newsletter have been determined. This will give the newsletter a clear focus, which will more effectively hold the reader's interest. Consider the following questions when planning a newsletter:

- What is the purpose or goal of the newsletter? Is it to sell, inform, explain, or announce something?

- Who will be the audience of the newsletter? What do they need to know? What do they want to know?

DTP POINTER

Examine as many newsletters as possible to get design ideas.

- What image should the newsletter project? How will this be achieved?

- Will the newsletter contain graphics, such as images, illustrations, and advertisements?

- How often will the newsletter be published? What items should be repeated in each issue?

- What is the budget for creating the newsletter? How much time can be devoted to creating it?

Understanding the Basic Elements of a Newsletter

Successful newsletters contain consistent elements in every issue. This makes it easy for readers to find what they need, and the ultimate goal of any newsletter is to effectively communicate the content. The basic elements of a newsletter are shown in Figure 6.1 and can be described as follows:

- **Nameplate:** Contains the newsletter's title and is usually located on the front page. The nameplate (also known as the *banner*) can include the company logo, a unique typeface, or an image to help reinforce an organization's identity.

- **Folio:** Contains the publication information that changes from issue to issue, including the volume number, issue number, and current date of the newsletter. The folio usually appears near the nameplate but can also be displayed at the bottom or side of a page. In desktop publishing, the term *folio* can also be used to refer to the page number.

- **Subtitle:** A short phrase describing the purpose and/or audience of the newsletter. The subtitle (or *tagline*) is usually located below the nameplate, near the folio.

- **Headlines:** Titles of articles, which organize the text and attract the reader's attention. Headlines can be set in 18-point type or larger and generally in a sans serif typeface.
- **Bylines:** Identify the authors of articles. The byline is usually located under the headline.
- **Body text:** The main content of a newsletter (also known as *body copy*).
- **Subheads:** Secondary headings that provide the transition from headlines to body text. Subheads may also be referred to as *section headings* because they are sometimes used to break up the text into sections. Subheads are usually set in bold and in a larger type size than the body text.
- **Graphics:** Images and illustrations added to a newsletter to support and expand on points made in the body text and to add interest to the document.

Figure 6.1 Identifying Basic Elements in a Newsletter

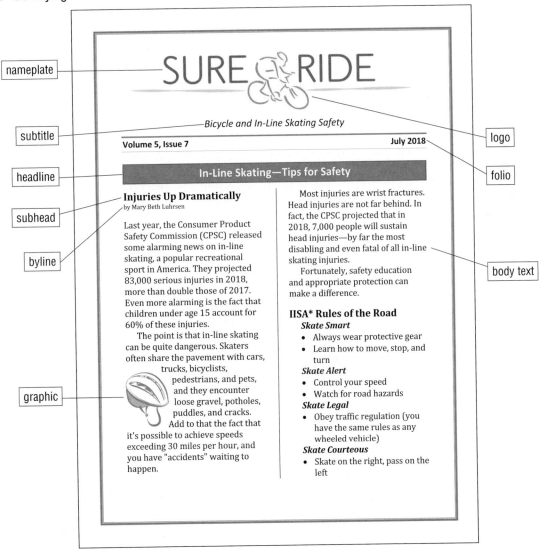

Designing the Page Layout of a Newsletter

The desktop publishing concepts and guidelines discussed in previous chapters provide the basic principles for designing a newsletter. These principles emphasize the use of consistency, balance, proportion, contrast, white space, focus, directional flow, and color. If designing a newsletter or any other document for a company or another organization, make sure the design coordinates with the organization's identity by using the same logos, typefaces, type sizes, column arrangements, and color choices that are used in other correspondence.

Typically, page layout begins with choosing the paper size and type and determining the margins for the newsletter. Next, decisions are made about the number, length, and width of columns. Typefaces, type sizes, and typestyles must also be considered, as well as graphics, ruled lines, borders, shading, and coloring. Also consider whether creating styles of the commonly used elements will be helpful for saving time and effort in creating a newsletter.

Applying Design Concepts

One of the biggest challenges in designing a newsletter is balancing change with consistency. A newsletter is typically reproduced on a regular basis—often monthly, bimonthly, or quarterly. Each new issue contains new ideas, articles, and graphic elements. However, for a newsletter to be effective, each issue must also have a consistent organization and appearance. Consistency contributes to the publication's identity and gives the reader a feeling of familiarity.

DTP POINTER
Newsletter design should be consistent from issue to issue.

Features that may be kept consistent among issues of a newsletter include the margins; column layout; nameplate formatting and location; logos; color; ruled lines; and formatting of headlines, subheads, and body text. Automate the process of formatting consistent elements by creating styles, which will be discussed later in this chapter.

DTP POINTER
Use no more than one or two images per page if possible.

Focus and balance can be achieved through the design and size of the newsletter's nameplate; the arrangement of text on the page; the use of graphics; and the careful placement of lines, borders, and backgrounds. When including graphics, use restraint. A single, large, well-placed image is usually preferred over many small images scattered throughout the document. Size images according to their relative importance to the content. Headlines and subheads can serve as secondary focal points as well as provide balance throughout the document as a whole.

As discussed in Chapter 1, white space creates contrast and attracts the reader's eyes. Surround text with white space to make it stand out. To draw attention to the nameplate or headline of the newsletter, consider choosing a bold typestyle, a larger type size, or a WordArt style in addition to surrounding the text with white space. Use sufficient white space throughout a newsletter to break up blocks of text and offer the reader visual relief.

DTP POINTER
Use graphic accents with discretion.

Good directional flow can be achieved by using ruled lines that guide the reader's eyes through the document. Graphic elements placed strategically throughout a newsletter can also provide a pattern for the reader's eyes to follow. If using color in a newsletter, do so sparingly. Establish focus and directional flow by using color to highlight key information and elements in the publication.

Analyze how all of these design concepts discussed were achieved in the newsletter shown in Figure 6.1 on page 187. What does this newsletter design do well? How could it be improved?

Choosing Paper Size and Type

The first considerations in designing a newsletter page layout are the type of paper and the paper size. The number of copies needed and the equipment available for creating, printing, and distributing the newsletter can affect this decision. Most newsletters are created on standard 8.5-by-11-inch paper, although some are printed on larger sheets, such as 8.5-by-14-inch paper. The most economical choice for printing is standard 8.5-by-11-inch paper. This size of paper is easier to hold and read, is cheaper to mail, and fits easily in standard file folders.

When deciding on the weight of the paper for a newsletter, consider the cost, the quality desired, and the images to be included. Typically, the heavier the stock, the more expensive the paper. In terms of color, note that white paper can create glare, making reading more difficult. If possible, investigate other more subtle colors. Another option is to purchase predesigned newsletter paper from a paper supply company. These papers come in many colors and designs and often contain differently shaded areas on a page to help separate and organize text.

Setting Margins in a Newsletter

After considering the paper that will be used for the newsletter, determine the margins of the pages. The sizes of the margins are linked to the number of columns needed, the formality desired, the visual elements to be used, the amount of text to be included, and the type of binding, if any. Keep the margins consistent throughout the newsletter. The following are a few general rules for setting newsletter margins:

- A wide right margin is considered formal. This approach positions the text at the left side of the page—the side where most readers tend to look first. If the text is justified, the newsletter will appear even more formal.
- A wide left margin is less formal. A table of contents or marginal subheads can be placed in the left margin to give the newsletter an airy, open appearance and make it easier for the reader to find what he or she needs.
- Equal left and right margins tend to create an informal look.

If creating a multiple-page newsletter with left-and-right facing pages, consider using **mirror margins**, whereby the outside margins of the pages are equal and the inside margins of the pages are equal, creating a mirror image, as shown in Figures 6.2 and 6.3. Often, the inside margins are wider than the outside margins; however, this may depend on the amount of space needed for the binding, as discussed in the next paragraph. To create facing pages with mirror margins, click the Margins button in the Page Setup group on the Layout tab and then click *Mirrored* at the drop-down list. Another method to insert mirrored margins is to click the Margins button and then click *Custom Margins* at the drop-down list. At the Page Setup dialog box with the Margins tab selected, click the *Multiple pages* option box arrow in the *Pages* section and then click *Mirror margins* at the drop-down list. If including page numbers, position the numbers on the outside edges of the pages.

When creating a multiple-page newsletter, increase the inside margins to create a **gutter** to accommodate the binding. Gutter space can be added to the left side or the top of a page. To bind a document such as a book with facing pages, adding gutter space to the inside margins may be necessary. This means adding space to the left margins of odd pages and the right margins of even pages. To add gutters, display the Page Setup dialog box with the Margins tab selected, specify whether

Figure 6.2 Understanding Mirror Margins with a Wider Outside Margin

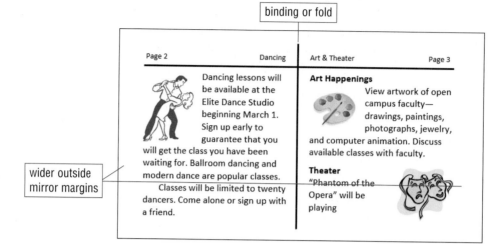

Figure 6.3 Understanding Mirror Margins with a Wider Inside Margin

DTP POINTER

Use extra-wide gutters or margins to counteract dense text.

to add gutter space to the left or top margin with the *Gutter position* option, and then enter the gutter measurement in the *Gutter* measurement box. To add gutter space to facing pages, first apply mirror margins and then enter a measurement in the *Gutter* measurement box.

Creating Columns in a Newsletter

column

A vertically oriented block of text with short lines; text flows from the bottom of one column to the top of the next

When preparing a newsletter, another important consideration is the readability of the document. The line length of the text can enhance or detract from readability. Setting the text in columns can make reading easier for the audience. **Columns** are vertically oriented blocks of text with short lines in which text flows from the bottom of one block to the top of the next. Columns will be used to format the newsletter created throughout this chapter; however, keep in mind that linked text boxes can be used to position text within a newsletter, which will be discussed later in the chapter.

Tutorial

Formatting Text into Columns

 Columns

Using columns in a newsletter promotes text organization and helps guide the reader's eyes. When the first column on the page is filled with text, the insertion point moves to the top of the next column on the same page in a snaking pattern. When the last column on the first page is filled, the insertion point moves to the beginning of the first column on the second page and so on.

Create columns by clicking the Columns button in the Page Setup group on the Layout tab. At the drop-down list, click *One, Two, Three, Left, Right,* or *More Columns.* The *Left* and *Right* options create columns of unequal width, providing an asymmetrical layout. Clicking the *More Columns* option displays the Columns dialog box, as shown in Figure 6.4. Options at this dialog box allow for customizing the widths of the columns and the white space between them.

Using Balanced and Unbalanced Columns

Word automatically lines up (balances) columns by filling every column to the last line. However, on the last page of a newsletter, there may not be enough text to balance the columns. For example, in a two-column layout, the text in the first column may flow to the bottom of the page, while the text in the second column may end near the top. Columns can be manually balanced by positioning the insertion point at the end of the text in the last column of the section to be balanced, clicking the Layout tab, clicking the Breaks button, and then clicking *Continuous* in the *Section Breaks* section.

Breaks

Figure 6.5A shows the last page of a document containing unbalanced columns. Figure 6.5B shows the same page after the columns have been balanced. To force a new page to start after the balanced columns, click after the continuous break and then manually insert a page break by pressing Ctrl + Enter.

Determining the Number of Columns

The number of columns used in a newsletter may vary from one column to two or more columns. The size of the paper used, the font and type size selected, the amount of text and other content available, and other design considerations will affect this decision.

A one-column newsletter is easy to produce because the articles simply follow each other. The one-column format is the simplest to design and work with because it allows for making changes and additions easily. A one-column newsletter requires a larger type size (usually 11 or 12 points) to accommodate the long line length.

Figure 6.4 Customizing Columns at the Columns Dialog Box

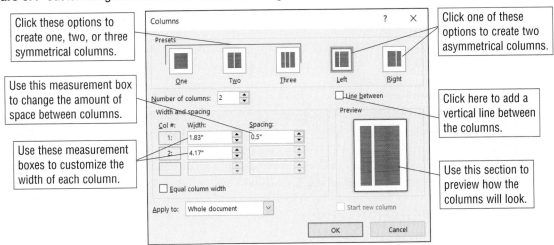

Figure 6.5 Comparing Unbalanced and Balanced Columns

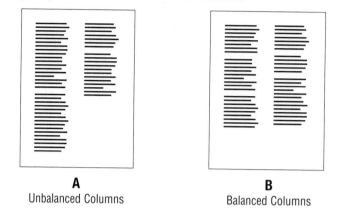

A
Unbalanced Columns

B
Balanced Columns

Be sure to use wide margins with a one-column layout. Consider including a table of contents, a schedule, or some other text box feature on one side of a one-column newsletter, as shown in Figure 6.6A.

tombstoning

Occurs when headlines or subheads display side by side in adjacent columns

The two-column format, shown in Figure 6.6B, is most commonly used for newsletters. It conveys a professional look, especially if used with justified text. Generally, use type sizes between 10 and 11 points when using a two-column layout. Be careful to avoid *tombstoning*, which occurs when headlines or subheads display side by side in adjacent columns. Adding graphic enhancements will make this classic two-column format more interesting.

Figure 6.6 Comparing One-Column and Two-Column Newsletters

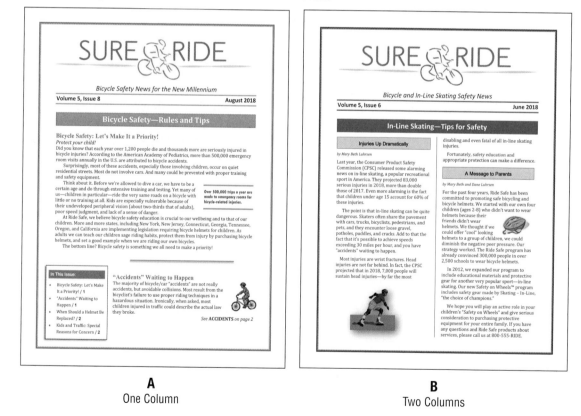

A
One Column

B
Two Columns

A three-column format can be successful because the nature of the layout prevents using too much text on the page. This popular format allows more flexibility for adding interesting design elements. Use a smaller type size (9 to 11 points) in this format if more text is necessary on a page. Placing headlines, subheads, text, and graphics across one, two, or three columns can create a distinctive flow. Often, one column on the first page of the newsletter is reserved for a table of contents, marginal subheads, or other design elements, thus allowing for more white space in the document and creating more visual interest.

A four-column format allows for even more flexibility than a three-column format; however, it may be more time consuming to lay out. Leaving one column fairly empty with a great deal of white space to offset more text-intensive columns is a visually appealing solution. This format provides many opportunities to display headlines, subheads, graphics, and other design elements across one or more columns. Using a small type size for the text (9 to 10 points) may be necessary. Also consider printing on larger-sized paper when using a four-column layout.

Using Varying Numbers of Columns

Section breaks can be used to vary the page layout within a single newsletter. For example, use a section break to separate a one-column nameplate from text that is formatted in three columns, as shown in Figure 6.7. Three methods are available for inserting section breaks in a document. The first method involves selecting from the break options at the Breaks button drop-down list. For the second method, insert a section break by selecting the *This point forward* option at the *Apply to* option box at the Columns dialog box. For the third method, select the text first and then apply column formatting.

To move the insertion point between columns, use the mouse or press Alt + Up Arrow to move the insertion point to the top of the previous column. Press Alt + Down Arrow to move the insertion point to the top of the next column.

When formatting text in columns, Word automatically breaks the columns to fit the page. If a column breaks in an undesirable location, insert a column break to control where one column ends and another begins on the page. To insert a column break, position the insertion point where the new column will begin and then press Ctrl + Shift + Enter. Another option is to click the Breaks button on the Layout tab and then click *Column* in the *Page Breaks* section of the drop-down list.

Figure 6.7 Using Section Breaks in a Newsletter

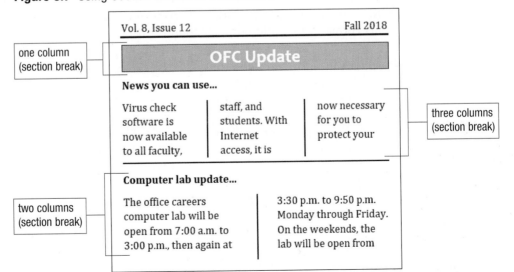

Changing the Number of Columns

To change the number of columns for an entire newsletter, select the newsletter text by pressing Ctrl + A. To change the number of columns for a portion of a document, select the text or sections to change. After selecting the text, click the Columns button and then select the number of desired columns at the drop-down list. To remove column formatting, select the sections to change, click the Columns button, and then click *One* at the drop-down list.

Changing Column Widths

If the newsletter is divided into sections, click in the section to be changed and then drag the column marker on the horizontal ruler. If an adjacent column is hampering efforts to change the width of another column, change the width of the adjacent column first. If the column widths are equal, all the columns will change. If the column widths are unequal, only the column being adjusted will change. To specify exact measurements for column widths, hold down the Alt key to display the column width measurements while dragging the column marker on the ruler. Another option is to display the Columns dialog box and then type exact measurements in the measurement boxes.

Adding Vertical Ruled Lines between Columns

To add a vertical ruled line between columns, position the insertion point in the section where the line is to be added. Display the Columns dialog box, click to insert a check mark in the *Line between* check box (see Figure 6.4 on page 191), and then close the dialog box.

Adding Borders and Horizontal Lines to Newsletter Pages

Change the appearance of pages of a newsletter by adding borders around pages, paragraphs, images, and text boxes and by adding horizontal lines between paragraphs. To add a page border, click the Page Borders button in the Page Background group on the Design tab. At the Borders and Shading dialog box with the Page Border tab selected, choose a particular line style, color, and width or select a predesigned art border. Make sure that *Whole document* displays in the *Apply to* option box.

To create a border around a paragraph of text, click the Borders tab at the Borders and Shading dialog box and then make desired changes to the line style, color, and width. Make sure that *Paragraph* displays in the *Apply to* option box. Use options in the Picture Styles group on the Picture Tools Format tab to add borders around images, and use options in the Shape Styles group on the Drawing Tools Format tab to add borders around text boxes.

Add a horizontal line to a document by clicking the Online Pictures button in the Illustrations group on the Insert tab, using the search text *horizontal line* at the Insert Pictures window, clicking a specific horizontal line, and then clicking the Insert button. Format the horizontal line with options on the Picture Tools Format tab. Another method for adding a horizontal or vertical line to a newsletter is by clicking the Shapes button in the Illustrations group on the Insert tab, clicking a line in the *Lines* section, and then drawing a line in the document. Customize the line with options on the Drawing Tools Format tab.

Using Drop Caps in a Newsletter

A *drop cap* is created by setting the first letter of the first word in a paragraph in a larger font size and then extending it down into the paragraph or out into the margin. Drop caps are typically used to identify the beginnings of major sections

Tutorial

Inserting a Page
Border

Tutorial

Applying Borders

Page
Borders

drop cap

Created by setting
the first letter of
the first word in
a paragraph in a
larger font size and
extending it down
into the paragraph
or out into the
margin

or parts of a document, and they can be used to enhance the appearance of publications such as magazines, brochures, and newsletters.

A drop cap looks best within a paragraph of text set in a proportional font. The drop cap can be set in the same font as the paragraph text or in a complementary font. For example, set a drop cap in a sans serif font and the paragraph text in a serif font. A drop cap can be limited to one character or the entire first word of a paragraph can be set as drop caps.

Create a drop cap with options at the Drop Cap button drop-down list in the Text group on the Insert tab. Choose to set the drop cap in the paragraph or in the margin. Click *Drop Cap Options* at the Drop Cap button drop-down list to display the Drop Cap dialog box. At this dialog box, specify the font, the number of lines the letter will drop, and the distance the letter will be positioned from the text of the paragraph.

Tutorial

Creating and Removing a Drop Cap

 Drop Cap

Using Styles in a Newsletter

Using styles is especially valuable for saving time, effort, and keystrokes in creating a newsletter. A newsletter contains elements that must remain consistent from page to page as well as from issue to issue. Using styles reinforces this consistency by saving formatting instructions with names so they can be applied over and over.

One method for creating a customized style is to apply formatting to text and then create a style based on that formatting. To create a style based on existing formatting, select the text or object, click the More Styles button in the Styles group on the Home tab, and then click *Create a Style* at the drop-down gallery. At the Create New Style from Formatting dialog box, type a name for the style and then click OK.

Creating a Newsletter

The initial steps in creating a newsletter involve designing its basic elements, including a nameplate, a folio, and a subtitle. The next section will discuss creating text elements, such as headlines, bylines, body text, and subheads, along with inserting and editing graphics. The following sections will provide guidance on creating and placing each element of the Summit Outreach newsletter created in Project 1.

Creating a Nameplate

nameplate

The artwork and/or type that includes the name of the newsletter; usually placed at the top of the first page; also called the *banner*

DTP POINTER

A nameplate should sell the contents of a newsletter.

Creating a nameplate is the first step in creating a newsletter. A **nameplate** (also known as a *banner*) is the artwork, such as a logo or other graphic, and/or type that includes the name of the publication and is usually placed at the top of the first page of a newsletter. It captures the reader's eyes and immediately identifies the newsletter. The choices of fonts and type sizes and the design of the name are important for several reasons. They help the reader form his or her first impression of the newsletter, and they are used in every issue.

The nameplate created in Project 1a consists of the organization's logo, the organization's name, and the newsletter name set in the same colors as those used in the logo (green and gold). The nameplate is generally the same from issue to issue. Saving the nameplate as a style is not necessary, but it should be saved in the newsletter template.

Figure 6.8 illustrates several examples of nameplates. Review the uses and different locations of elements. Looking at other newsletters can help to develop skills in newsletter design and layout.

Figure 6.8 Illustrating Sample Nameplates

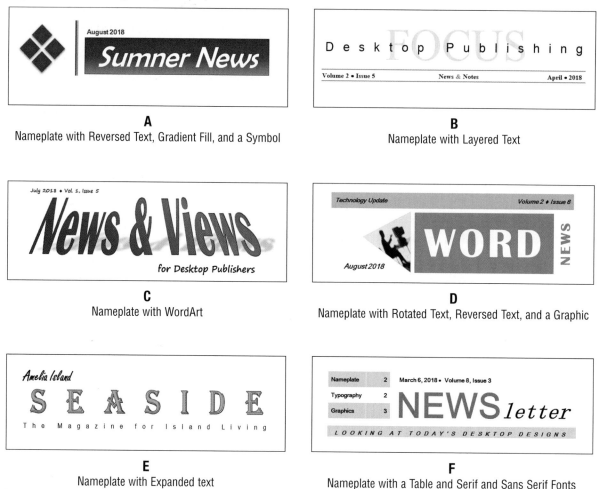

A
Nameplate with Reversed Text, Gradient Fill, and a Symbol

B
Nameplate with Layered Text

C
Nameplate with WordArt

D
Nameplate with Rotated Text, Reversed Text, and a Graphic

E
Nameplate with Expanded text

F
Nameplate with a Table and Serif and Sans Serif Fonts

Project 1a Creating a Nameplate for a Newsletter

Part 1 of 8

1. Display a blank document and then save it with the name **6-Nameplate**.
2. Change the top, bottom, left, and right margins to 0.5 inch. *Hint: Click the* **Narrow** *option at the Margins button drop-down list.*
3. Apply the Organic theme and the Franklin Gothic theme fonts.
4. With the insertion point positioned at the beginning of the document, press the Enter key 10 times. Press Ctrl + Home to position the insertion point back at the top of the document and then insert **SOLogo.png** from the C6 folder.
5. Format, size, and position the logo as shown in Figure 6.9 on page 211 by completing the following steps:
   a. With the logo selected, apply Square text wrapping.
   b. Resize the logo by typing 1.4 in the *Shape Height* measurement box in the Size group on the Picture Tools Format tab.
   c. Position the logo as shown in Figure 6.9.

6. Draw a text box to the right of the logo that measures approximately 1 inch in height and 5.4 inches in width and then format the text box, and the text within the text box, by completing the following steps:

   a. With the text box selected, type 1 in the *Shape Height* measurement box in the Size group on the Drawing Tools Format tab. Next, type 5.4 in the *Shape Width* measurement box, and then press the Enter key.

   b. Position the insertion point inside the text box, change the paragraph alignment to right, and then type Summit Outreach.

   c. Select *Summit*, change the font to 60-point Haettenschweiler, and then apply the Gold, Accent 6 font color.

   d. Select the text *Outreach* and then change the font to 60-point Haettenschweiler.

   e. Click the Font Color button arrow and then click *More Colors* at the drop-down gallery. At the Colors dialog box, click the Custom tab, type 40 in the *Red* measurement box, 160 in the *Green* measurement box, and 75 in the *Blue* measurement box. Click OK to close the dialog box.

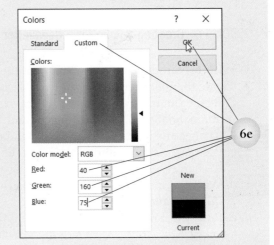

   f. Select *Summit Outreach* and then click the Font group dialog box launcher.

   g. At the Font dialog box, click the Advanced tab, change the *Spacing* option to Expanded, and then type 3 in the *By* measurement box right of the *Spacing* option box.

   h. Click the *Kerning for fonts* check box to insert a check mark, type 14 in the *Points and above* measurement box, and then click OK.

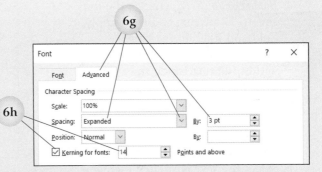

   i. Drag the text box containing *Summit Outreach* to a position similar to that shown in Figure 6.9 on page 211.

   j. Remove the shape fill and shape outline from the text box.

7. Draw a text box and then format it and the text within it by completing the following steps:

   a. With the text box selected, change the shape height to 0.6 inch and the shape width to 3.8 inches.

   b. Position the insertion point inside the text box, change the paragraph alignment to right, and then type Community Connections.

   c. Select *Community Connections,* change the font to 28-point Bell MT, apply italic formatting, and then turn on kerning for fonts 14 points and above.

   d. Remove the shape fill and shape outline from the text box and then position it as shown in Figure 6.9.

8. Save **6-Nameplate.docx**. *Note: You do not need to print until you are finished with the entire newsletter.*

Check Your Work

Creating a Folio

folio

Contains publishing information that changes from issue to issue, such as the volume number, issue number, and date

The *folio* in a newsletter consists of publishing information that changes from issue to issue, such as the volume number, issue number, and date. However, the formatting applied to the folio should remain consistent across all the issues. Frequently, the folio is preceded or followed by a graphic that sets the information apart from the rest of the nameplate. The folio may appear above or below the nameplate.

Reversed text can be used to add emphasis and interest. Using a thick font or applying bold formatting will make the font stand out against a shaded background, as in the Summit Outreach newsletter shown in Figure 6.9 on page 211.

Project 1b Creating a Folio for a Newsletter   Part 2 of 8

1. With **6-Nameplate.docx** open, save the document with the name **6-Folio**.
2. Create the folio for the newsletter in Figure 6.9 by completing the following steps:
   a. Below the text box containing *Community Connections*, draw a text box that measures approximately 0.3 inch in height and 7.5 inches in width.
   b. Change the shape height of the text box to 0.37 inch and the shape width to 7.5 inches.
   c. Position the insertion point inside the text box and then type Navigating Community Resources.
   d. With the insertion point still inside the text box, set a right tab at 7.2 inches. ***Hint: Use the Tabs dialog box.***
   e. Press the Tab key and then type Summer/Fall 2018.
   f. Select *Navigating Community Resources* and *Summer/Fall 2018*, change the font size to 12 points, and then apply bold and italic formatting.
   g. With the insertion point positioned within the text inside the text box, click the Paragraph group dialog box launcher, type 2 in the *Before* measurement box and 10 in the *After* measurement box in the *Spacing* section, and then click OK.

   h. Select the text box, click the More Shape Styles button in the Shape Styles group on the Drawing Tools Format tab, and then click the *Colored Fill - Gold, Accent 6* style option (last column, second row in the *Theme Styles* section). The text should automatically display in white.

   i. Position the text box as shown in Figure 6.9.

3. Create a style from existing formatting by completing the following steps:
   a. Select the folio text box.
   b. Click the More Styles button in the Styles group on the Home tab and then click *Create a Style* at the drop-down gallery.
   c. At the Create New Style from Formatting dialog box, type Folio in the *Name* text box and then click OK. **Hint: The Folio style is added to the list of styles in this document.**

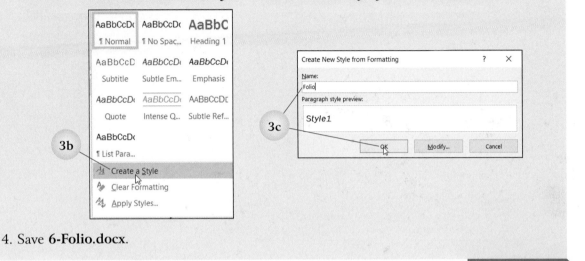

4. Save **6-Folio.docx**.

Check Your Work

Creating a Subtitle

subtitle

A short phrase that describes the purpose and/ or audience of a newsletter; usually appears below the nameplate and near the folio

The *subtitle* (or *tagline*) is a short phrase that describes the purpose and/or intended audience of the newsletter. The subtitle usually appears below the nameplate and near the folio. The text in the subtitle remains consistent from issue to issue. Creating a style for this element is not necessary because it should be saved as part of the newsletter template. A subtitle is usually set in a sans serif typeface of 14 to 24 points, and kerning should be turned on.

Project 1c Creating a Subtitle for a Newsletter   Part 3 of 8

1. With **6-Folio.docx** open, save the document with the name **6-Subtitle**.
2. Format the subtitle by completing the following steps:
   a. Above the text box containing *Summit Outreach*, draw a text box that measures approximately 0.3 inch in height and 5.25 inches in width.
   b. With the text box selected, change the shape height to 0.3 inch and the shape width to 5.25 inches.
   c. With the insertion point positioned inside the text box, change the font size to 10 points and the paragraph alignment to right.
   d. Type Published for the Volunteers of Summit Outreach Community Services.
   e. Remove the shape fill and shape outline from the text box and then position it as shown in Figure 6.9 on page 211. **Hint: Make sure the last characters in all the text boxes align vertically near the right margin.**

3. Group all the nameplate elements by completing the following steps:
   a. Press and hold down the Shift key and click to select each element.
   b. Click the Group button in the Arrange group on the Drawing Tools Format tab and then click *Group* at the drop-down list.

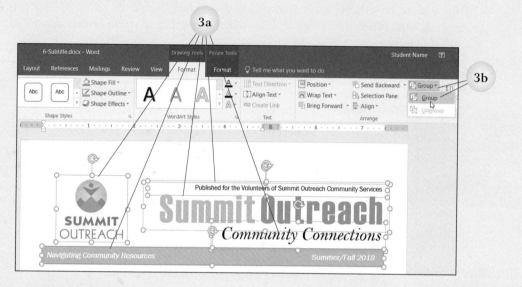

4. Save **6-Subtitle.docx**.

Check Your Work

Creating a Headline

headline

Describes the content of an article and helps organize the text of a newsletter

Headlines organize the text and tell the reader what information individual articles will communicate. To set the headlines apart from the text, use a larger type size, a heavier weight, and/or a different typeface. When determining the type size for headlines, start with 18 points and then increase the size until it is the desired size for the newsletter. As a guideline, choose a sans serif typeface for headlines; however, this is not a hard-and-fast rule.

Multiline headings often look better and are easier to read if the leading (the white space between lines) is reduced. Using all caps (sparingly) or small caps automatically reduces the leading below headlines because capital letters do not have descenders. A headline should have more space above than below. This indicates that the headline goes with the text that follows it, rather than the text that precedes it. Because headlines may be used several times in a newsletter, reinforce consistency and promote efficiency in formatting the document by creating a style.

Project 1d **Creating a Headline for a Newsletter**   Part 4 of 8

1. With **6-Subtitle.docx** open, save the document with the name **6-Headline**.
2. Create a section break between the folio and the headline by completing the following steps:
   a. Turn on the display of nonprinting characters by clicking the Show/Hide ¶ button in the Paragraph group on the Home tab.

b. Position the insertion point on the paragraph symbol below the folio, as shown at the right.

c. Click the Layout tab and then click the Breaks button in the Page Setup group.

d. Click the *Continuous* option at the drop-down list. This will insert a continuous section break below the folio at the bottom of the nameplate. ***Hint: If you cannot see the continuous section break in your document, move the nameplate up until the break is visible***.

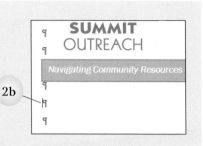

3. Turn on the columns feature by completing the following steps:

a. With the insertion point still positioned at the paragraph symbol below the folio (and below the continuous section break), click the Columns button in the Page Setup group on the Layout tab.

b. Click *More Columns* at the drop-down list.

c. At the Columns dialog box, click *Right* in the *Presets* section. This will create two asymmetrical columns where the left column is twice as wide as the right one.

d. Type 0.4 in the *Spacing* measurement box for column 1 in the *Width and spacing* section.

e. Click OK to close the dialog box.

f. Click the Show/Hide ¶ button in the Paragraph group on the Home tab to turn off the display of nonprinting characters.

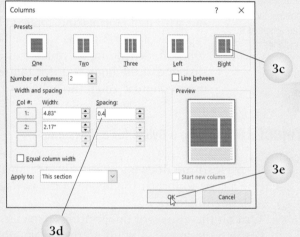

4. Create the headline by completing the following steps:

a. Change the font size to 28 points and apply bold formatting.

b. Change the font to the green color used in the banner (Red 40, Green 160, Blue 75).

c. Type New Era in Client Choice.

d. Select *New Era in Client Choice*, display the Font dialog box with the Advanced tab selected, and then turn on kerning for type 14 points and above.

e. With the headline still selected, click the Text Effects and Typography button, point to *Shadow* at the drop-down list, and then click the *Offset: Right* option at the side menu (first column, second row in the *Outer* section).

f. Position the insertion point in the headline and then click the Layout tab.

g. Type 12 in the *Before* measurement box in the Paragraph group, type 0 in the *After* measurement box, and then press the Enter key.

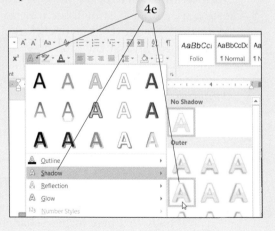

5. Create a style from existing formatting by completing the following steps:
   a. Position the insertion point anywhere in the headline text, click the More Styles button in the Styles group on the Home tab, and then click *Create a Style* at the drop-down gallery.
   b. At the Create New Style from Formatting dialog box, type Headline in the *Name* text box and then click OK. **Hint: The Headline style is added to the list of styles saved with this document.**
6. Save **6-Headline.docx**.

Check Your Work ▶

Creating a Byline

byline

Identifies the author of an article in a newsletter

The next step in building a newsletter is to create the byline. The **byline** identifies the author of an article and is often set in the same typeface as the body text but with italic formatting applied. The byline may be the same size as the body typeface or 1 or 2 points smaller. The byline may appear below the headline or subhead, depending on which is the title of the article, or it may appear as the first line of the body text if it follows a headline or subhead that spans two or more columns. Align the byline at the left margin or at the right side of a column.

Project 1e Creating a Byline for a Newsletter   Part 5 of 8

1. With **6-Headline.docx** open, save the document with the name **6-Byline**.
2. Create a style to format the byline in the newsletter as shown in Figure 6.9 on page 211 by completing the following steps:
   a. Turn on the display of nonprinting characters.
   b. Position the insertion point on the paragraph symbol below the headline text.
   c. Type By Cindy Lopez.
   d. Press the Enter key once if a paragraph symbol does not display after the byline.
   e. Select the byline *By Cindy Lopez,* change the font size to 9 points, and then apply italic formatting.
   f. With the byline still selected, click the Layout tab, type 6 in the *After* measurement box in the *Spacing* section in the Paragraph group, and then press the Enter key.
   g. Turn off the display of nonprinting characters.
3. Create a style from existing formatting by completing the following steps:
   a. With the byline text selected, click the More Styles button in the Styles group and then click *Create a Style* at the drop-down gallery.
   b. At the Create New Style from Formatting dialog box, type Byline in the *Name* text box and then click OK. **Hint: The Byline style is added to the list of styles saved with this document.**
4. Save **6-Byline.docx**.

Check Your Work ▶

Formatting Body Text

body text

The main content of the newsletter

The **body text** (or *body copy*) is the main content of a newsletter. Formatting the body text may include changing paragraph alignment, indenting the text, and controlling where the text breaks between pages.

Changing Paragraph Alignment

The type of paragraph alignment chosen for a newsletter influences the tone of the publication. Paragraphs can be aligned using buttons in the Paragraph group on the Home tab in a variety of ways: at the left margin; at the right margin; at both the left and right margins (justified); and centered between the margins, causing both the left and right margins to be ragged.

Justified text (text that aligns at both the left and right margins) is common in publications such as textbooks, newspapers, newsletters, and magazines. It is more formal than left-aligned text, but for justified text to convey a professional appearance, the line length must be appropriate. If the line length is too short, the words and/or characters in a paragraph may be widely spaced. When several consecutive lines have wide spaces between words, a channel of white space, or **river**, may run through the text. Remedying this situation requires increasing the line length, changing to a smaller type size, and/or hyphenating multisyllable words. Text aligned at the left margins is the easiest to read and is popular for publications of all kinds. Center alignment should be used only for small blocks of text.

Indenting Paragraphs with Em Spaces

In typesetting, tabs are generally measured by em spaces rather than inches. An **em space** is a space as wide as the point size of the surrounding type. For example, if the type size is 12 points, an em space is 12 points wide. Typically, the first lines of paragraphs in a newsletter should be indented one or two em spaces.

Em space indentations can be created in two ways. One way is to type an increment at the *Left* or *Right* indent measurement box in the Paragraph group on the Layout tab. Alternatively, create an em space at the Tabs dialog box. In Project 1f, the default tab setting will be changed to a 1.5 em space indentation for each paragraph that begins with a tab. This is accomplished by typing *18 pt* in the *Default tab stops* measurement box at the Tabs dialog box. Word will convert this point measurement to 0.25 inch because 1 horizontal inch contains 72 points. Be sure to use increments of em spaces for all the paragraph indentations in a newsletter. Also use em spaces around bullets and any other indented text.

Generally, the first paragraph after a headline or subhead is not indented even though all the remaining paragraphs are indented. Notice the paragraph formatting in Figure 6.9 on page 211.

Applying the Widow/Orphan Control Feature

The Widow/Orphan control feature in Word is turned on by default. This feature prevents the first and last lines of paragraphs from being separated across pages. A **widow** is a single line of a paragraph, headline, or subhead that is pushed to the top of the next page. A single line of text that appears by itself at the bottom of a page is called an **orphan**. The Widow/Orphan control option is located in the *Pagination* section of the Paragraph dialog box with the Line and Page Breaks tab selected.

Even with the Widow/Orphan control feature on, watch for subheads that are inappropriately separated from the text at the end of a column or page. To keep a heading or subhead with the text that follows it, consider inserting a check mark in the *Keep with next* check box in the Paragraph dialog box with the Line and Page Breaks tab selected. Another option is to select the text to keep together and then insert a check mark in the *Keep lines together* check box.

Align Left

Center

Align Right

Justify

river

A channel of white space in the text caused by having wide spaces between words in several consecutive lines

em space

A space as wide as the point size of the surrounding type

widow

A single line of a paragraph or heading that is pushed to the top of the next page

orphan

A single line of text that appears by itself at the bottom of a page

1. With **6-Byline.docx** open, save the document with the name **6-Body**.
2. Position the insertion point on the blank line below the byline text. Using the Object button on the Insert tab, insert the text file **ClientChoice.docx** from the C6 folder.
3. Format the body text by completing the following steps:
   a. Select the text from *Saturday, September 8* to the end of the document and then verify that the font is 11-point Franklin Gothic Book.
   b. With the text still selected, click the Paragraph group dialog box launcher to display the Paragraph dialog box.
   c. Click the Tabs button in the bottom left corner of the Paragraph dialog box.
   d. At the Tabs dialog box, type 18 pt in the *Tab stop position* text box, make sure *Left* is selected in the *Alignment* section, and then click the Set button. (Eighteen points is 1.5 em spaces, which is equal to approximately 0.25 inch.)

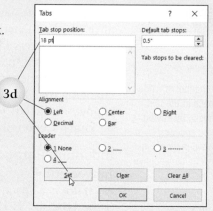

   e. Click OK to close the Tabs dialog box.
   f. One paragraph at a time (except the first paragraph), position the insertion point at the beginning of the paragraph and then press the Tab key.
4. Create a style to format the body text by completing the following steps:
   a. Position the insertion point in one of the indented paragraphs in the body of the newsletter. ***Hint: Do not position the insertion point in the first paragraph because it is not indented.***
   b. Click the More Styles button in the Styles group and then click *Create a Style* at the drop-down gallery.
   c. At the Create New Style from Formatting dialog box, type Body in the *Name* text box and then click OK. ***Hint: The Body style is added to the list of styles saved with this document.***
5. Add a drop cap to the first paragraph by completing the following steps:
   a. Position the insertion point in the word *Saturday* in the first paragraph.
   b. Click the Insert tab, click the Drop Cap button in the Text group, and then click *Drop Cap Options* at the drop-down list.
   c. At the Drop Cap dialog box, click the *Dropped* option in the *Position* section, change the *Font* option in the *Options* section to Bell MT, and then click OK.

6. Save **6-Body.docx**.

> **Check Your Work**

Creating a Subhead

subhead

A secondary heading that provides the transition between the headline and the body text

Subheads are secondary headings that provide the transition from headlines to body text. They help organize the text and give readers clues about the content. In addition, subheads provide contrast on text-intensive pages. Marginal subheads are sometimes placed in the left margin or in a narrow column left of the body text, providing an airy, open appearance. Subheads can be set in a larger type size, a different typeface, or a heavier weight than the text. They can be centered, left aligned, right aligned, or formatted in shaded boxes.

Inserting and Editing Graphics

graphic

An image or illustration added to support or expand on a point made in the text

Graphics, such as images and illustrations, are added to a newsletter to support and expand on points made in the text and to add interest to the document. Choose graphics carefully and use them sparingly. Also edit graphics to make them suitable for a particular newsletter, as will be done in Project 1g. Customize an image with options on the Picture Tools Format tab.

Project 1g   Inserting Graphic Elements into a Newsletter

Part 7 of 8

1. With **6-Body.docx** open, save the document with the name **6-Graphics**.
2. Position the insertion point at the beginning of the second column of text. (If necessary, turn on the display of nonprinting characters to determine where the column begins.)
3. Insert and format the image of a shopping cart as shown in Figure 6.9 on page 211, by completing the following steps:
   a. Click the Insert tab and then click the Pictures button in the Illustrations group.
   b. At the Insert Picture dialog box, navigate to the C6 folder and then double-click **shoppingcart.png**.
   c. With the image selected, click the Color button in the Adjust group on the Picture Tools Format tab and then click *Gold, Accent color 6 Light* (last column, last row in the *Recolor* section).
   d. With the image selected, click the Rotate button in the Arrange group and then click *Flip Horizontal* at the drop-down gallery. *Note: In most cases, graphics should face the text.*

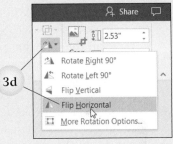

   e. Change the height of the image to 2.1 inches.
   f. Apply Square text wrapping to the image and then position it as shown in Figure 6.9.
   g. Turn on the display of nonprinting characters and then make sure that a paragraph symbol displays below the image. If not, move the image up until the paragraph symbol displays below it.
   h. Position the insertion point at the beginning of the paragraph below the image, click the Layout tab, type 18 in the *Before* measurement box in the *Spacing* section in the Paragraph group, and then press the Enter key.
   i. Turn off the display of nonprinting characters.
4. Insert the text box in the bottom right corner of the newsletter, as shown in Figure 6.9, by completing the following steps:
   a. With the insertion point positioned on the line below the image, click the Insert tab, click the Text Box button in the Text group, click the *Draw Text Box* option at the drop-down list, and then click in the document immediately right of the insertion point.
   b. Change the height of the text box to 2 inches and the width to 2.5 inches.
   c. With the insertion point positioned in the text box, change the spacing after paragraphs to 0 points, change the paragraph alignment to center, and then type the following:
      Our Vision (Press the Enter key.)
      Navigating Community Resources (Press the Enter key two times.)
      Our Mission (Press the Enter key.)
      Summit Outreach provides resource referrals and leadership in the community by coordinating and uniting resources to empower people to be self-sufficient.
   d. Select *Our Vision*, press and hold down the Ctrl key and select *Our Mission*, apply bold formatting, and then change the font color to the green used earlier in the newsletter (Red 40, Green 160, Blue 75).

e. Select *Summit*, apply bold formatting, and then change the font color to Gold, Accent 6.

f. Select *Outreach*, apply bold formatting, and then change the font color to the green used in Step 4d.

g. Click the text box border to select the text box, click the Borders button arrow in the Paragraph group on the Home tab, and then click *Borders and Shading* at the drop-down list.

h. At the Borders and Shading dialog box, change the *Color* option to the green used in this newsletter, change the *Width* option to 4 ½ pt, and then click the top border in the *Preview* section.

i. Change the *Color* option to Gold, Accent 6, change the *Width* option to 2 ¼ pt, click the bottom border in the *Preview* section, and then click OK to close the dialog box.

j. Remove the shape outline from the text box.

k. Apply Square text wrapping to the text box.

l. Position the image near the center of the right column, as shown in Figure 6.9 on page 211.

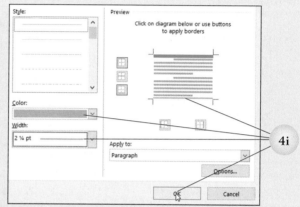

5. Insert a column break by completing the following steps:

a. Position the insertion point at the beginning of the last paragraph in the left column (begins *All distribution sessions*). Make sure the insertion point is positioned at the left margin (before the tab) rather than in the first word.

b. Click the Layout tab, click the Breaks button in the Page Setup group, and then click the *Column* option in the *Page Breaks* section of the drop-down list. The last paragraph of text should now display just below the shopping cart image in the right column. If necessary, reposition the shopping cart image and text box so they appear as shown in Figure 6.9.

6. Save **6-Graphics.docx**.

Check Your Work

Distributing Newsletters

Many methods are available for distributing a newsletter. Add addresses to newsletters and distribute them through the mail, or, save the costs of printing and mailing a newsletter by sending it as an email attachment or posting it on the web.

Mailing a Newsletter

self-mailer

A document that can be mailed without using an envelope

In Project 1h, the back of the newsletter created earlier will be formatted to create a self-mailer. A *self-mailer* is a document that can be mailed without using an envelope. After creating a self-mailer, insert merge codes into the self-mailer section of the newsletter and then merge the newsletter with an existing data source file. Use options on the Mailings tab to merge a newsletter with a data source file.

After completing the merge, fold the newsletter to send it through the mail. Before mailing a self-mailer newsletter, fold the newsletter in half or in thirds and attach a label or sticker to bind the halves or thirds together. Even though the U.S. Postal Service allows some stapled documents to be mailed, it is better not to use staples to close mail pieces. Staples can slow down sorting and delivery; they may require the mail piece to be handled manually instead of automatically and therefore increase the cost of processing the mailing.

Sending a Newsletter as an Email Attachment

DTP POINTER ❯

Email newsletters should be brief—typically no more than 1,000 words in length.

An inexpensive, easy, and effective alternative to mailing a newsletter is to send it as an email attachment. One option is to send the newsletter Word document as an email attachment. However, a better option is to save the newsletter in PDF format and then send it as an email attachment. The PDF format captures all the elements of a printed document as an electronic image that others can view, print, and forward, even if they do not have Word or another word processing software installed on their computers.

Save a Word document in PDF format by clicking the File tab, clicking the *Export* option, clicking the Create PDF/XPS button, making sure that *PDF (*.pdf)* displays in the *Save as type* option box at the Publish as PDF or XPS dialog box, and then clicking the Publish button.

Viewing a Newsletter on the Web

HTML

Stands for *Hypertext Markup Language*; a formatting and organizational language for displaying text, simple graphics, and hyperlinks on the web

 Web Page Preview

MHTML

Stands for *MIME HTML*; a file format that creates a single HTML document out of a web page and its supporting files; also known as *.mht* and *Single File Web Page*

A newsletter created in Word can be saved in a web format, such as **HTML** or **MHTML**, that allows for viewing the document in a web browser. If the newsletter is formatted in a table, the structure of the newsletter will stay in place when it is viewed on the web.

To save a newsletter in MHTML, click the File tab and then click the *Export* option. At the Export backstage area, click the *Change File Type* option, click the *Single File Web Page (*.mht, *.mhtml)* option, and then click the Save As button. At the Save As dialog box, type the file name and then specify where to save the document. Click the Change Title button, type a page title, (such as the title of the newsletter, which will display in the title bar of the browser) and then click OK. Click the Save button at the Save As dialog box and, if necessary, click the Continue button at the Microsoft Word Compatibility Checker.

To view the newsletter in a web browser, add the Web Page Preview button to the Quick Access Toolbar. Begin by clicking the Customize Quick Access Toolbar button at the right of the Quick Access Toolbar and then clicking the *More Commands* option at the drop-down list. At the Word Options dialog box with the *Quick Access Toolbar* option selected, click the *Choose commands from* option box arrow and then click *All Commands*. Scroll down the list, click the *Web Page Preview* option, click the Add button, and then click OK. Open the newsletter in Word and then click the Web Page Preview button to view the document as it will display on a web page in a chosen browser. Depending on the formatting applied to the newsletter in Word, elements in the newsletter may not appear in the same locations when saved in the MHTML format.

Project 1h Changing the Newsletter Layout, Saving the Newsletter in PDF Format,
and Merging to a Data Source   Part 8 of 8

1. With **6-Graphics.docx** open, save the document with the name **6-SummitNewsletter**.
2. Press Ctrl + End to position the insertion point at the end of the document (above the vision text box), click the Insert tab, and then click the Page Break button in the Pages group. *Hint: If the hard returns at the bottom of the first page automatically generate another page, you will not need to insert a page break.*
3. Click the Layout tab, click the Breaks button in the Page Setup group, and then click the *Continuous* option in the *Section Breaks* section of the drop-down list.
4. Change the column layout by completing the following steps:
    a. Click the Columns button in the Page Setup group and then click *More Columns* at the drop-down list.
    b. Click *Left* in the *Presets* section.
    c. Type 0.4 in the *Spacing* measurement box for column 1 in the *Width and spacing* section.
    d. Click OK to close the dialog box.

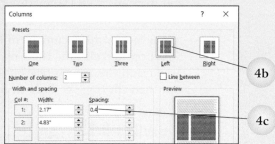

4b
4c

5. Insert the text box shown in the left column of page 2 of the newsletter in Figure 6.9 (page 211) by completing the following steps:
    a. With the insertion point positioned in the left column of the second page, click the Insert tab, click the Text Box button in the Text group, click *Draw Text Box*, and then click in the document right of the insertion point.
    b. Change the height of the text box to 2.1 inches and the width to 2.4 inches.
    c. With the insertion point positioned in the text box, change the spacing after paragraphs to 0 points, change the paragraph alignment to center, and then type the following text:
        Summit Outreach (Press the Enter key.)
        884 Alder Lane (Press the Enter key.)
        Bellingham, WA 98225 (Press the Enter key.)
        Phone: 360.555.8110 (Press the Enter key.)
        Fax: 360.555.8115 (Press the Enter key.)
        summit@emcp.com (Press the Enter key.)
        www.emcp.net/summit (Press the Enter key.)
        As we are a registered 501(c)(3) charity, all donations are fully tax deductible.
        Hint: If the (c) *typed in the last line automatically changes to a copyright symbol, immediately press Ctrl + Z to undo the change. Also, allow the email address and web address to display automatically as hyperlinks (light-green text with an underline).*
    d. Apply the green and gold font colors and then apply bold formatting as shown in Figure 6.9.
    e. Apply the green 4 ½ point border to the top of the text box and the gold 2 ¼ point border to the bottom of the text box, as instructed in Steps 4g through 4i in Project 1g.
    f. Remove the shape outline from the text box.
    g. Apply Square text wrapping to the text box and then position it as shown in Figure 6.9.
6. Create the text in the next column by completing the following steps:
    a. Position the insertion point below the text box on the second page and then press Ctrl + Shift + Enter to move the insertion point to the top of the next column. If necessary, move the text box back to the left side of the document and make sure it is positioned above the column break. You may need to turn on the display of nonprinting characters to view the column break.

b. At the top of the right column, type Client Nutrition and Supply and then press the Enter key.

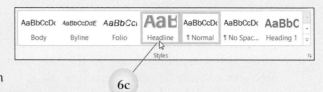

6c

c. Position the insertion point in *Client Nutrition and Supply* and then click the *Headline* option in the Styles group.

d. Click below the heading and then insert **NutritionandSupply.docx** from the C6 folder.

e. Select *By Cindy Lopez* and then apply the Byline style in the Styles group.

f. Select the article text and then apply the Body style in the Styles group.

g. Position the insertion point in the first word in the first paragraph, and then insert a drop cap in the Bell MT font that extends down into the paragraph, as shown in Figure 6.9 on page 211.

7. Create the mailing text by completing the following steps:

a. Position the insertion point at the end of the nutrition and supply text (after the period that follows *upon the available supply*).

b. Click the Layout tab, click the Breaks button in the Page Setup group, and then click the *Continuous* option in the *Section Breaks* section.

c. Click the Columns button in the Page Setup group and then click *One* at the drop-down list.

d. Insert **SOLogo.png** from the C6 folder.

e. With the logo selected, change the text wrapping to Square and then size and position the logo as shown on the second page of the newsletter in Figure 6.9.

f. Draw a text box for the Summit Outreach return address as shown in Figure 6.9.

g. Type the return address text in the text box. (Refer to Figure 6.9 for the return address text. Press Shift + Enter at the end of each line of the address.)

h. Remove the shape fill and shape outline from the text box.

i. Position the text box right of the logo, as shown in Figure 6.9.

j. Draw another text box for the merged mailing address in a location similar to that shown in Figure 6.9.

8. Insert the merge codes by completing the following steps:

a. Position the insertion point inside the mailing address text box, click the Mailings tab, click the Start Mail Merge button in the Start Mail Merge group, and then click *Normal Word Document* at the drop-down list.

b. Click the Select Recipients button in the Start Mail Merge group and then click *Use an Existing List* at the drop-down list.

8b

c. Navigate to the C6 folder and then double-click **BellinghamClients.mdb**.

d. Click in the empty mailing address text box, if necessary, and then click the Address Block button in the Write & Insert Fields group.

e. At the Insert Address Block dialog box, click OK.

f. Select the «Address Block» merge code in the text box, click the Layout tab, type 0 in the *After* measurement box in the *Spacing* section in the Paragraph group, and then press the Enter key. (This results in single-spacing the address.)

g. Remove the shape fill and shape outline from the text box.

h. Click the Finish & Merge button in the Finish group on the Mailings tab and then click *Edit Individual Documents* at the drop-down list.

i. Make sure that *All* is selected in the *Merge records* section of the Merge to New Document dialog box and then click OK.

9. Save the merged newsletter with the name **6-MergedNewsletter**.

10. Print only the merged newsletter addressed to Jansen Dell and then close **6-MergedNewsletter.docx**.

11. Save **6-SummitNewsletter.docx**.

12. Save the newsletter in PDF format by completing the following steps:

a. Click the File tab and then click the *Export* option.

b. Click the Create PDF/XPS button in the *Create a PDF/XPS Document* section.

c. At the Publish as PDF or XPS dialog box, navigate to the C6 folder and then type 6-SummitNewsletterPDF in the *File name* text box.

d. Insert a check mark in the *Open file after publishing* check box and then click the Publish button.

e. View the newsletter in PDF format and then close Adobe Acrobat Reader.

13. Save and then close **6-SummitNewsletter.docx**.

14. ***Optional:*** Create a circular label to be used when the newsletter is folded in half and sent through the mail. At a blank document, display the Label Options dialog box, choose Avery US Letter - 8293 High Visibility Round Labels, insert **SOLogo.png** from the C6 folder, and then copy the logo into each label. Save the label as **6-MailingLabel**. Print and then attach the label to the folded newsletter.

Check Your Work

Saving a Newsletter as a Template

To save time in creating future issues of a newsletter, save the newsletter as a template. To do this, delete all the text, pictures, and objects that will not remain the same in future issues. Conversely, leave the nameplate and all of the text, images, symbols, and so on that will remain the same (or use the same style) in each issue of the newsletter. For example, to save the Summit Outreach newsletter as a template, keep the following items and delete the rest:

- Folio (The month and volume/issue numbers will change but the titles will remain—use the folio text as placeholder text.)

- Nameplate

- Subtitle

- Headline (The headline text will change but the position and formatting will remain—use the headline text as placeholder text.)

- Byline (The byline text will change but the position and formatting will remain—use the byline text as placeholder text.)

- Body text (The body text will change but the formatting will remain— leave a paragraph as placeholder text.)

After the text and elements that will change with each issue have been deleted and replaced with placeholders (if desired), press the F12 function key to display the Save As dialog box. At the Save As dialog box, change the *Save as type* option to *Word Template (*.dotx)*. Navigate to the folder where the newsletter template will be saved, type a name for the template, and then click the Save button.

Figure 6.9 Summit Outreach Newsletter Created in Project 1

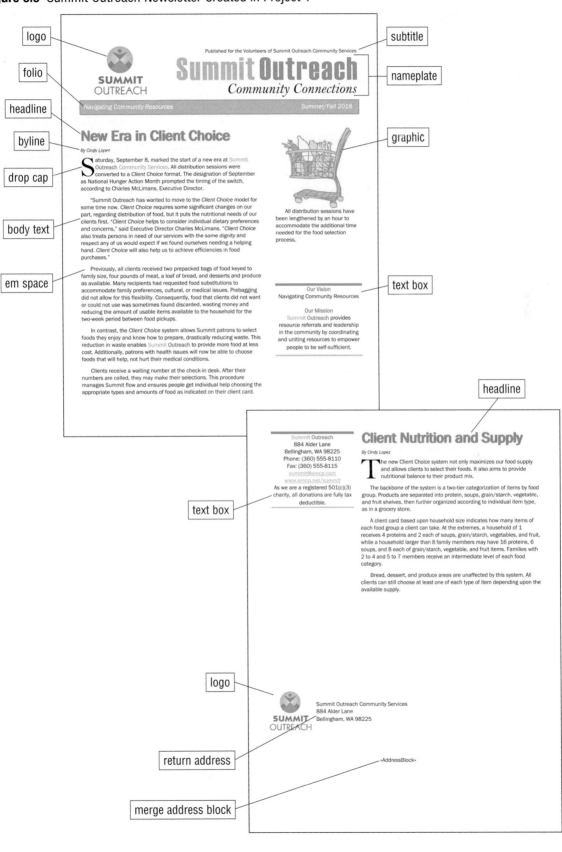

logo

folio

headline

byline

drop cap

body text

em space

subtitle

nameplate

graphic

text box

headline

text box

logo

return address

merge address block

Published for the Volunteers of Summit Outreach Community Services

Summit Outreach
Community Connections

Navigating Community Resources　　　　　　　*Summer/Fall 2018*

New Era in Client Choice

By Cindy Lopez

Saturday, September 8, marked the start of a new era at Summit Outreach Community Services. All distribution sessions were converted to a *Client Choice* format. The designation of September as National Hunger Action Month prompted the timing of the switch, according to Charles McLimans, Executive Director.

"Summit Outreach has wanted to move to the *Client Choice* model for some time now. *Client Choice* requires some significant changes on our part, regarding distribution of food, but it puts the nutritional needs of our clients first. "*Client Choice* helps to consider individual dietary preferences and concerns," said Executive Director Charles McLimans. "*Client Choice* also treats persons in need of our services with the same dignity and respect any of us would expect if we found ourselves needing a helping hand. *Client Choice* will also help us to achieve efficiencies in food purchases."

Previously, all clients received two prepacked bags of food keyed to family size, four pounds of meat, a loaf of bread, and desserts and produce as available. Many recipients had requested food substitutions to accommodate family preferences, cultural, or medical issues. Prebagging did not allow for this flexibility. Consequently, food that clients did not want or could not use was sometimes found discarded, wasting money and reducing the amount of usable items available to the household for the two-week period between food pickups.

In contrast, the *Client Choice* system allows Summit patrons to select foods they enjoy and know how to prepare, drastically reducing waste. This reduction in waste enables Summit Outreach to provide more food at less cost. Additionally, patrons with health issues will now be able to choose foods that will help, not hurt their medical conditions.

Clients receive a waiting number at the check-in desk. After their numbers are called, they may make their selections. This procedure manages Summit flow and ensures people get individual help choosing the appropriate types and amounts of food as indicated on their client card.

All distribution sessions have been lengthened by an hour to accommodate the additional time needed for the food selection process.

Our Vision
Navigating Community Resources

Our Mission
Summit Outreach provides resource referrals and leadership in the community by coordinating and uniting resources to empower people to be self-sufficient.

Summit Outreach
884 Alder Lane
Bellingham, WA 98225
Phone: (360) 555-8110
Fax: (360) 555-8115
summit@emcp.com
www.emcp.net/summit
As we are a registered 501(c)(3) charity, all donations are fully tax deductible.

Client Nutrition and Supply

By Cindy Lopez

The new Client Choice system not only maximizes our food supply and allows clients to select their foods. It also aims to provide nutritional balance to their product mix.

The backbone of the system is a two-tier categorization of items by food group. Products are separated into protein, soups, grain/starch, vegetable, and fruit shelves, then further organized according to individual item type, as in a grocery store.

A client card based upon household size indicates how many items of each food group a client can take. At the extremes, a household of 1 receives 4 proteins and 2 each of soups, grain/starch, vegetables, and fruit, while a household larger than 8 family members may have 16 proteins, 6 soups, and 8 each of grain/starch, vegetable, and fruit items. Families with 2 to 4 and 5 to 7 members receive an intermediate level of each food category.

Bread, dessert, and produce areas are unaffected by this system. All clients can still choose at least one of each type of item depending upon the available supply.

Summit Outreach Community Services
884 Alder Lane
Bellingham, WA 98225

«AddressBlock»

Project 2 **Create a Newsletter for Sure Ride** 9 Parts

You will create a newsletter that contains a header, footer, sidebar, table of contents, pull quote, kicker, end sign, jump line, image, caption, and masthead. The newsletter will also include linked text boxes and spot color.

Preview Finished Project

Understanding Newsletter Design and Formatting Techniques

The basic design elements and formatting techniques used in creating a newsletter have been introduced in this chapter. Additional design elements—such as tables, headers and footers, sidebars, table of contents, pull quotes, kickers, and end signs—can be included in a newsletter to maximize its impact on the intended audience.

Understanding Advanced Newsletter Design Elements

The most effective newsletters contain an appealing and well-positioned blend of text and visual elements. In Project 2, visual elements such as a table of contents, kicker, and sidebar will be used as focal points to draw the reader into the content of the newsletter. Design elements such as headlines, subheads, ruled lines, jump lines, and end signs can be used to indicate the directional flow of information in the document, and still other elements, such as page borders and pull quotes, can be used to provide balance, proportion, and contrast. All of these elements, if used in a consistent format and manner, can create unity within a single newsletter and among different issues of a newsletter.

Formatting a Newsletter Using Columns, Text Boxes, and Tables

Most newsletters are formatted in a two- or three-column layout. As discussed earlier in this chapter, the columns can be equal in width, providing a symmetrical design, or of varying widths, providing an asymmetrical design. In Word, three methods are available for creating columns in a newsletter: columns, text boxes, and tables.

Using the columns feature may seem like the simplest choice, especially when laying out a newsletter similar to the one created in Project 1. However, placing text within text boxes and tables allows changing the position or dimensions of an article, as is often required when trying to arrange elements in a newsletter. Another benefit to using text boxes is that they can be linked.

In a table, text will wrap around a graphic or text box inserted in a cell, whereas text will not wrap around elements such as shapes and additional text boxes if the original text is also contained within a text box. However, compared with text boxes, tables are not as easy to position, and trying to insert a text box within a table may produce unpredictable results.

Using Online Newsletter Templates

While creating a newsletter template provides more control over the design and layout of the document, it can be time consuming. To save time, consider choosing one of the online newsletter templates from Microsoft that are available at the New backstage area, as shown in Figure 6.10. (Note that the number of available online newsletter templates may vary from one time to the next because new ones are occasionally added to the collection.)

Previewing the newsletter templates in Word will show that most of them use linked text boxes as their underlying structures. The newsletter templates are also formatted using styles to reinforce consistency. In addition, the basic design and colors used in each newsletter remain consistent from page to page, and each newsletter includes many preformatted design elements, such as a nameplate, table of contents, pull quotes, picture captions, headers and footers, and sidebars.

Adding Design Elements to a Newsletter

As discussed earlier in the chapter, a number of basic elements are included in a newsletter. Enhance both the design and content of the newsletter by adding elements such as headers and footers, spot color, sidebars, a table of contents, pull quotes, kickers, end signs, linked text boxes, captions for images, and a masthead.

Figure 6.10 Choosing Online Newsletter Templates at the New Backstage Area

Type *newsletter* in the search text box to find online newsletter templates.

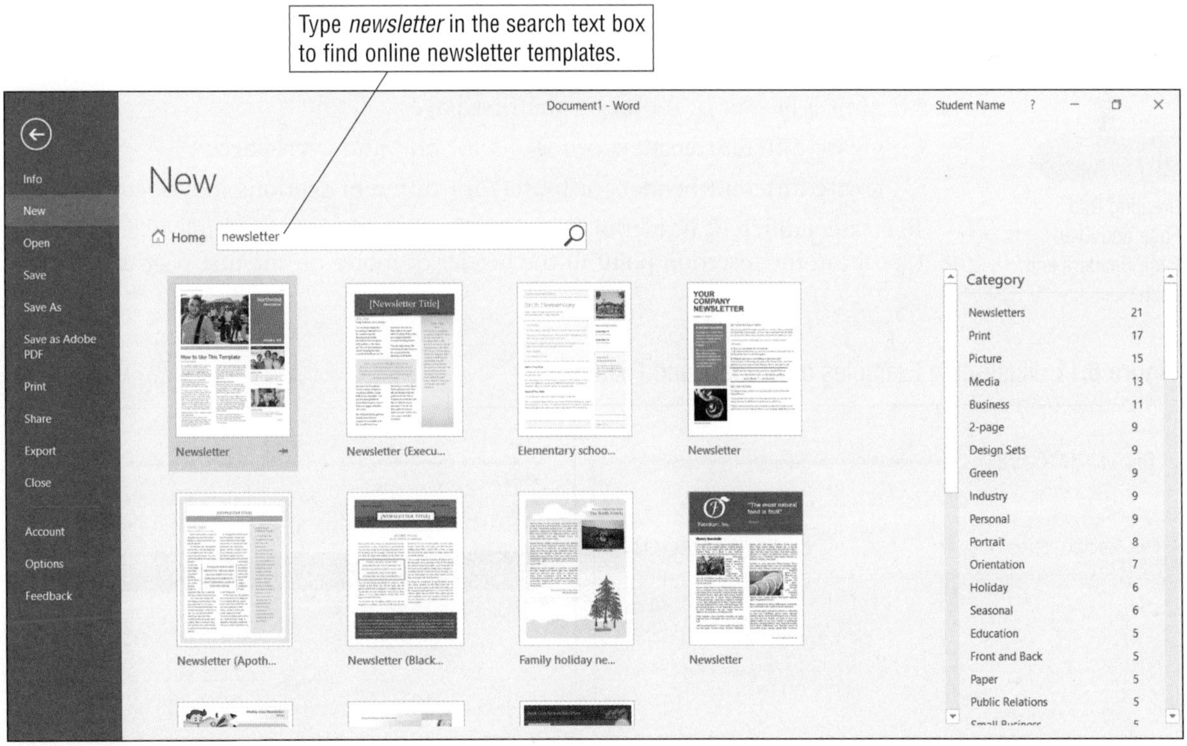

Creating Headers and Footers

Tutorial

Creating a
Custom Header
and Footer

 Header

Headers and footers (text repeated at the top and bottom of every page) are commonly used in newsletters, manuscripts, textbooks, reports, and other publications. A predesigned header or footer can be inserted in a document or a customized header or footer can be created from scratch.

To create a customized header, click the Insert tab, click the Header button in the Header & Footer group, and then click *Edit Header* at the drop-down list. Type text or insert objects in the Header pane and then click the Close Header and Footer button in the Close group on the Header & Footer Tools Design tab. Complete similar steps to create a customized footer.

DTP POINTER

Use a header and/or
footer to reinforce
the company or
organization identity.

DTP POINTER

Consistent
formatting of
the header and
footer helps to
establish unity in a
publication.

In a newsletter, information such as the page number, a slogan, the name of the newsletter, the issue number or date of the newsletter, and the name of the organization producing the newsletter are commonly placed in the header and/or footer, as illustrated in Figure 6.11. Because the header and footer are commonly repeated on every page (starting with the second page), they provide the perfect places to reinforce the identity of a company or organization. For example, including the company or organization name or a smaller version of the nameplate or logo in the header or footer can increase the reader's awareness of the brand identity. In Figure 6.11A, the Sure Ride header (the bottom header) includes both the company logo and the slogan. In Figure 6.11B, the Community News footer (the middle footer) includes the newsletter name and the page number set in reversed text in a green bar that ties in the colors used throughout the newsletter.

Creating Different Headers and Footers within a Newsletter

Tutorial

Creating a
Different First
Page Header and
Footer

Tutorial

Creating Odd
Page and Even
Page Headers and
Footers

By default, Word inserts a header and/or footer on every page in the document. However, different headers and footers can be created within the same document. For example, it is possible to do any of the following:

- create a unique header or footer on the first page
- omit a header or footer on the first page
- create different headers or footers for odd and even pages
- create different headers or footers for different sections in a document

To create a different header or footer on the first page of a multiple-page document, position the insertion point in the header or footer on the first page and then

Figure 6.11 Illustrating Examples of Headers and Footers

TRAINING*NEWS*

FINANCIAL SPOTLIGHT   NOVEMBER 2018

Winners wear helmets!

Page 2   Fly with Sunshine Air

COMMUNITY NEWS   3

3

A
Header Examples

B
Footer Examples

click the *Different First Page* check box in the Options group on the Header & Footer Tools Design tab to insert a check mark. The Header pane on the first page will be labeled *First Page Header,* and the Footer pane on the first page will be labeled *First Page Footer*. The first-page header or footer can include text or be left blank. To display a header or footer on the first page, type the text for the header or footer and then click the Next button in the Navigation group to move to the Header or Footer pane on the second page of the document. (Click the Previous button to edit the first-page header or footer after moving to the second page.) Type the text to be included in the header or footer for all the other pages in the document. Use the Go to Header or Go to Footer button in the Navigation group to move back and forth between the Header and Footer panes. When finished creating and editing headers and footers, click the Close Header and Footer button in the Close group.

Being able to provide different headers and footers on odd and even pages is useful when inserting page numbers in a multiple-page newsletter that has spreads (pages that face one another). Odd page numbers can be placed on the right sides of the pages, and even page numbers can be placed on the left sides of the pages. To create different odd and even page headers and footers, insert a check mark in the *Different Odd & Even Pages* check box in the Options group on the Header & Footer Tools Design tab. Be sure to keep the formatting consistent for both the odd- and the even-page headers and footers.

A new header or footer can be created for a new section of a newsletter. If the header or footer should print only on pages in a specific section and not on pages in previous sections, turn off the Link to Previous feature. This tells Word that the new header or footer applies exclusively to the current section. Break a section link by clicking the Link to Previous button in the Navigation group on the Header & Footer Tools Design tab.

Saving Headers and Footers

A customized header created from scratch is saved with the document. To make the header available for future documents, save it as a building block in the Header gallery. To do this, select the header, click the Header button on the Header & Footer Tools Design tab, and then click *Save Selection to Header Gallery* at the drop-down list. At the Create New Building Block dialog box, type a name for the header in the *Name* text box and then click OK. Complete similar steps to save a footer in the Footer gallery.

A header saved to the Header gallery is available at the Header button drop-down list or the Building Blocks Organizer dialog box. A footer saved to the Footer gallery is available at the Footer button drop-down list or the Building Blocks Organizer dialog box.

Adding Spot Color to a Newsletter

Adding *spot color* involves using one color as an accent in a black-and-white publication. Spot color can be applied to such elements as ruled lines, graphics, borders, background fills, headings, special characters, and end signs, as shown in Figure 6.12A. Spot color can also be applied to the background of a text box or to a drop cap. If a logo or organizational seal contains a particular color, consider using that color as a unifying element throughout the publication. Variations of a spot color can be obtained by *screening*, or producing a lighter shade of the same color. Refer to Figure 6.12 to see how spot color can add to the visual appeal of a publication.

Next

Previous

Go to Header

Go to Footer

Close Header and Footer

DTP POINTER

Right pages should have odd page numbers and left pages should have even page numbers.

 Link to Previous

spot color

One color added as an accent in a black-and-white publication

screening

Producing a lighter shade of a color

Figure 6.12 Comparing Versions of a Newsletter with and without Spot Color

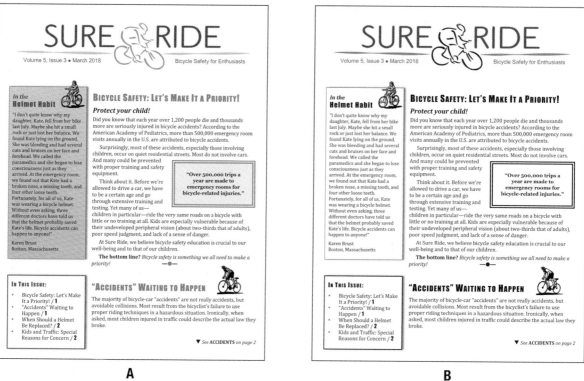

A
With Spot Color

B
Without Spot Color

Another way to incorporate spot color into a newsletter is by adding color to all or part of a black-and-white image. To add color to an entire image, select the image, click the Color button in the Adjust group on the Picture Tools Format tab to display a drop-down gallery of colors and effects, and then click an option. To add color to a specific part of an image, select the image, click the Group button in the Arrange group on the Picture Tools Format tab, and then click *Ungroup*. For many images, this will make it possible to select and apply color to each part of the image individually.

Some image formats, such as bitmap (.bmp), will not allow ungrouping an image. However, some changes can be made to the image by using the *Set Transparent Color* option at the Color button drop-down gallery, as shown in Figure 6.13A. After clicking the *Set Transparent Color* option, click the desired area of the image to make it transparent, as shown in Figure 6.13B. With the image selected, apply the new color by clicking the Shading button in the Paragraph group on the Home tab and then clicking the desired color, as shown in Figure 6.13C. To make more sophisticated changes to a bitmapped image, use a photo-editing program.

Make sure to use spot color sparingly. Just as an all black-and-white page may appear gray, using too much spot color can change the whole look of the document and fail to achieve the emphasis or contrast that was intended. Using spot color can make a black-and-white publication look brighter and more appealing, but keep in mind that using color always adds to the cost of printing. Be sure to price the cost of color printing during the planning stages of a project.

Figure 6.13 Using the *Set Transparent Color* Option to Change the Color in a Bitmapped Image

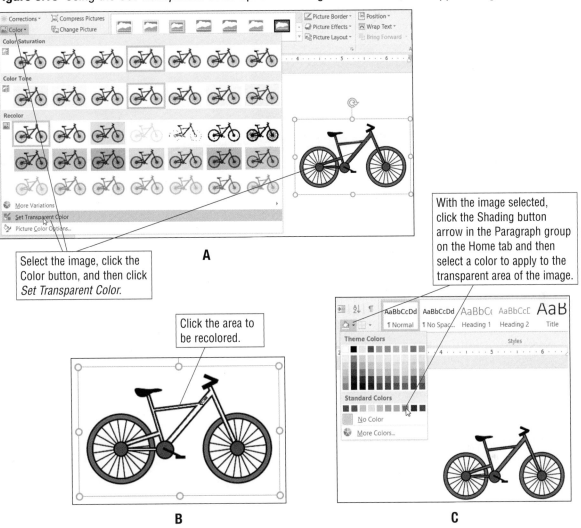

Select the image, click the Color button, and then click *Set Transparent Color*.

A

With the image selected, click the Shading button arrow in the Paragraph group on the Home tab and then select a color to apply to the transparent area of the image.

Click the area to be recolored.

B

C

Project 2a Creating a Header and Footer with Spot Color in a Newsletter

1. Open **NewsletterBanner.docx** from the C6 folder and then save it with the name **6-Header&Footer**.
2. Change the spot color in the Sure Ride logo in the banner by completing the following steps:
   a. Click on the bicycle logo. (This selects the entire banner. The banner contains four separate objects grouped together.)
   b. Click the Picture Tools Format tab.
   c. Click the Group button in the Arrange group and then click *Ungroup* at the drop-down list.
   d. Click outside the banner to deselect the objects and then click the bottom of the front bicycle tire. (This will select the part of the banner that contains the bicycle image and the two horizontal lines.)

2c

e. Click the Color button in the Adjust group and then select Green, Accent color 6 Light at the drop-down gallery (last column, bottom row in the *Recolor* section).

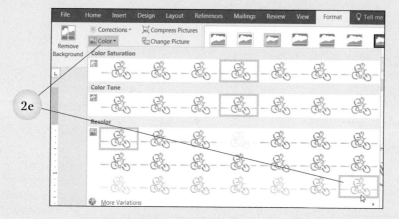

3. Create two uneven columns using the columns feature by completing the following steps. *Note: These columns are being set up for future projects and to avoid potential problems.*

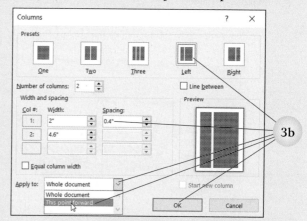

   a. Press Ctrl + End to position the insertion point below the newsletter banner, click the Layout tab, click the Columns button in the Page Setup group, and then click *More Columns* at the drop-down list.
   b. At the Columns dialog box, click *Left* in the *Presets* section, change the spacing after column 1 in the *Width and spacing* section to 0.4 inch, change the *Apply to* option to This point forward, and then click OK.
   c. Click the Breaks button in the Page Setup group on the Layout tab and then click the *Column* option in the *Page Breaks* section of the drop-down list.

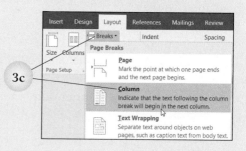

   d. With the insertion point positioned at the top of the column at the right, repeat the previous step to insert one more column break. This will produce a second page, which is necessary to create the headers and footers as described in Steps 4 and 5.
   e. Press Ctrl + Home to position the insertion point at the beginning of the document.
4. Create a different first-page header and footer by completing the following steps:
   a. Click the Insert tab, click the Header button in the Header & Footer group, and then click *Edit Header* at the drop-down list.
   b. On the Header & Footer Tools Design tab, click in the *Different First Page* check box in the Options group to insert a check mark. **Hint: The Header pane should be labeled First Page Header -Section 1-.**

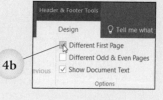

5. Create the header for the rest of the newsletter by completing the following steps:
   a. Click the Next button in the Navigation group. *Hint: The Header pane should be labeled **Header -Section 2-**.*
   b. Click the Link to Previous button in the Navigation group to turn off this feature. *Hint: If a prompt displays asking you to delete this header/footer and connect to the header/footer in the previous section, click No. You should not see **Same as Previous** displayed in the upper right corner of the header.*
   c. Click the Pictures button in the Insert group.
   d. At the Insert Picture dialog box, navigate to the C6 folder and then double-click *SureRideLogo.png*.

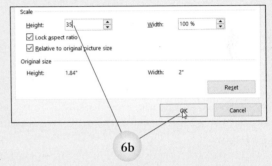

6. Format the image by completing the following steps:
   a. With the image selected, click the Size group dialog box launcher on the Picture Tools Format tab.
   b. At the Layout dialog box with the Size tab selected, click in the *Height* measurement box in the *Scale* section, type 35, and then click OK. (The width will automatically adjust to 35%.)
   c. With the image still selected, click the Color button in the Adjust group and then select the Green, Accent color 6 Light color at the drop-down gallery (last column, bottom row in the *Recolor* section).
   d. Click right of the image to deselect it.

7. In the Header pane on page 2, draw a text box right of the Sure Ride logo that will accommodate the dotted line and slogan shown on page 2 of the newsletter in Figure 6.19 on page 240. The text box should measure approximately 0.4 inch high by 6.5 inches wide.

8. On the Drawing Tools Format tab, make the following changes to the text box:
   a. Remove the shape fill and shape outline from the text box.
   b. Click the Position button in the Arrange group and then click *More Layout Options* at the drop-down gallery.
   c. At the Layout dialog box with the Position tab selected, change the *Absolute position* measurement in the *Horizontal* section to 1.4 inches and then change the *to the right of* option to Page.
   d. Change the *Absolute position* measurement in the *Vertical* section to 0.7 inch, change the *below* option to Page, and then click OK.
   e. Click the Shape Styles group task pane launcher.

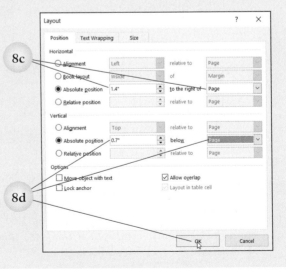

f. At the Format Shape task pane, make sure that *Shape Options* is selected at the top of the task pane, click the Layout & Properties icon, and then click *Text Box* to display the options.

g. Change the *Left margin* and *Right margin* measurements to 0 inches and then close the task pane.

9. Insert the dotted-line leader and the slogan by completing the following steps:

a. With the insertion point positioned in the text box, click the Home tab and then click the Paragraph group dialog box launcher.

b. At the Paragraph dialog box, click the Tabs button.

c. At the Tabs dialog box, type 6.5 in the *Tab stop position* text box, click the *Right* option in the *Alignment* section, click the *2 ....* option in the *Leader* section, click the Set button, and then click OK to close the dialog box.

d. Press the Tab key and then type Helmets save lives!

e. Select the slogan text and then change the font to Tempus Sans ITC and apply bold formatting.

f. Select the leader line dots and then change the font size to 14 points and the font color to Green, Accent 6, Darker 25%.

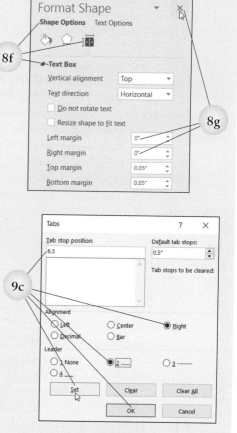

10. Create the footer that will begin on the second page by completing the following steps:

a. Click the Header & Footer Tools Design tab and then click the Go to Footer button in the Navigation group.

b. Verify that the left side of the Footer pane is labeled *Footer -Section 2-*. If *Same as Previous* displays at the right side of the Footer pane, click the Link to Previous button in the Navigation group to turn off this feature.

c. Click the Page Number button in the Header & Footer group, point to *Bottom of Page* in the drop-down list, scroll down the side menu, and then click the *Tildes* option.

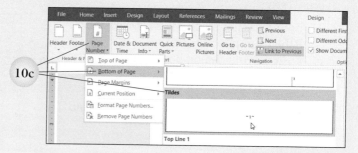

d. Select *2* in the footer and then change the font to Tempus Sans ITC.

e. Click the Close Header and Footer button in the Close group.

11. Preview the newsletter at the Print backstage area, comparing both pages against those shown in Figure 6.19 on page 240. Make sure that no header or footer text displays on page 1 and that the header and footer text correctly display on page 2. **Hint: You may need to adjust the bottom margin if the footer does not print properly.**

12. Save **6-Header&Footer.docx**.

Check Your Work

Creating Sidebars

A *sidebar* is a block of information or a related story that is set off from the body text using some type of box or border. A sidebar may include a photograph or another graphic along with the text. Frequently, a sidebar contains a shaded or screened background in an accent color that is used throughout the newsletter. A sidebar can be set in any position relative to the body text. In Word, a sidebar can easily be created by drawing a text box or by inserting a predesigned text box from the Text Box button drop-down list in the Text group on the Insert tab.

Project 2b Inserting a Sidebar into a Newsletter   Part 2 of 9

1. Insert a sidebar containing the *In the Helmet Habit* feature in the newsletter you started in Project 2a by completing the following steps:
   a. With **6-Header&Footer.docx** open, save the document with the name **6-Sidebar**.
   b. Turn on the display of nonprinting characters.
   c. Position the insertion point left of the first column break in the left column on page 1 and then turn on kerning at 14 points and above.

   d. Draw a text box just below the column break in the left column that is approximately the same size and in the same position as the sidebar shown in Figure 6.19 on page 240.
   e. Change the height of the text box to 4.7 inches and the width to 2.2 inches.
   f. Position the insertion point in the text box and then insert **HelmetHabitText.docx**. from the C6 folder. Do not be concerned if all the text is not visible at this point.
   g. Make sure the font size of the sidebar text is 10 points.
   h. Select the text box, click the Drawing Tools Format tab, click the Position button in the Arrange group, and then click *More Layout Options* at the drop-down gallery.
   i. At the Layout dialog box with the Position tab selected, click the *Alignment* option in the *Horizontal* section to select it, make sure that *Left* displays in the *Alignment* option box, and then change the *relative to* option to Margin.
   j. In the *Vertical* section, verify that the *Absolute position* option is selected, change the *Absolute position* measurement to 2.5 inches, change the *below* option to Page, and then click OK.

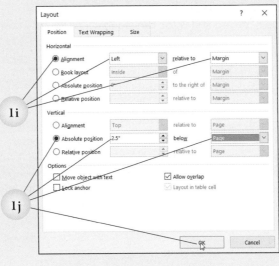

k. With the text box still selected, click the More Shape Styles button in the Shape Styles group and then click the *Subtle Effect - Green, Accent 6* option (last column, fourth row in the *Theme Styles* section).

l. With the text box still selected, click the Shape Effects button in the Shape Styles group, point to *Shadow*, and then click the *Offset: Right* option (first column, second row in the *Outer* section).

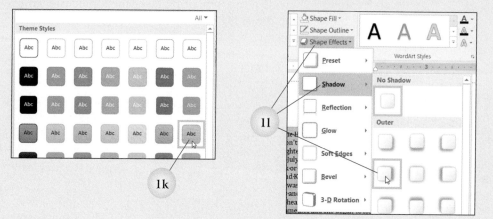

m. Click the Shape Outline button arrow in the Shape Styles group and then click the *Green, Accent 6, Darker 50%* option (last column, bottom row in the *Theme Colors* section).

2. Format the text inside the sidebar by completing the following steps:

a. Position the insertion point at the beginning of the title *In the Helmet Habit* and then press the Enter key.

b. Select *In the* and then change the font to 12 points, apply bold and italic formatting, and change the font color to Green, Accent 6, Darker 50%.

c. Position the insertion point in front of the word *Helmet* in the title, delete the space before *Helmet*, and then press the Enter key.

d. Select *Helmet Habit*; change the font to 14-point Impact; apply the Green, Accent 6, Darker 50% font color; and then expand the character spacing by 1.2 points.

e. Position the insertion point within the title text *In the*, display the Paragraph dialog box, change the *Line spacing* option to Exactly, type 10 in the *At* measurement box, and then click OK.

f. Position the insertion point within the title text *Helmet Habit* and then change the spacing after paragraphs to 6 points.

3. For use in future issues, create styles for the sidebar heading by completing the following steps:

a. Position the insertion point within the title text *In the* and then click the Home tab if necessary to make it active.

b. Click the More Styles button in the Styles group.

c. Click *Create a Style* at the drop-down gallery.

d. At the Create New Style from Formatting dialog box, type Sidebar Heading-1 in the *Name* text box and then click OK.

e. Position the insertion point within the title text *Helmet Habit* and then follow Steps 3b through 3d, naming this style *Sidebar Heading-2*.

4. Position the insertion point after . . . *anyone!"* in the last line of the sidebar text, press the Delete key to eliminate the extra hard return below this line, and then change the spacing after paragraphs to 6 points.

5. Insert the bicyclist image by completing the following steps:
   a. Deselect the text box and then make sure that the insertion point is not positioned in the text box containing the sidebar text.
   b. Click the Insert tab and then click the Pictures button.
   c. At the Insert Picture dialog box, navigate to the C6 folder and then double-click *bicyclist.jpg*. (Do not be concerned if parts of the newsletter move out of place. Adjustments will be made in the next step.)
6. Format the bicyclist image by completing the following steps:
   a. With the bicyclist image selected, click the Color button in the Adjust group, click the *Set Transparent Color* option at the drop-down list, and then click in the white background of the image.
   b. Click the Wrap Text button in the Arrange group on the Picture Tools Format tab and then click the *In Front of Text* option at the drop-down list.
   c. Use the corner sizing handles to reduce the size of the image so it is similar to the bicyclist image shown at the right and in Figure 6.19 on page 240.
   d. Click and drag the image so that it extends above the upper right corner of the sidebar text box, as shown in Figure 6.19.
7. Save **6-Sidebar.docx**.

Check Your Work

Creating a Table of Contents

table of contents

A list of articles, features, and other major elements and their page numbers

Tutorial

Customizing and Updating a Table of Contents

A **table of contents** is a list of the articles, features, and other major elements of a newsletter and their corresponding page numbers. Having a table of contents is optional in a one- or two-page newsletter, but in a multiple-page newsletter, a table of contents is an important and necessary element. The information presented in the table of contents may strongly influence whether the reader will read beyond the front page of the newsletter. Consequently, the table of contents should stand out from the surrounding information and be legible and easy to follow. Figure 6.14 shows a few examples of tables of contents in newsletters.

A table of contents is usually located on the front page of a newsletter. It is often placed in the lower left or lower right corner of the page. It can, however, be placed closer to the top of the page—on either side of or even within an asymmetrically designed nameplate. If a newsletter is designed to be a self-mailer (no envelope), the table of contents can be placed near the mailing address so the reader is invited into the newsletter before he or she even opens it.

The table of contents in the newsletter created in Project 2 is located in the lower left corner. The green border, bullets, bold title, and numbers make the table of contents easily identifiable and adds visual interest to the page. The table of contents, along with the drop-shadowed text box that contains it, will add weight to the left side of the page and balance to the page as a whole once the body text is added to the right side.

Figure 6.14 Understanding Tables of Contents in Newsletters

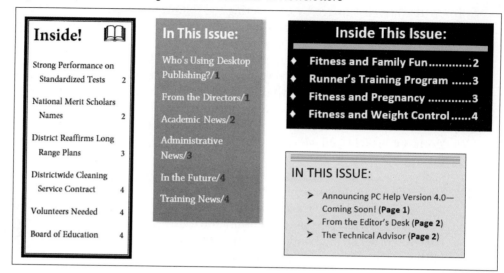

Project 2c Inserting a Table of Contents in a Newsletter

Part 3 of 9

1. With **6-Sidebar.docx** open, save the document with the name **6-TableofContents**.
2. Insert the table of contents text in a text box by completing the following steps:
   a. Draw a text box that is approximately the same size and in the same position as the table of contents text box shown in Figure 6.19 on page 240.
   b. Position the insertion point in the text box and then insert **TableofContentsText.docx** from the C6 folder.
   c. With the text box selected, click the Drawing Tools Format tab to make it active and then apply the Green, Accent 6, Darker 50% shape outline.
   d. Change the weight of the outline to 1½ points.
   e. Change the height of the text box to 2 inches and the width to 2.2 inches.
   f. Click the Position button in the Arrange group and then click *More Layout Options* at the drop-down list.
   g. At the Layout dialog box with the Position tab selected, change the *Absolute position* measurement in the *Horizontal* section to 0.03", and then change the *to the right of* option to Margin.
   h. In the *Vertical* section, verify that the *Absolute position* option is selected, change the *Absolute position* measurement to 6.9 inches, change the *below* option to Margin, and then click OK.

 i. Click the Shape Effects button in the Shape Styles group, point to *Shadow*, and then click the *Offset: Right* option at the side menu (first column, second row in the *Outer* section).

3. Select the title text *In This Issue:* and then apply the following formatting:

 a. Click the Home tab, click the More Styles button, and then click the *Subtle Reference* option.

 b. Change the font to 12-point Impact and apply the Green, Accent 6, Darker 50% font color.

 c. Expand the character spacing by 1.2 points.

 d. Change the spacing before paragraphs to 6 points and the spacing after paragraphs to 8 points.

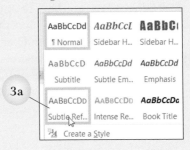

4. Select the remaining text below the title and then apply the following formatting:

 a. Change the font to 11-point Cambria. **Hint: Do not be concerned if some of the text is not visible at this point.**

 b. Display the Paragraph dialog box, type 2 in the *After* measurement box in the *Spacing* section, change the *Line Spacing* option to Exactly, type 12 in the *At* measurement box (if necessary), and then click OK.

 c. Click the Bullets button arrow in the Paragraph group and then click *Define New Bullet* at the drop-down gallery.

 d. At the Define New Bullet dialog box, click the Symbol button, select *Wingdings* in the *Font* option box, click the round bullet shown in the image below (character code 159, located in approximately the eighth row), and then click OK to close the Symbol dialog box.

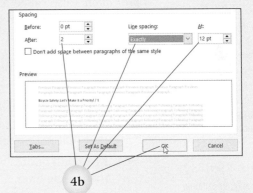

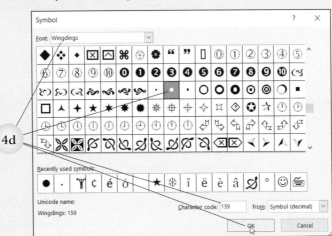

 e. At the Define New Bullet dialog box, click the Font button to display the Font dialog box; change the bullet color to Green, Accent 6, Darker 25%; and then click OK two times to close both dialog boxes.

f. Change the bullet position by displaying the Paragraph dialog box, typing 0 in the *Left* measurement box in the *Indentation* section, making sure that *Hanging* displays in the *Special* option box, typing 0.3 in the *By* measurement box, and then clicking OK.

g. Select each page number in the table of contents text box and change the font to Impact.

5. Save **6-TableofContents.docx**.

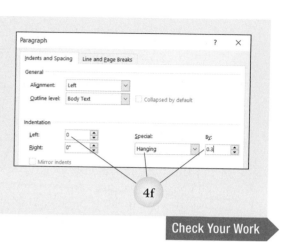

4f

Check Your Work

Creating Pull Quotes

A **pull quote** (also called a *pullout* or *callout*) is a direct phrase, summarizing statement, or important point associated with the body text of a newsletter. A pull quote acts as a focal point, helps to break up lengthy blocks of text, and provides visual contrast. Effective pull quotes are interesting, brief, and formatted to stand out from the rest of the body text. Using pull quotes is an excellent way to draw readers into an article.

Keep in mind the following tips when creating pull quotes for a newsletter:

- Include relevant and interesting text in pull quotes. Edit direct quotes so they will not be taken out of context when read individually as pull quotes.

- Keep pull quotes brief—approximately 10 to 15 words and never longer than a few lines.
- Set pull quotes in a font or font style that contrasts with the font used for the body text.
- Increase the type size to make pull quotes stand out from the body text.
- Apply bold and/or italic formatting to pull quotes.
- Set off pull quotes from the body text with ruled lines or graphics boxes.
- Use at least one element in the pull quote design that establishes a visual connection with the rest of the newsletter.
- Be consistent. Use the same format for all the pull quotes throughout one issue of the newsletter and throughout future issues of the same newsletter.

Project 2d Creating Styles and a Pull Quote in a Newsletter   Part 4 of 9

1. With **6-TableofContents.docx** open, save the document with the name **6-PullQuote**.
2. Position the insertion point left of the column break in the right column, press the Enter key, and then insert **BicycleSafetyText.docx** from the C6 folder.
3. Select the article heading *Bicycle Safety: Let's Make It a Priority!* and then make the following changes:
   a. Change the font to 18-point Impact; change the font color to Green, Accent 6, Darker 25%; and apply small caps formatting (Ctrl + Shift + K).
   b. Expand the character spacing by 1.2 points.
   c. Change the spacing after the paragraph to 6 points.

4. Create a style from this formatting to use with future article headings by completing the following steps:
   a. Position the insertion point in the article heading.
   b. Click the More Styles button in the Styles group on the Home tab and then click *Create a Style* at the drop-down gallery.
   c. At the Create New Style from Formatting dialog box, type Article Head in the *Name* text box and then click OK.
5. Format the article text by completing the following steps:
   a. Position the insertion point at the beginning of the line *Did you know* and then select all the article text.
   b. Change the font size to 11 points.
   c. Display the Paragraph dialog box, type 3 in the *After* measurement box in the *Spacing* section, change the *Special* option to First line, type 0.2 in the *By* measurement box, and then click OK.

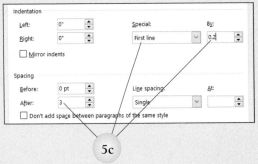

5c

6. With the article text still selected, create a style and name it Article Text.
7. Create a style for the first paragraph of the article that eliminates the first-line indentation by completing the following steps:
   a. Position the insertion point within the first paragraph of article text.
   b. Display the Paragraph dialog box, make sure the Indents and Spacing tab is selected, change the *Special* option to (none) in the *Indentation* section, and then click OK.
   c. Create a style and name it 1st Paragraph.
8. Create a pull quote by completing the following steps:
   a. Click the Insert tab, click the Text Box button in the Text group, scroll down the drop-down list, and then click the *Grid Quote* option.

   8a

   b. With the text placeholder selected in the pull quote text box, type "Over 500,000 trips a year are made to emergency rooms for bicycle-related injuries."
   c. Select the text in the pull quote text box, change the font to 10-point Georgia, apply bold formatting, remove italic formatting, change the font color to Black, Text 1, and then change the case to Sentence case. **Hint: Use the Change Case button in the Font group on the Home tab.**
   d. Select the pull quote text box; change the shape fill to Gold, Accent 4, Lighter 80%; and then change the shape outline to Green, Accent 6, Darker 25%.
   e. Change the height of the pull quote text box to 1.2 inches and the width to 2.3 inches.
   f. Drag the pull quote to a position similar to that shown in Figure 6.19 on page 240.
9. In the last paragraph of the article text, select *The bottom line?* and then apply bold formatting. Select the last sentence, *Bicycle safety is something we all need to make a priority!*, and then apply italic formatting.
10. Save **6-PullQuote.docx**.

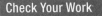

Creating Kickers and End Signs

kicker

A brief sentence or phrase that leads into an article

A *kicker* is a brief sentence or phrase that leads into an article. Generally, a kicker is set in a size smaller than the headline but larger than the body text. It is often stylistically distinct from both the headline and the body text. A kicker can be placed above or below the headline or article heading. In the newsletter shown in Figure 6.19 on page 240, the kicker is placed above the first article heading and serves as a lead-in to the first article.

end sign

A symbol or special character that indicates the end of an article

Symbols and special characters used to indicate the end of a section of text, such as the end of an article, are known as *end signs*. In the newsletter shown in Figure 6.19, an end sign follows the last paragraph in the first article. The end sign is the same color as the accent color in the newsletter, which contributes to the unified appearance of the publication. The end sign shown in the figure also mimics the dots in the header. Appropriate special characters or combinations of these characters—such as ௸, ◎, ✳, ❖, ✪, and ✄ from the Wingdings and Webdings fonts—may be used as end signs.

Project 2e   Creating a Kicker and an End Sign in a Newsletter   Part 5 of 9

1. With **6-PullQuote.docx** open, save the document with the name **6-EndSign**.
2. Create the kicker by completing the following steps:
   a. Position the insertion point at the beginning of the first paragraph below the article heading *Bicycle Safety*.
   b. Type Protect your child! and then press the Enter key.
   c. Select *Protect your child!* and then change the font size to 14 points and apply bold and italic formatting.
3. Create a style for the kicker formatting by completing the following steps:
   a. Position the insertion point within the kicker.
   b. Create a style and name it Kicker.
4. Create the end sign by completing the following steps:
   a. Position the insertion point before the paragraph mark at the end of the article (right of the exclamation point after the word *priority*) and then press the Tab key three times. *Hint: Make sure that italic formatting is turned off.*
   b. Click the Insert tab, click the Symbol button in the Symbols group, and then click *More Symbols* at the drop-down list.
   c. At the Symbol dialog box, click the Special Characters tab.
   d. Double-click the *Em Dash* option and then click the Symbols tab.
   e. Change the *Font* option to Wingdings 2 and then double-click the round bullet in approximately the eighth row (character code 152).
   f. Click the Special Characters tab again, double-click the *Em Dash* option, and then click the Close button.
   g. Select the end sign (the three new symbols you inserted) and then change the font to Impact.
   h. Select the round bullet and then change the color to Green, Accent 6, Darker 25%.
5. Save **6-EndSign.docx**.

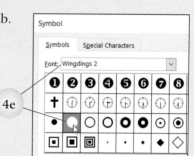

4e

Check Your Work

Using Linked Text Boxes in Newsletters

Featuring the beginnings of several articles on the first page of a newsletter increases the chance of attracting readers. Also, an article may be too lengthy to fit on one page, so continuing it on another page is necessary. This can be hard to manage when the body text of the newsletter is set in columns or a table, but it is easy to achieve using text boxes because of the text box linking feature in Word. This feature allows text to flow from one text box to another, even if the text boxes are not adjacent or even on the same page.

At least two text boxes are needed to create a link; however, any number of text boxes can be added to the chain of linked text boxes. When the first text box is filled, the text automatically flows into the second text box and then into the third text box and so on. If text is added to or deleted from one of the text boxes, the remaining article text in the other text boxes adjusts to the change.

Establish as many chains of linked text boxes in a newsletter as needed. For example, create one chain of linked text boxes for an article that begins on page 1 and continues on pages 3 and 4. For an article that begins on page 2 and continues on page 4 of the same newsletter, create another chain of linked text boxes.

Creating and Breaking the Link

Create two or more text boxes to link them. For example, if an article begins on page 1 and is to continue on page 2, create a text box on page 1 and then create another text box on page 2. Size the text boxes to fit within the column width and then position them as desired. If necessary, readjust the sizes and positions of the boxes later, after the text has been added.

To create a link between the two text boxes, complete the following steps:

1. Select the text box that is to be first in the chain.
2. Click the Drawing Tools Format tab, if necessary, to select it.
3. Click the Create Link button in the Text group. The mouse pointer will display as a small upright pitcher.
4. Position the mouse pitcher over the text box to be linked. The pitcher appears tipped with letters spilling out of it when it is over a text box that can receive the link, as shown in Figure 6.15. Click once to complete the link.
5. To create a link from the second text box to a third text box, select the second text box and then repeat Steps 2 through 4. Repeat these steps to add more links to the chain.
6. To break the chain of linked text boxes, click in the text box that precedes the text box to which the link will break and then click the Break Link button in the Text group on the Drawing Tools Format tab.

Create Link

Break Link

Creating Jump Lines

When starting an article on one page and continuing it on another, direct the reader to where he or she should go to read the rest of the text. A *jump line* is used to indicate that a newsletter article or feature continues on another page or is being continued from another page. To serve as an aid in the directional flow of information in a document, a jump line must be easily distinguishable from the surrounding text so the reader can find it. A jump line is commonly set in small italic type, approximately 2 points smaller than the body text. A jump line can also be enclosed in parentheses.

jump line

Text informing the reader that an article continues on another page or is being continued from another page

Figure 6.15 Linking Text Boxes

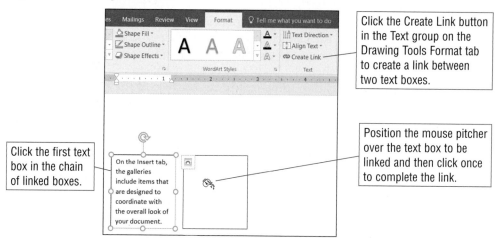

Click the Create Link button in the Text group on the Drawing Tools Format tab to create a link between two text boxes.

Position the mouse pitcher over the text box to be linked and then click once to complete the link.

Click the first text box in the chain of linked boxes.

On the Insert tab, the galleries include items that are designed to coordinate with the overall look of your document.

Project 2f Creating Linked Text Boxes and a Jump Line in a Newsletter

1. With **6-EndSign.docx** open, save the document with the name **6-JumpLine**.
2. Insert linked text boxes by completing the following steps:
   a. Make sure that nonprinting characters display and then scroll to the bottom of page 1.
   b. Draw a text box below the column break to hold the beginning of the second article. Adjustments will be made to the size and position of the text box in future steps so that it displays as shown in Figure 6.19 on page 240.
   c. Click to position the insertion point at the top of the left column on page 2 and then draw a text box to hold the remaining article text. Using the horizontal ruler as a guide, limit the width of the text box to the width of the left column. Adjustments will be made to the formatting, size, and position of this text box in Project 2i.
3. Create a link between the two text boxes so that text will automatically flow from one box to another by completing the following steps:
   a. Select the first text box (located on page 1), click the Drawing Tools Format tab, and then click the Create Link button in the Text group.
   b. Position the mouse pointer, which now displays as an upright pitcher, over the second text box (located on page 2), until it displays as a pouring pitcher and then click to complete the link.

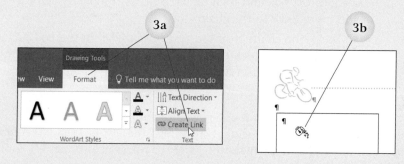

   c. Remove the shape outline in the first text box that is linked (at the bottom of page 1, second column).
   d. Change the height of the first text box to 1.8 inches and the width to 4.7 inches.
   e. Move the first text box to a position similar to that shown in Figure 6.19.

f. Click the Shape Styles group task pane launcher, click *Shape Options* if necessary to select it at the Format Shape task pane, click the Layout & Properties icon, and then click *Text Box* to display the options.

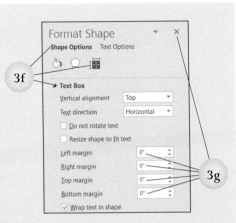

g. Change the left, right, top, and bottom margins to 0 inches and then close the task pane.

h. Click inside the first text box to position the insertion point and then insert **AccidentText.docx** from the C6 folder.

i. Check the text box on page 2 and make sure that the remaining article text is visible. If not, use the sizing handles to enlarge the text box.

j. Position the insertion point in the title *"Accidents" Waiting to Happen* in the first text box and then apply the Article Head style (from the Styles gallery). **Hint: If the Article Head style does not display in the Styles gallery, click the More Styles button in the Styles group.**

4. Format the article text by completing the following steps:

a. Double-click to select the word *The* at the beginning of the line *The majority of bicycle-car "accidents,"* press and hold down the Shift key, and then press Ctrl + End to select all the article text in both text boxes. **Hint: The text in the second text box will not appear highlighted, even though it is selected.**

b. With the text selected, apply the Article Text style (from the Styles gallery).

c. Position the insertion point in the first paragraph and then apply the 1st Paragraph style.

5. Create a jump line by completing the following steps:

a. Position the insertion point at the end of the first paragraph and press the Enter key two times.

b. Change the paragraph alignment to right.

c. Display the Symbol dialog box, change the *Font* option to Wingdings 3, insert the triangle symbol shown in the image below (character code 113, located in approximately the fifth row), and then click the Close button.

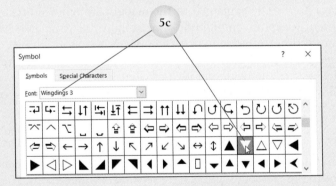

d. Press the spacebar and then type See ACCIDENTS on page 2. If the beginning of the second paragraph is visible below the jump line, press the Enter key to force this text to appear at the beginning of the linked text box on page 2.

e. Select *See* in the new jump line on page 1 and then apply italic formatting.

f. Select *ACCIDENTS* and then apply bold formatting.

g. Select *on page 2* and then apply italic formatting.

h. Select the entire jump line text (not the triangle symbol) and then change the font size to 10 points.

i. Click the Layout tab and make sure that the *After* option in the *Spacing* section in the Paragraph group is set to 3 pt.
6. Save the formatted jump line as a quick part by completing the following steps.
  Note: You are saving the jump line as a quick part instead of creating a style because the jump line contains mixed formatting and text that can be used in other jump lines.
  a. Select the entire jump line, including the triangle symbol.
  b. Click the Insert tab, click the Quick Parts button in the Text group, and then click *Save Selection to Quick Part Gallery* at the drop-down list.
  c. At the Create New Building Block dialog box, type jump line in the *Name* text box and then click OK.

7. Insert the image of the man riding a bicycle in the article subhead by completing the following steps:
  a. Position the insertion point above the column break in the right column on page 1.
  b. Display the Insert Picture dialog box, navigate to the C6 folder, and then double-click **biker.png**.
  c. With the image selected, change the text wrapping to In Front of Text.
  d. Click the Color button in the Adjust group and then click the *Green, Accent color 6, Dark* option (last column, second row in the *Recolor* section).
  e. Size and position the image as shown in Figure 6.19 on page 240.
8. Save **6-JumpLine.docx**.

Check Your Work

Creating Captions

Tutorial

Creating and Customizing Captions

caption

A description or explanation that accompanies a chart, diagram, illustration, or photograph

Insert Caption

When looking at a photograph in a newspaper, newsletter, or magazine, most people will read the accompanying text that describes the photograph. While some images can stand on their own, most photographs, illustrations, diagrams, and charts need to be explained to the reader through a short description known as a ***caption***. A caption should not only explain the associated image but also establish a connection to the body text. The reader's eyes are drawn to elements such as images that stand out on the page. Adding a descriptive caption to an image quickly gives the reader an idea of what it is about, as shown in Figure 6.16. A well-written caption can entice a reader to read the corresponding article and maybe even the rest of the newsletter.

Make the caption text look different from the body text by applying bold or italic formatting, decreasing the type size, and perhaps changing the font color. As always, legibility is key. Keep captions as short as possible and focus on explaining what the reader will immediately see and wonder about. Make sure to write and format captions in a consistent manner throughout a newsletter.

The easiest way to insert a caption is by using the captions feature. To do this, select the image and then click the Insert Caption button in the Captions group on the References tab. Another option is to right-click the image and then click *Insert Caption* at the shortcut menu. This displays the Caption dialog box, with several different caption settings that can be adjusted, as shown in Figure 6.17.

When the Caption dialog box displays for the first time in a document, the text *Figure 1* has already been inserted in the *Caption* text box. A caption label such as *Figure 1* or *Table 1* is useful when creating more detailed, technical newsletters that may contain tables, SmartArt graphics, or even an Excel worksheet or PowerPoint slide. These elements should be captioned with labels and either numbers or letters (Figure 3, Table C, etc.) so that they can be easily referenced within the text. The caption feature automatically numbers the figures in a document.

Change the type of label (Figure, Table, etc.) by clicking the *Label* option box arrow and then selecting a new label type. Add label options to this option box by clicking the New Label button. Change the style of numbering by clicking the Numbering button, and change the position of the caption by clicking the *Position* option box arrow. Once the appropriate label and position for the caption have been selected, add a title, description, or other text in the *Caption* text box and then click OK to close the dialog box. Add or edit the caption text in the text box that appears near the image after the Caption dialog box has been closed.

If the images in a newsletter do not need to be labeled, create captions without labels by clicking to insert a check box in the *Exclude labels from caption* check box in the Caption dialog box. This will remove the label from the *Caption* text box.

Another option is to create captions from scratch. To do this, simply insert a text box, type the caption text, and then size and position the text box near the image. This option is best used in documents that contain only a few images because it can be much more time consuming than using the captions feature.

Figure 6.16 Understanding Captions

Table 1 The Greek Alphabet

Letter name	Uppercase	Lowercase	Letter name	Uppercase	Lowercase
Alpha	A	α	Nu	N	ν
Beta	B	β	Xi	Ξ	ξ
Gamma	Γ	γ	Omicron	O	o
Delta	Δ	δ	Pi	Π	π
Epsilon	E	ε	Rho	P	ρ
Zeta	Z	ζ	Sigma	Σ	σ
Eta	H	η	Tau	T	τ
Theta	Θ	θ	Upsilon	Υ	υ
Iota	I	ι	Phi	Φ	φ
Kappa	K	κ	Chi	X	χ
Lambda	Λ	λ	Psi	Ψ	ψ
Mu	M	μ	Omega	Ω	ω

Figure 1 Mt. Rainier, Washington State

captions

Figure 6.17 Using the Caption Dialog Box

Caption dialog box:
- Caption: Figure 1: Helmets Save Lives!
- Options
  - Label: Figure
  - Position: Below selected item
  - Exclude label from caption
  - New Label...
  - Delete Label
  - Numbering...
  - AutoCaption...
  - OK
  - Cancel

Type the caption text here.

Click here to change the type of label.

Click here to change the position of the caption.

Click here to change the numbering style.

Click here to remove the label from the caption.

Click here to add a new label to the *Label* option list.

1. With **6-JumpLine.docx** open, save the document with the name **6-Picture**.
2. Insert a picture title, as shown in Figure 6.19 on page 240, by completing the following steps:
   a. Press Ctrl + End to position the insertion point at the top of page 2 and then press Ctrl + Shift + Enter to position the insertion point at the top of the right column.
   b. Draw a text box at the top of the right column that is 0.5 inch in height and 4.5 inches in width. *Note: You may have to resize the linked text box in the left column on the second page.*
   c. Remove the shape outline from the new text box.
   d. Click once in the new text box to position the insertion point inside it.
   e. Type Who Says Helmets Aren't Cool?
   f. Insert the arrow symbols at the beginning and end of the heading as shown in Figure 6.19. (The arrows are in the Wingdings font, character codes 201 and 202.)
   g. Apply the Article Head style to *Who Says Helmets Aren't Cool?* and the arrow symbols, then change the paragraph alignment of the text in the text box to center.
   h. Drag and position the text box as shown in Figure 6.19.
   i. If the text box in the left column and the text box you just inserted in the right column overlap, reduce the width of the text box in the left column so it is approximately the same width as the column. Use the horizontal ruler as a guide.
3. Insert and format a picture as shown in Figure 6.19 by completing the following steps:
   a. Position the insertion point at the top left corner of page 2 and then insert *children.jpg* from the C6 folder.
   b. Change the text wrapping to In Front of Text.
   c. Change the width of the picture to 4.4 inches.
   d. Apply the Simple Frame, White picture style.
   e. Position the image as shown in Figure 6.19.
4. Create a picture caption by completing the following steps:
   a. With the picture selected, click the References tab and then click the Insert Caption button in the Captions group.
   b. At the Caption dialog box, make sure that *Figure 1* displays in the *Caption* text box and *Below selected item* displays in the *Position* option box and then click OK.
   c. With the insertion point positioned inside the caption text box and to the right of *Figure 1*, type a colon and then press the spacebar.
   d. Insert **PictureText.docx** from the C6 folder at the location of the insertion point.
5. Select the entire caption—including the figure label, the figure number, and the text you just inserted—and then change the font to 10-point Cambria and apply bold and italic formatting.
6. Save **6-Picture.docx**.

Check Your Work

Creating a Newsletter Masthead

masthead

Contains information about the publication of a newsletter

The *masthead* contains information about the publication of a newsletter. A masthead usually contains the following items (see Figure 6.18):

- Name and address of the company or organization that produces the newsletter
- Newsletter publication schedule, such as weekly, monthly, or biannually
- Names of the individuals that contribute to the production of the newsletter, such as editors, authors, and graphic designers
- Copyright information

The masthead may also contain a small logo, seal, or other graphic identifier. Although a masthead is commonly located on the back page of a newsletter, it can sometimes be found on the first page. Wherever the masthead is placed, its design, layout, and location should be consistent from issue to issue.

DTP POINTER ❯

Be consistent in the design, layout, and placement of the masthead from issue to issue.

Figure 6.18 Illustrating Examples of Masthead Designs

Desktop Designs

Editor:
Martha Ridoux

Design and Layout:
Grace Shevick

Contributing Authors:
Jonathan Dwyer
Taylor Shipley
Christine Johnson

Published Monthly by:
DTP Training, Inc.
4550 North Wabash St.
Chicago, IL 60155
(312) 555-9366
emcp.net/dtp

©**Copyright 2018 by:**
DTP Training, Inc.
All rights reserved.

Desktop Designs

Editor:
Martha Ridoux

Design and Layout:
Grace Shevick

Contributing Authors:
Jonathan Dwyer
Nancy Shipley
Christine Johnson

Published Monthly by:
DTP Training, Inc.
4550 North Wabash St.
Chicago, IL 60155
(312) 555-9366
emcp.net/dtp

©**Copyright 2018 by:**
DTP Training, Inc.
All rights reserved.

1. With **6-Picture.docx** open, save the document with the name **6-Masthead**.
2. Insert a predesigned text box to hold the masthead text by completing the following steps:
   a. Position the insertion point at the beginning of the second page of the newsletter.
   b. Click the Insert tab, click the Text Box button in the Text group, and then scroll down and click the *Simple Quote* option at the drop-down list.

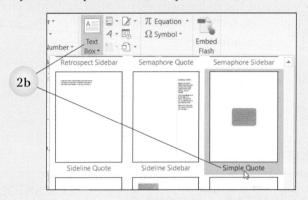

   c. With the new text box selected, change the shape height to 2.2 inches and the shape width to 3.1 inches.
   d. Drag the text box to the bottom left corner of page 2 to a location similar to that shown in Figure 6.19 on page 240.
   e. With the text box selected, apply the Subtle Effect - Green, Accent 6 effect in the Shape Styles gallery on the Drawing Tools Format tab.
   f. Change the shape outline color to Green, Accent 6, Darker 50%.
   g. Click once inside the text box to select the placeholder and then insert **MastheadText.docx** from the C6 folder.
   h. Press Ctrl + A to select all the masthead text in the text box, click the Layout tab, type 0 in the *After* option in the *Spacing* section in the Paragraph group, and then press the Enter key.
   i. Click in the title of the text box, *Sure Ride*, and then change the spacing after paragraphs to 6 points.
3. Save **6-Masthead.docx**.

Check Your Work

Understanding Copyfitting

Publications such as magazines and newsletters contain information that varies from issue to issue. Although the articles and stories are laid out on the page according to a structure (such as the asymmetrical two-column format in the Sure Ride newsletter), an article or story may sometimes take up more or less space than is allotted to it. Arranging text and design elements so they fit in a fixed amount of space is referred to as *copyfitting*.

copyfitting

Arranging the text and design elements so they fit in a fixed amount of space

Many methods are available for copyfitting a newsletter, depending on the challenges encountered. When more space is necessary for text, try the following common copyfit methods:

- Reduce the margins.
- Change the alignment.
- Change the typeface, typestyle, or type size, but limit the body type size to a minimum of 9 points (preferably, 10 or 11 points).

- Reduce the spacing before and after paragraphs (or hard returns) to reduce the spacing around the nameplate, headlines, subheads, frames, and text boxes.
- Reduce the spacing between paragraphs.
- Turn on hyphenation.
- Condense the spacing between characters.
- Reduce the line spacing in the body text.
- Remove a sidebar, pull quote, kicker, or end sign.
- Edit the text, including rewriting and eliminating sections.

DTP POINTER ❯

Don't go overboard when making copyfitting changes—small adjustments can make a big difference.

When space needs to be filled, try the following copyfitting methods:

- Increase the margins.
- Change the alignment.
- Change the font size, but limit the body type size to a maximum of 12 points.
- Increase the spacing between paragraphs.
- Adjust the character spacing.
- Increase the line spacing in the body text.
- Increase the spacing around the nameplate, headlines, subheads, text boxes, and graphics.
- Add a sidebar, pull quote, kicker, end sign, graphic lines, clip art, or photo.
- Add text.

Be consistent when making adjustments by copyfitting. For example, if the white space after one headline is increased, the white space after all the headlines should be increased. Alternatively, if the type size of the body text in one article is decreased, the type size of the body text in all the articles should be decreased. Adjustments are less noticeable when made uniformly. Also, small adjustments can often make a big difference. For instance, rather than reducing the type size by 1 whole point, try reducing it by 0.25 or 0.5 point.

Project 2i Adding Articles, Applying Styles, and Using Copyfitting Techniques   Part 9 of 9

1. With **6-Masthead.docx** open, save it with the name **6-SureRideNewsletter**.
2. Add content to the second page of the newsletter as shown in Figure 6.19 on page 240, by completing the following steps. Make your own minor adjustments if necessary to fit the articles in their respective locations:
   a. To make room for the article *The Light Bulb Test* at the beginning of page 2, click and drag the linked text box on page 2 that contains the remaining text from the *Accidents* article to just above the Sure Ride masthead. (This text box will be formatted in future steps.)
   b. Position the insertion point at the top left side of page 2 (at the beginning of column 1) and then draw a text box to hold the article *The Light Bulb Test*.
   c. Remove the shape outline and shape fill from the text box.
   d. Change the size of the text box to 4 inches in height and 2.4 inches in width.
   e. Drag the text box to a position similar to that shown in Figure 6.19.
   f. Change the left, right, top, and bottom margins of the text box to 0 inches.
      Hint: Change the internal margins at the Format Shape task pane with the Layout & Properties icon selected.

g. Click once inside the text box to position the insertion point and then insert **LightBulbText.docx** from the C6 folder.

h. Position the insertion point in the heading *The Light Bulb Test* and then apply the Article Head style.

i. Position the insertion point in the first paragraph and then apply the 1st Paragraph style.

j. Position the insertion point in the second paragraph (begins with **Caution:** *This experiment*) and then apply the Article Text style.

3. Insert the light bulb image in the article heading by completing the following steps:

a. Position the insertion point between *Light* and *Bulb* in the heading and then delete the space between the words.

b. With the insertion point positioned between the two words, display the Insert Picture dialog box, navigate to the C6 folder, and then double-click *lightbulb.png*.

c. With the light bulb image selected, size it similarly to the image shown in Figure 6.19 on page 240. Make sure the light bulb is small enough so that the article heading fits on one line and the article text fits within the text box.

4. Create the end sign at the end of the article by completing the following steps:

a. On page 1, select the end sign at the end of the first article and then press Ctrl + C to copy the end sign.

b. Position the insertion point right of the period in the last sentence at the end of the article *The Light Bulb Test*, press the spacebar three times, and then press Ctrl + V to paste the end sign into the text box.

5. Select the linked text box that contains the remaining text from the *Accidents* article and then make the following changes with options on the Drawing Tools Format tab:

a. Remove the shape outline and shape fill from the text box.

b. Change the size of the text box to 2 inches in height and 2.4 inches in width.

c. Change the internal text box margins to 0 inches at the Format Shape task pane.

d. Drag the text box to a position similar to that shown in Figure 6.19.

6. Insert and format the "continued" jump line at the beginning of the text in the linked text box on page 2 by completing the following steps:

a. Position the insertion point at the beginning of the text in the linked text box on page 2.

b. Click the Insert tab, click the Quick Parts button in the Text group, and then click the *jump line* option in the *General* section of the drop-down list.

c. Delete the word *See* in the jump line.

d. Select the word *on* and then type from.

e. Select the number *2* and then type 1.

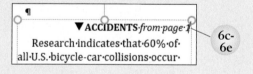

7. Insert the horizontal line above the jump line by completing the following steps:

a. Position the insertion point in the jump line, click the Home tab, click the Borders button arrow in the Paragraph group, and then click *Borders and Shading* at the drop-down gallery.

b. At the Borders and Shading dialog box with the Borders tab selected, change the *Width* option to *1 pt*. Click the top border of the diagram in the *Preview* section, make sure that no borders display on the remaining sides of the diagram, and then click OK.

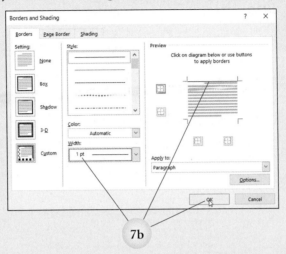

7b

8. Copy and paste the end sign from the article THE LIGHT BULB TEST three spaces after the end of the article. (Drag down the masthead text box slightly if necessary.)
9. Adjust the two text boxes and the masthead as necessary so they display as shown in Figure 6.19.
10. Save **6-SureRideNewsletter.docx**.
11. Insert an article in the remaining space in the right column of page 2 by completing the following steps:
    a. Draw a text box to hold the article *When Should a Helmet Be Replaced?* that is approximately the same size and in the same location as that shown in Figure 6.19.
    b. Remove the shape outline and shape fill from the text box.
    c. Change the size of the text box to 4.1 inches in height and 4.5 inches in width.
    d. Change the left, right, top, and bottom margins to 0 inches at the Format Shape task pane.
    e. Click once inside the text box to position the insertion point and then insert **ReplaceHelmetText.docx** from the C6 folder.
    f. Drag the text box to a position similar to that shown in Figure 6.19.
12. Apply styles to the article text you just inserted by completing the following steps:
    a. Position the insertion point in the title *When Should a Helmet Be Replaced?* and then apply the Article Head style.
    b. Select all the paragraph text and then apply the 1st Paragraph style.
13. Insert a bullet and emphasize the text at the beginning of each paragraph by completing the following steps:
    a. Select all the article text paragraphs (excluding the title).
    b. Click the Bullets button in the Paragraph group on the Home tab.
    c. Click the Decrease Indent button in the Paragraph group to move the bullets to the edge of the text box.
    d. Select the first sentence in each bulleted paragraph and then change the font to Impact.
14. Scroll through the newsletter and make any copyfitting adjustments that are necessary.
15. Turn off the display of nonprinting characters.
16. Save, print, and then close **6-SureRideNewsletter.docx**.

Check Your Work

Figure 6.19 Sure Ride Newsletter Created in Project 2

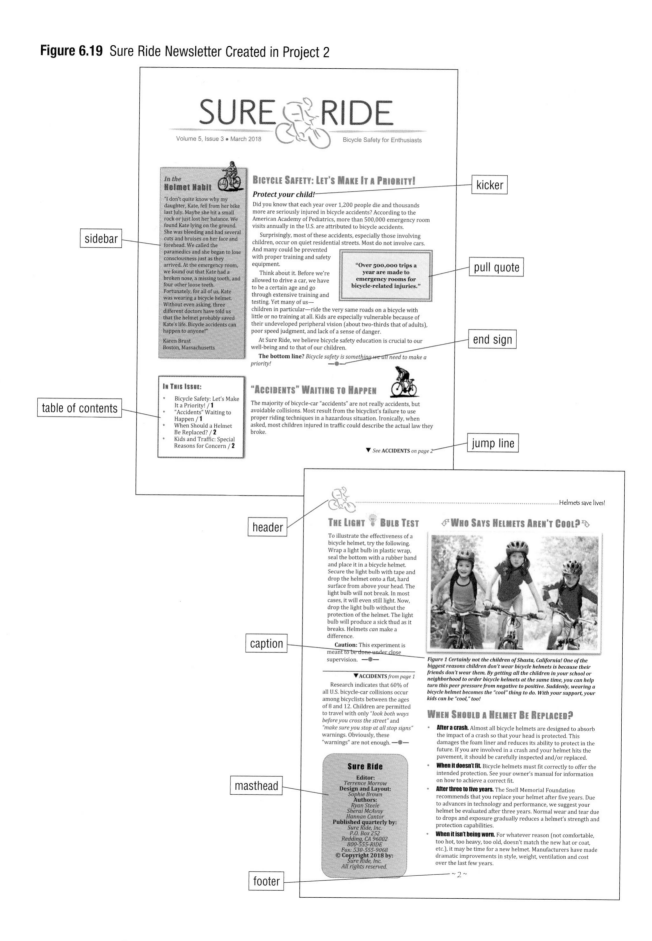

kicker

sidebar

pull quote

table of contents

end sign

jump line

header

caption

masthead

footer

Chapter Summary

- When planning a newsletter, consider the purpose or goal, the audience, the image that should be projected, how to use graphics, the frequency of publication, and the budget for the newsletter.

- A successful newsletter contains consistent elements in every issue, making it easy for readers to find what they need. Basic newsletter elements include a nameplate, logo, subtitle, folio, headlines, subheads, bylines, body text, and graphics.

- The nameplate, or banner, consists of the artwork and/or type that includes the newsletter's name and is usually located on the front page.

- The folio consists of the publication information that changes from issue to issue, including the volume number, issue number, and date.

- The subtitle is a short phrase describing the purpose and/or audience of the newsletter.

- Headlines are the titles of articles and should be distinguished from the body text to attract the reader's attention.

- The byline identifies the author of an article.

- The main content of a newsletter is the body text or body copy. Formatting the body text may include changing paragraph alignment, indenting the text, and controlling where the text breaks between pages.

- Subheads organize the text and expand on headlines; they also provide contrast on text-intensive pages.

- Graphics, such as pictures and clip art, are added to a newsletter to support and expand on points made in the text.

- Focus and balance can be achieved in a newsletter through the design and size of the nameplate; the arrangement of text on the page; the use of graphics; and the careful placement of lines, borders, and backgrounds.

- Consider creating a gutter to accommodate the bindings of a multiple-page newsletter. Create a gutter by displaying the Page Setup dialog box with the Margins tab selected, specify the location of the gutter (left or top margin) with the *Gutter position* option, enter the gutter measurement in the *Gutter* measurement box, and then click OK.

- When determining the paper size and type of a newsletter, consider the number of copies needed, the equipment available, the cost, and the quality desired.

- The sizes of the margins for a newsletter are linked to the number of columns needed, formality desired, visual elements to be used, and amount of text to be included. Keep margins consistent throughout a newsletter.

- If creating a multiple-page newsletter with facing pages, consider using Word's mirror margins feature, which accommodates wider inside or outside margins.

- The line length of text in a newsletter can enhance or detract from the readability of the text. Setting text in columns may improve readability. Set columns with options at the Columns button drop-down list in the Page Setup group on the Layout tab or with options at the Columns dialog box.

- The columns on the last page of a document can be balanced by inserting a continuous section break at the end of the text. Insert a continuous section break by clicking the Breaks button in the Page Setup group on the Layout tab and then clicking *Continuous* at the drop-down list.

- The number of columns in a newsletter may vary from one to two or more, but the two-column format is most common. Avoid tombstoning, which occurs when headings or subheads display side by side in adjacent columns.
- Section breaks can be used to vary the page layout within a single newsletter.
- Change the number of columns, modify the column widths, and add vertical lines between columns with options at the Columns dialog box. Display this dialog box by clicking the Columns button in the Page Setup group on the Layout tab and then click *More Columns* at the drop-down list.
- Add borders and horizontal lines to newsletter pages, text, and images to enhance the appearance of the newsletter. Add borders around paragraphs of text with options at the Borders and Shading dialog box, add horizontal lines to a document with options at the Insert Pictures window, use options in the Picture Styles group on the Picture Tools Format tab to add borders around images, and use options in the Shape Styles group on the Drawing Tools Format tab to add borders around text boxes.
- To enhance the appearance of text in a newsletter, use a drop cap to identify the beginning of a major section or article. Create a drop cap with the Drop Cap button in the Text group on the Insert tab or with options at the Drop Cap dialog box.
- Using styles helps maintain consistency across the recurring elements in a newsletter. Styles are created for a particular newsletter and saved with it.
- Control the appearance of body text in a newsletter using formatting options such as paragraph alignment, paragraph indents (i.e., em spaces), and the Widow/Orphan control feature.
- Create a newsletter as a self-mailer, which is a document that can be mailed without using an envelope.
- A newsletter can be saved and then sent as an email attachment. Saving the newsletter in PDF file format ensures that the formatting will remain intact and that anyone will be able to view, print, and forward the document.
- A newsletter can be created in Word, saved in HTML or MHTML, and then viewed in Web Page Preview. Formatting a newsletter as a table will keep the structure of the newsletter in place when it is viewed on the web.
- To establish consistency from one issue to the next and to save time creating future issues, save a newsletter as a template.
- Newsletters can be formatted using columns, tables, or text boxes.
- Search for available online newsletter templates by typing the search text or category in the search text box at the New backstage area and then pressing the Enter key. Double-click the desired template to open a document based on it.
- Elements that can be added to a newsletter to enhance the visual impact include tables of contents, headers and/or footers, mastheads, kickers, sidebars, pull quotes, captions, ruled lines, jump lines, page borders, and end signs.
- Headers and footers are commonly used in newsletters. Headers and footers can be placed on specific pages, only odd pages, or only even pages, and they can include page numbering, slogans, logos, and horizontal ruled lines.
- Use spot color—a single color in a black-and-white document—as an accent. Add color to features such as ruled lines, graphics, borders, backgrounds, headings, and end signs.

- A sidebar is a block of information or a related story that is set off from the body text using some type of box or border. It can include an image along with text. A sidebar can be created from scratch by drawing and then enhancing a text box, or a predesigned sidebar can be inserted from the Text Box button drop-down list.

- In a multiple-page newsletter, a table of contents is an important and necessary element. It is generally formatted to stand out from the surrounding information and located on the front page in the lower left or lower right corner.

- A pull quote is a direct phrase, summarizing statement, or important point associated with the body text. It acts as a focal point, helps to break up lengthy blocks of text, and provides visual contrast.

- A kicker is a brief sentence or phrase that leads into an article. It is typically set in a type size smaller than the headline but larger than the body text and is placed above or below the headline or article heading.

- A symbol or special character used to indicate the end of a section of text is referred to as an end sign.

- If an article begins on one page and continues onto another page, link the text boxes containing the article text to allow it to flow from one text box to another.

- In a newsletter, a jump line indicates that an article or feature is being continued on or from another page. As an aid in the directional flow of information, a jump line should be easy to distinguish from the surrounding text.

- A short, descriptive caption can be added to an image to give the reader an idea of what the image is about and to establish a connection to the body text. Apply bold or italic formatting to the caption and set it in a smaller point size to make it different from the body text.

- Add predesigned Word captions to tables and figures, or create designs from scratch using text boxes.

- The masthead contains information about publication of the newsletter, such as the company address, newsletter publication schedule, names of those contributing to the production, and copyright information. The masthead is generally placed on the back page of the newsletter and should have a consistent design, layout, and location.

- Copyfitting refers to arranging and adjusting text and design elements so that they fit in a fixed amount of space.

Commands Review

FEATURE	RIBBON TAB, GROUP	BUTTON, OPTION	KEYBOARD SHORTCUT
align left	Home, Paragraph		Ctrl + L
align right	Home, Paragraph		Ctrl + R
break link	Drawing Tools Format, Text		
caption	References, Captions		

FEATURE	RIBBON TAB, GROUP	BUTTON, OPTION	KEYBOARD SHORTCUT
center	Home, Paragraph		Ctrl + E
column break	Layout, Page Setup	, *Column*	Ctrl + Shift + Enter
columns	Layout, Page Setup		
continuous section break	Layout, Page Setup	, *Continuous*	
drop cap	Insert, Text		
footer	Insert, Header & Footer		
go to footer	Header & Footer Tools Design, Navigation		
go to header	Header & Footer Tools Design, Navigation		
header	Insert, Header & Footer		
justify	Home, Paragraph		Ctrl + J
link text boxes	Drawing Tools Format, Text		
link to previous	Header & Footer Tools Design, Navigation		
margins	Layout, Page Setup		
next section	Header & Footer Tools Design, Navigation		
page borders	Design, Page Background		
page numbers	Header & Footer Tools Design, Header & Footer		
previous section	Header & Footer Tools Design, Navigation		
quick parts	Insert, Text		
symbol	Insert, Symbols		
text box	Insert, Text		

Workbook

Chapter study tools and assessment activities are available in the workbook pages of the ebook. These resources are designed to help you further develop and demonstrate mastery of the skills learned in this chapter.

Creating Brochures and Booklets

Performance Objectives

Upon successful completion of Chapter 7, you will be able to:

1 Plan brochures and booklets

2 Create brochures after making key decisions about page layout and printing

3 Use columns to format brochures and booklets

4 Understand and practice duplex printing

5 Create booklets using a book fold

6 Create brochures and booklets using the 2 Pages per Sheet feature

Desktop Publishing Terms

booklet	letter fold
brochure	map fold
dummy	panel
duplex printing	parallel folds
gate fold	

Word Features Used

Book fold	orientation
column breaks	section breaks
columns	styles
Draft view	style sets
manual duplex printing	2 Pages per Sheet

 Data Files

Before beginning chapter work, copy the C7 folder to your storage medium and then make C7 the active folder.

Project 1 **Create a Brochure**   **3 Parts**

You will create a trifold brochure using the columns and duplex printing features to provide the framework for the brochure.

Preview Finished Project

Planning Brochures and Booklets

brochure

A short informational or promotional publication; created on one sheet that is later folded to create multiple pages

A *brochure* is a small informational or promotional publication that often contains both text and graphics. A brochure is produced on one sheet of paper that is then folded to create different pages. A *booklet* is similar to a brochure in content and length, but its pages are bound (with staples, stitches, or glue) rather than folded. As with any other desktop publication, it is important to plan a brochure or booklet before beginning to create it.

booklet

A short informational or promotional publication; differs from a brochure in that it is bound rather than folded

Defining the Purpose

The purpose of a brochure or booklet can be to inform, educate, promote, or sell. Consider the purpose driving each of the following publications:

- A city agency mails brochures to community members that explain a local recycling program.
- A doctor displays brochures on childhood immunizations in the patient waiting room.
- A car salesperson hands out a brochure on a current model to a potential buyer.
- A new management consulting firm sends out brochures introducing its services.
- A professional organization mails booklets to its members listing membership information: addresses, telephone numbers, fax numbers, email addresses, and so on.
- A homeowners' association prepares a directory of names, addresses, and services provided by residents (babysitting, pet sitting, garage cleaning, and so on).
- Volunteers for a local theater prepare a playbill (formatted as a booklet) for distribution during a theatrical production.

Notice that some brochures and booklets have more than one purpose, which is fairly normal. For example, the goals of a brochure on childhood immunizations may be to inform and educate, and the goals of a brochure about a car's current model may be to inform and promote sales of the car. Alternatively, the goals of a playbill (booklet) may be to inform an audience of facts about a play, introduce people who are playing the roles, and promote organizations that support the community theater.

Keep in mind that brochures and booklets are yet other documents that can help establish an organization's identity and image. Incorporating design elements from other business documents into the design of a brochure or booklet reinforces the brand among readers.

Determining the Content

Before creating the layout and design of a brochure or booklet, determine what the content will be. A brochure or booklet should include the following items:

- A clearly stated description of the topic, product, service, or organization
- A description of the people or company doing the informing, educating, promoting, or selling
- A description of how the reader will benefit from this information, product, service, or organization
- A clear indication of what action the audience should take after reading the brochure or booklet
- An easy way for readers to carry out the desired action, such as providing a phone number to call, a detachable postcard to send in for more information, or a form to fill in

Creating Brochures

Before working on the content for a brochure, make a few key decisions regarding page layout and printing. These decisions include determining the size and type of paper, determining the page layout, setting the margins, and determining the panel widths and margins.

Determining the Size and Type of Paper

Determining the paper size is an important first step in planning a brochure because it helps to determine the number and size of panels the brochure will have. **Panels** are the "pages" of a brochure that are created by the folds in the paper.

A brochure can be folded in several different ways. The manner in which a brochure is folded determines the order in which the panels are set on the page and read by the recipient. All brochures are folded using **parallel folds**, or folds that run in the same direction. The most common brochure fold is called a **letter fold**, also known as a *trifold*. A letter fold creates a three-panel brochure, as shown in Figure 7.1A. Other brochure folds that can easily be created using standard-size 8.5-by-11-inch paper in landscape orientation include an accordion fold and a single fold (see Figures 7.1B and 7.1C). Standard legal-size paper (8.5 by 14 inches) can be used to create a brochure with a **map fold** or a **gate fold**, as shown in Figures 7.1D and 7.1E. Different paper sizes can be used to create variations of these folds. In addition, folds do not always have to create equal panel sizes. Experiment with different paper sizes and brochure folds to find the one that is best suited to the content and audience.

Figure 7.1 Understanding Brochure Folds

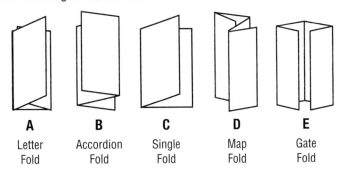

A	B	C	D	E
Letter Fold	Accordion Fold	Single Fold	Map Fold	Gate Fold

Sidebar definitions

panel

A "page" in a brochure created by folds in the paper

parallel folds

Folds that run in the same direction

letter fold

A fold that creates a three-panel brochure in which the sides of the paper fold in toward the middle; the paper is folded two times

map fold

A fold in which the paper is folded three times: the first two folds face inward and the third faces outward

gate fold

A fold in which the paper is folded three times—all three folds face inward

Brochures are usually printed on both sides of the page and can be printed on a variety of paper stocks. The paper stock may vary in size, weight, color, and texture. Some papers made especially for brochures also contain guidelines that indicate where to fold. The type of paper selected for a brochure affects the total production cost. When selecting the paper stock for a brochure, consider the following factors:

- A standard-size brochure, such as a three-panel brochure created from 8.5-by-11-inch paper stock, can fit easily in a #10 business envelope.
- A standard-size brochure designed as a self-mailer satisfies postal regulations and is therefore less costly to mail.
- Paper stocks in nonstandard sizes may be more expensive to purchase and to mail.
- Heavier-weight papers are more expensive to purchase and to mail.
- Higher-quality paper stocks are more expensive to purchase.
- Colored paper is more costly than standard white, ivory, cream, or gray.
- Paper stocks with preprinted designs are more expensive than plain paper stock.

Although cost is an important factor when choosing paper stock, other factors should be considered, as well, including how the brochure will be distributed, how often each copy will be handled, and the level of quality required. If the target audience is expected to keep the brochure for a period of time or to handle it often, plan to purchase a higher-quality, heavier paper stock. Similarly, choose a paper within the budget that enhances the overall image of the publication in the reader's mind.

DTP POINTER

View mailing regulations at www.usps.gov.

If personally printing a brochure or booklet, conduct a test with extra paper to ensure the printing works as intended. Some papers are better suited for laser and inkjet printers than others. If unsure about what type of paper to purchase, take a master copy of a brochure to a printer for advice on the best type of paper for the situation. Print shops can also fold brochures and booklets on commercial folding equipment. If a brochure is designed as a self-mailer, take a sample of the paper stock to the post office to see if it meets U.S. Postal Service mailing regulations.

Determining Brochure Page Layout

DTP POINTER

The way a brochure is folded helps to determine how the content should be organized.

The folds within a brochure create distinct sections that specific blocks of text can be placed in. For example, a three-panel brochure actually has six panels available for text: three panels on one side of the paper and three more on the other side. The way a brochure is folded determines the order in which the reader will view each panel and thus how the content should be organized. Notice how the panels are labeled in the letter-fold brochure layout illustrated in Figure 7.2. Panels 1, 2, and 3 are on the inside of the brochure, moving from left to right. Panel 4 is visible when the cover is opened. Panel 5 is the back of the folded brochure, which may be used for mailing purposes. Panel 6 is the cover of the brochure. The main content of the brochure is contained in panels 1, 2, and 3.

dummy

A mockup document that is laid out, folded, trimmed, and/or labeled in the same way as the actual publication

It can be confusing to figure out how to arrange the content in a Word document to achieve the final brochure layout. To avoid making mistakes, it is a good idea to create a mockup, or *dummy*, of a brochure. A dummy is created using the same size of paper as the final document and is also folded in the same manner.

Figure 7.2 Understanding Panel Layout in a Letter-fold Brochure

PANEL 1 (inside)	PANEL 2 (inside)	PANEL 3 (inside)

Side 1—Inside

PANEL 4 (first flap viewed when cover is opened)	PANEL 5 (back/ mailing)	PANEL 6 (cover)

Side 2—Outside

DTP POINTER ❯

Keep a dummy of the folded brochure nearby and refer to it when creating the content for each panel.

A dummy can be as simple or as detailed as desired. For visual verification that items are correctly placed in panels, fold a piece of paper in the chosen style and then label each panel (similar to what is shown in Figure 7.2). Make a more detailed dummy with specific margin, column, and spacing settings as a guide for placing text in each panel.

A simple brochure dummy can be created by hand, but it is best to create a more complex dummy in Word. A brochure dummy can be created in Word using columns, tables, text boxes, or the 2 Pages per Sheet feature (applicable only to single-fold brochures). For example, to create a standard-size, three-panel brochure, create a dummy by changing the page orientation to landscape and then dividing the page into three columns using the columns feature or into three columns and one row using the table feature. Alternatively, three text boxes can be sized and positioned on the page to represent three panels. Once the order in which the panels of a brochure will be seen is understood, plan the content that will go on each panel.

Setting Page Margins for a Brochure

Tutorial ❯

Changing Margins

Because brochure panels are small, the page margins should be set as narrow as possible to create more space for content. Many home and office printers require a minimum 0.5-inch left or right margin (depending on the page orientation) because a certain amount of space is needed for the printer to grab the paper and eject it from the printer.

🔲 Margins

If margins are set at less than the minimum, Word will prompt the user with the following message: *One or more margins are set outside the printable area of the page. Choose the Fix button to increase the appropriate margins.* Click the Fix button to change the margins to the printer's minimum setting. Check the new margin setting by clicking the Margins button in the Page Setup group on the Layout tab. If landscape is the selected paper orientation, the right margin will be the only margin "fixed" by Word because that is the side of the paper the printer grabs to eject the paper.

Even if Word fixes only one margin in a document, the opposite-side margin should be adjusted to match. For example, if a printer requires a minimum 0.5 inch for the right margin in landscape orientation, set the left and right margins at 0.5 inch.

If the Ignore button is clicked in response to the prompt to fix the margins, the program will ignore the printer's minimum requirement and accept whatever margins have been set. However, the printer will not print anything in its nonprinting area, which will result in content being cut off. Use the Print Preview area of the Print backstage area to view the results of setting margins that are less than the printer's minimum requirements.

Determining Panel Widths and Margins

In most brochure layouts, the panels cannot all be the same width, because some panels need to fold and lay flat inside other panels. If equal-size panels are used, the margins on some of the panels will appear uneven and the brochure folds will not fall properly in relation to the text. To solve this problem, individually size the text box for each panel to allow the appropriate placement of the text and the folds to achieve the desired result. Experiment and make adjustments to find the appropriate panel widths.

Several methods can be used to create the panels of a brochure. The letter-fold brochure template, shown in Figure 7.3, uses a table as the underlying structure, as do most online templates. Other templates use text boxes for the panels, as shown in Figure 7.4. Columns can also be used as the underlying structure of a brochure, as taught in Project 1b. Choosing a method for structuring a letter-fold brochure should be based on what is easiest to use and what is most appropriate for the design of the brochure.

Figure 7.3 Using an Online Brochure Template (Formatted with a Table)

Figure 7.4 Using an Online Brochure Template (Formatted with Text Boxes)

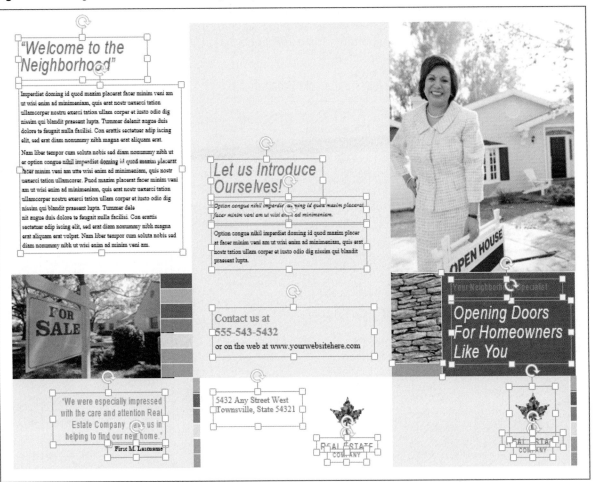

When designing a letter-fold brochure with three panels, as shown in Figure 7.5, consider the following steps for determining the widths of the panels and the spaces between them:

1. Fold the brochure paper stock into the desired configuration which in this example is a letter-fold layout. Measure the width of each panel. The width obtained will be approximate because a ruler cannot measure hundredths of an inch, but it will be a good starting point.

2. Establish the left and right margins for the whole page. (See the previous section on setting page margins for a brochure.)

3. The left margin for the whole brochure page is also the left margin for panel, so, subtract the left margin setting from the total width of panel 1. Estimate how much of the remaining amount is needed for the text and other content and for an appropriate amount of white space on the right side of the panel. For example, if panel 1 measures approximately 3.7 inches and the left page margin is 0.55 inch, subtract 0.55 inch from 3.7 inches. From the 3.15 inches that remain, estimate how much of that space will be occupied by text and how much needs to be allotted for the right margin of panel 1 (i.e., the white space before the fold). The method used to create the white space between columns depends on the method used to create the columns, as explained in Table 7.1.

DTP POINTER

Saving a blank brochure as a template will save time if a second brochure is needed at a later date.

4. For panel 2, use the whole panel width to estimate how much space is needed for the content and appropriate amounts of white space on the left and right sides of the panel. The column width in panel 2 will be wider than the column widths in panels 1 and 3.

Figure 7.5 Determining Panel Widths for a Letter-fold Brochure

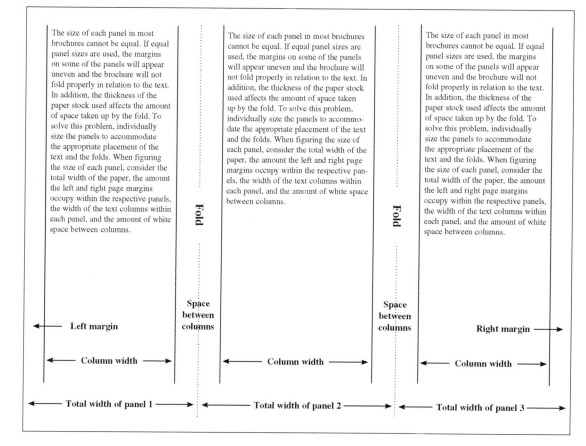

Table 7.1 Methods Used to Create Spacing between Columns

Method used to create columns	Method used to create spacing between columns
Columns	At the Columns dialog box in the *Width and spacing* section, adjust the amount in each *Spacing* text box.
Table	Create blank columns between the columns that contain the text for each panel.
Text boxes	Size and position the text box containing the text for each panel, leaving the desired amount of white space between text boxes.
Book Fold	Adjust the margin settings and the gutter space.
2 Pages per Sheet	Adjust the margin settings. (This method is applicable only to single-fold brochures.)

5. For panel 3, use the same measurements determined for panel 1. Keep in mind that the margins are flipped from what they were in panel 1: the right margin for the whole brochure page is also the right margin for the panel.

6. After establishing the text column widths and the amounts of white space between panels 1 and 2 and panels 2 and 3, reverse the measurements for panels 4, 5, and 6. For example, panels 1 and 6 will be the same width, panels 2 and 5 will be the same width, and panels 3 and 4 will be the same width. If using the columns feature, insert a section break to vary the column formatting on the second page. (See the *Inserting and Removing Section Breaks* section later in this chapter for more information.) If using the table feature, create another table for the second page of the brochure, reversing the column measurements from panels 1, 2, and 3. If using text boxes, remember to reverse the measurements as stated previously.

7. Use the previous suggestions to create a dummy. Insert random text in every panel and then print the brochure. To insert random text, type *=rand()* and then press the Enter key. Fold the page as the brochure will be folded and check the amounts of space between columns. As illustrated in Figure 7.5 on the previous page, the space between two panels is divided by the fold, allowing white space on either side of the fold. In other words, the space between two columns defines the margins for two different panels. Is the text positioned correctly within each panel? If not, adjust the spaces between columns and/or the column width settings and then print and fold the brochure again.

DTP POINTER

To create a dummy using a table, insert a table with five columns and one row: three columns for the panels and two columns for the spaces between them.

DTP POINTER

To insert random text in a document, type =rand() and then press the Enter key.

Using Columns to Format Brochures and Booklets

By default, all Word documents are automatically set up in a one-column format. However, a document can include as many columns as can fit on the page. Word determines the column widths based on the number of columns specified and the page width, margin settings, and spacing between columns. Column formatting can be assigned to a document before the text is typed, or it can be applied to existing text.

Creating Columns Using the Columns Dialog Box

Columns

To create columns, begin by clicking the Columns button in the Page Setup group on the Layout tab to display the Columns button drop-down list, which contains preset designs. When one of these designs is selected, the column feature is applied to the whole document, to the section where the insertion point is located (if the document has been divided into sections), or to the selected text (if text has been selected). Remember that each column will contain the content for one panel of the brochure.

To customize columns, click *More Columns* at the bottom of the Columns button drop-down list to display the Columns dialog box, as shown in Figure 7.6. Experiment with changing the width between columns and note how the changes affect the text in each panel. For example, in a letter-fold brochure, increasing the space between columns 1 and 2 will cause the text in panel 2 to shift to the right, whereas decreasing the space between columns 1 and 2 will cause the text in panel 2 to shift to the left.

Figure 7.6 Reviewing Options at the Columns Dialog Box

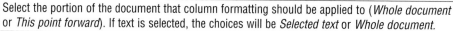

Click or type the number of columns desired.

Enter a measurement for the width of each column.

Enter the amount of space between columns.

Remove the check mark to create columns of unequal width.

Insert a check mark to add a vertical line between the columns.

Select the portion of the document that column formatting should be applied to (*Whole document* or *This point forward*). If text is selected, the choices will be *Selected text* or *Whole document*.

To remove column formatting, position the insertion point in the section containing columns and then change the column format to one column using either the Columns button drop-down list or the Columns dialog box.

Using the Horizontal Ruler to Adjust Column Widths

After columns have been created, the width and spacing can be changed with the column markers on the horizontal ruler (see Figure 7.7). To do this, make sure the horizontal ruler is displayed. (Click to insert a check mark in the *Ruler* check box in the Show group on the View tab.) Position the arrow pointer in the middle of the Left Margin or Right Margin column marker on the horizontal ruler until it turns into a left-and-right-pointing arrow. Click and hold down the left mouse button, drag the column marker to the left or right to make the column narrower or wider, and then release the mouse button. Press and hold down the Alt key while dragging the column marker to view the exact measurements on the ruler.

Figure 7.7 Adjusting Column Widths on the Horizontal Ruler

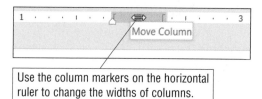

Use the column markers on the horizontal ruler to change the widths of columns.

Inserting and Removing Section Breaks

Tutorial

Inserting and Deleting a Section Break

 Breaks

By default, any column formatting is applied to the whole document. However, a document can be divided into sections to allow each section to have custom column styles. For example, a brochure may contain a title or headline that will span the entire width of the page instead of just one column. To accomplish this, type and format the title, position the insertion point at the left margin of the first line of text to be formatted into columns, click the Breaks button in the Page Setup group on the Layout tab, and then click one of the section break options, as shown in Figure 7.8. Additionally, use the Columns dialog box to apply a section break automatically from the location of the insertion point to the end of the document or until other column formatting is encountered. To do this, change the *Apply to* option at the bottom of the Columns dialog box from *Whole document* to *This point forward*.

Section breaks are used to allow layout and formatting changes within a document. Use them between sections that have different margins, paper sizes or orientations, page borders, headers and footers, columns, page numbering, line numbering, footnotes, and endnotes.

Section breaks can also be used to balance the text in columns. For example, if there is one full-length column and one very short one, insert a section break to divide the content evenly between the two columns. To do this, position the insertion point at the end of the last column, click the Breaks button, and then click the *Continuous* option at the drop-down list.

To delete a section break, click the View tab and then click the Draft View button in the Views group or click the Show/Hide ¶ button in the Paragraph group on the Home tab to turn on the display of nonprinting characters. The section break will display as a dotted line with the text *Section Break*. Position the insertion point left of the section break and then press the Delete key to remove it.

Figure 7.8 Inserting Section Breaks with Options at the Breaks Button Drop-down List

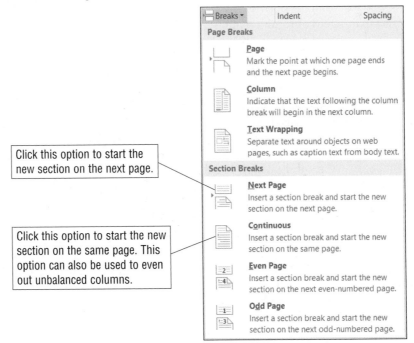

Click this option to start the new section on the next page.

Click this option to start the new section on the same page. This option can also be used to even out unbalanced columns.

Inserting a Column Break

DTP POINTER

While creating a brochure, continually evaluate the column breaks to make sure they are in appropriate locations.

When formatting text into columns, Word automatically breaks the columns to fit the page. At times, text may wrap from one column to another in an undesirable way. For example, a heading may appear at the bottom of the column while the text that follows the heading begins at the top of the next column. Change automatic column breaks by manually inserting column breaks at the desired locations.

To insert a column break, position the insertion point where the new column should begin and then press Ctrl + Shift + Enter. Another option is to click the Breaks button in the Page Setup group on the Layout tab and then click *Column* in the *Page Breaks* section.

Project 1a Creating a Dummy of a Letter-fold Brochure Using Columns

Part 1 of 3

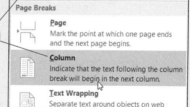

1. At a blank document, change the page orientation to landscape.
2. Change the left and right margins to 0.5 inch.
3. Change to a three-column format by clicking the Layout tab, clicking the Columns button in the Page Setup group, and then clicking *Three* at the drop-down list.
4. Insert the panel labels by completing the following steps:
   a. Change the paragraph alignment to center.
   b. Type PANEL 1, press the Enter key, and then type (inside) in the first panel (column 1).
   c. Click the Breaks button in the Page Setup group on the Layout tab and then click *Column* in the *Page Breaks* section.
   d. Using Figure 7.2 on page 249, as a guide, repeat Steps 4b through 4c until all six panels are labeled as shown in the figure. **Hint: Press Ctrl + Shift + Enter to insert a column break.**
5. Print the dummy by completing the following steps:
   a. Press Ctrl + Home to position the insertion point on the first page (containing panels 1, 2, and 3).
   b. Display the Print backstage area.
   c. At the Print backstage area, click the down-pointing arrow to the right of the first gallery in the *Settings* section (contains the text *Print All Pages*) and then click the *Print Current Page* option.
   d. Click the Print button.
   e. Put the first printed page back in the printer so the second page will be printed on the back of the first page. **Note: You may need to experiment to find the proper way to put the page back into the printer so that the dummy prints as it should. You will learn more about printing on both sides of the paper later in this chapter.**
   f. Position the insertion point on the second page (containing panels 4, 5, and 6) and then print it.
6. Fold the dummy as you would the real brochure.
7. Save the dummy brochure with the name **7-Dummy**.
8. Close **7-Dummy.docx**.
9. **Optional:** Open the documents in the SampleBrochures folder located in the C7 folder and then practice the different folds.

Check Your Work

When working on a brochure, remember to save the document often. Creating even a simple brochure involves many steps, and having to redo lost work is time consuming. Also view the document frequently to assess the overall layout and design. Adjustments often need to be made that can affect other parts of the document not visible in the document window.

Project 1b Creating Panels 1, 2, and 3 of a Letter-fold Brochure

1. At a blank document, change the page orientation to landscape. (You will be creating an informational brochure on a safari, similar to the one shown in Figure 7.9 on page 260.)
2. Click the Margins button in the Page Setup group on the Layout tab and then click *Narrow* to change the top, bottom, left, and right margins to 0.5 inch.
3. Apply the Facet theme.
4. Apply the Orange theme colors.

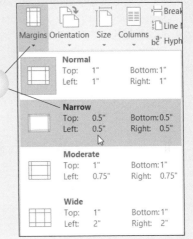

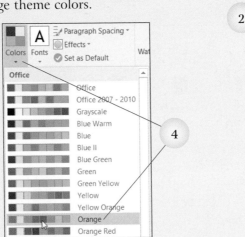

5. Apply the Casual style set.
6. With the insertion point positioned at the top of the page, insert **SafariIntro.docx** from the C7 folder.
7. Position the insertion point in the heading *WHAT ARE THE BIG 5?* and then make the following changes:
   a. Apply the Heading 1 style and then change the paragraph alignment to center.
   b. Insert a bottom border by clicking the Borders button arrow in the Paragraph group on the Home tab and then clicking *Bottom Border* at the drop-down gallery.
   c. Change the spacing before paragraphs to 0 points and the spacing after paragraphs to 10 points.
8. Select the paragraph of text (which begins *The "Big 5" refers to*), apply the Intense Emphasis style, and then apply the Tan, Accent 5, Darker 50% font color.
9. Press Ctrl + End to move the insertion point to the end of the document and then press the Enter key.

10. Click the *No Spacing* style option in the Styles group on the Home tab.
11. Change to a three-column format by completing the following steps:
    a. Click the Layout tab.
    b. Click the Columns button in the Page Setup group and then click *More Columns* at the drop-down list.
    c. At the Columns dialog box, click *Three* in the *Presets* section.
    d. Select the current measurement in the column 1 *Width* measurement box and then type 2.47.
    e. Click in the column 1 *Spacing* measurement box and make sure that *1.29"* displays.
    f. Click the *Apply to* option box arrow and then click *This point forward* at the drop-down list.
    g. Click OK.

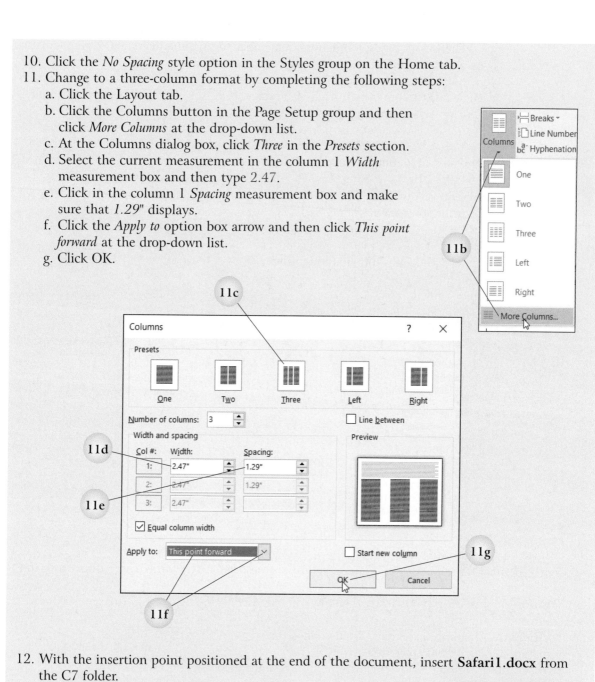

12. With the insertion point positioned at the end of the document, insert **Safari1.docx** from the C7 folder.
13. Select the text from the paragraph that begins *Large, robust* through the paragraph that begins *Adolescent males roam*. Click the Home tab and then click the Bullets button in the Paragraph group.
14. Position the insertion point at the beginning of the text *Lion* and then insert **lion.png** from the C7 folder.
15. Make the following changes to the lion image:
    a. Apply Square text wrapping.
    b. Click the More Picture Styles button in the Picture Styles group and then click the *Rotated, White* option.

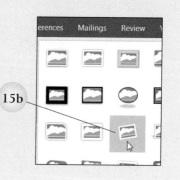

16. Position the insertion point in the text *Lion*, apply the Heading 2 style, and then insert a bottom border.
17. Position the insertion point at the end of the first column (in the blank line below the last bulleted item) and then insert a column break by pressing Ctrl + Shift + Enter.
18. Complete steps similar to Steps 12 through 17 to insert the following text files and images and then apply the picture styles. ***Hint: Insert a column break after formatting each panel. After changing the text wrapping to Square, move down the images of the leopard and the rhinoceros as shown in Figure 7.9 to make sure that the animal names line up horizontally.***

	Text File	Graphic File	Picture Style
Panel 2	**Safari2.docx**	**leopard.png**	Beveled Matte, White
Panel 3	**Safari3.docx**	**rhino.png**	Bevel Perspective Left, White

19. Insert the safari graphic behind the text on the page as shown in Figure 7.9 by completing the following steps:
   a. Press Ctrl + Home.
   b. Click the Insert tab and then click the Pictures button in the Illustrations group.
   c. Navigate to the C7 folder and then double-click *safariborder.png*.
   d. Change the width of the image to 11 inches.
   e. Change the text wrapping to Behind Text.
   f. Drag the image so it is positioned approximately 0.25 inch from the bottom edge of the page, as shown below.

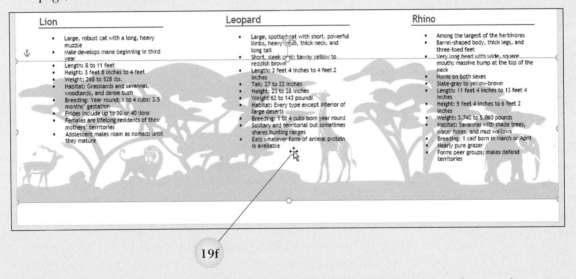

19f

20. Make any necessary adjustments so that your document looks similar to the one shown in Figure 7.9.
21. Save the brochure with the name **7-Panels1-3**.

Check Your Work

Figure 7.9 Front of Brochure Created in Project 1b (Panels 1–3)

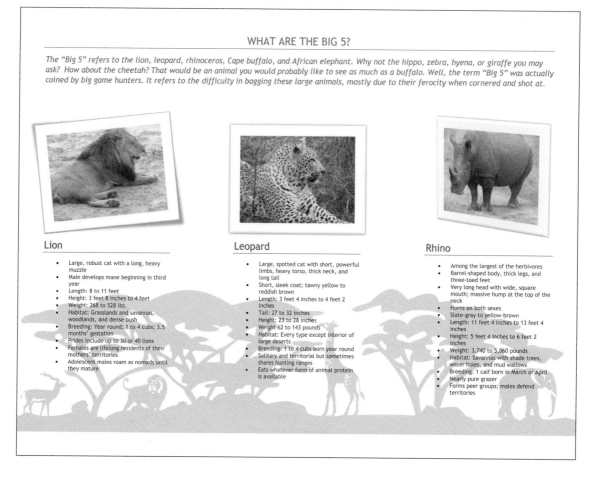

WHAT ARE THE BIG 5?

The "Big 5" refers to the lion, leopard, rhinoceros, Cape buffalo, and African elephant. Why not the hippo, zebra, hyena, or giraffe you may ask? How about the cheetah? That would be an animal you would probably like to see as much as a buffalo. Well, the term "Big 5" was actually coined by big game hunters. It refers to the difficulty in bagging these large animals, mostly due to their ferocity when cornered and shot at.

Lion
- Large, robust cat with a long, heavy muzzle
- Male develops mane beginning in third year
- Length: 8 to 11 feet
- Height: 3 feet 8 inches to 4 feet
- Weight: 268 to 528 lbs.
- Habitat: Grasslands and savannas, woodlands, and dense bush
- Breeding: Year round; 1 to 4 cubs; 3.5 months' gestation
- Prides include up to 30 or 40 lions
- Females are lifelong residents of their mothers' territories
- Adolescent males roam as nomads until they mature

Leopard
- Large, spotted cat with short, powerful limbs, heavy torso, thick neck, and long tail
- Short, sleek coat; tawny yellow to reddish brown
- Length: 3 feet 4 inches to 4 feet 2 inches
- Tail: 27 to 32 inches
- Height: 23 to 28 inches
- Weight 62 to 143 pounds
- Habitat: Every type except interior of large deserts
- Breeding: 1 to 4 cubs born year round
- Solitary and territorial but sometimes shares hunting ranges
- Eats whatever form of animal protein is available

Rhino
- Among the largest of the herbivores
- Barrel-shaped body, thick legs, and three-toed feet
- Very long head with wide, square mouth; massive hump at the top of the neck
- Horns on both sexes
- Slate-gray to yellow-brown
- Length: 11 feet 4 inches to 13 feet 4 inches
- Height: 5 feet 4 inches to 6 feet 2 inches
- Weight: 3,740 to 5,060 pounds
- Habitat: Savannas with shade trees, water holes, and mud wallows
- Breeding: 1 calf born in March or April
- Nearly pure grazer
- Forms peer groups; males defend territories

Understanding Duplex Printing

Printing a brochure or booklet almost always requires printing on both sides of the paper. This process is known as ***duplex printing***. Some printers offer automatic duplex printing, while others provide instructions to manually reinsert a page to print on the second side. Some printers do not support duplex printing at all. To determine whether a specific printer supports duplex printing, check the printer manual or review the options in the *Settings* section of the Print backstage area. The printer properties can also be displayed by clicking the <u>Printer Properties</u> hyperlink below the Printer gallery.

If a printer supports duplex printing manually (not automatically), select the *Manually Print on Both Sides* option in the second gallery in the *Settings* section of the Print backstage area in Word, as shown in Figure 7.10. All the pages that appear on one side of the paper will print and then a prompt will say to turn the stack over and feed the pages into the printer again. Alternatively, print on both sides by printing the odd and then the even pages. To do this, display the Print backstage area and then click the *Only Print Odd Pages* option at the first gallery in the *Settings* section. After the odd pages have been printed, flip the stack of pages over, click the *Only Print Even Pages* option, and then click the Print button. Depending on the printer, the pages may need to be rotated and/or reordered to print the other side of the stack correctly.

duplex printing

Printing on both sides of a sheet of paper

DTP POINTER

When placing the printed first page in the printer tray, make sure to orient it so that the second page prints on the blank side.

Figure 7.10 Setting Up Manual Duplex Printing at the Print Backstage Area

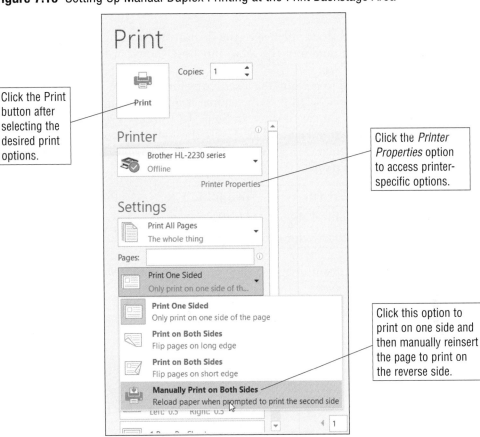

Click the Print button after selecting the desired print options.

Click the *Printer Properties* option to access printer-specific options.

Click this option to print on one side and then manually reinsert the page to print on the reverse side.

DTP POINTER

Do not reverse the page order in both Word and the printer's properties, or the two settings will cancel out each other.

In addition, the order that the pages print in can be changed by clicking the File tab and then clicking *Options*. At the Word Options dialog box, click *Advanced* in the left panel and then add a check mark next to the option to print on the front or the back of the page, as shown in Figure 7.11. If changes are made in the Word Options dialog box, make sure to change them back before printing a regular document.

Figure 7.11 Changing Printing Options at the Word Options Dialog Box

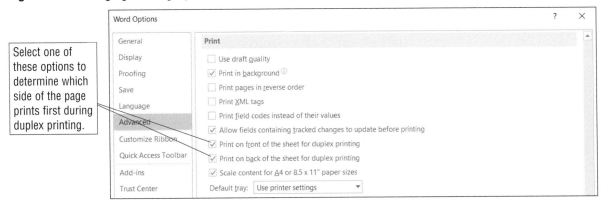

Select one of these options to determine which side of the page prints first during duplex printing.

1. With **7-Panels1-3.docx** open, save the document with the name **7-Safari**.
2. Create panels 4, 5, and 6 of the safari brochure shown in Figure 7.12 by completing the following steps:
   a. Press Ctrl + End to position the insertion point at the end of the page containing panels 1, 2, and 3 and then press Ctrl + Shift + Enter to insert a column break.
   b. Complete steps similar to those in Steps 12 through 17 in Project 1b to format panels 4 and 5 as shown in Figure 7.12. Insert the following text files and photographs and then apply the following picture styles. *Hint: Remember to insert a column break after formatting each panel.*

	Text File	Graphic File	Picture Style
Panel 4	**Safari4.docx**	**buffalo.png**	Rotated, White
Panel 5	**Safari5.docx**	**elephant.png**	Beveled Matte, White

   c. Position the elephant image so the heading *African Elephant* aligns horizontally with the heading *Cape Buffalo*.

3. Create the title text in panel 6 (the cover) by completing the following steps:
   a. At the top of panel 6, press the Enter key six times. *Hint: Make sure the No Spacing style is selected in the Styles gallery.*
   b. Type the following:

      Out of (Press Enter.)
      Africa (Press Enter.)
      Safari at (Press Enter.)
      Kruger (Press Enter.)
      National (Press Enter.)
      Park

   c. Select the text you just typed; change the font to 26-point Castellar; apply the Tan, Accent 5, Darker 50% font color; and then change the paragraph alignment to center.
   d. Add a reversed text effect to *AFRICA* in panel 6 as shown in Figure 7.12 by selecting the text *AFRICA* (including the nonprinting paragraph symbol after the word) and then applying the Tan, Accent 5, Lighter 80% font color.
   e. With *AFRICA* still selected, click the Shading button arrow in the Paragraph group on the Home tab and then click the *Orange, Accent 1, Darker 25%* option (fifth column, fifth row in the *Theme Colors* section).

4. Click anywhere in the brochure to deselect the text *AFRICA* and then insert and format a text box in panel 6 by completing the following steps:
   a. Draw a text box in the panel that is approximately 1 inch in height and 1.75 inches in width.
   b. With the insertion point inside the text box, type In search of the BIG.
   c. Select the text *In search of the BIG*, change the font to 24-point Gloucester MT Extra Condensed, and then apply the Orange, Accent 1, Darker 25% font color.
   d. Change the paragraph alignment in the text box to right.
   e. Remove the shape fill and shape outline from the text box.
5. Insert and format another text box in panel 6 by completing the following steps:
   a. Draw a text box that is approximately 2 inches in height and 1 inch in width.
   b. With the insertion point inside the text box, type 5.
   c. Select *5*, change the font to 100-point Papyrus, and then apply the Tan, Accent 5, Darker 50% font color.
   d. Remove the shape fill and shape outline from the text box.
   e. Position the two text boxes as shown in Figure 7.12.
6. Copy the safari graphic from the bottom of the first page and then paste it in the same location at the bottom of the second page (approximately 0.25 inch above the bottom of the page).
7. Make any necessary adjustments so that your document looks similar to the one shown in Figure 7.12.
8. Save **7-Safari.docx** and then print the first page of the brochure. (You may want to print the brochure on parchment- or beige-colored paper.) Reinsert the first page into the printer and then print the second page on the back of the first page or print using the manual duplex feature at the Print backstage area.
9. Close **7-Safari.docx**.

Check Your Work

Figure 7.12 Back of Brochure Created in Project 1c (Panels 4–6)

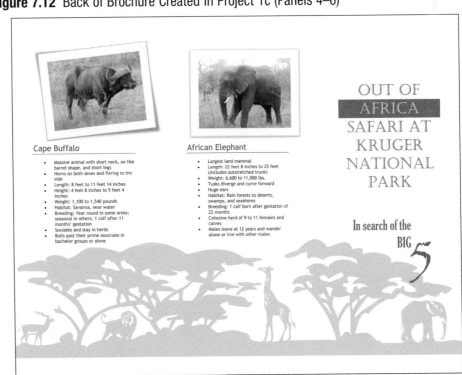

Project 2 Create a Booklet

1 Part

You will create an eight-page booklet and then fold it after it has been printed using features learned in this chapter.

Preview Finished Project

Creating Booklets

Booklets are often used for menus, manuals, directories, invitations, and programs. Various types of booklets can be created in Word. In this section, a folded booklet will be created, in which each sheet of standard-size 8.5-by-11-inch paper contains two pages of the booklet. The booklet will be enhanced by adding headers, footers, and page numbers.

DTP POINTER

A book fold can be added to an existing document, but remember to check and reposition some of the elements.

To create a folded booklet in Word, start at a blank document and then change the orientation to landscape. Display the Page Setup dialog box with the Margins tab selected, click the *Multiple pages* option box arrow, and then click *Book fold* at the drop-down list.

When *Book fold* is selected at the Page Setup dialog box, Word sets up the document to print two pages on one side of the paper. The paper is then folded so that it opens like a book. When planning the placement of text, consider how the document will print and how the booklet will be assembled. For example, in an eight-page booklet, pages 8 and 1 are next to each other on the same side of the same sheet of paper, as are pages 2 and 7, 6 and 3, and 4 and 5, as shown in Figure 7.13. This can get confusing to keep track of, so as with a brochure, create a dummy booklet first. When additional pages are required for a booklet, insert a page break to create a new page with the existing book-fold setting.

When using the book-fold setting, a document will display with facing pages. This means that the margins of the left page mirror those of the right page (i.e., the inside margins are the same width and the outside margins are the same width). The *Gutter* measurement box at the Page Setup dialog box is not available when using the *Mirror margins*, *2 pages per sheet*, or *Book fold* option.

Figure 7.13 Understanding Page Placement within an Eight-page Booklet

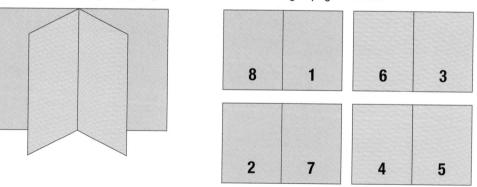

1. Open a blank document and save it with the name **7-GolfBookFold**.
2. Apply page formatting by completing the following steps:
   a. Click the Layout tab, click the Margins button in the Page Setup group, and then click the *Custom Margins* option at the drop-down list.
   b. At the Page Setup dialog box with the Margins tab selected, change the top, bottom, right, and left margins to 0.5 inch.
   c. Change the gutter measurement to 0.25 inch.
   d. Click the *Multiple pages* option box arrow in the *Pages* section and then click *Book fold* at the drop-down list. ***Hint: When you select*** **Book fold***, the page orientation changes automatically to landscape.*
   e. Click the *Sheets per booklet* option box arrow and then click *8* at the drop-down list.
   f. Click OK to close the dialog box.

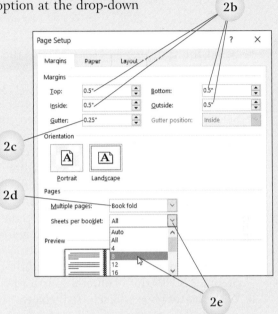

3. Press Ctrl + Enter seven times to generate a total of eight pages in the booklet.
4. Apply the Dividend theme.
5. Position the insertion point in the first page and then insert the images as shown on the cover of the booklet in Figure 7.14 by completing the following steps:
   a. Use the Pictures button in the Illustrations group on the Insert tab to insert **womangolfer.png** from the C7 folder.
   b. With the image selected, change the text wrapping to In Front of Text.
   c. Apply the Beveled Matte, White picture style (second option in the Picture Styles group) and then drag the image to a position similar to that shown in Figure 7.14 on page 268.

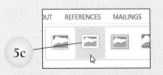

   d. Use the Pictures button to insert **golfclub.png** from the C7 folder.
   e. Change the height of the image to 2 inches.
   f. Change the text wrapping to Behind Text.
   g. Click the Artistic Effects button in the Adjust group on the Picture Tools Format tab and then click the *Texturizer* effect (second column, fourth row).
   h. Click the More Picture Styles button in the Pictures Styles group and then click the *Rotated, White* option (third column, third row).
   i. Drag the image to a position similar to that shown in Figure 7.14.

6. Add the text at the bottom of the cover page by completing the following steps:
   a. Draw a text box that measures 1.25 inches by 3.5 inches.
   b. Position the text box at the bottom of the cover page and then type the following in the text box:

   > Midwest Golf Club (Press Shift + Enter.)
   > Women's 9-Hole Directory (Press Shift + Enter.)
   > Summer 2018

   c. Select the text *Midwest Golf Club* and then click the *Title* style option in the Styles group on the Home tab.
   d. Select the text *Women's 9-Hole Directory*, change the font to 14-point Trebuchet MS, and turn on kerning for fonts 14 points and above.
   e. Select the text *Summer 2018* and then change the font to 14-point Trebuchet MS.
   f. With the text *Summer 2018* still selected, apply the Fill: White; Outline: Plum, Accent color 2; Hard Shadow: Plum, Accent color 2 text effect (fourth column, third row) using the Text Effects and Typography button in the Font group on the Home tab.
   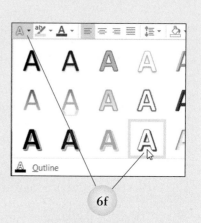
   g. Select the text box, click the Drawing Tools Format tab, click the More Shape Styles button in the Shape Styles group, and then select the Subtle Effect - Plum, Accent 2 style (third column, fourth row).
   h. With the text box still selected, change the paragraph alignment to center.
   i. Save the document.
7. Position the insertion point at the top of page 2, press Ctrl + E, and then type Notes. **Hint: Turn on the display of nonprinting characters and position the insertion point before the Page Break mark.**
8. Position the insertion point on page 3 (making sure that the insertion point is positioned before the Page Break mark) and then insert **Welcome.docx** from the C7 folder.
9. Select the text *Welcome to the 2018 golf season!* and then apply the Intense Quote style.

10. Select the text beginning with *All scores are to be posted* to the end of the text and then click the Bullets button in the Paragraph group.
11. With the text still selected, display the Paragraph dialog box with the Indents and Spacing tab selected. Remove the check mark from the *Don't add space between paragraphs of the same style* check box in the *Spacing* section and then click OK.

12. Position the insertion point on page 4 (before the Page Break mark) and then insert **MemberNames.docx** from the C7 folder.
13. Insert **MemberNames.docx** from the C7 folder on page 5 and on page 6.
14. Position the insertion point on page 7 and then insert **Schedule.docx** from the C7 folder.
15. Apply the Intense Quote style to the text *Ladies 9-Hole Golf Schedule*.
16. Position the insertion point at the top of page 8, press Ctrl + E, and then type More Notes.
17. Add page numbering by completing the following steps:
    a. Press Ctrl + Home to position the insertion point at the beginning of the document.
    b. Click the Insert tab and then click the Page Number button in the Header & Footer group.
    c. Point to the *Bottom of Page* option at the Page Number button drop-down list and then click the *Plain Number 2* option in the *Simple* section of the side menu.
    d. Click the *Different First Page* check box in the Options group on the Header & Footer Tools Design tab to insert a check mark.

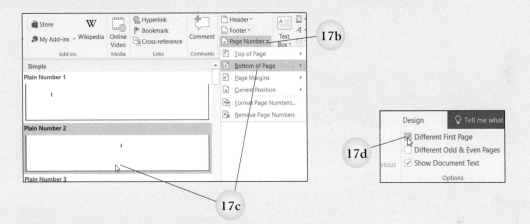

    e. Click the Close Header & Footer button in the Close group.
18. Print the document by completing the following steps:
    a. Display the Print backstage area.
    b. Click the second gallery in the *Settings* section (which contains the text *Print One Sided*) and then click *Manually Print on Both Sides* at the drop-down list.
    c. Click the Print button.
    d. Word will print all the pages that appear on one side of the paper and then prompt you to turn the stack over and feed the pages into the printer again. Once you have turned the stack of papers over, click the OK button. ***Hint: You may have to experiment with reloading your pages properly.***

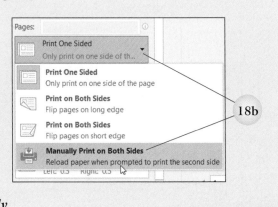

19. Fold the pages to assemble the booklet.
20. Save and close **7-GolfBookFold.docx**.

Check Your Work

Figure 7.14 Booklet Created in Project 2

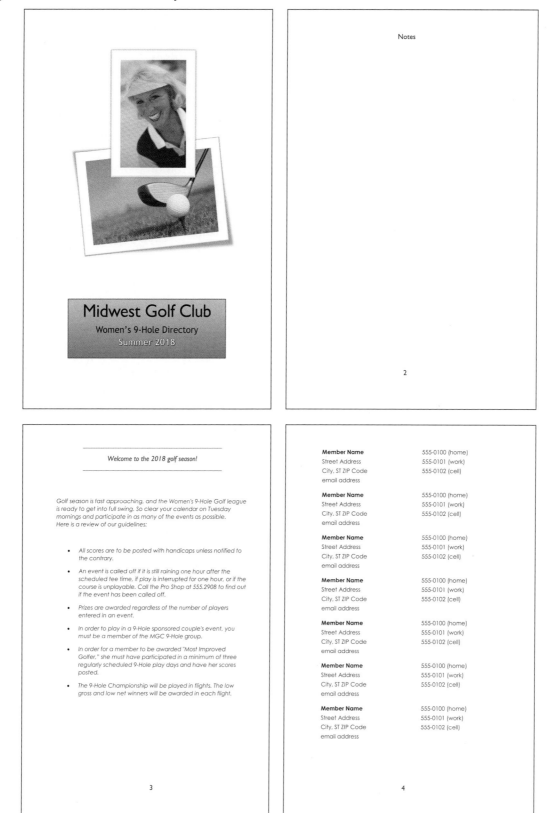

Notes

2

Welcome to the 2018 golf season!

Golf season is fast approaching, and the Women's 9-Hole Golf league is ready to get into full swing. So clear your calendar on Tuesday mornings and participate in as many of the events as possible. Here is a review of our guidelines:

- All scores are to be posted with handicaps unless notified to the contrary.

- An event is called off if it is still raining one hour after the scheduled tee time, if play is interrupted for one hour, or if the course is unplayable. Call the Pro Shop at 555.2908 to find out if the event has been called off.

- Prizes are awarded regardless of the number of players entered in an event.

- In order to play in a 9-Hole sponsored couple's event, you must be a member of the MGC 9-Hole group.

- In order for a member to be awarded "Most Improved Golfer," she must have participated in a minimum of three regularly scheduled 9-Hole play days and have her scores posted.

- The 9-Hole Championship will be played in flights. The low gross and low net winners will be awarded in each flight.

3

Member Name	555-0100 (home)
Street Address	555-0101 (work)
City, ST ZIP Code	555-0102 (cell)
email address	

Member Name	555-0100 (home)
Street Address	555-0101 (work)
City, ST ZIP Code	555-0102 (cell)
email address	

Member Name	555-0100 (home)
Street Address	555-0101 (work)
City, ST ZIP Code	555-0102 (cell)
email address	

Member Name	555-0100 (home)
Street Address	555-0101 (work)
City, ST ZIP Code	555-0102 (cell)
email address	

Member Name	555-0100 (home)
Street Address	555-0101 (work)
City, ST ZIP Code	555-0102 (cell)
email address	

Member Name	555-0100 (home)
Street Address	555-0101 (work)
City, ST ZIP Code	555-0102 (cell)
email address	

Member Name	555-0100 (home)
Street Address	555-0101 (work)
City, ST ZIP Code	555-0102 (cell)
email address	

4

continues

Figure 7.14 Booklet Created in Project 7.3—*continued*

Member Name	555-0100 (home)
Street Address	555-0101 (work)
City, ST ZIP Code	555-0102 (cell)
email address	
Member Name	555-0100 (home)
Street Address	555-0101 (work)
City, ST ZIP Code	555-0102 (cell)
email address	
Member Name	555-0100 (home)
Street Address	555-0101 (work)
City, ST ZIP Code	555-0102 (cell)
email address	
Member Name	555-0100 (home)
Street Address	555-0101 (work)
City, ST ZIP Code	555-0102 (cell)
email address	
Member Name	555-0100 (home)
Street Address	555-0101 (work)
City, ST ZIP Code	555-0102 (cell)
email address	
Member Name	555-0100 (home)
Street Address	555-0101 (work)
City, ST ZIP Code	555-0102 (cell)
email address	
Member Name	555-0100 (home)
Street Address	555-0101 (work)
City, ST ZIP Code	555-0102 (cell)
email address	

5

Member Name	555-0100 (home)
Street Address	555-0101 (work)
City, ST ZIP Code	555-0102 (cell)
email address	
Member Name	555-0100 (home)
Street Address	555-0101 (work)
City, ST ZIP Code	555-0102 (cell)
email address	
Member Name	555-0100 (home)
Street Address	555-0101 (work)
City, ST ZIP Code	555-0102 (cell)
email address	
Member Name	555-0100 (home)
Street Address	555-0101 (work)
City, ST ZIP Code	555-0102 (cell)
email address	
Member Name	555-0100 (home)
Street Address	555-0101 (work)
City, ST ZIP Code	555-0102 (cell)
email address	
Member Name	555-0100 (home)
Street Address	555-0101 (work)
City, ST ZIP Code	555-0102 (cell)
email address	
Member Name	555-0100 (home)
Street Address	555-0101 (work)
City, ST ZIP Code	555-0102 (cell)
email address	

6

Ladies 9-Hole Golf Schedule

Tuesday	April 24	Opening Luncheon
Tuesday	May 8	Opening Scramble
Tuesday	May 15	9-Hole Event, Front
Tuesday	May 22	9-Hole Event, Back
Friday	May 25	9-Hole Couple's Golf
Wednesday	May 30	Women's Rally for the Cure
Tuesday	June 5	9-Hole Event, Front
Tuesday	June 12	9-Hole Event, Back
Tuesday	June 15	9-Hole Event, Crazy Days
Tuesday	June 26	9-Hole Event, Front
Tuesday	July 3	9-Hole Guest Day
Tuesday	July 10	9-Hole, Championship
Friday	July 20	9-Hole, Couples Golf
Tuesday	July 24	Closing Lunch

7

More Notes

8

Project 3 **Create a Brochure and Booklet with 2 Pages per Sheet** **2 Parts**

You will create a brochure and booklet using the 2 Pages per Sheet feature to create the framework for each document.

Preview Finished Project

Using the 2 Pages per Sheet Feature to Create Brochures and Booklets

Word's 2 Pages per Sheet feature can be used to create both brochures and booklets. This feature divides each page in half, as shown in Figure 7.15. The printed page can then be folded in half and used as a single-fold brochure, or several pages can be folded and bound at the fold to create a booklet. Word displays and numbers each half page as a separate page. Any page formatting—such as margins, paper size, and orientation—can be applied to each half page. Headers and footers, page numbering, and page borders can also be inserted.

To use the 2 Pages per Sheet feature, click the Layout tab and then click the Page Setup group dialog box launcher. At the Page Setup dialog box with the Margins tab selected, click the *Multiple pages* option box arrow and then click *2 pages per sheet* at the drop-down list. In addition, select *Portrait* or *Landscape* in the *Orientation* section and then enter the desired margin measurements. Refer to Figure 7.15 to see where the outside and inside margins are located when portrait or landscape orientation is selected.

Figure 7.15 Using the 2 Pages per Sheet Feature

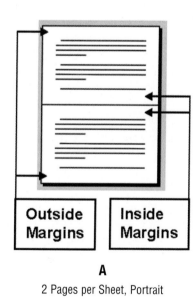

A

2 Pages per Sheet, Portrait

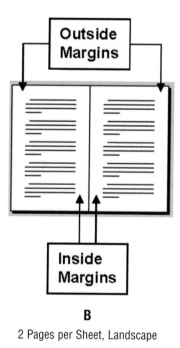

B

2 Pages per Sheet, Landscape

1. Open **SingleFoldLandscape.docx** in the SampleBrochures folder and then print the document on both sides of a sheet of paper. Use this as a dummy for Project 3a.
2. At a blank document, create the inside panels of a single-fold brochure as shown in Figure 7.16 on page 274 by completing the following steps:
   a. Click the Layout tab and then click the Page Setup group dialog box launcher.
   b. At the Page Setup dialog box with the Margins tab selected, change the top, bottom, left, and right margins to 0.7 inch; change the page orientation to landscape; and then click the *Multiple pages* option box arrow and click *2 pages per sheet* at the drop-down list. (When you click the *2 pages per sheet* option, the left and right margins change to the outside and inside margins.)
   c. Click OK to close the dialog box.
   d. With the insertion point positioned at the beginning of the document, insert **HeartText.docx** from the C7 folder.
   e. Press Ctrl + A to select all the text in the document, click the Home tab, and then click the *No Spacing* style.

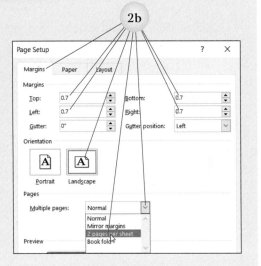

3. Apply a style to the first paragraph of text and then modify the style by completing the following steps:
   a. Select the first paragraph of text.
   b. Click the *Heading 1* style in the Styles group on the Home tab.
   c. Change the font to 14-point Lucinda Sans Unicode, apply bold and italic formatting, and then apply the Blue, Accent 5, Darker 25% font color.
   d. Right-click the Heading 1 style in the Styles gallery and then click *Update Heading 1 to Match Selection*.

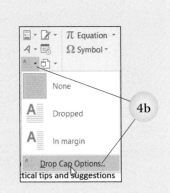

4. Insert and format the paragraph with the drop cap as shown in Figure 7.16 by completing the following steps:
   a. Click anywhere in the first paragraph to deselect it, position the insertion point within it, and then click the Insert tab.
   b. Click the Drop Cap button in the Text group and then click *Drop Cap Options* at the drop-down list.

c. At the Drop Cap dialog box, click *Dropped* in the *Position* section, change the font to Harrington, make sure that *3* displays in the *Lines to drop* measurement box, and then change the value in the *Distance from text* measurement box to 0.1 inch.

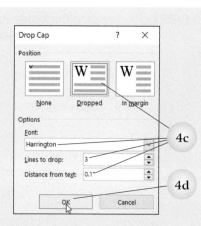

d. Click OK to close the dialog box.

e. With the drop cap selected (gray sizing handles display around the letter), change the font color to Orange, Accent 2, Darker 25% and then remove italic formatting.

f. Click the Line and Paragraph Spacing button in the Paragraph group and then click *Remove Space Before Paragraph* at the drop-down list.

5. Apply a style and then modify the style by completing the following steps:

a. Select the text *Diabetes: The Latest News* and apply the Heading 2 style.

b. Right-click the *Heading 2* style in the Styles group and click *Modify*.

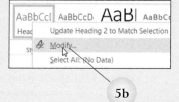

c. At the Modify Style dialog box, change the font to 16-point Cambria, apply bold formatting, and then apply the Orange, Accent 2, Darker 25% font color.

d. Apply small caps formatting by clicking the Format button in the lower left corner of the dialog box and then clicking *Font* at the pop-up list.

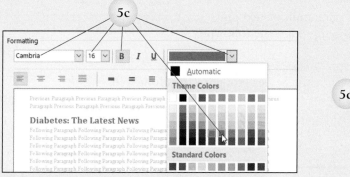
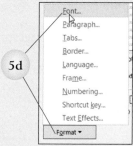

e. At the Font dialog box with the Font tab selected, insert a check mark in the *Small caps* check box and then click OK.

f. Add 18 points of spacing before the paragraph by clicking the Format button and then clicking *Paragraph* at the pop-up list. At the Paragraph dialog box, type 18 in the *Before* measurement box in the *Spacing* section and then click OK.

g. Click OK to accept the modifications to the Heading 2 style. (The modified Heading 2 style has replaced the previous Heading 2 style, which is saved with the document.)

6. Copy the Heading 3 style and the Heading 4 style from the **HeartTemplate.dotx** template into the current document by completing the following steps:

a. Click the Styles group task pane launcher.

b. Click the Manage Styles button at the bottom of the Styles task pane.

c. At the Manage Styles dialog box, click the Import/Export button in the bottom left corner.

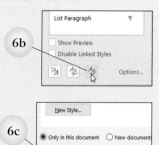

d. At the Organizer dialog box, click the Close File button below the option box that contains the text *Normal.dotm (global template)*.

e. Click the Open File button (previously the Close File button), navigate to the C7 folder, and then double-click **HeartTemplate.dotx** in the Content pane.

f. Select the Heading 3 and the Heading 4 styles in the *In HeartTemplate.dotx* list box (hold down the Ctrl key while clicking *Heading 3* and *Heading 4*) and then click the Copy button.

g. If a Word message box displays asking if you want to override the Heading 3 style, click the Yes to All button. At the Organizer dialog box, click the Close button.

h. Close the Styles task pane.

7. Select the text *Tuesday, March 20, 2018* and then apply the Heading 3 style.

8. Select the text *Katherine Dwyer, M.D.* and then apply the Heading 4 style.

9. Create a style based on formatting by completing the following steps:

a. Select the paragraph beginning *One of the best ways*, change the font to 12-point Calibri, and then add 12 points of spacing before the paragraph.

b. Right-click the text, click the Styles button on the Mini toolbar, and then click *Create a Style* at the side menu.

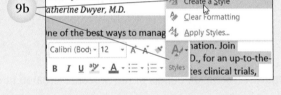

c. At the Create New Style from Formatting dialog box, type HeartBody in the *Name* text box and then click OK.

10. Apply the Heading 2, Heading 3, Heading 4, and HeartBody styles to the remaining headings and paragraphs as shown in Figure 7.16.

11. Position the insertion point before the text *All lectures:* and add 9 points of spacing before the paragraph.

12. Select the text from *All lectures:* to the end of the document. With the text selected, change the font to 12-point Calibri, apply bold formatting, and then apply the Blue, Accent 5, Darker 25% font color.

13. Use the existing tabs and the Tab key to align the lecture information (time and location) as shown in Figure 7.16.

14. Position the insertion point before *The talk is* and then add 9 points of spacing before the paragraph.

15. Select the text *FREE* and then change the font color to Orange, Accent 2, Darker 25%.
Note: If the text in the last paragraph at the bottom of the second page continues to a third page, adjust the paragraph spacing to avoid creating the new page.

16. Save the modified style set by completing the following steps:

a. Click the Design tab.

b. Click the More Style Sets button in the Document Formatting group.

c. At the drop-down gallery, click *Save as a New Style Set*.

d. At the Save as a New Style Set dialog box, type XX-HeartStyles (replacing the *XX* with your initials) in the *File name* text box and then click the Save button.

17. Add the image on the first page of the brochure by completing the following steps:

a. Position the insertion point before the text *DIABETES: THE LATEST NEWS* and then click the Pictures button in the Illustrations group on the Insert tab.

b. At the Insert Picture dialog box, navigate to the C7 folder.

c. Double-click the file **healthcare.png**.

d. With the image selected, click the Crop button arrow in the Size group on the Picture Tools Format tab, point to *Crop to Shape*, and then click the *Heart* option at the side menu (sixth column, third row in the *Basic Shapes* section).

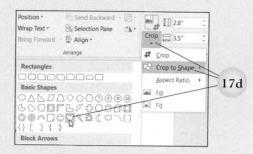

e. Change the text wrapping to In Front of Text and then size and position the image as shown in Figure 7.16. Make sure that the heart displays on the left page of the brochure. *Hint: The image will display on only one of the pages and it will show as only half an image. Do not worry; it will print properly!*

f. With the image selected, click the Color button in the Adjust group and then click the *Blue, Accent color 5 Light* option (sixth column, third row in the *Recolor* section).

g. Click the Corrections button in the Adjust group and then click *Sharpen: 25%* in the *Sharpen/Soften* section.

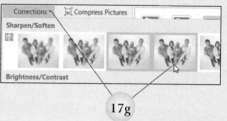

h. Change the text wrapping to Behind Text.

18. Save the document with the name **7-Panels1,2**.

19. Print and then close **7-Panels1,2.docx**.

Check Your Work

Figure 7.16 Inside Panels of the Brochure Created in Project 3a

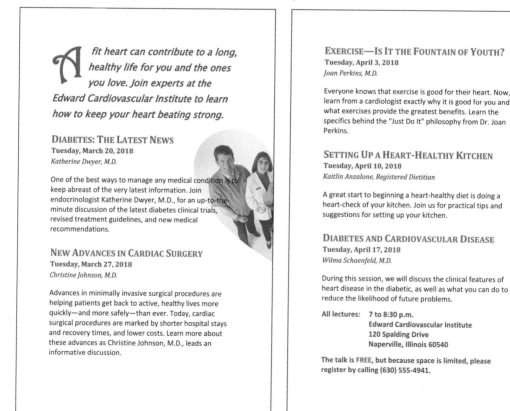

A fit heart can contribute to a long, healthy life for you and the ones you love. Join experts at the Edward Cardiovascular Institute to learn how to keep your heart beating strong.

DIABETES: THE LATEST NEWS
Tuesday, March 20, 2018
Katherine Dwyer, M.D.

One of the best ways to manage any medical condition is to keep abreast of the very latest information. Join endocrinologist Katherine Dwyer, M.D., for an up-to-the-minute discussion of the latest diabetes clinical trials, revised treatment guidelines, and new medical recommendations.

NEW ADVANCES IN CARDIAC SURGERY
Tuesday, March 27, 2018
Christine Johnson, M.D.

Advances in minimally invasive surgical procedures are helping patients get back to active, healthy lives more quickly—and more safely—than ever. Today, cardiac surgical procedures are marked by shorter hospital stays and recovery times, and lower costs. Learn more about these advances as Christine Johnson, M.D., leads an informative discussion.

EXERCISE—IS IT THE FOUNTAIN OF YOUTH?
Tuesday, April 3, 2018
Joan Perkins, M.D.

Everyone knows that exercise is good for their heart. Now, learn from a cardiologist exactly why it is good for you and what exercises provide the greatest benefits. Learn the specifics behind the "Just Do It" philosophy from Dr. Joan Perkins.

SETTING UP A HEART-HEALTHY KITCHEN
Tuesday, April 10, 2018
Kaitlin Anzalone, Registered Dietitian

A great start to beginning a heart-healthy diet is doing a heart-check of your kitchen. Join us for practical tips and suggestions for setting up your kitchen.

DIABETES AND CARDIOVASCULAR DISEASE
Tuesday, April 17, 2018
Wilma Schaenfeld, M.D.

During this session, we will discuss the clinical features of heart disease in the diabetic, as well as what you can do to reduce the likelihood of future problems.

All lectures: 7 to 8:30 p.m.
Edward Cardiovascular Institute
120 Spalding Drive
Naperville, Illinois 60540

The talk is FREE, but because space is limited, please register by calling (630) 555-4941.

To make this brochure self-mailing, the back will be used for the mailing address, return address, and postage. This newly created material will be printed on the reverse side of the content created in Project 3a and will appear as shown in Figure 7.17 on page 277.

Project 3b **Creating the Back (Panel 3) and Cover**
(Panel 4) of a Single-fold Brochure Part 2 of 2

1. Open **HeartCoverandBack.docx** and then save the document with the name **7-Panels3,4**.
2. Apply the style set you created in Project 3a by completing the following steps:
   a. Click the Design tab.
   b. Click the More Style Sets button in the Document Formatting group.
   c. At the drop-down gallery, click the *XX-HeartStyles* style set option in the *Custom* section (where *XX* has been replaced with your initials).
3. Apply and then modify the Title style by completing the following steps:
   a. Position the insertion point in the text *Spring 2018* on the cover (panel 4) of the brochure and then apply the Title style.
   b. Select the text *Spring 2018* and then change the paragraph alignment to right.
   c. Change the font to 24-point Calibri, apply small caps formatting (Ctrl + Shift + K), and then apply the Blue, Accent 5, Darker 25% font color.
   d. Click the Borders button arrow and then click *Borders and Shading* at the drop-down list.
   e. At the Borders and Shading dialog box, change the line color to Orange, Accent 2, Darker 25% and the line width to 2¼ pt.
   f. Click to add the line to the bottom of the paragraph in the *Preview* section and then click OK.

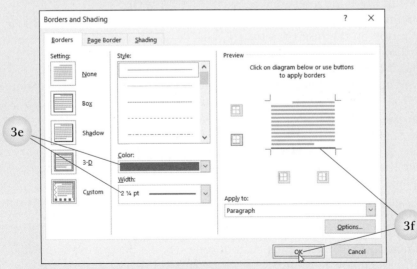

   g. With the text still selected, right-click the *Title* style thumbnail in the Styles gallery and then click *Update Title to Match Selection* at the shortcut menu.

4. Remove the shape outline and shape fill from the title text box.
5. Select the text *Heart's*; change the font to 36-point Harrington; apply bold formatting; apply the Orange, Accent 2, Darker 25% font color; apply small caps formatting; and then turn on kerning for fonts 14 points and above.
6. With the text still selected, change the paragraph alignment to right.
7. Select the text *For your* and *Sake...,* change the font to 18-point Calibri, apply all caps formatting, and then change the paragraph alignment to right. ***Hint: Select For Your**, **press and hold down the Ctrl key, and then select Sake....***

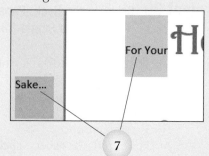

8. Press Ctrl + Home to position the insertion point at the beginning of the document and then insert the same healthcare professionals image used in Project 3a. (Substitute a different image if necessary.)
9. Crop the image to a heart shape by making sure that the image is selected, clicking the Crop button arrow on the Picture Tools Format tab, pointing to *Crop to Shape*, and then clicking the *Heart* option in the *Basic Shapes* section of the drop-down list.
10. With the image still selected, click the Picture Effects button in the Picture Styles group, point to *Shadow*, and then click the *Inside: Top Right* effect (third column, first row in the *Inner* section).

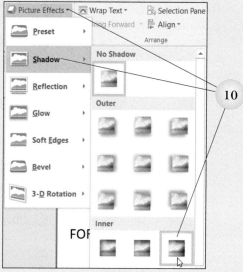

11. Change the height of the image to 3.3 inches and the width to 4.13 inches.
12. Change the text wrapping to In Front of Text and then drag the image to the position shown in Figure 7.17.
13. Insert the logo on the front cover by completing the following steps:
    a. Press Ctrl + Home to move the insertion point to the beginning of the document.
    b. Use the Pictures button on the Insert tab to insert **edwardcardio.png** from the C7 folder.
    c. Change the height of the logo to 0.7 inch and the width to 1.88 inches.
    d. Change the text wrapping to In Front of Text and then drag the image to the position shown in Figure 7.17.
14. Select the text *EDWARD CARDIOVASCULAR INSTITUTE* in the return address (on the back cover, or panel 3, of the brochure) and then apply the Heading 3 style. ***Hint: If the Heading 3 style is not visible in the Styles group, click the More Styles button. You may need to apply the Heading 2 style first to display the Heading 3 style in the Styles gallery.***
15. Save **7-Panels3,4.docx**.
16. Reinsert the page you printed in Project 3a (**7-Panels1,2.docx**) into the printer and then print **7-Panels3,4.docx** on the back side.
17. Close both documents.
18. Open a blank document and then delete the custom style set you created in the previous exercise by completing the following steps:
    a. Click the Design tab.
    b. Click the More Style Sets button in the Document Formatting group.

c. In the *Custom* section, right-click the style set containing your initials.
d. Click *Delete* at the shortcut menu and then click the Yes button when a message box appears asking if you want to delete the style set.
e. Close the blank document without saving changes.

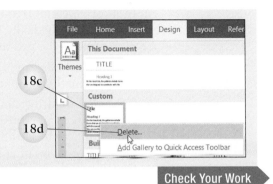

18c

18d

Check Your Work

Figure 7.17 Back and Cover of Brochure Created in Project 3b

Chapter Summary

- Brochures and booklets can be used to inform, educate, promote, and sell. These documents also provide another means of establishing an organization's identity and image.

- The manner in which a brochure is folded determines the order in which the panels are set on the page. The most common brochure fold is called a *letter fold* or *trifold*.

- When choosing the paper stock for a brochure, consider how the brochure will be used. If it will be passed around and used heavily, print on higher quality paper stock to create a more durable brochure. If a brochure will be mailed to a household and lightly used, print on lighter, less durable paper.

- The folds within a brochure create distinct sections in which specific blocks of text can be placed. The main content is contained in panels 1, 2, and 3.

- A dummy is a mockup of a document created using the same size of paper as the final document and folded in the same manner. Create a dummy to help determine where text and objects are placed on the brochure page layout.

- Because the panels in a brochure tend to be small, the page margins should be set as narrow as possible to create more space for content.

- In most brochure layouts, the panels cannot all be the same width. Size text boxes individually for different panels to accommodate the appropriate placement of the text and the folds to achieve the desired result.
- Several methods can be used to create the panels of a brochure. The most common methods are using text boxes, columns, or a table.
- Column formatting can be varied within the same document by using continuous section breaks to separate the sections that will be formatted with different column settings. Divide a document into sections to create different numbers or styles of columns within the same document with options at the Breaks button drop-down list or at the Columns dialog box.
- Printing a booklet or brochure almost always requires printing on both sides of the paper. This is known as *duplex printing*. Depending on the printer, pages may need to be rotated and/or reordered to print the other side of the stack correctly.
- When *Book fold* is selected at the Page Setup dialog box with the Margins tab selected, Word sets up the document to print two pages on one side of the paper. After the paper is folded, it opens like a book.
- Use the 2 Pages per Sheet feature to create a page divided in half, which can be folded. Each side of the page can include individual page settings, headers and footers, page numbers, and so on.
- A style can be modified and any occurrence of the style in the document is automatically updated to reflect the changes. A modified style can be saved to the Styles gallery as a replacement of the original style or it can be saved with a new name. Styles are saved in the document in which they are created.
- If the styles in a document have been created or modified, they can be saved as a style set. A saved style set can then be used in other documents. Styles can be copied from one document or template into another document or template with options at the Organizer dialog box.

Commands Review

FEATURE	RIBBON TAB, GROUP	BUTTON	KEYBOARD SHORTCUT
breaks	Layout, Page Setup		
columns	Layout, Page Setup		
new style	Home, Styles		
styles	Home, Styles		
style sets	Design, Document Formatting		
Styles task pane	Home, Styles		Alt + Ctrl + Shift + S

Creating Specialty Promotional Documents

Performance Objectives

Upon successful completion of Chapter 8, you will be able to:

1   Use Word to create promotional documents

2   Create raffle tickets by using Word's table feature and choosing the appropriate paper

3   Create registration forms that include lines on which to type using Word's underline feature and shapes feature, as well as a table and tab leaders

4   Create postcards by using Word's labels feature and choosing the appropriate paper

5   Merge promotional documents for mailing

6   Create and print invitations, greeting cards, and custom envelopes

7   Create and print a promotional poster

Desktop Publishing Terms

bond paper   newsprint paper
book paper   offset paper
cover paper   tag paper
leader

Word Features Used

fields   shapes
headers and footers   tables
labels   tab leaders
Mail Merge   themes
Printer Properties

Precheck

Check your current skills to help focus your study.

Data Files

Before beginning chapter work, copy the C8 folder to your storage medium and then make C8 the active folder.

SNAP

If you are a SNAP user, launch the Precheck and Tutorials from your Assignments page.

You will create raffle tickets using a table as the framework and adding an *AutoNum* field to the tickets to make them sequentially numbered.

Preview Finished Project

Using Word to Create Promotional Documents

DTP POINTER

Well-organized and clearly written promotional documents inspire confidence in the reader.

In addition to newsletters, flyers, announcements, brochures, and booklets, the "promotional documents" category includes tickets, registration forms, gift certificates, postcards, bookmarks, name tags, invitations, and greeting cards, among many others. These types of documents are considered promotional because they often display a business or organization name or promote an item or service that is for sale. Figure 8.1 illustrates a few promotional documents created with the basic design concepts and Word features used in most of the projects in this chapter. Figure 8.2 illustrates online templates that can be used to promote business interests.

Figure 8.1 Creating Specialty Promotional Documents in Word

Bookmarks

Ticket

Door Hanger

Discount Coupon

Coaster

Gift Certificate

Figure 8.2 Using Word Online Templates to Create Specialty Promotional Documents

Bookmarks

Open House Announcement

Club Membership Card

Gift Certificate

Punch Card

Thank You Card

Menu

The focus of this chapter is on creating several different types of promotional documents: raffle tickets, a registration form, postcards and postcard labels, a greeting card, and a promotional poster. As with any other desktop publishing document, it is important to take the time to plan and design specialty promotional materials. Think about the purpose and audience and determine what content the document needs to communicate. Create a thumbnail sketch and/or dummy to help visualize your design before beginning to work. Take time to carefully select fonts, images, and other design elements. Remember that the content is the most important part of any document.

Creating Raffle Tickets

Raffle tickets are considered specialty promotional documents because they are often used to help raise money for an organization or a cause. Use the table feature in Word to quickly and easily create raffle tickets. Printing the tickets on a thicker paper stock will make them more substantial and durable.

Using Tables to Create Promotional Documents

A table is especially well suited to be used as a framework while creating raffle tickets. With a table, the sizes of the rows and columns can be adjusted to create uniformly sized tickets, and an extra column can be added to create the stub portion of the ticket.

Quick Parts

Word also simplifies the process of numbering the raffle tickets with the *AutoNum* field code. This field code is entered in a document when automatic page numbers are inserted, and it can be used to number the tickets and stubs sequentially. To insert this field code, click the Quick Parts button on the Insert tab and then click *Field* at the drop-down list. This opens the Field dialog box, as shown in Figure 8.3. Make sure that *(All)* displays in the *Categories* option box and then click *AutoNum* in the *Field names* list box. Choose a format for the numbers (e.g., 1, 2, 3) at the *Format* list box.

Figure 8.3 Inserting an *AutoNum* Field Code

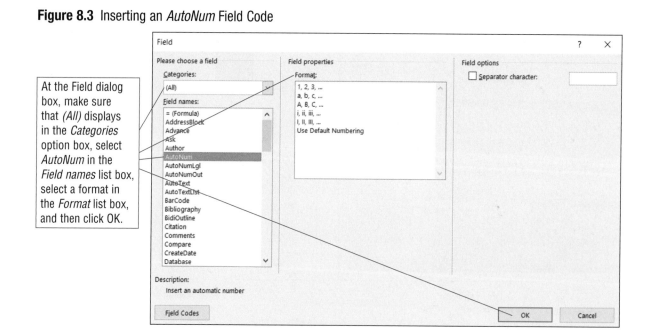

At the Field dialog box, make sure that *(All)* displays in the *Categories* option box, select *AutoNum* in the *Field names* list box, select a format in the *Format* list box, and then click OK.

Understanding Paper Types

Picking the appropriate paper for a project can be challenging. Each type of paper has special characteristics.

Two characteristics that vary from paper to paper are stiffness and grain. The term *stiffness* refers to how easily the paper can bend, and the term *grain* refers to the direction in which the wood fibers in the paper align. It is important to consider the grain if the paper is to be folded; folding against the grain in a stiff sheet can cause the paper to crack. Stiff paper is often scored so it is easier to fold. Another important characteristic of paper is how durable it is and whether or not it can be used in printer press machines, which prints ink on the paper at a very high rate.

One of the most common types of paper is **bond paper**, which is used for a variety of applications from business forms to home and office stationery. It is a strong type of paper, and its cotton fiber content (which usually ranges from 25 to 50 percent) contributes to its good ink absorption. However, bond paper is thin and tends to jam easily in printers.

Book paper is another common paper type. It is durable, inexpensive, and more opaque than bond paper, which makes it well suited to two-sided printing.

Several other common types of paper are available. **Cover paper**, also known as *cardstock*, is a heavy, stiff sheet that is durable and folds easily in the direction of the grain. It is commonly used for folders, postcards, business cards, greeting cards, and book covers. **Newsprint paper** is used almost exclusively for newspapers and is generally inexpensive. This off-white paper, which is thin and porous, is mainly made from recycled paper. Newsprint paper is cut oversized and is durable for running through high speed/volume printers. **Offset paper** is used in offset printing because it is strong and resists tearing when used in large, fast printers. **Tag paper** is dense and strong; it is used for merchandise tags. Other types of specialty papers include onionskin paper (also known as *tissue paper*) and rice paper.

Sidebar glossary

bond paper
A common type of paper; is strong and has good ink absorption

book paper
A common type of paper; is durable, inexpensive, and opaque; well suited for two-sided printing

cover paper
A heavy, stiff, durable type of paper; folds easily in the direction of the grain; also known as *cardstock*

newsprint paper
An inexpensive type of paper; used for printing newspapers

offset paper
A strong type of paper used in offset printing; resists tears when used in large, fast printers

tag paper
A dense, strong type of paper; used for merchandise tags

Project 1 Creating Raffle Tickets and Stubs with Sequential Numbering   Part 1 of 1

1. At a blank document, begin creating the tickets shown in Figure 8.4 on page 286 by changing the top and bottom margins to 0.75 inch.
2. Create a table with two columns and one row.
3. Change the row height and column widths in the table by completing the following steps:
   a. With the insertion point positioned in the first cell in the table, click the Table Tools Layout tab.
   b. Select the current measurement in the *Height* measurement box in the Cell Size group, type 2, and then press the Enter key.
   c. Select the current measurement in the *Width* measurement box in the Cell Size group, type 4, and then press the Enter key.

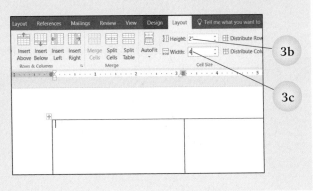

d. Click in the second cell (column) in the table.

e. Select the current measurement in the *Width* measurement box in the Cell Size group, type 2.25, and then press the Enter key.

4. Select the first column and then change the right cell border line to a dashed line by completing the following steps:

a. Click the Table Tools Design tab.

b. Click the Borders button arrow in the Borders group and then click *Borders and Shading* at the drop-down list.

c. At the Borders and Shading dialog box with the Borders tab selected, make sure that *Cell* is selected in the *Apply to* option box.

d. Click the right border line in the *Preview* box to remove the line.

e. Click the third line (dashed line) from the top in the *Style* list box and then click where the previous line displayed in the *Preview* box.

f. Click OK to close the dialog box.

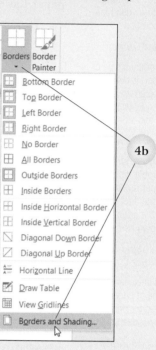

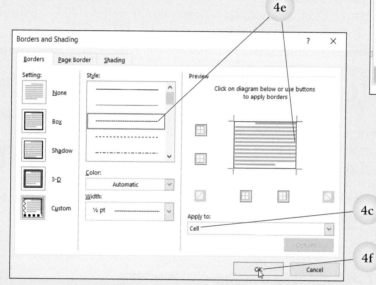

5. Save the document in the C8 folder with the name **8-Raffle**.

6. Insert the ticket and stub text by completing the following steps:

a. Position the insertion point in the first cell and then insert **Raffle.docx** from the C8 folder.

b. Press the Backspace key to remove the blank line.

c. Position the insertion point in the second cell and then insert **Stub.docx** from the C8 folder.

d. Press the Backspace key to remove the blank line.

7. Insert the Summit Outreach logo by completing the following steps:

a. Position the insertion point in the first cell in the first row and then insert **SOLogo.png** from the C8 folder.

b. Apply Tight text wrapping.

c. Position the logo as shown in Figure 8.4.

d. With the logo selected, copy it to the stub section of the ticket by pressing and holding down the Ctrl key while dragging and dropping the logo to the stub section.

e. Click the Color button in the Adjust group on the Picture Tools Format tab and then click the *Washout* option in the *Recolor* section.

f. Apply Behind Text text wrapping.

g. Position the logo in the stub section as shown in Figure 8.4.

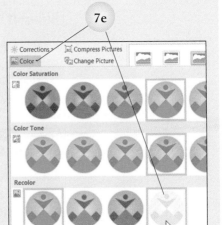

8. Insert sequential numbering by completing the following steps:

   a. Position the insertion point right of *No.* in the first cell and then press the spacebar once.

   b. Click the Insert tab, click the Quick Parts button in the Text group, and then click *Field* at the drop-down list.

   c. At the Field dialog box, make sure that *(All)* displays in the *Categories* option box.

   d. Click *AutoNum* in the *Field names* list box.

   e. Click OK to close the dialog box.

   f. Position the insertion point right of *No.* in the second cell (stub), press the spacebar once, and then insert the *AutoNum* field code as you did in Steps 8b through 8e.

9. Copy the table row three times by completing the following steps:

   a. Select the table row.

   b. Press Ctrl + C to copy the row.

   c. Press Ctrl + End to move the insertion point below the table.

   d. Press Ctrl + V three times. (This inserts three additional rows in the table.)

   Note: If the dashed right border of the first column does not copy to the next three rows, complete Step 4 again to apply the dashed right border.

10. Horizontally center the table by completing the following steps:

    a. Select the entire table.

    b. Click the Table Tools Layout tab.

    c. Click the Properties button in the Table group.

    d. At the Table Properties dialog box, make sure that the Table tab is selected and then click the *Center* option in the *Alignment* section.

    e. Click OK to close the dialog box.

11. Save, print, and then close **8-Raffle.docx**.

Check Your Work

Figure 8.4 Raffle Tickets Created in Project 1

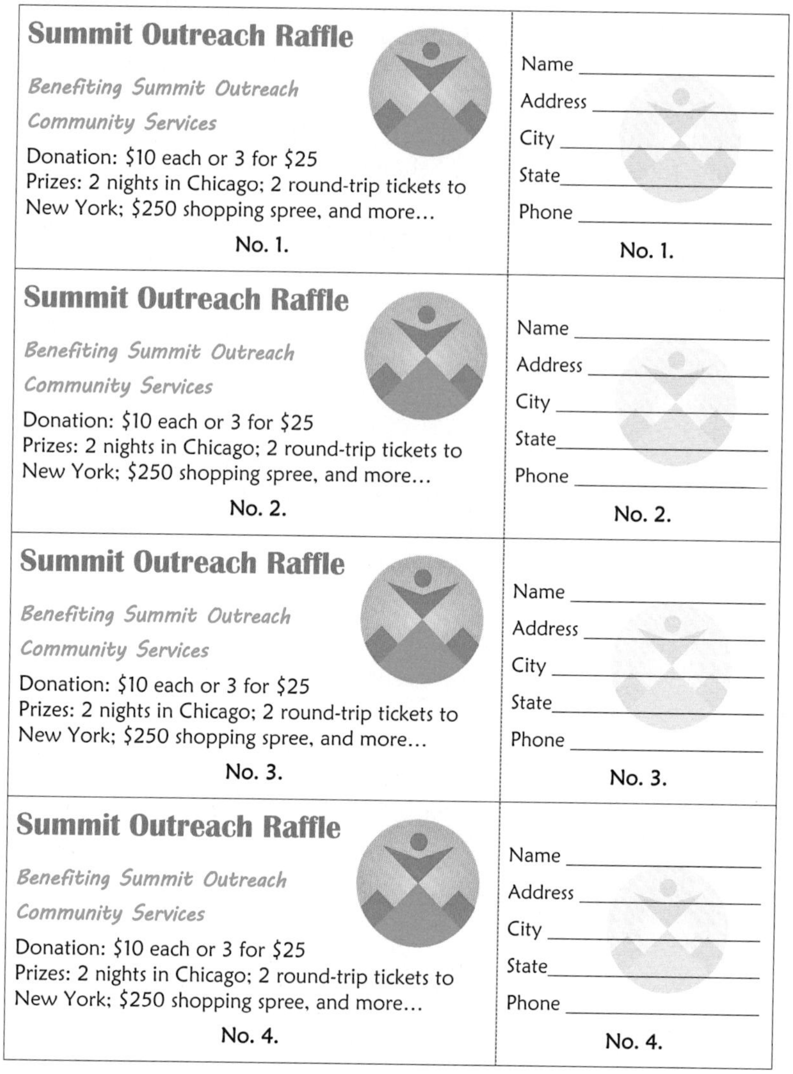

Project 2 Create a Registration Form

1 Part

You will create a registration form that includes lines on which the user can enter data. The lines will be created using tabs, tables, and line objects.

Preview Finished Project

Creating Registration Forms

Registration forms and application forms can be used to gather information for promotional purposes, such as mailings, events, and contests. These forms can be printed and then filled in by users, or users can complete them electronically. Although the main purpose of this type of document is to gather information, design elements should be added to create interest and anticipation among users.

If a form is to be filled in electronically, it should be as user friendly as possible. One problem common to many forms is the inability for the user to type on a line meant for data entry. Typing often moves the line farther along, instead of inserting the data above the line. Several methods can be used to create lines on which data can be entered.

Creating Lines Using the Underline Feature

The first method for creating a line that data can be entered on requires the use of the Underline button and the Tab key. To create a line using the Tab key and the Underline button, complete the following steps:

1. Create tab stops at the points that the line starts and stops.
2. Press the Tab key to align the insertion point at the first tab.
3. Click the Underline button in the Font group on the Home tab to turn on underlining.
4. Press the spacebar once. This creates a location (placeholder) where text can be entered on the line. (Turn on the display of nonprinting characters to view the spacebar placeholder.)
5. Press the Tab key to create the line.
6. Click the Underline button to turn off underlining.
7. Press the Enter key to move to the next line, or press the Tab key to move to the next column.

Figure 8.5 shows the tab settings on the horizontal ruler and the use of the Underline button and Tab key. Make sure that data can be entered on the created line by moving the insertion point to the position after the spacebar and then typing some text. The text should appear typed above the line.

To type on the line that was created using the underline and tab method, turn on the display of nonprinting characters and then position the insertion point immediately right of the space created as a placeholder (which displays as a small dot in the middle of the line) and then type text. If the insertion point is placed before the placeholder, the line will be pushed to the right as data is entered using the keyboard. When a form is created using the Underline button, a note should be provided that instructs the person filling out the form to position the insertion point one space right of the beginning of the underline.

Figure 8.5 Using the Underline Button and Tab Key to Create Fill-in Lines

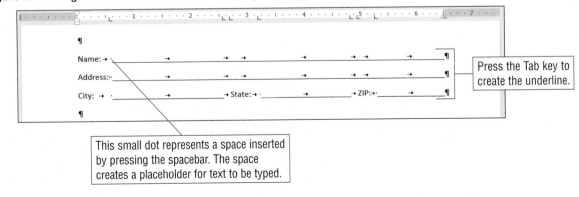

Press the Tab key to create the underline.

This small dot represents a space inserted by pressing the spacebar. The space creates a placeholder for text to be typed.

Creating Lines Using the Shapes Feature

The second method for creating a line that data can be entered on involves creating a line shape using options from the Shapes button drop-down list in the Illustrations group on the Insert tab. Data can be entered in both the hard-copy and electronic copy without disturbing the line's settings. When a line (or any other shape) is placed within a document, it can be moved around by selecting it and then pressing the arrow keys or using the mouse to drag it to the desired location. The shape will move along the lines of the invisible drawing grid that exists within each document, as discussed in earlier chapters. Each time an arrow key is pressed, the shape will move in that direction to the next line of the drawing grid. Often, the default spacing between the gridlines of a document is larger than desired for moving an object; the spacing setting can be adjusted to overcome this problem.

Align

Use the Align button in the Arrange group on the Drawing Tools Format tab to adjust the placement of the lines and make sure that they are all uniform. For example, select two or more lines and then align them at the left by clicking the Align button and then clicking *Align Left* at the drop-down list. Or align the lines between the left and right margins by clicking *Align Center*. If three or more lines are selected, distribute the lines vertically by clicking the *Distribute Vertically* option at the Align button drop-down list.

Creating Lines Using Tables

DTP POINTER

To indent text within a table cell, press Ctrl + Tab to insert a tab.

The third method for creating lines that data can be entered on is to insert a table into the document, as shown in Figure 8.6A, and then add and remove border lines. Using tables allows for easy alignment and placement of the elements within a form. Whether a document is being created to be printed out and filled in by hand or filled in at a computer, use a table as an underlying structure for organizing the text. Type the labels (such as *Name:* and *Date:*) in cells and then remove unnecessary border lines, such as the left, top, and right borders, as shown in Figure 8.6B.

Figure 8.6 Using a Table to Create Lines in a Form

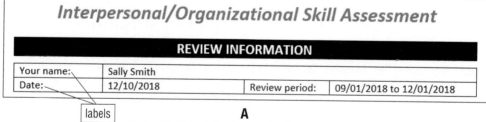

A
Table with Default Borders on All Sides of the Cells

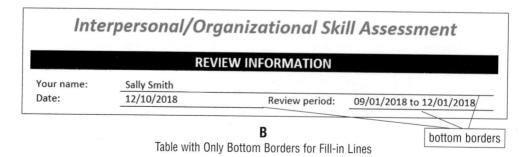

B
Table with Only Bottom Borders for Fill-in Lines

Creating Lines Using Tab Leaders

leader

A line that leads the reader's eyes across a space on the page

Another method for creating lines that align is to use *leaders*, which are lines that guide the reader's eyes across a space on the page. Several types of leaders can be created in Word by using tabs. To do this, display the Tabs dialog box, set a tab where the lines are to end, and then click the desired leader option. Click the Set button and then click OK to close the dialog box. In the document, type the label text and then press the Tab key. A leader will display from the text to the tab setting. Text cannot be inserted on a leader line because the typed text will replace the leaders.

Project 2 Creating a Conference Registration Form
Part 1 of 1

1. Open **Registration.docx** and then save the document with the name **8-Registration**. (You will customize the registration document so it appears as shown in Figure 8.7 on page 292.)
2. Position the insertion point at the left margin, two lines below the text *CONFERENCE REGISTRATION*.
3. Make sure that the horizontal ruler is visible. (If it is not, click the View tab and then click the *Ruler* check box in the Show group to insert a check mark.)
4. Display the Tabs dialog box, set left tabs at 0.75 inch and 6.5 inches, and then click OK to close the dialog box.
5. Type Name: and then press the Tab key to align the insertion point at the first tab setting. (This is where the underline will begin.)
6. Click the Underline button in the Font group on the Home tab and then press the spacebar once. (This creates a placeholder for the starting point of the line.)
7. Press the Tab key. (A line is created between the insertion point and the tab marker at 6.5 inches.)
8. Click the Underline button to turn off underlining.
9. Press the Enter key and then type Address:.
10. Press the Tab key to align the insertion point at the first tab.
11. Click the Underline button and then press the spacebar once to create the placeholder.
12. Press the Tab key to create the line.
13. Click the Underline button to turn off underlining.
14. Press the Enter key.
15. Use a table to create the *City*, *State*, and *Zip* lines by completing the following steps:
    a. Click the Insert tab.
    b. Click the Table button in the Tables group and then drag over the grid to create a table with six columns and one row.
    c. Select the table.
    d. Click the Borders button arrow in the Borders group on the Table Tools Design tab and then click *No Border* at the drop-down gallery. *Hint: Make sure that table gridlines are turned on.*

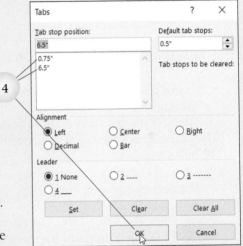

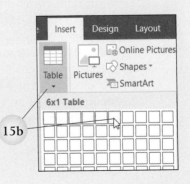

e. Type City: in the first cell.

f. Type State: in the third cell.

g. Type ZIP: in the fifth cell.

h. Click in the cell containing *City:*, click the Table Tools Layout tab, select the current measurement in the *Width* measurement box in the Cell Size group, type 0.75, and then press the Enter key.

i. Change the widths of the remaining columns as follows:

Column 2 = 2 inches

Column 3 = 0.6 inch

Column 4 = 1.75 inches

Column 5 = 0.5 inch

Column 6 = 0.9 inch

j. Position the insertion point inside the second cell and then click the Table Tools Design tab.

k. Make sure that the *Line Style* option box in the Borders group shows a solid line. If it does not, click the *Line Style* option box arrow and then click the first line style option at the drop-down gallery. Choosing a line style makes the Border Painter button active. Click the Border Painter button to deactivate it.

l. Click the Borders button arrow and then click *Bottom Border* at the drop-down gallery.

m. Position the insertion point inside the fourth cell and then click the Borders button.

n. Position the insertion point inside the sixth cell and then click the Borders button.

o. Change the margin for the first cell by completing the following steps:

1) Click in the first cell.

2) Click the Table Tools Layout tab.

3) Click the Properties button in the Table group.

4) At the Table Properties dialog box, click the Cell tab.

5) Click the Options button in the lower right corner of the dialog box.

6) At the Cell Options dialog box, click the *Same as the whole table* check box to remove the check mark.

7) Select the current measurement in the *Left* measurement box, type 0, and then press the Enter key.

8) Click OK to close the Table Properties dialog box.

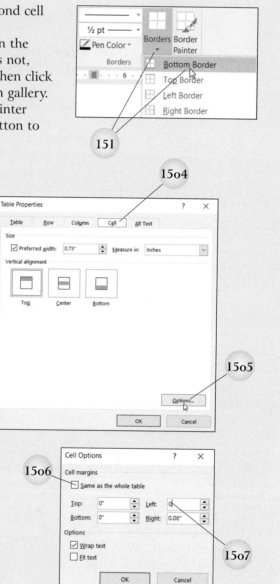

16. Create the *Phone* and *Email* lines using line shapes by completing the following steps:
    a. Position the insertion point on the blank line below the table and then press the Enter key.
    b. Type Phone: and then press the Enter key.
    c. Type Email: and then press the Enter key.
    d. Click the Insert tab, click the Shapes button in the Illustrations group, and then click the *Line* option (first option in the *Lines* section).
    e. Position the crosshairs right of *Phone:* and visually align it with the left edge of the *City:* fill-in line.
    f. Press and hold down the Shift key and then click and drag to create a line that is approximately 2 inches long (approximately the same length as the *City:* fill-in line).
    g. Click the *Subtle Line - Dark 1* thumbnail in the Shape Styles gallery on the Drawing Tools Format tab (the first thumbnail).

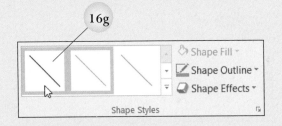

    h. Press Ctrl + D to duplicate the line.
    i. Drag the duplicated line after *Email:* and visually align it with the left edge of the *Phone:* fill-in line.
    j. Check the positions of the two drawn lines in the document and make any needed adjustments so the lines display as shown in Figure 8.7.
17. Position the insertion point on the blank line below the text *Check one:*.
18. Create and format a table by completing the following steps:
    a. Insert a table with three columns and three rows.
    b. Change the width of the first column to 0.3 inch, the width of the second column to 0.5 inch, and the width of the third column to 3 inches.
    c. Remove the border lines from the table. (Do this by selecting the entire table, clicking the Table Tools Design tab, clicking the Borders button arrow, and then clicking *No Border* at the drop-down gallery.)
    d. Insert bottom borders in the three cells in the first column.
    e. Center the table horizontally by clicking the Table Tools Layout tab and then clicking the Properties button. At the Table Properties dialog box, click the Table tab, click the *Center* option in the *Alignment* section, and then click OK.
    f. Type the text in the cells as shown in Figure 8.7.
19. Save and then print **8-Registration.docx**.
20. Save the document with the name **8-RegistrationComplete**.
21. Insert information in the form as shown in Figure 8.8 on page 293. ***Hint: Press the Tab key when entering the phone number and email address.***
22. Save and then print **8-RegistrationComplete.docx**. (You may notice that the lines created using different methods are not the same weight; therefore, choosing one method of creating lines throughout a document is a good idea. The three methods were used in this exercise for demonstration and practice purposes.)
23. Close **8-RegistrationComplete.docx**.

Check Your Work

Figure 8.7 Registration Form Created in Project 2

Best Sellers of the Western Region

Spring Conference, March 17, 2018

CONFERENCE REGISTRATION

Name: _____

Address: _____

City: _____ State: _____ ZIP: _____

Phone: _____

Email: _____

Registration deadline: February 22, 2018

Check one:

_____ $100   Participant from member institution
_____ $125   Participant from non-member institution
_____ $150   Institutional membership dues

Your check must accompany registration

Make check payable to:

Storyteller Books

Mail registration to:

Storyteller Books
123 Main Street
Glen Ellyn, IL 60137

Figure 8.8 Completed Registration Form Created in Project 2

Best Sellers of the Western Region

Spring Conference, March 17, 2018

CONFERENCE REGISTRATION

Name: Sasha Kovich

Address: 13442 South Elmhurst Drive

City: Chicago   State: IL   ZIP: 60605

Phone: (312) 555-4826

Email: skovich@emcp.net

Registration deadline: February 22, 2018

Check one:

x	$100	Participant from member institution
	$125	Participant from non-member institution
	$150	Institutional membership dues

Your check must accompany registration

Make check payable to:

Storyteller Books

Mail registration to:

Storyteller Books
123 Main Street
Glen Ellyn, IL 60137

You will create postcards using the labels feature. The front will include generic information, and the back will include addresses that will be merged with the document.

Preview Finished Project

Creating Postcards

Postcards are inexpensive to create and mail, and they provide an appropriate means of delivering a brief message to customers or prospective customers. Postcards can be used as appointment reminders, change-of-address notifications, reply cards, display cards, thank-you cards, and invitations. Predesigned and printed postcards with attractive borders and color combinations can be purchased in different sizes and weights that meet US Postal Service standards. Any US Postal Service location will have prestamped 3.5-by-5.5-inch postcards.

Word provides predesigned postcard templates that include placeholder text to provide instructions on how to use the template. To locate these templates, click the File tab and then click the *New* option. Enter *postcard* in the search text box, press the Enter key, and then double-click the desired postcard template. A postcard template can be customized to include promotional images and text by simply adding an appropriate photo, logo, or clip art illustration, along with a promotional statement that reinforces the identity of the company or organization or promotes a service or product that it provides. In addition, the Mail Merge feature can be used to create postcards for mass mailing.

Labels

Alternatively, postcards can be created using the Labels button to access the labels feature, which provides postcard labels such as Avery US Letter 3256 Postcards, 5689 Postcards, and 8387 Postcards. Each of these options includes four postcards per page; each postcard measures 4.25 inches by 5.5 inches. The Avery US Letter 8386 Postcards label creates two postcards per page; each postcard measures 4 inches by 6 inches.

Most postcards are created on cover paper (also known as *cardstock*). The weight or thickness of the paper must be strong enough to hold up in the mail. The front side of the postcard is used for the return address and the recipient's address and includes an area reserved for the postage. On the reverse side, create a headline and use a graphic, photo, or watermark to emphasize the message. Make sure to leave room for the message and optional signature.

Project 3a Creating Postcards Using the Labels Feature

Part 1 of 2

1. At a blank document, create postcards using a label (see Figure 8.9 on page 296) by completing the following steps:
   a. Click the Mailings tab and then click the Labels button in the Create group.
   b. At the Envelopes and Labels dialog box with the Labels tab selected, click the Options button toward the bottom of the dialog box.

c. At the Label Options dialog box, select *Avery US Letter* in the *Label vendors* option box, select *8386 Postcards* in the *Product number* list box, and then click OK.

d. At the Envelopes and Labels dialog box, click the New Document button.

2. Insert the image into the top postcard and format it as shown in Figure 8.9 by completing the following steps:

a. Use the Pictures button on the Insert tab to insert **visions.png** from the C8 folder into the postcard.

b. Change the width of the image to 4 inches.

c. Apply Square text wrapping.

d. Position the image as shown in Figure 8.9. *Hint: Make sure table gridlines are turned on.*

3. Insert the text by completing the following steps:

a. Draw a text box in the top postcard that measures 2 inches in height and 3.5 inches in width.

b. Type See the world a little clearer and a little brighter with regular eye examinations. in the text box.

c. Select *See the world* and then change the font to 24-point Bauhaus 93 and the font color to Blue.

d. Select the rest of the text, change the font to 24-point Harlow Solid Italic, and then change the font color to Green, Accent 6.

e. Select the text box, change the paragraph alignment to center, and then remove the shape fill and shape outline.

f. Position the text box as shown in Figure 8.9.

4. Group the image and text box by completing the following steps:

a. Click the image to select it.

b. Press and hold down the Shift key and then click the text box. (The image and the text box should both be selected.)

c. Click the Picture Tools Format tab.

d. Click the Group button in the Arrange group and then click *Group* at the drop-down list.

5. Copy the grouped object in the first postcard and paste it into the second postcard. Position the pasted object in the same position on the second postcard as the object in the first postcard (refer to Figure 8.9).

6. Save the document with the name **8-Postcards**.

7. Print two copies of **8-Postcards.docx** and then close the document.

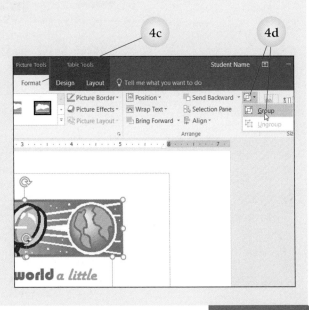

Check Your Work

Figure 8.9 Postcards Created in Project 3a

See the world *a little clearer and a little brighter with regular eye examinations.*

See the world *a little clearer and a little brighter with regular eye examinations.*

Merging Promotional Documents for Mailing

In Chapter 6, a newsletter was merged with a main document using an existing data source file. To create a new data source file, use the Select Recipients button in the Start Mail Merge group on the Mailings tab.

Creating a Data Source File

Creating a Data Source File

 Select Recipients

To create a data source file with the Select Recipients button, click the button and then click the *Type a New List* option at the drop-down list. At the New Address List dialog box, shown in Figure 8.10, use the predesigned fields offered by Word and type the required data, or edit the fields by deleting and/or inserting custom fields and then type the data. When all the records have been entered, click OK. At the Save Address List dialog box, navigate to the desired folder, type a name for the data source file, and then click OK. Word saves a data source file as an Access database, but having the Access application on a computer to complete a merge with a data source file is not necessary.

Merging Documents

Tutorial

Previewing and Merging Documents

 Finish & Merge

When the main document and the data source file have been created, complete the merge by clicking the Finish & Merge button in the Finish group on the Mailings tab. At the drop-down list that displays, choose to merge the records and create a new document, to send the merged documents directly to the printer, or to send the merged documents by email.

To merge the documents and create a new document with the merged records, click the *Edit Individual Documents* option at the Finish & Merge button drop-down list. Identify specific records to be merged with options at the Merge to New Document dialog box. Select the *All* option to merge all the records in the data source. Select the *Current record* option if only the current record is to be merged. Use the *From* and *To* text boxes to specify a range of records for merging. For example, to merge only records 1 through 3, enter *1* in the *From* text box and *3* in the *To* text box.

Figure 8.10 Using the New Address List Dialog Box

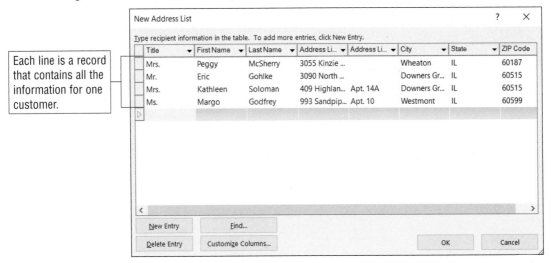

Merging Postcard Labels

Tutorial

Merging Labels

Start Mail
Merge

DTP POINTER

The US Postal
Service recommends
typing addresses in
ALL CAPS with no
punctuation.

Update
Labels

Address
Block

To merge postcard labels, specify the data source file by clicking the Mailings tab, clicking the Select Recipients button, and then clicking *Use an Existing List* at the drop-down list. At the Select Data Source dialog box, navigate to the folder containing the data source file and then double-click the file.

Next, create the postcard label main document, which is the front side of the postcard that contains the mailing information. To do this, click the Start Mail Merge button in the Start Mail Merge group and then click *Labels* at the drop-down list. At the Label Options dialog box that displays, select the desired label vendor and product number and then click the OK button.

At the label document, type any text in the first postcard, such as the return address, insert the «*AddressBlock*» field in the appropriate location in the postcard, and then click the Update Labels button in the Write & Insert Fields group on the Mailings tab to update the labels so each postcard contains the «*AddressBlock*» field. Merge the label main document with the specified data source file by clicking the Finish & Merge button in the Finish group, clicking *Edit Individual Documents*, selecting the desired option in the Merge to New Document dialog box, and then clicking OK to close the dialog box.

Project 3b   Creating a Data Source and Merging Labels for a Postcard Mailing   Part 2 of 2

1. Create a data source for merging with a postcard label by completing the following steps:
   a. At a blank document, click the Mailings tab.
   b. Click the Select Recipients button in the Start Mail Merge group and then click *Type a New List* at the drop-down list.
   c. At the New Address List dialog box, predesigned fields display in the list box. Delete fields by completing the following steps:
      1) Click the Customize Columns button.
      2) At the Customize Address List dialog box, click *Company Name* to select it and then click the Delete button.
      3) At the message informing you that any information in the field will be deleted when you delete the field, click Yes.
      4) Complete steps similar to Steps 1c2 and 1c3 to delete the following fields:
         Country or Region
         Home Phone
         Work Phone
         E-mail Address
      5) Click OK to close the Customize Address List dialog box.

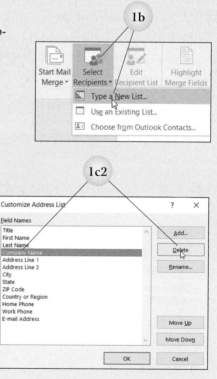

d. At the New Address List dialog box, enter the information for the first customer listed in Figure 8.11 by completing the following steps:

1) Type Mrs. in the *Title* field and then press the Tab key.
2) Type Peggy and then press the Tab key.
3) Type McSherry and then press the Tab key.
4) Type 3055 Kinzie Court and then press the Tab key two times.
5) Type Wheaton and then press the Tab key.
6) Type IL and then press the Tab key.
7) Type 60187 and then press the Tab key. (This moves the insertion point to the *Title* field in the next record.)

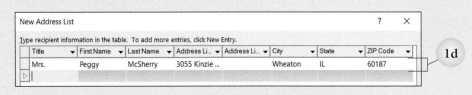

e. Type the information for the three remaining patients in Figure 8.11 in this order: Gohlke, Soloman, Godfrey. After entering the ZIP code for the last patient, Margo Godfrey, click OK to close the New Address List dialog box.

f. At the Save Address List dialog box, save the data source file to the C8 folder with the name **NaperGrovePatientList**. (Word saves this document as a database file with the *.mdb* file extension.)

2. Create a postcard label main document by completing the following steps:

a. Click the Start Mail Merge button in the Start Mail Merge group on the Mailings tab and then click *Labels* at the drop-down list.

b. At the Label Options dialog box, make sure that *Avery US Letter* is selected in the *Label vendors* option box, make sure that *8386 Postcards* is selected in the *Product number* list box, and then click OK.

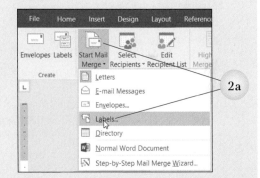

3. With the insertion point positioned in the top postcard, make the following changes:

a. Display the Paragraph dialog box, remove the spacing before paragraphs, make sure that single line spacing is selected, and then click OK to close the dialog box.

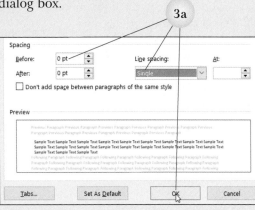

b. At the postcard, press the spacebar once and then press the Enter key. (If you do not press the spacebar before pressing the Enter key, the insertion point will move above the postcard label.) With the insertion point positioned in the label, type the following text:

> Naper Grove Vision Care (Press the Enter key.)
> 5018 Fairview Avenue (Press the Enter key.)
> Downers Grove, IL 60515 (Press the Enter key two times.)
> Just a friendly reminder! (Press the Enter key two times.)
> Please call our office now for your (Press the Enter key.)
> appointment (630) 555-3932.

c. Select *Naper Grove Vision Care*, change the font to 16-point Calibri, apply bold and small caps formatting, change the font color to Blue, and turn on kerning for fonts 16 points and above.

d. Select *Just a friendly reminder!* and then change the font to 16-point Harlow Solid Italic and the font color to Light Green.

4. Insert the *«AddressBlock»* field in the top postcard and update the labels to copy the top label and paste its contents into the second label by completing the following steps:

a. Position the insertion point immediately right of the period after the telephone number and then press the Enter key two times.

b. Click the Layout tab, select the current measurement in the *Left* measurement box in the Paragraph group, type 2.5, and then press the Enter key.

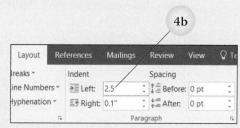

c. Click the Mailings tab and then click the Address Block button in the Write & Insert Fields group.

d. At the Address Block dialog box, click OK to accept the default settings.

e. Click the Update Labels button in the Write & Insert Fields group.

5. Merge the postcard main document with the **NaperGrovePatientList.mdb** data source file by completing the following steps:

a. Click the Finish & Merge button in the Finish group on the Mailings tab and then click *Edit Individual Documents* at the drop-down list.

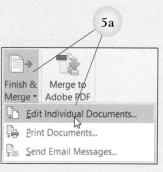

b. At the Merge to New Document dialog box, make sure that *All* is selected and then click OK. (Your merged document should appear similar to what is shown in Figure 8.12.)

6. Save the merged postcard document with the name **8-MergedPostcards**.

7. Insert the two pages you printed of **8-Postcards.docx** correctly into the printer and then print **8-MergedPostcards.docx**.

8. Close **8-MergedPostcards.docx**.

9. Save the main document with the name **8-PostcardMainDoc**.

10. Close **8-PostcardMainDoc.docx**.

Check Your Work

Figure 8.11 Information for Data Source Fields Used in Project 3b

Title	=	Mrs.		*Title*	=	Mr.
First Name	=	Peggy		*First Name*	=	Eric
Last Name	=	McSherry		*Last Name*	=	Gohlke
Address Line 1	=	3055 Kinzie Court		*Address Line 1*	=	3090 North Orchard Road
Address Line 2	=			*Address Line 2*	=	
City	=	Wheaton		*City*	=	Downers Grove
State	=	IL		*State*	=	IL
ZIP Code	=	60187		*ZIP Code*	=	60515
Title	=	Mrs.		*Title*	=	Ms.
First Name	=	Kathleen		*First Name*	=	Margo
Last Name	=	Soloman		*Last Name*	=	Godfrey
Address Line 1	=	409 Highland Drive		*Address Line 1*	=	993 Sandpiper Lane
Address Line 2	=	Apt. 14A		*Address Line 2*	=	Apt. 10
City	=	Downers Grove		*City*	=	Westmont
State	=	IL		*State*	=	IL
ZIP Code	=	60515		*ZIP Code*	=	60599

Figure 8.12 Merged Postcards Created in Project 3b

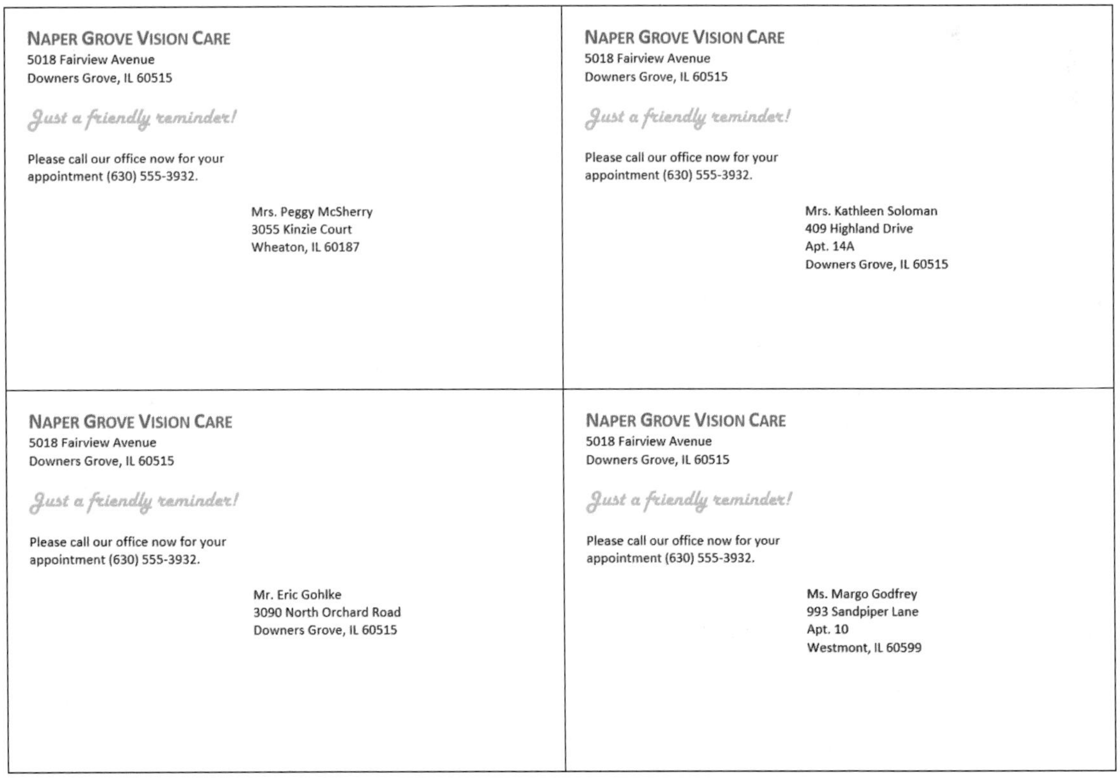

NAPER GROVE VISION CARE
5018 Fairview Avenue
Downers Grove, IL 60515

Just a friendly reminder!

Please call our office now for your
appointment (630) 555-3932.

Mrs. Peggy McSherry
3055 Kinzie Court
Wheaton, IL 60187

NAPER GROVE VISION CARE
5018 Fairview Avenue
Downers Grove, IL 60515

Just a friendly reminder!

Please call our office now for your
appointment (630) 555-3932.

Mrs. Kathleen Soloman
409 Highland Drive
Apt. 14A
Downers Grove, IL 60515

NAPER GROVE VISION CARE
5018 Fairview Avenue
Downers Grove, IL 60515

Just a friendly reminder!

Please call our office now for your
appointment (630) 555-3932.

Mr. Eric Gohlke
3090 North Orchard Road
Downers Grove, IL 60515

NAPER GROVE VISION CARE
5018 Fairview Avenue
Downers Grove, IL 60515

Just a friendly reminder!

Please call our office now for your
appointment (630) 555-3932.

Ms. Margo Godfrey
993 Sandpiper Lane
Apt. 10
Westmont, IL 60599

You will create the cover, inside, and back of an invitation using features and techniques covered in this textbook.

Creating Invitations and Greeting Cards

DTP POINTER

Promote consistency among company documents by inserting a logo and using colors found in the logo.

Invitations and greeting cards are typically one-page documents with a horizontal or vertical book fold. An invitation is used to tell an audience about an event and ask them to attend, and a greeting card can be used for a variety of promotional purposes.

Planning Invitations and Greeting Cards

In planning a card, whether an invitation or a greeting card, consider focus, balance, consistency, proportion, contrast, and directional flow. While including plenty of white space is always a good design practice, it is especially important when working within a small area, such as a card. If using a graphic for focus, be sure that the graphic relates to the subject of the card. Promote consistency through the use of color, possibly picking one or two colors from the graphic used in the card to use in the text. Include the company logo, if one is available. Select one or two fonts that match the tone of the document.

Designing Invitations and Greeting Cards

Since a card is often smaller than a standard-size sheet of paper, it is possible to produce more than one card on each page. There are a few different ways to do this. Use the 2 Pages per Sheet feature covered in Chapter 7, or use a table to divide the Word document page into quadrants, as shown in Figure 8.13. These quadrants represent the front, back, and inside panels of the card. After the page is printed, fold it horizontally and vertically along the fold lines, as shown in the figure. A table can also be used to create two cards on one page in landscape orientation, as shown in Figure 8.14.

Word templates can also be used to create cards. Locate templates by entering *greeting cards* in the search text box in the New backstage area. Select a template and then customize it to suit the company or organization's identity. Consider including the company or organization's logo or one of the graphics from the card on the envelope.

Printing Invitations, Greeting Cards, and Custom Envelopes

When choosing the paper for a card, consider a heavy-weight stock, such as 60- or 65-pound uncoated cardstock. Professional-quality cardstock can be purchased at an office supply store for printing invitations and greeting cards. Greeting card envelopes can also be purchased and come in varying sizes, such as 5.75 inches by 8.75 inches and 4.38 inches by 5.75 inches.

Figure 8.13 Creating One Card per Sheet in Portrait Orientation

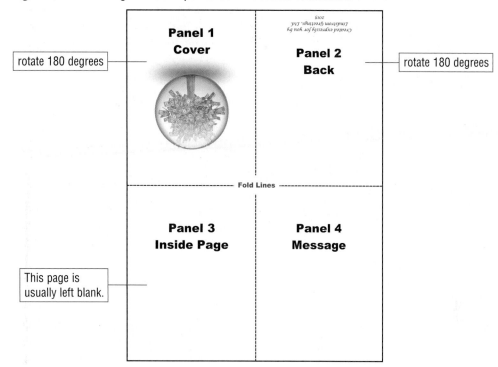

rotate 180 degrees

rotate 180 degrees

This page is usually left blank.

Figure 8.14 Creating Two Cards per Sheet in Landscape Orientation

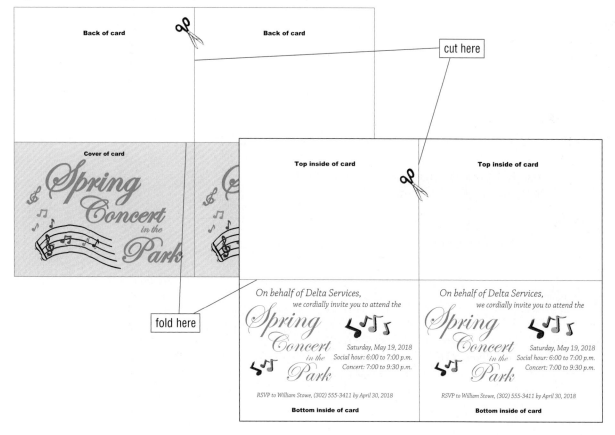

cut here

fold here

Figure 8.15 Creating a Custom-Size Envelope

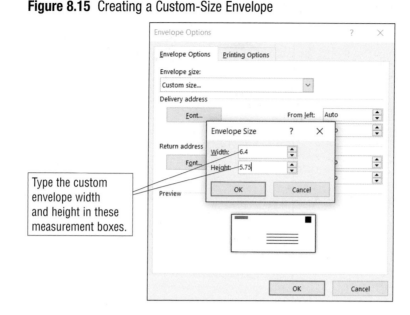

Type the custom envelope width and height in these measurement boxes.

To print a custom-size envelope, click the Envelopes button in the Create group on the Mailings tab, click the Options button at the Envelopes and Labels dialog box with the Envelopes tab selected, click the arrow right of the *Envelope size* list box, and then scroll down and click *Custom size* at the bottom of the list box. Type the desired dimensions at the Envelope Size dialog box, as shown in Figure 8.15. Refer to the printer documentation to determine the correct way to load envelopes for a specific printer.

If the list of recipients is long, consider creating a master copy of the card and taking it to a commercial printer to have it reproduced and machine folded. For the mass mailing of an invitation or a holiday card, consider creating a data source consisting of names and addresses and then merging this information onto envelopes or mailing labels, as covered in Project 3b.

Project 4 Creating the Cover, Back, and Inside of an Invitation

Part 1 of 1

1. At a blank document, change the top margin to 6 inches and the left, bottom, and right margins to 0.7 inch.
2. Use the Pictures button in the Illustrations group on the Insert tab to insert **blue-green-border.png** from the C8 folder. (See Figure 8.16A on page 307.)
3. With the border selected, make the following changes:
   a. Click the Rotate button in the Arrange group on the Picture Tools Format tab and then click *Rotate Left 90°* at the drop-down list.
   b. Click the Size group dialog box launcher.

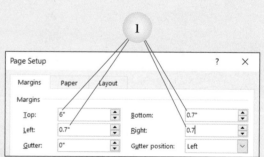

c. At the Layout dialog box with the Size tab selected, remove the check mark from the *Lock aspect ratio* check box in the *Scale* section.

d. Select the current measurement in the *Absolute* measurement box in the *Height* section and then type 6.6.

e. Select the current measurement in the *Absolute* measurement box in the *Width* section, type 4.2, and then click OK.

f. Click the Position button in the Arrange group and then click *Position in Bottom Center with Square Text Wrapping* at the drop-down gallery.

g. Click the Wrap Text button in the Arrange group and then click *Behind Text* at the drop-down gallery.

4. Use the Pictures button on the Insert tab to insert **phonathon.png** from the C8 folder.

5. With the picture selected, make the following changes:

a. Change the width of the picture to 4 inches.

b. Apply In Front of Text text wrapping.

c. Position the image as shown at the right and in Figure 8.16A on page 307.

6. Create the text boxes on the border by completing the following steps:

a. Draw a text box that measures 0.8 inch in height and 2.9 inches in width.

b. Apply the Facet theme.

c. Type Sharing, Inc. in the text box.

d. Select *Sharing, Inc.*; apply the Fill: Dark Green, Accent color 2; Outline: Dark Green, Accent color 2 effect using the Text Effects and Typography button on the Home tab; and then change the font size to 32 points.

e. With the text still selected, change the paragraph alignment to center.

f. Click the Drawing Tools Format tab and then remove the shape outline from the text box.

g. Click the Shape Fill button arrow, point to *Gradient*, and then click *More Gradients* at the bottom of the side menu.

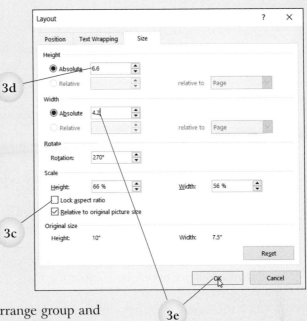

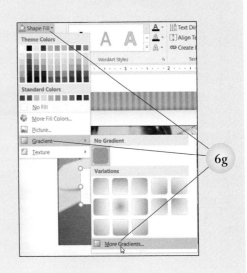

h. At the Format Shape task pane, click the *Gradient fill* option to select it.

i. Click the Direction button in the task pane and then click the *Linear Up* option (second column, second row).

j. Close the Format Shape task pane.

k. Drag the text box so it is positioned on the top border, as shown in Figure 8.16A.

l. Drag a copy of the text box and position it on the bottom border.

m. In the copied text box, replace the text by typing Phonathon 2018.

n. Change the width of the text box to 3.7 inches.

o. Position the text box on the bottom border, as shown in Figure 8.16A.

7. Create the WordArt logo on the back of the cover as shown in Figure 8.16A by completing the following steps:

a. Click the Insert tab, click the Header button in the Header & Footer group, and then click *Edit Header* at the drop-down gallery.

b. Click the Insert tab, click the WordArt button in the Text group, and then click *Fill: Dark Green, Accent color 2; Outline: Dark Green, Accent color 2* (third column, first row).

c. Type Desktop Designs.

d. Click the Text Effects button in the WordArt Styles group, point to *Transform*, and then click the *Triangle: Up* option (third column, first row in the *Warp* section).

e. Change the height of the WordArt to 0.7 inch and the width to 2.2 inches.

f. Click the Align button in the Arrange group on the Drawing Tools Format tab and then click *Align Center* at the drop-down gallery.

g. Rotate the WordArt image by clicking the Rotate button and then clicking *Flip Vertical* at the drop-down gallery.

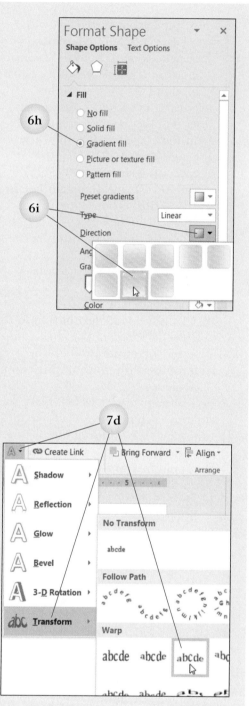

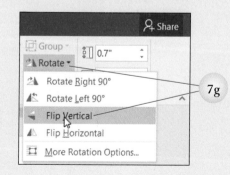

8. Save the document with the name **8-Cover**.
9. Print and then close **8-Cover.docx**.
10. Open **Sharing.docx** from the C8 folder and then save it with the name **8-InsideText**.
11. Insert and format the clip art image shown in Figure 8.16B by completing the following steps:
    a. Use the Pictures button on the Insert tab to insert **family.png** from the C8 folder.
    b. Change the height of the image to 1.7 inches.
    c. Apply Square text wrapping.
    d. Crop the bottom of the image as shown at the right.
    e. Position the image as shown in Figure 8.16B.
12. Save **8-InsideText.docx**.
13. Place the printed cover into your printer. *Hint: Be careful to position the paper correctly so the inside document will print on the reverse side of the cover, with the text appearing right-side up when you lift up the cover.*
14. Print and then close **8-InsideText.docx**.
15. Finish the invitation by folding the top of the page to the bottom of the page.

Check Your Work

Figure 8.16 Card Created in Project 4

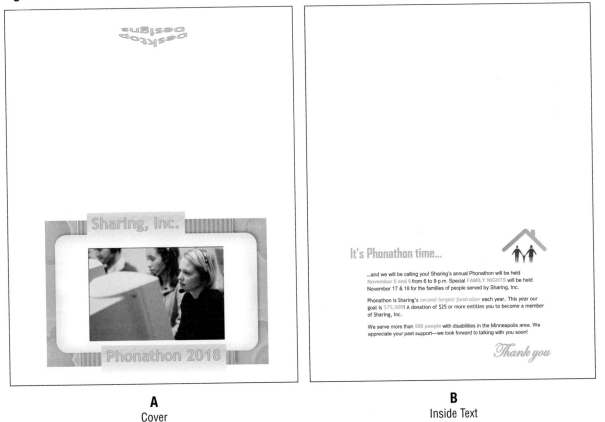

A
Cover

B
Inside Text

You will open a poster, add an image, and then format the poster. You will also use the Printer Properties feature to print the document on four pages and then cut and assemble the poster.

Preview Finished Project

Creating and Printing a Promotional Poster

DTP POINTER

Do not let the graphics in a poster overpower the message.

DTP POINTER

Resist using fancy typefaces in a poster; they make content hard to read.

DTP POINTER

A poster with spelling and grammar errors will lack credibility with the reader.

A poster is generally a large, illustrated sheet of paper designed to advertise or publicize an event or activity. Posters vary in size and are usually attached to walls and other vertical surfaces.

Before creating a poster, take the time to determine the theme or subject matter. A poster should convey information clearly without a lot of clutter. Consider the following guidelines when creating a poster:

- Written content should be edited so that it explains the important points of the subject matter without being wordy.
- Include graphics if they will help to spark interest and illustrate or complement the information in the poster.
- Use no more than two or three fonts in the poster, and make sure that they are legible both close up and from a distance.
- Carefully check for and correct spelling or grammatical errors.

Printing a Promotional Poster

The directions for printing the poster created in Project 5 apply to a Brother color laser printer. Follow the directions for printing this poster based on the printer options for the specific printer that is being used. Some experimentation may be necessary.

Figure 8.17 shows an advanced options dialog box, where access is provided to the appropriate poster size for printing. To display a dialog box similar to the one shown in Figure 8.17, click the File tab and then click the *Print* option. At the Print backstage area, click the *Printer Properties* option directly below the name of the printer in the *Printer* section. Select the appropriate tab or click an Advanced button to display options for printing poster-size documents. Select an option that will print the poster at the desired size. To create a poster measuring 15 inches by 9 inches on letter-size paper, which is 8.5 inches by 11 inches, select an option that prints the poster in four parts on four separate sheets of paper. Select the desired orientation for the poster and then click OK.

Trimming and Assembling a Poster

As mentioned in Chapter 5, most printers have a nonprinting area, which means that text and graphics cannot be printed to the very edge of the page. Because of this, the edges of the pages will most likely need to be trimmed before taping

Figure 8.17 Printing a Promotional Poster

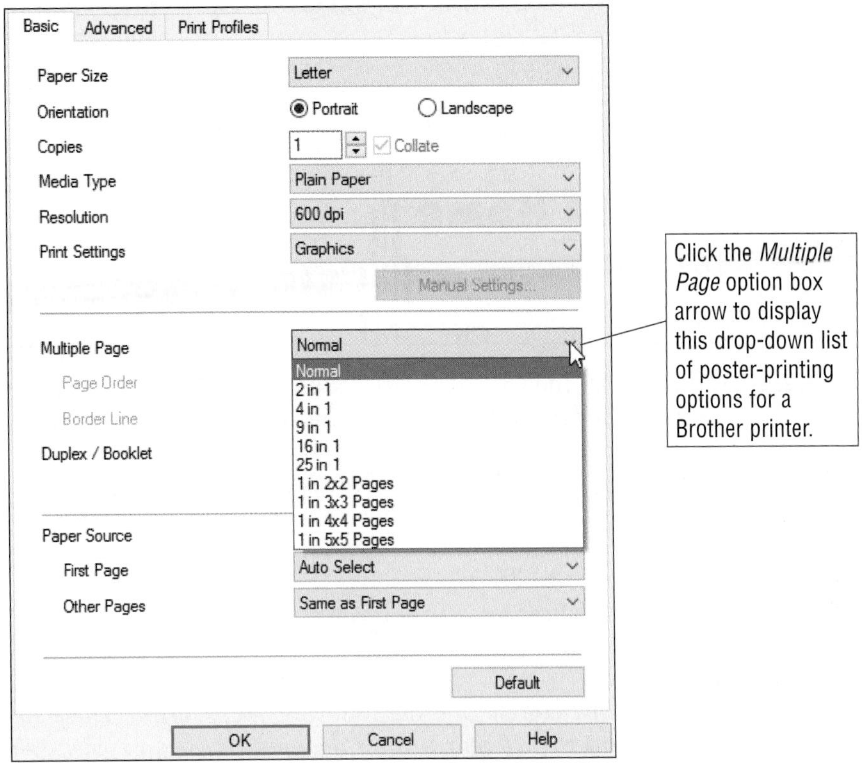

Click the *Multiple Page* option box arrow to display this drop-down list of poster-printing options for a Brother printer.

them together to create the complete poster. As an alternative to cutting off the edges, fold them toward the back of the paper and then tape the pages together. This may provide more support for the taped area, but it may also make the poster heavier and bulkier.

Consider having a poster professionally printed at a print shop, office supply store, or similar type of business, instead of assembling it and using multiple sheets of paper.

Project 5 Creating and Printing a Poster

Part 1 of 1

1. Open **Poster.docx** in the C8 folder and then save it with the name **8-Poster**.
2. With the insertion point positioned at the beginning of the document, insert and format the image shown in Figure 8.18 on page 311 by completing the following steps:
   a. Use the Pictures button on the Insert tab to insert **Chicago.png** from the C8 folder.
   b. Change the width of the image to 4.5 inches.
   c. Apply the Position in Top Center with Square Text Wrapping postion to the image.
3. Draw a text box that measures 0.8 inch in height and 3 inches in width and then type Sweet Home in the text box.
4. Select *Sweet Home* and then change the font to 36-point Bauhaus 93 and apply the Dark Red font color.
5. Remove the shape fill and shape outline from the text box and then drag the text box so it is positioned as shown in Figure 8.18.

Chapter 8 | Creating Specialty Promotional Documents

309

6. Drag a copy of the text box (which you will use for the word *Chicago*) to a position similar to that shown in Figure 8.18 and below. Select *Sweet Home* in the new copy of the text box and then type Chicago.

7. Increase the height of the text box to 0.9 inch so that the *g* is not cut off at the bottom.
8. Select the text in the text box below the Chicago skyline image, change the font to 18-point Calibri, and then change the paragraph alignment to center.
9. Select *Midwest Golf Club Ladies 9-Hole Guest Day* and then apply the following formatting:
   a. Use the Text Effects and Typography button in the Font group on the Home tab to apply the Fill: Blue, Accent color 1; Shadow (second column, top row).
   b. Change the font size to 26 points.
   c. Display the Font dialog box with the Advanced tab selected, turn on kerning for fonts 26 points and above, expand the spacing by 0.5 points, and then close the dialog box.
10. Save **8-Poster.docx**.
11. Print the document by completing the following steps. ***Hint: These steps may vary depending on your printer. If your printer does not include a poster-printing option, check with your instructor.***
   a. Click the File tab and then click the *Print* option.
   b. At the Print backstage area, click the *Printer Properties* option.
   c. At the printer Document Properties dialog box, click the Advanced button. (Or click a tab that provides an option to print a poster in four parts, on four separate pages.)
   d. Click the *Multiple Page* option box arrow and then click *1 in 2x2 Pages*. (This step will vary depending on your printer.)

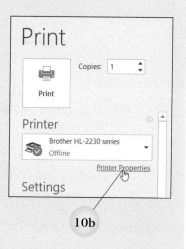

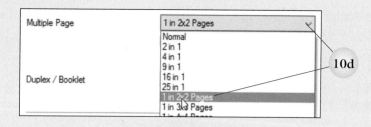

   e. Click OK to close the dialog box pages, and if necessary, click OK to close the printer Document Properties dialog box.
   f. At the Print backstage area, click the Print button.
12. Trim and then tape together the pages of the poster.
13. Return the printer settings back to the default settings.
14. Close **8-Poster.docx**.

Check Your Work

Figure 8.18 Poster Created in Project 5

Prints document on four pages.

Sweet Home Chicago

Midwest Golf Club

Ladies 9-Hole Guest Day

June 23, 2018

7:30 a.m. – Light breakfast
8:20 a.m. – To the links
11:30 a.m. – A taste of Chicago

Wear a "Chicago" costume...your favorite Chicago hot
spot...famous Chicagoan...sports figures...
be creative and win the prize!

Chapter Summary

- Documents such as tickets, registration forms, postcards, invitations, greeting cards, and posters are considered promotional because they often display the name of a business or organization or promote an item or service that is for sale.

- Create and format promotional documents using templates or from scratch using tables or text boxes.

- Tables are especially well suited to be used as a framework for creating tickets, as well as other promotional documents.

- Insert an automatic numbering command in a ticket document by adding an *AutoNum* field code.

- Registration and application forms are used to gather information and can be printed out and filled in by hand or completed electronically on a computer.

- To create lines that data can be entered on, design a document by using tables, inserting fields, drawing a line shape, drawing lines using the Underline command and tab settings, or using tab leaders.

- Postcards are an appropriate means of delivering a brief message to customers or prospective customers. Predesigned and printed postcards can be purchased in sizes and weights that meet US Postal Service standards.

- Create a postcard using a predesigned postcard template or use Word's labels feature, which provides predefined postcard labels. The labels feature formats documents so they can be printed on designated label sheets.

- To merge promotional documents for mailing, create a data source file with the Select Recipients button in the Start Mail Merge group on the Mailings tab.

- When creating a data source file, use predesigned fields provided by Word at the New Address List dialog box. Delete predesigned fields not needed for a data source file and create custom fields, if necessary.

- Word saves a data source file as an Access database with the *.mdb* file extension, but having Access installed on the computer is not necessary to complete a merge with a data source file.

- Merge a main document with a data source file to create a new document, send the merged documents directly to the printer, or send the merged documents by email.

- When merging postcard labels, insert the *«AddressBlock»* field in the appropriate location in the postcard main document and then click the Update Labels button so that each postcard contains the *«AddressBlock»* field.

- Invitations and greeting cards are typically one-page documents with a horizontal or vertical book fold.

- Create cards by inserting text in text boxes, using a table to create each panel of a card, or using a Word template.

- A poster is generally a large, illustrated sheet of paper designed to advertise or publicize an event or activity.

- A poster can be printed by accessing a specific printer's properties dialog box and selecting an option to print the poster on four sheets of paper or more. The number of pages selected will determine the size of the overall poster.

- Once the poster pages have been printed, cut off the page margins and assemble the poster.

Commands Review

FEATURE	RIBBON TAB, GROUP	BUTTON, OPTION
Address Block field	Mailings, Write & Insert Fields	
align	Drawing Tools Format, Arrange	
borders	Table Tools Design, Borders	
Field dialog box	Insert, Text	, *Field*
finish merge	Mailings, Finish	
labels	Mailings, Create	
New Address List dialog box	Mailings, Start Mail Merge	, *Type a New List*
select recipients	Mailings, Start Mail Merge	
start mail merge	Mailings, Start Mail Merge	
table	Insert, Table	
Table Properties dialog box	Table Tools Layout, Table	
update labels	Mailings, Write & Insert Fields	

Workbook

Chapter study tools and assessment activities are available in the workbook pages of the ebook. These resources are designed to help you further develop and demonstrate mastery of the skills learned in this chapter.

Unit assessment activities are also available in the workbook pages of the ebook. These activities are designed to help you demonstrate mastery of the skills learned in this unit.

Index